Eliza Fenwick

Eliza Fenwick

EARLY MODERN FEMINIST

LISSA PAUL

University of Delaware Press

NEWARK

Distributed by the University of Virginia Press

University of Delaware Press
© 2019 by Lissa Paul
All rights reserved
Printed in the United States of America on acid-free paper

First published 2019

ISBN 978-1-64453-009-2 (cloth)
ISBN 978-1-64453-010-8 (paper)
ISBN 978-1-64453-011-5 (e-book)

1 3 5 7 9 8 6 4 2

Library of Congress Cataloging-in-Publication Data is available for this title.

Cover art: Cross-written letter from Elizabeth Rutherford to
Adeline Moffat, January 1834. (Fenwick Family Correspondence,
MS211, box 2, folder 1; courtesy of the New-York Historical Society)

To Murray Wilcox,

for bringing order and coherence to the search for Eliza's life

Contents

Illustrations

Acknowledgments

Although Eliza managed her transatlantic moves—from Britain to Barbados to North America—with apparently confident grace, my search for her required a great deal of support from a large number of people and institutions In order to write confidently about her in the context of the revolutionary times in which she lived, I had to become fluent in a range of otherwise unrelated subject areas including the early Methodism of her childhood, the radical literary, feminist and political cultures of late eighteenth and early nineteenth century Britain, the transatlantic slave trade, the lives and resistance strategies of enslaved people in Barbados especially as the era of legal enslavement came to an end, and the intimacies of early nineteenth-century urban life in New Haven, New York, Niagara and Toronto. Although my first thanks are to all the dedicated librarians in the thirty-six archives and historical societies I consulted in the course of my research I will single out a few for special mention: Alissandra Cummins, Barbados Historical Society; Carlyle Best, University of West Indies Cave Hill Library, Cave Hill, Barbados; Sandra Boyce, National Library Barbados; Stephen Hebron, Bodleian Special Collections, Oxford; Andrea Immel, Cotsen Children's Library, Princeton; Peter Nockles, John Rylands Library, Manchester; Martha Scott, Osborne Collection of Early Children's Books, Toronto; Frances Skelton, New Haven Museum and Historical Society; David Wykes, Dr. Williams's Library London, and Angela Barc, Victoria College Library, University of Toronto.

In addition to the librarians and archivists who helped me navigate their collections, I want to thank scholars in a wide range of disciplines who have generously given of their time and expertise. Among the eighteenth-century studies scholars, I want to thank Isobel Grundy, for her constant encouragement from the very beginning; Janet Todd, for her advice and support especially through my first draft written during my fellowship at Lucy Cavendish Cambridge in the fall of 2013; William McCarthy, whose work on Anna Barbauld and personal advice helped me figure out how to shape the narrative; and Matthew Grenby, for providing me with opportunities, especially during the wonderful British Society for Eighteenth-Century Studies conferences in Oxford, to try out my earliest attempts at telling Eliza's story to scholars in the field. Thanks also go to Michèle Cohen, Mark Burden, Michael Dobson, Shelley King, Paul Stevens, Carol Percy for their research tips, to Jill

Shefrin for her early edits of my manuscript and to Jack Lynch for suggesting the University of Delaware Press as a good "home" for Eliza. And thanks to John Lenton for all his help in understanding the lives of John Wesley's itinerant preachers in the formative stages of Methodism in the mid-eighteenth century.

The section on Eliza's life in Barbados was the most difficult to write and I want to thank a number of scholars of Caribbean history, particularly histories of enslavement and resistance, for their assistance and their patience. In particular, I'd like to thank Evelyn O'Callaghan, Sir Hilary Beckles, Tara Inniss, Pedro Welch, and Rodney Worrell for their insights and for the opportunities to present early stages of my work at UWI. And with thanks to Karl Watson for his tours of Bridgetown, his intimate knowledge of the history of the island, and his support for my first published piece on Eliza in Barbados in *The Journal of the Barbados Museum & Historical Society Journal*.

Besides the scholars who provided direct subject-specific expertise to my research, I want to acknowledge friends, scholars and graduate assistants whose research support, copyediting, thoughtful comments and insights have contributed as well. With thanks to Deirdre Baker, Aidan Chambers, Nancy Chambers, Nina Christensen, Gerry Clarke, Martin, the taxi driver in Cork who knew who owned Lee Mount, Michael Joseph, Mick Gowar, Jhonel Morvan, Ann Kember, Barbara Lazar, Philip Nel, Jennifer Pazienza, Mark Poulin for his thoughtful and meticulous copyediting, Mike Ferguson and Tanner Bisson from Morro Images for their brilliant work on the art files, and Kim Reynolds, Morag Styles, Joseph T. Thomas, Stephanie Tuckonic, Lynne Vallone, Katherine Wakely-Mulroney and Jack Zipes.

The painstaking research involved in finding Eliza in sources that were often unreferenced and/or unindexed would not have been possible without the generous, consistent support I've received from the Social Sciences and Humanities Research Council of Canada (SSHRC). Special thanks to the reviewers of my applications, especially to the one who described Eliza's story as "gobsmakingly interesting." The research support I've received at my home institution, Brock University, has always been wonderful. With thanks especially to Tressie Dutchyn, Tracey Naldjieff, Philip Thomas and Snezana Ratkovic for their faith and support. With thanks, too, to the anonymous readers of the manuscript; to my editors at UDP, Robin Runia and Julia Oestreich; to my indexer, Nancy Will; and to my agent, Caitlin McDonald.

As is typically the case in acknowledgements, the people who have endured the most are near the end. First thanks to my collaborator, Murray Wilcox, who has been with me on the "Eliza" adventure from very near the beginning. The credit for organizing Eliza's letters and managing the huge amount of related material, especially biographical material, goes to him. The entire project would not have been possible without him. And with thanks to my patient, wonderful husband, Geoff Bubbers, and our sons, Matt and Jeremy, for editorial advice, editing and enduring my insistence on dogged persistence.

One of the major pleasures in writing Eliza's story is that I now know what happened to her descendants, how they settled into North American life, put down roots, and succeeded in establishing themselves socially, economically, and culturally, just as Eliza had wished for, worked for, and imagined. I am particularly grateful for support from Eliza's living Canadian descendants: Brett Rutherford and Dave Rutherford, both descended from Eliza's youngest grandson Roland, and from John Cornell, an American descendent of Eliza's granddaughter, Elizabeth.

Images from *The Seraph* were obtained from the Archives of American Art, Smithsonian Institution, Thomas Casilear Cole Papers, 1750–1976.

All images of Barbados marriage and baptismal certificates were obtained from the University of North Carolina (UNC) Southern Historical Collection, Wilson Library, University of North Carolina at Chapel Hill.

The excerpt from "East Coker" is reprinted by permission of Faber and Faber, London, and by Houghton Mifflin Harcourt Publishing Company, from *Collected Poems 1909-1963* by T. S. Eliot; © 1936, renewed 1964 by Thomas Stearns Eliot, all rights reserved. The excerpt from "This Be the Verse" is reproduced by permission of Faber and Faber, London, and by permission of Farrar, Straus and Giroux, from *The Complete Poems of Philip Larkin*, edited by Archie Burnett; © 2012 by the estate of Philip Larkin.

Thanks also to Murray Wilcox for the photograph of the plaque commemorating the Negro Burial Ground and the photograph of William and Susannah Steward House. Every effort has been made to contact those involved in creating the images and quotations reproduced in this volume.

Notes on the Text

As the given names of Eliza, her daughter, Eliza Ann, and her granddaughter, Bessie, are all variations of Elizabeth, I made an editorial decision in order to distinguish between them in the text. I use "Eliza" when referring to Eliza Fenwick (1766–1840), "Eliza Ann" when referring to Eliza Ann Rutherford (1789–1828), and "Elizabeth" or "Bessie" when referring to Elizabeth Rutherford Savage (1817–1899). One more note on names: when referring to Eliza Fenwick, I use "Eliza" throughout, rather than the more conventional "Fenwick," as it reads as too formal, distant, and somehow too masculine. "Mrs. Fenwick" would have been customary in the eighteenth century, but it is too quaint for a twenty-first-century biography. And I rejected the option of writing out "Eliza Fenwick" repeatedly as it is just too clumsy.

Most of the extant letters included here are by Eliza, though some are by her daughter and granddaughter. Those with ties to these women at first carefully kept and treasured the letters, which provided material links to people whom they had known and loved. Over time, however, the letters entered a different phase of existence. They became historical artifacts and that is when their perceived significance changed. Letters that end up in library archives usually do so because of their connections either with famous people and/or famous events. Eliza's letters and those of her descendants occupy a kind of twilight zone, an in-between place. A few letters survive in the William Godwin archive in the Abinger Collection at the Bodleian Library in Oxford, a few in the Henry Crabb Robinson archive in Dr. Williams's Library in London, England, and in the Pforzheimer Collection of Shelley and His Circle at the New York Public Library. All survive because they connect Eliza immediately with other famous people of her age. The letters to Mary Hays, the ones dated between 1798 and 1828 that formed the basis of A. (Annie) F. Wedd's *The Fate of the Fenwicks,* survive in the New-York Historical Society because Wedd sold them to A. D. Savage for one hundred pounds.[1] That transaction came about only after Annie Wedd discovered, just before her volume was published in 1927, that Eliza's living descendants in the United States cared about the material. That archive also contains correspondence between Wedd and Elizabeth's son A. D. Savage, including his objections to some of Wedd's omissions. There is no explicit reference to the ways the letters to the Moffat family made their way back to Eliza's family, except through an earlier reference to the "younger generation of those to whom the letters had been sent."

In addition to the letters to the Moffats, there are some to Mrs. Massa and Mrs. Winslow. A note dated May 11, 1844, written in red ink, offers an explanation: "Mrs. Massa and Mrs. Winslow were the daughters of Mr. Barrell, originally of Barbados, but who moved to New York around 1830 and were friends of Mrs. Fenwick and were long friends of ERS [Elizabeth Rutherford Savage, Eliza's granddaughter]."[2] Unlike letters saved to provide glimpses of famous people—people who have made a significant public impact—the letters to Mrs. (Dora) Massa and Mrs. Winslow testify to intimate family friendships sustained across long periods of time and distances. Eliza and her family had left Barbados in 1822, but the bonds between the two families remained, and the letters speak to the ways in which immigrant families supported each other.

Thomas Casilear Cole, who had been the keeper of the family history, divided up his cache of family history sometime in the 1970s. He put most of the material related directly to Eliza in the New-York Historical Society archive, but he did put other items, including a few manuscript letters, in two related archives, one in North Carolina and the other in Washington, D. C. Items related primarily to William Rutherford Savage, one of Elizabeth's sons, survive in the archives of the University of North Carolina at Chapel Hill. There, I found among other items handwritten copies of the official records of Eliza Ann's marriage to William Rutherford, and the birth certificates of her four Barbados-born children, all dated 1822, indicating that Eliza and Eliza Ann had wanted to ensure that they had an official record of the legitimacy of all the children, important as William Rutherford had long separated from his family by that time. The third archive, the Thomas Casilear Cole papers at the Archives of American Art at the Smithsonian in Washington, contains eighteen boxes of material, mostly related to Cole and his career as a portrait painter. There, I found the one physical object that had belonged personally to Eliza: a leather-bound book of sacred music, with her name embossed in gold on the cover. It was in box 17 of the eighteen boxes, with no explanatory note about how it got there or why, but it felt like a breathtaking gift to hold something that had actually belonged to her, something both personal and physically beautiful, something that connected to her life in London in the 1790s.

Besides the deposits of family-related material Thomas Casilear Cole made to archives in New York, Chapel Hill, and Washington, unreferenced and unindexed manuscript letters by Eliza and Elizabeth turned up in the Baldwin Collection of the Toronto Public Reference Library, just a short walk away from my own home. The collection is named for Robert Baldwin, "who established responsible government in pre-Confederation Canada."[3] One part contains, according to the archivist, "1000 pieces bound in 13 volumes and 532 pieces unbound" (L11, 1749–1850), and the other part contains "2 volumes and 268 unbound" (L12, section II 1797–1843). The finding aids look comprehensive and, in addition to the online information, there are three closely packed card-catalogue drawers. Although someone had carefully and manually cross-referenced people who appear in the letters, there are no references to Eliza or any members of her family anywhere. On my initial search, I took the absence as being accurate and did not look further. Later, I decided to go back and just order up boxes from the date range (mid-1830s) when I knew Eliza and her family had been in Upper Canada. That's when handwritten letters from Eliza surfaced, as did references to her and to Elizabeth in an unpublished manuscript, *The Bonnet-Box Letters*, written by descendants of Robert Baldwin, based on letters they had found dating from the 1830s.[4]

Some closing notes on the text. First, all quotations from Eliza's letters and those of her daughter and granddaughter are from my own transcriptions of original manuscript versions. The names of two of the people in A. F. Wedd's 1927 edition of *The Fate of the Fenwicks* have been corrected throughout: Eliza worked as a governess for the Honner (not Honnor) family in Ireland, and she hired Mr. Houley (not Houry) as a teacher in Barbados. The corrections were made by cross-referencing property records in Ireland and newspaper records in Barbados. And second, because I'm arguing for Eliza's historical relevance, I've written—as a wise editor used to say—for "the general interested reader" rather than for specialists in eighteenth-century studies or Caribbean or Canadian studies. To that end, I've sometimes used what eighteenth-century specialists disdainfully describe as "presentism," employing anachronistic current references to capture a feeling or an idea from the past. For example, when trying to convey what it was like for Methodist itinerants (such as Eliza's father, Peter Jaco) in the mid-eighteenth century to preach, sometimes to thousands of people on stony beaches or muddy fields, I suggest that they were like rock stars performing at open-air concerts. I know, of course, that rock concerts did not exist in the eighteenth century, but if I invoke a comparison to Woodstock or Glastonbury (in the UK), the reference instantly conjures the exuberant joy, the sense of community, the wonder at being enthralled by the performance, and the sheer thrill of being a participant. Overwhelmingly, those were the impressions conveyed in the first-hand accounts by John Wesley's original itinerant preachers of their experiences with the people they were bringing to Methodism.[5] In the eighteenth century, "enthusiasm" was often used in a derogatory way to describe what went on at some of those Methodist sessions on beaches and in fields, so though it would be the term preferred by scholars, it would be relatively meaningless to the twenty-first-century readers to whom this book is addressed. At the heart of my biographical account of the life and letters of Eliza Fenwick is a commitment to the idea that her two-hundred-year-old story of adaptation, endurance, imagination, and persistence during a period of seismic social and political change will inspire and ring true to contemporary readers.

Abbreviations

EF	Eliza Fenwick
EAR	Eliza Ann Rutherford
ER	Elizabeth (Bessie) Rutherford
HCR	Henry Crabb Robinson
JM	John Moffat
LCS	London Corresponding Society
MH	Mary Hays
SCI	Society for Constitutional Information

Eliza Fenwick

Prelude

Out at sea the dawn wind
Wrinkles and slides. I am here
Or there, or elsewhere. In my beginning.
—T. S. Eliot, "East Coker," *Four Quartets*

Like T. S. Eliot, crime writers know that the clues to a story's beginnings are best detected at the end, in the mysteries surrounding the dead. My story about the mysterious and adventurous literary life of Eliza Fenwick (1766–1840) begins at an end, not her end—that is, not with her death—but in her account of the deaths of her two eldest grandsons, William and Thomas Rutherford. When they drowned together in the frigid early-spring waters of Lake Ontario on April 12, 1834, William was just twenty-one and Tom nineteen. The day after their deaths, Eliza squeezed the news into a small empty space at the bottom of a letter she had been ready to post to her New York friends, the Moffats:

> This letter oddly remained unsealed though seemingly finished in my desk, til now—and now I resume it to tell you that our deep, *deep* tragedy is ended—William & Tom have lived together—have suffered together and have died together—Tom lies a corpse in the next room but the blue waters of the Lake still cover the body of poor William where they yesterday met their end. They were both at breakfast more than usually cheerful—I went about my usual household affairs & Elizabeth to her duties. I was occupied in the kitchen & laundry til after 12 & then on enquiring for them learned they had gone out together, & William had his gun. There is an island about 2 mile across the bay abounding in wild chickens & William's object no doubt was to go there. They applied for a boat, it appears, but was refused, the owner perceiving th [there is a hole in the page here where some unknown later hand attempted to erase the words]. They were seen on the Lake in a very, *very* small canoe which had been lying on the shore. A young man was rowing his wife & sick child for air on the lake & as he approached he observed one seem to start violently, fall overboard, when the other clasped his hands in evident agony & plunged. (Eliza Fenwick to John Moffat, 13 April 1834)[1]

Eliza's narrative, written in a tiny even hand, is both compelling and mystifying: the details of the deaths of her grandsons raise questions begging

1

York from Gibraltar Point, 1828. (Courtesy of the Toronto Public Library)

for clarification, investigation, and interpretation. Why, for instance, is her "deep, deep tragedy" *ended* with the deaths of Will and Tom? Why isn't their drowning the tragedy? What caused one to "start violently"? What does "start violently" mean? Did one brother have some kind of epileptic fit? Did something frighten him? Or were there earlier hints that the morning jaunt Will and Tom took was doomed? That something in their manner, something erased, constituted evidence enough for the boat owner to decide that the two young men embarking on a short trip across the bay posed too "great a risk to be trusted with his boat? Were they drunk? Is that what Eliza meant when she said that they were "more than usually cheerful" at breakfast? Even if they were drunk, once they had been refused the boat, why would they chance a "very, *very* small canoe" in Lake Ontario in mid-April? The ice would have only just melted and the water would barely have been above freezing. Why would anyone stand up in a small (thus presumably unstable) canoe? Those are just the questions raised by Eliza's story about the deaths of her grandsons.

Did Will and Tom die by misadventure? Or suicide? Did one, on seeing the other doomed, make a split-second decision to follow? Or was the dive by the second a rescue attempt? A report of the deaths in *The Kingston Chronicle and Gazette* leans toward the second conclusion, recording that the two were on a "shooting excursion in a skiff, when one of them was seen to fall overboard," and that "the other brother jumped into the water to his rescue and both were drowned."[2] My intention here is not to answer the questions surrounding the mysterious deaths of young Will and Tom, but rather to foreground their grandmother as an author worth reading.

Eliza was a compelling writer and she had an uncanny knack for landing in moments later characterized as defining episodes of social and cultural change. She wrote about them with the same narrative grace and skill that characterized her published work and her personal letters. From literary London in the years around 1800 to the shores of Lake Ontario in the 1830s, Eliza's travels took her, as a single working mother, then grandmother, from Britain to Barbados, to New Haven, to New York, to Niagara and then to Toronto, before she finally retired and died in Rhode Island in 1840.

Although the number of published literary works confirmed as having been written by Eliza remains small—one novel, *Secresy* (1795), and ten books for children in the early 1800s—her letters testify to her literary gifts. The surviving letters Eliza wrote between September 12, 1797, when she was a young wife, mother, and writer in London, England, and November 30, 1840, just days before she died on December 8 in Providence, Rhode Island provide the basis for her story as told here. But first, a short overview, or plot summary, to set the stage and provide literary and historical context.

From her early life in the 1770s—she was born in 1766, the daughter of one of John Wesley's original itinerant preachers in the period when Methodism was advancing—Eliza moved with her husband John Fenwick into the radical 1790s London circles of William Godwin and Mary Wollstonecraft. When John proved too given to drink and debt to support his wife and two children (Eliza Ann, born 1789, and Orlando, born 1798), Eliza left him in the early 1800s, trying her hand briefly at shopkeeping, writing for children, and working as a governess in order to support herself and her family. By financing lessons in singing, dancing, and French, Eliza prepared her daughter Eliza Ann to be a self-supporting actress, an occupation she took up in her late teens. Eliza Ann's acceptance of a contract in late 1811 to act in a new repertory company in Bridgetown, Barbados, set Eliza's colonial journey into motion. In quick succession, following her arrival in Barbados, Eliza Ann married another expatriate Englishman, William Rutherford, started a family (William was born in 1813, Tom two years later), and suggested to her mother that they open an elite school for girls in Bridgetown. The school would, she thought, provide the financial and social security that had eluded them throughout their years of struggle in Britain. In late 1814, Eliza and her teenage son Orlando set sail for Barbados. Neither Eliza nor her children would see Britain again.

At the heart of this book is Eliza's colonial immigration success story: from Britain via the Caribbean to North America, hers was a transnational journey through the social, political, and cultural shifts that transformed the late Enlightenment world of the eighteenth century into the Romantic/industrial world of the nineteenth. It is a story of failure and success, of hopes for the future and despair when hope dissolves. It is a story of literary and pedagogical innovation, endurance, and persistence. The schools Eliza ran in the Caribbean and North America were informed by the late Enlightenment radical philosophies of education promoted by Mary Wollstonecraft, William Godwin, Anna Barbauld, Maria Edgeworth, and Mme de Genlis. Eliza shared their faith in the possibility of nurturing a generation of socially and politically engaged thinking adults, women as well as men, and her pedagogical practices were infused with their philosophies. As William Godwin explained so beautifully in 1802, the goal of education should be the development of "an active mind and a warm heart."[3]

Yet, the financial and social gains Eliza was able to make with her first school in Barbados were outweighed by personal losses. Orlando died in November 1816 of yellow fever. Though Eliza Ann bore two more children, Elizabeth (Bessie) Rutherford was born on April 6, 1817, just five months after Orlando's death, and Orlando (Roland) Rutherford was born on July 16, 1818, the day his father William (who, like his father-in-law John Fenwick, was given to drink and debt) abandoned his family and returned to Britain.

Eliza's determination to keep trying despite repeated loss and failure stands as remarkable. As her daughter's health declined around 1820 and slave-dependent Barbados started to crumble in the years before slavery was finally abolished in 1834, Eliza and Eliza Ann moved with the four young children in 1822, first to New Haven, then to New York, with the intention of running schools for girls based on their progressive Barbados model. Both of their first American schools were short-lived and Eliza Ann died in 1828, leaving Eliza with the sole responsibility of raising and educating her grandchildren.

The move to the colony of Upper Canada in 1829, to start a school with the recently widowed Mary Breakenridge, proved to be the turning point for Eliza. It was in Niagara and York (which became Toronto in 1834), in what was then Upper Canada, that Eliza was finally able to establish social and financial security and create viable futures for her two surviving grandchildren. Both put down roots in the "new" world—Roland in the backwoods of Upper Canada (now Tillsonburg), and Elizabeth in the United States. Eliza left Toronto in 1838 to retire at the invitation of her friend, Alexander Duncan, and it was at his home in Rhode Island that she died in 1840. Through her combination of intelligence, perseverance, networking, and entrepreneurial gifts, during her nine years in Upper Canada Eliza was able to leverage the possibilities offered in the burgeoning colony and become an immigration success story. As this brief précis of Eliza's life shows, she had little time to write, given that her days were consumed by teaching, running schools, and childrearing. Her letters became the place where she could exercise her talents when her need to earn a living crowded out the literary life she had started to live in the 1790s and early 1800s.

Almost two hundred years after the deaths of Will and Tom in the unforgiving waters of Lake Ontario—too long ago for anyone now living to feel personal sorrow at their loss—it is Eliza's report of their untimely deaths that remains. She creates narrative gaps in her story, the kinds of missing pieces that alert modern readers of mystery stories and detective fiction to possible clues.[4] Though photography was still experimental in the 1830s and moving pictures decades away, Eliza's narrative reads cinematically, the composition uncannily true to what has become the formulaic structure of hour-long television murder-mystery dramas. She begins with the fact of the still and silent Tom, lying, as she says, "a corpse in the next room." By putting herself in the picture, in the act of writing her letter in such close proximity to the body of her nineteen-year-old grandson, she invokes her own presence and his absence. The fact that the body of her eldest grandson Will is still covered by what she terms "the blue waters of the Lake" underlines her sense of an ending and the split between life and death. As in the now familiar genre of cinematic storytelling, Eliza quickly cuts to an interior domestic scene from the beginning of the previous day, emphasizing its safe, routine ordinariness, the daily bustle of cooking, washing, and chores in which she and her granddaughter Elizabeth had been engaged. Recollections of the everyday nature of the moments preceding life-changing catastrophic events are exactly the narrative tools people instinctively employ when their lives are suddenly split apart. Witnesses to the tragedy of the planes crashing into the Twin Towers in New York on 9/11, for example, frequently noted the beauty of the early fall day, the clear blueness of the sky.[5] Eliza too, in her note, tries to recapture, if just for a moment, that uneventful time before the day fell apart. In the act of retelling, she suspends time, briefly holding the physical solidity of the presence of the day and of her grandsons in that moment.

Eliza moves quickly, however, from the safety of the domestic interior to the precise components of the outdoor setting that provide the reason and location for the deaths of her grandsons: the description of the wild chickens on the island, and of Will's gun and his desire to cross the open stretch of water and use it to shoot them.[6] The backstory to the day occupies only an instant in Eliza's account. She shifts, changes her narrative position, and reconstructs, out of fragments that had been reported to her after Tom's body had been recovered and returned, the actual sequence of events that had led to the deaths of her grandsons. In cinematic terms, it is as if she had backed away from the scene and moved out for a wide-angled long shot. Narratively, Eliza is removed from the scene, only able to report helplessly from the perspective of the "young man" who was "rowing his wife & sick child for air" on the lake. He was obviously too far away to rescue Will and Tom, but by invoking his view of the events, Eliza positions herself, by association, as also too far away to help. The scene unfolds and there is nothing she or anyone else can do to stop it. All that is left is the end, the observation by the young man that "one seem[ed] to start violently & fall overboard," and the other "clasped his hands in evident agony & plunged." The whole passage fits into just a few handwritten lines and there are no crossings-out or hesitations. And despite the fact that Eliza wrote in the immediate aftermath of her grandsons' deaths, her literary skill stands, captured in her eye for character and setting and her narrative sense of action and drama. The passage reads with the economical structure and sharply focused style of an accomplished novelist, which is exactly what she had been forty years earlier in Britain when her debut epistolary novel, *Secresy,* was published in 1795.

By beginning the story of the life and letters of Eliza Fenwick with a close reading of the passage from her 1834 letter on Will and Tom's death, the fact that she remained a gifted writer throughout her long life comes sharply into focus. Her letters are integral to her literary legacy and constitute what is now called "life writing."[7] Even though Eliza's time in Upper Canada was marked by loss, it was the place where she fulfilled the dream of establishing a life for herself, her grandchildren, and ultimately her descendants. Her overwhelmingly positive, optimistic, and beautifully written views of Upper Canadian life distinguish her from the acknowledged foremothers of Canadian literature: Susanna Moodie (1803–85), her sister Catherine Parr Traill (1802–99), and Anna Jameson (1794–1860), with whom Eliza overlapped in the 1830s. In contrast to Moodie's schizophrenic stories of the miseries of "roughing it" in the bush, Traill's bucolic meditations on the natural world, or Jameson's pompous, condescending descriptions of her amusing encounters with bumbling colonials, Eliza writes with sharp clarity about Upper Canada as a place of opportunity, a place where she can thrive, a place in polite society where she can engage in the cultural life of a community that celebrates music, intellectual life, and literature. Her private letters confirm that she was, as her friend Henry Crabb Robinson described her, a writer "of remarkable talent."[8] As he became best known as the first chronicler of the Romantic poets, particularly William Wordsworth and Samuel Taylor

Coleridge (both of whom Eliza also knew), Crabb Robinson's informed opinion counts. By way of contrast, he did not like Anna Jameson, either as a writer or as a person.

Because Eliza composed *Secresy*—her only published work unmarked as being for children—as an epistolary novel, it is perhaps unsurprising that her letters should read as fiction. A. F. Wedd, the editor of *The Fate of the Fenwicks* (1927), a collection of letters from Eliza to her ancestor, author Mary Hays, thought so too. In her introduction, Annie (as she was called) Wedd explains that she had found a bundle of Eliza's letters "torn, mouse-eaten and discoloured" and "closely written on large sheets of paper," and determined that the collection, though composed a century earlier, was worth editing and publishing. At the time of writing her introduction, however, Wedd did not know that Eliza's descendants were living in the United States and Canada. But she did recognize Eliza's talent for reporting on the people and events she had encountered as she moved from London at the end of the eighteenth century (just as her marriage was breaking up), through the early stages of her colonial adventure in Barbados, including the death of her son, and finally to New York where she experienced the death of her daughter. Instead of organizing the volume of letters conventionally by date, Wedd arranged and heavily edited the manuscript letters as a five-part, eighty-six-chapter novel in order to make the collection read like an adventure-romance: "Eliza makes Progress," "Slavery in Skinner Street," "Mary Hays to the Rescue," "A Favourable Turn of Fortune's Wheel," and "An Adventurous Journey," are a few of the chapter titles.

When *The Fate of the Fenwicks* was published in 1927, reviewers validated Wedd's creative rearrangement of the letters. In *The Daily News* of Friday, December 23, 1927, for instance, Robert Lyn wrote that "if this story were fiction it would be among the most moving novels of the season." The reviewer in *The Woman's World* (July 1928) confirmed the assessment: "you can hardly fancy a novel more delightful and entertaining than we find in *The Fate of the Fenwicks.*"[9]

Only by comparing the original manuscript letters, word-by-word, against the published version of *The Fate of the Fenwicks* does the extent of Wedd's editing—designed to ratchet up the adventure and situate Eliza as incompetent and unable to manage her own affairs—come into focus. In order to set up a dramatic foil, Wedd positions her own ancestor, as evidenced in the chapter title "Mary Hays to the Rescue," as heroic, ready to save Eliza every time she fell. If the phrase had been available to Wedd, she would have described Eliza as someone who could not get her act together.

To be fair, Wedd's assessment of Eliza's failure is consistent with the typical received version of her in eighteenth-century studies, where, to quote an early reader of this biography, she is on "the outskirts of literary history." If Eliza figures at all, it is as a one-hit wonder with *Secresy,* or as the person who cared for Mary Wollstonecraft as she was dying after giving birth to Mary Shelley, or in children's book histories as one of the authors children's book historian F. J. Harvey Darton dismisses in his "moral tale didactic" category as only worth mentioning in passing.[10] For twenty-first-century readers, however, Eliza's story reads differently. It's a colonial success story, one that potentially maps, as Marilyn Butler says, a "new mythology." By restoring passages from Eliza's letters that Wedd left out, both Eliza Fenwick and Mary Hays surface as literary women attempting to articulate a modern, feminine-inflected worldview.

There is no direct evidence that Eliza composed her letters with publication in mind, though it was a relatively common practice in the period for letters, or parts of letters, to be copied and circulated privately within circles of friends and families. Epistolary travel writing is a genre with which Eliza would have been familiar. Her friend Mary Wollstonecraft's *Letters Written During a Short Residence in Sweden, Norway and Denmark,* published in 1796, proved an immediate popular success. Composed of letters written to her lover Gilbert Imlay (also the father of her daughter Fanny), Wollstonecraft prepared her letters for publication during the period in the mid-1790s that coincided with her most intense friendship with Eliza; their young daughters, Fanny and Eliza Ann, played together. A generation later, in 1816, Fanny became the recipient of the letters her half-sister Mary Godwin had written when on the run to Geneva with her lover Percy Bysshe Shelley. According to Janet Todd, Mary Shelley had been writing "lengthily and in detail to Fanny," with their mother Wollstonecraft's travel writing in mind. Shelley, explains Janet Todd, was "copying out much of what she wrote; she had a shrewd eye to the publication she would make of these and her accounts of her previous trip. Together they would form a travelogue catching impressions of the war-torn countryside and people. . . ."[11] Eliza's letters, like Mary Wollstonecraft's and Mary Shelley's, read with what looks like a calculated mix of the personal and the political, the intimate and the public. They were contributing to the letter-writing genre Jürgen Habermas describes as giving rise to "the public sphere" of the eighteenth century.[12] Eliza would also have understood that letters could be used as tools of political action. In the 1790s, her own husband, John Fenwick, had been active in The London Corresponding Society (LCS), a society built on letters used to argue, in the wake of the French Revolution, for English parliamentary reform. And Eliza's own epistolary novel, *Secresy*, argues for the rights of women to be educated.

Eliza herself copied and circulated letters by her daughter, Eliza Ann, written between 1811 and 1813, from Barbados. Some of those lively letters detailing day-to-day life in slave-dependent Barbados are in *The Fate of the Fenwicks*, and they are as vivid and arresting as Eliza's. The letters were long and it must have taken hours for Eliza to copy each one and send it on to Mary Hays. Wedd had no compunctions about splitting Eliza Ann's letters apart and rearranging them in order to foreground the point that her marriage to William Rutherford would be as ill-starred as her mother's marriage to the feckless John Fenwick was. Unlike Wedd's, my project is about positioning Eliza not as tragic heroine, but rather as a literary woman worth reading—an innovative, adventuring woman who confidently negotiated rapidly shifting social and political contexts as she moved across the globe.

Besides restoring the parts of Eliza's story omitted by Wedd in her fashioning of *The Fate of the Fenwicks*, I've immersed myself in the scholarly literature of a wide range of fields (eighteenth- and nineteenth-century studies, as well as Methodist, feminist, Caribbean, American, and Canadian literary and social histories) and mined literature, letters, newspapers, and other archival sources (such as army records, Methodist archives, theater archives, and published memoirs) from the period in order to locate the personal in relation to the seismic political and cultural shifts of the day. What the story of Eliza's life offers to twenty-first-century readers is a glimpse of how her private day-to-day life of teaching, writing, running schools, negotiating friendships, providing a home, and raising children and grandchildren was determined by and intersected with the historic events of the times and places in which she lived.

I have introduced Eliza on the shores of Lake Ontario, busy with her "household affairs" in the kitchen and laundry, because my book is also partly about how she got there, in the 1830s, so very far away from her radical literary life in the 1790s and early 1800s among the influential authors, actors, publishers, and politicians of her day. The room from which Eliza wrote the news of her grandsons' deaths was located in King's College, the precursor to the University of Toronto, as that was where Eliza still was working, as a sixty-eight-year-old woman, supporting herself as a boarding-house matron for the recently formed Upper Canada College. In Toronto, Eliza knew the Lieutenant Governor, John Colborne, Bishop Strachan, the family of William Warren Baldwin, and others influential in making the town a financial, cultural, and political center for the quickly growing colony of Upper Canada. Eliza's friendship with those powerful Toronto figures testifies to her enduring gift for what was called sociability, an art she seems to have cultivated throughout her life.[13]

A list of Eliza's friends and acquaintances in Britain still reads like a who's who of the late eighteenth and early nineteenth centuries. In varying degrees of intimacy, she knew, among others: the third American Vice President Aaron Burr (1756–1836)[14]; poet Samuel Taylor Coleridge (1772–1834); author and philosopher William Godwin (1756–1836); author and actor Elizabeth Inchbald (1753–1821); actor Stephen Kemble (1758–1822); essayist William Hazlitt (1778–1830); author Charles Lamb (1775–1834) and his sister and collaborator, Mary Lamb (1765–1847); publisher Joseph Johnson (1738–1809); author Amelia Opie (1769–1853); author Jane Porter (1776–1850); author and biographer of the Romantic poets, Henry Crabb Robinson (1775–1867); actor, poet, and mistress of the Prince of Wales, Mary Robinson (1757–1800); author Charlotte Smith (1749–1806); poet Percy Bysshe Shelley (1792–1822); poet Robert Southey (1774–1843); author and philosopher Mary Wollstonecraft (1759–97); and poet Dorothy Wordsworth (1771–1855). That is a partial list.[15] Eliza attended the birth of the daughter of Mary Wollstonecraft and William Godwin in 1797, and knew her as the child who grew up to become, famously, Mary Shelley (1797–1851), author of *Frankenstein; or, the Modern Prometheus* (1818). Even my sampling of people who made up the everyday community of Eliza's social and cultural life in Britain speaks to her intellectual vitality and accomplishment. And the list speaks to how very far she had traveled from that life by the time her grandsons died in the cold April waters of Lake Ontario in 1834.

The narrative trajectory of Eliza's lived story, as she moved from literary London to Upper Canada via Ireland, Bridgetown, New Haven, and New York, combines some of the most attractive conventions of adventure romance, mystery, and travel journalism: photogenic locations, riveting characters, and page-turning plot. Her personal quest for happiness, stability, security, and a home for her family played out in the context of the revolutions marking the beginnings of early modern shifts toward parliamentary democracy, social responsibility, and the abolition of slavery in the increasingly globalized world. As the new century began in 1800, Eliza took up what would become her working life as an essentially single mother and later grandmother. In so doing, she deserves recognition as a pioneering figure on the long road toward independent, enfranchised lives for women.

Although the word "plot" is a freighted term to use in describing the trajectory of a life, Eliza's life was so fueled by a desire to succeed as an independent woman, so driven by maternal love and a desire for personal and financial stability, that the narrative arc of her story does feel like the plot of a novel, literally an adventure. Fittingly, the adventure story genre had come to mean, by the eighteenth century, a physically and financially hazardous enterprise, so related to "venture" capital. As the word "adventure" is rooted in the Latin *adventus* (meaning "arrival"), the fact that Eliza literally arrives at success in Upper Canada provides a kind of well-earned happy ending for a story about her ability to persevere through failure and loss. There is something worth honoring, praising, recognizing, and remembering about Eliza's resilience, her willingness to pick herself up after each failure and start again, relying on her wit, entrepreneurship, sociability, and ingenuity to set a new course into an uncertain future.

Eliza's lifelong adaptability remains inspiring. She navigated, often at close range, events shaping the modern world: John Wesley's creation of evangelical Methodism; the emergence of the American Republic; the fall of the Bastille and the beginning of the French Revolution in 1789 (coinciding with the birth of her first child); the publication of *A Vindication of the Rights of Woman* in 1792, by Mary Wollstonecraft, at a time when they were close friends; and the long slow ending of slavery, from William Wilberforce's first failed attempt at legislation in 1791, through the abolition of the trade in the British Empire and the United States in 1807, to the final abolition of slavery in the British Colonies in 1834. Eliza was in Barbados when the slave uprising of 1816 closed down the island, and she was in Toronto when William Lyon Mackenzie's failed rebellion of 1837 heralded the beginning of political reform in Upper Canada. In order to cope, Eliza had to move from the left to the right of the political spectrum, the irony being that, though her radical life in 1790s London provided her with the intellectual tools she needed to be self-supporting, she had to align herself with the elite right-wing in order to market her suitability as a teacher to their daughters.

My own interest in Eliza began when, as a children's literature specialist, I encountered her *Visits to the Juvenile Library; or, Knowledge Proved to be the Source of Happiness* (1805). As the novel is about children and their (enslaved) nanny who achieve liberation through literacy via the books they discover in Tabart's Juvenile Library, an upmarket children's book shop in Central London, it is a prescient form of what we now call product placement, though in its own time it would have been described as an extended advertising "puff." Eliza's other books for children, including *The Life of Carlo* (1804), her "celebrity bio" of a real dog who performed in London's Drury Lane Theatre, and her interactive paint-by-number or parse-by-color grammar book *Rays from the Rainbow* (1812), demonstrated both her consistent narrative skill and her instinct for quirky, original, and marketable ideas. My starter book on Eliza, *The Children's Book Business: Lessons from the Long Eighteenth Century* (2011), came out of my early interests in her children's books. I used *Visits to the Juvenile Library* to ground my discussion on the burgeoning children's book publishing industry of the early nineteenth century, though I used *Secresy*—with its arguments on educational philosophy and the rights of women to be educated—as a counterpoint. It was in Isobel Grundy's introduction to the 1998 modern Broadview edition of *Secresy* that I first read that Eliza had lived in Toronto, where I live, and in Niagara-on-the-Lake, about a twenty-minute drive from where I work at Brock University. That's when I found myself wanting to know what Eliza, who had been so much a part of the radical literary, cultural, and political life in London in the 1790s and early 1800s, was doing in my neighborhood in the 1830s.

In the summer of 2008, I was consulting the New York Public Library's Pforzheimer Collection of Shelley and His Circle, doing some background research for what became *The Children's Book Business*. In my off hours, I was reading *Mary Hays: The Growth of a Woman's Mind* (2006), a biography by Gina Luria Walker, and noticed an endnote saying that the manuscript letters from Eliza to Mary—the ones Annie Wedd had used for *The Fate of the Fenwicks*—were in the New-York Historical Society Library. There was no reason given for why they were there, but as it was a nice day in June and the route from the New York Public Library to the New-York Historical Society involved a stroll through Central Park, I emailed the library saying that I was interested in seeing the Fenwick Family Papers. When I arrived the librarian asked me which box I wanted. As I had not anticipated that there would be more than one, I asked for all three boxes, and that's when I had the gift of an extraordinarily lucky break.[16]

The first box contained *The Fate of the Fenwicks* manuscript letters, the ones written to Mary Hays between 1798 and 1828. That box also contained a folder marked "unpublished" and another called "undated." Both included letters and fragments Annie Wedd had omitted. The third box held photographs of Eliza's descendants, recording their lives in the United States and in Canada through the late nineteenth century and well into the twentieth. The photograph of Eliza's granddaughter, Elizabeth, taken in 1876 when she was a very old woman, is particularly compelling.

Without any surviving images of Eliza or her children, the photograph of her granddaughter provides the closest link I could find. The second box in the New-York Historical Society archive was the one that proved

Photograph of Elizabeth (Bessie) Rutherford Savage, 1876. (Fenwick Family Correspondence, MS 211, box 3, folder 11; courtesy of the New-York Historical Society)

a revelation. It held about sixty letters (some are fragments and some are by her granddaughter) unreferenced in any of the scholarly material I had found on Eliza, and apparently unknown at that time by other researchers. The letters written by Eliza are dated between 1829 (when she arrived in Niagara) and 1840 (when she died), though the box contains letters dated to 1855, written by her granddaughter Elizabeth. A few are to members of the family of Theodore Barrell (1771–1846), as Eliza had known them in Barbados. For the most part, however, the letters in the third box were written to John Little Moffat (1788–1865), a New York silversmith, and his wife and children. Those letters speak to a friendship that apparently started when Eliza and her family moved to New York in about 1825 and endured through the lifetimes of her grandchildren.

The Moffats had befriended Eliza and her family when, after a brief three-year stint in New Haven, they had moved to New York to make a second attempt at establishing a school for girls in America. Eliza Ann's health was deteriorating. Her death in New York in 1828, left Eliza with the sole responsibility for raising and educating her four young Barbados-born grandchildren. Eliza couldn't sustain the New York school on her own and for a time she ran an upmarket boarding house instead. John Moffat and his family provided emotional and practical support, as references to that period in the letters attest. When the possibility of running a new school in Niagara came up, the Moffats encouraged Eliza to make the move: a new start in a new school in a new country. The extant letters in the archive from the period are filled with compelling, upbeat, detailed accounts of the people, politics, and communities in Upper Canada, decades before the British colony became Ontario, one of the four provinces (the others were Quebec, Nova Scotia, and New Brunswick) joined at confederation in 1867 to become the Dominion of Canada. The happy final letters in the archive are ones Eliza wrote while in retirement, when she lived with the family of Alexander Duncan (1805–1891). Those letters were written from Canandaigua and Sodus Bay in Upper New York State, and finally from Providence, Rhode Island where she died in 1840.

Besides the complete letters in the second New-York Historical Society box, there were fragments, including a folder labeled "undated," made up entirely of letters that had been cut apart, indicating that some long-ago hand had made explicit decisions about what should stay and what should go. I tried not to dwell on what had been irrevocably lost, but judging from the remaining fragments, it looks as if they contained details about why Eliza described the lives of her two eldest grandsons, Will and Tom, as tragic, and why their tragedy "ended" with their deaths.[17] There are tantalizing glimpses of what those anonymous editorial hands decided to keep and what to cut. There is, for instance, a fragment from a June 10, 1832 letter, a thin strip of text, containing just two handwritten lines. On one side is the section clearly meant to be kept, as it begins with Eliza saying to the Moffats that to save them from "the troublesome business" of "hunting for Mrs. Fenwick's writing," she will provide them with her "history of authorship." On the other side of that thin strip of paper, however, is a line from a section of the same letter that was not kept. The line reads: ". . . debt through mistake or misfortune, must expect these snubs & be thankful it is no worse" followed by an emphatic, underlined *Far worse indeed. . . .*"[18] But that's it. The page potentially containing information about the snub and the burden of debt is gone, while the page connecting to the information about Eliza's literary London life survives. As material that has long been deliberately destroyed stands only as evidence of earlier presence, as ghost material, I concentrate instead on what survives: manuscript letters in Eliza's hand, material providing answers to the questions I had asked when I had first tried seriously to find her, soon after arriving at Brock University in Niagara in 2005 and realizing I was close to Eliza's last known whereabouts.

In my initial funding application to the Social Sciences and Humanities Research Council of Canada (SSHRC)—for what I came to call my "Eliza" project—I framed my research proposal as a question about what Eliza Fenwick, who had been so much a part of the radical, literary London life of the 1790s, was doing in Niagara and Toronto between, as far as I could guess at the time, about 1829 and 1834.[19] In retrospect, I can safely confess now that I silently feared that I might have been asking a rhetorical question, and would be lucky if I could find public documents relating to the school or schools in which she taught in Upper Canada. In the summer of 2008, when I found myself staring at Eliza's own words in her own hand telling me exactly what she had been doing in my neighborhood in the 1830s, I had an odd *Alice Through the Looking-Glass* moment. As Alice had wondered if she was a thing in the Red King's dream or he a thing in hers, I wondered if Eliza had imagined me or if I had conjured her. Did Eliza foresee that someone in the future might find her letters and bring them to light? Or did my research question provide the right words, the magical incantation that would unlock her past? The letters from Eliza to Mary Hays in *The Fate of the Fenwicks* begin in London in 1798 and end in 1828, when Eliza was in New York with her grandchildren. The letters to the Moffat family, written from Niagara, begin in 1829, not long after the letters to Mary Hays conclude. Curiously, though not stated in A. F. Wedd's edition of Eliza Fenwick's letters, a scrap survives pointing to why the volume was titled *The Fate of the Fenwicks*. In a postscript of a letter to Mary Wollstonecraft Godwin Shelley, Mary Hays writes: "Have you, or Mrs. [Mary Jane] Godwin, ever learned the fate of my friend & yr mother's friend, Mrs. Fenwick? After the death of her daughter, her mind seemed broken up. She ceased to answer my letters, & all my enquiries respecting her proved fruitless" (Mary Hays to Mary Shelley, 30 November 1836).[20] The letters to the Moffats and the Barrell family detailing Eliza's North American life answer Hays's question about the "fate" of the Fenwicks.

Like the 1798–1828 letters to Mary Hays, the 1829–1840 letters survived through a complex web of chance, the recognition that they were, in some way, of literary merit and worth saving, and, of course, because they happened to have come into the possession of people who held onto things rather than people who disposed of them. In one of the New-York Historical Society file boxes there is a note by Thomas Casilear Cole (1888–1976), one of Eliza's direct descendants through her granddaughter Elizabeth's line.[21] Handwritten, in blue ballpoint ink, the note begins:

> I came into the possession of these letters on the death of my uncle, A. D. Savage (1848–1935) [one of Elizabeth's sons] in August 1935. They had been given to him, fortunately saved, by a younger generation of those to whom the letters had been sent, and who had valued and saved them. My uncle at sometime long ago had put them away for safe keeping in a trunk in storage. I don't know why he had never mentioned them to me. Perhaps he had forgotten about them.[22]

Cole's note was attached to a sheaf of carbon copies of typed transcripts dated 1935, when he had arranged to have the manuscript originals of a few of Eliza's letters from Niagara transcribed. He explains that he had painstakingly read the selected letters aloud to a typist, and then manually corrected the transcripts with a view to persuading a publisher to produce a follow-up volume to *The Fate of the Fenwicks*. No one was interested; America was in the darkest days of the Depression when he first tried, and the country then plunged into the Second World War. He returned the letters and the few transcripts he had made to storage, where they stayed until he put them into the care of public archives.

The New-York Historical Society archive does contain information about what has been irrevocably lost. There is another note in Cole's hand saying that his sister Dorothy Macomber had thrown out the artifacts that had been given to her for safekeeping. His note seethes with disgust at her lack of appreciation for the history she had forever consigned to oblivion. There is also a message from Jessie Savage Cole (1858–1940), Elizabeth's youngest daughter, saying that all the letters to Eliza (her great-grandmother) and to Eliza Ann (her grandmother) from Charles Lamb had been destroyed by her mother immediately after Eliza's death in 1840.[23]

Given that the handwritten letter is a vanishing artifact, an account of the ways in which Eliza and her correspondents engaged in letter writing is a necessary interlude. On one level, people writing letters in the late eighteenth and early nineteenth centuries used them much as we do email now. Even people who were close enough to walk to each other's homes or offices would send letters to arrange meetings, as well as to work out personal and professional issues, conflicts, or ideas. In London there typically would be postal delivery twice a day, so it was possible to write a note in the morning and have a reply by the afternoon. Unlike composing on a laptop computer, the act of writing required a lot of physical effort, skill, and material paraphernalia: paper, sealing wax, ink, an ink pot, feather quills, a penknife, and possibly a shaker of sand to blot wet ink. Paper was expensive and heavy, quill pens had to be sharpened, and ink stored carefully, and postage was also costly. The materiality of the act of letter writing occasionally manifests itself, a direct connection to the moment of composition. In a letter dated December 1811, for example, Eliza begins with a parenthetical comment in her note to Mary: "I have thrown down my ink," she writes, "Excuse the blot." Yet it was only on seeing the large fist-sized blot of blue-black ink on the manuscript letter that I had a visceral sense of the potential messiness of letter writing. As there were no separate envelopes in the period, the page on which the letter was written was then folded and sealed with sealing wax. Care had to be taken by the writer to ensure that a blank space would be left where the dime-sized space of the seal would be put, because anything written there would be obliterated.

Unlike letters typed on a screen, handwritten letters provide a tangible, intimate link to the individual living hands of their authors. That physical connection was especially important for people who were oceans apart, and who depended on "packet ships," as they were called, for their letters. In late 1811, Eliza's daughter Eliza Ann sailed to take up her position as a member of the new Theatre Royal Company in Barbados. Several of her long, intensely observed letters found their way into *The Fate of the Fenwicks* because Eliza, as I've explained, copied them out carefully and sent them to Mary Hays, who preserved them. Even two hundred years after the letters were composed, the close bond between Eliza Ann and her mother remains. There is a particularly moving passage offering a glimpse of how much those letters mattered. In February 1812, on a "Tuesday night," Eliza wrote that she could not sleep as she was so excited about having received a letter from her daughter: "I have got a letter from Eliza [Ann] & as it seems like herself come back to me! I cannot bear to part with it. . . ."

In keeping with the feminine-inflected worldview of my biographical subject, my writing about Eliza is characterized by the rhetorical structures of feminist-inflected scholarship. That means that it is personal; the connections between Eliza's late Enlightenment life and the contemporary life from which I write are entwined. As Janet Todd helpfully affirms in *Feminist Literary History*, "one of the strengths of feminist criticism has been its welcoming of the personal."[24] By way of contrast, masculine-inflected scholarship tends toward elevation of the abstract and objective while typically scorning the material (especially the domestic details associated with feminine experience) and the subjective. At the center of debate about what stands as viable scholarly discourse—as Lynne Pearce argues in *The Rhetorics of Feminism*—is the use of the personal pronoun, the "I." That is why it is worth pointing out here the graphic symbolism embodied in the use of the upper case "I" in supporting the structure of a scholarly work: as the steel I-beam is an essential structural support in the construction of buildings and bridges, the "strategic first person," the strategic "I," is used as Pearce (citing Elspeth Probyn's argument) explains, to "both signal, and enact, a new set of relationships between the speaker, his/her audience and the 'object of utterance'" (86).[25] By invoking "the first person strategic," I am bridging the gap between twenty-first century readers and the world of Eliza's late eighteenth- and early nineteenth-century life and letters.

Eliza lived her life with the narrative drive of fiction, but in telling the story of her life, I was faced with the genre question of how best to convey that story. A standard literary biography tracing the author's life from birth to death with a big section in the middle devoted to the literary publications that made the author famous would not work. Everything in that kind of narrative is devoted to demonstrating how an author's life story contributed to the development of his or her literary life. Given the relatively small number of literary works that can definitely be attributed to Eliza, her letters had to be at the heart of this project, as they constitute a valid literary genre in themselves; her life writing speaks to her ability to reinvent herself, to live the roles she had taken on in order to adapt to the political and social contexts shaping the life she lived. Although Eliza does not comment in any of the extant letters about the genre in which she was writing, it does feel like what her friend William Godwin described as "individual history," that is, a personal, philosophical story. As Gina Luria Walker and Pamela Clemit claim in the introduction to their edition of Godwin's *Memoirs of the Author of the Vindication of the Rights of Woman*, he promoted a personal narrative that could potentially "foster gradual social change by transforming the moral consciousness of readers."[26] "[G]radual social change" was also the hallmark of the schools Eliza ran. Her aim was to teach girls to become "thinking" women in the very terms Mary Wollstonecraft had outlined both in the *Thoughts on Education of Daughters* (1787) and in *A Vindication of the Rights of Woman* (1792).

In addition to employing Godwin's "individual history" as a structural model for my telling of Eliza's story, I have also taken cues from mystery, detective, and adventure genre fictions: Edmund de Waal's *The Hare with Amber Eyes: A Hidden Inheritance* (2010), A. S. Byatt's *Possession: A Romance* (1990), and John le Carré's *Tinker, Tailor, Soldier, Spy* (1974). From de Waal come structural lessons about telling a family story that takes place over a long period of time, across several cultures and countries, and is shaped by world-changing historical events.[27] As Byatt's *Possession* is simultaneously the story of a (fictional) late Romantic poet's life and love, and the story of the search for her by (also fictional) modern scholars and biographers, I've adapted the strategy of entwining the story of the biographical subject and the scholarly biographical search focused on that subject. John le Carré's use of the nursery verse—tinker, tailor, soldier, sailor / rich man, poor man, beggar man, thief / doctor, lawyer, Indian chief—is a playful list of occupations available to boys. For le Carré's spy novel, the allusion is to the chameleon-like way spies change their occupations. The less well-known and less promising female version of the nursery verse—lady, baby, gypsy, queen / elephant, monkey, tangerine—provides the inspiration for my biography by focusing attention on the changing roles that shaped Eliza's life.

My chapters, for the most part, follow Eliza's life chronologically as she traveled from Britain to the Caribbean to North America: from "Daughter of Methodism," "Mother and Author," "Children's Book Writer and Friend," to "Governess and Networker," "Colonist and Slaveholder," "School Owner and Mourner," and finally "North American Grandmother." Though the chronology of Eliza's life's story emerges naturally, it doesn't dominate. By focusing on her shifting roles, several types of transnational and cross-temporal narratives emerge. For instance, the schools in Bridgetown, New Haven, New York grew from the pedagogical values Eliza developed in concert with her literary cohort—the best known of that group being Catharine Macaulay, Mary Wollstonecraft, Mme de Genlis, Maria Edgeworth, Anna Barbauld, Charlotte Smith, and Jane Porter—on what an intellectually informed educational program of instruction might look like. By discussing the influences behind Eliza's educational philosophy, the ideas that shaped her beliefs about female education come into focus. The overarching agenda is to argue that Eliza has a place among canonical late Enlightenment literary, philosophical women, and among the writers and practitioners of maternal pedagogies. She was a terrific writer and her literary remains still pulse with life and passion, both with delight in the details of the everyday and with acutely observed critiques of the world in which she lived.

To read Eliza's writing in the context of public, global political events is to have a rare glimpse of what it was like for a woman without financial means or connections to move not just across oceans but also across varied and rapidly shifting social and cultural conditions, and to adapt successfully. Eliza was conscious of the strangeness of her nomadic life. As a relatively elderly woman of sixty-nine, writing in a March 30, 1835, letter to the Moffats in New York, she remembered how easy it had been when she lived there in the late 1820s, "to command a social evening together," as they had been just "a short walk" away from each other. In the letter, Eliza then shifts to abstract comments about how they are all living on a "floating world," and adds existentially: "we are but the particles moving with the general Mass." Perhaps Eliza had been recalling lines from Mary Wollstonecraft's 1796 *Letters Written During a Short Residence in Sweden, Norway and Denmark*, musing on her feelings of loss and injustice, describing herself similarly "as a particle broken off from the grand mass of mankind."[28] In writing almost forty years after Wollstonecraft's untimely death in 1797, Eliza knew intimately what it meant to be a "particle" on a "floating world," a participant in a "global economy" a couple of centuries before the phrase would become common currency.

1

Daughter of Methodism

At age seventy-four, Eliza wrote to her twenty-one-year-old friend, Reuben Moffat (1818–1894), reflecting generally on family life, values, and ties that bind. She reminisced about her childhood, claiming that her own "family ties" had all too early been torn apart. "They scarcely ever existed," she wrote, "for being when almost an infant the only remaining one of *16*, I had no brothers or sisters to struggle with me for supremacy of affection or yet to check my grasping self-love by the realisement of mutual sacrifices." Warming to her theme, Eliza developed her affecting family portrait: "Losing my father while very young & continuing a spoiled child of prosperity I still had sense enough to see the beauties of family union & often in my day dreams have pictured to myself a group of brothers & sisters & fancied how I should divide & distribute among them the lavish supplies which were mistakenly lavished on me" (EF to Reuben Moffat, 26 May 1840). Everything about the picture has the ring of authenticity—a perfect backstory for the cultured person Eliza was at seventy-four. As a gentlewoman who had been able to rely on her own resources, having been well-educated and well-nurtured, she fit the profile of a woman whose girlhood had been shaped by a moneyed, stable, loving, intellectual late-Enlightenment family. A talented writer, fluent in French, accomplished in music and dancing, and well-versed in art, literature, philosophy, and politics, Eliza must have had the look and sound of a "spoiled child of prosperity," the sole recipient of "lavish supplies." Any man, husband, or father assumed to have been a part of Eliza's early life in Britain would have been relegated by her young American correspondent Reuben Moffat—or by any other correspondent—to some distant, misty past. Far removed from the genteel 1770s girlhood to which Eliza alluded, her story must have made matter-of-fact sense to Reuben, something to be taken at face value. The historical evidence, however, suggests a different story.

In order for Eliza to have been "almost an infant" when she was the "the only remaining of *16*," her fifteen phantom siblings had to have died before she was born or when she was very young. But the dates don't appear to work. Eliza's father, Peter Jaco (1728–81), did not marry Eliza's mother, Elizabeth Hawksworth (1727–94), until 1763. He would have been thirty-five and she thirty-six and that just doesn't leave enough time for so many other children to have been born and died while Eliza was still "almost an infant" (she was born in 1766), unless Hawksworth had borne and lost most of those children before marrying Jaco.

The only clear information about Jaco's meeting with and marriage to Hawksworth comes primarily from a group of letters in the John Rylands Library, Manchester, where some of the Methodist archives are kept. According to a note in the manuscript, the letters written by Jaco in the 1760s to his friend George Merryweather (another of John Wesley's itinerant preachers) are "copies made from the originals" and given by Merryweather's daughter to an early Methodist archivist, James Werrell, in 1829.[1] In a letter dated February 26, 1764, Jaco refers to his future wife as "Mrs. Hawksworth," suggesting that she might have been previously married, but even that is not certain because the honorific "Mrs." was commonly used in the period for older women in general. Mrs. Hawksworth was a housekeeper and what was called a "class leader," a kind of lay, spiritual den mother, at the Methodist headquarters in Bristol, the Bristol New Room.[2] Built in 1742, the New Room was the meeting place John and Charles Wesley established after the Methodist societies, formed just four years earlier in 1739, had started to expand exponentially. What the Wesley brothers had needed was a central place of congregation, a venue suited for Christian worship and study, but not designated as a church.[3] Although Charles and John Wesley did encourage women who showed talent to take up leadership roles in their local religious study groups, Mrs. Hawksworth must have been particularly gifted in order to take her place at the center of Methodist life in Bristol. Jaco would have regularly visited the New Room as it was the organizational hub for the movement, the place where the evolving brotherhood of Methodist preachers would gather. It is where the Wesley brothers planned preaching "circuits" to the clusters of towns to which they would send their small rotating teams of preachers. And it was in the New Room that the traveling preachers would find a little respite before going on the road again.

Jaco, in the 1764 letter to Merryweather, sketched the events leading up to his marriage. He began with a profile of his ideal mate: "Ever since I first knew God," he wrote, "I thought that an agreeable companion must certainly sweeten many of the afflictions incident to this fluctuating state of things, & that this companion must be *truly pious*, independent of Riches, beauty or any personal accomplishment as any of these seldom meet in the same person. I therefore determined to chuse the former and leave all other events to God." Elizabeth Hawksworth fit the bill. She also fit Wesley's profile of the ideal candidate for the position of an itinerant's mate: "A preacher's wife," says Wesley, "should be a pattern of cleanliness, in her person, clothes and habitation. Let nothing slatternly be seen about her, no rags, no dirt, no litter. And she should be always at work, either for herself, her husband or for the poor."[4] In describing his first encounter with his future wife, Jaco used terms that were almost identical to Wesley's:

> Accordingly, four years ago [presumably in 1760 since the letter is dated 1764] I became acquainted with Mrs. Hawksworth the Housekeeper at Bristol Room, a serious, useful woman, & after a critical observation of her conduct I thought she was the most likely woman to make my Life agreeable that I had ever met with. After some time I communicated my thoughts to Mr. Charles Wesley who told me that it would be a sin to re- move her from the place she was in, that she was surprisingly blest in her classes, and in short gave me so much discouragement that I determined I would make no more confidents, but as she had nothing and I did not like her [text is unclear] to the church, we agreed to wait for a more favourable prospect.

Charles Wesley was obviously reluctant to lose someone who was contribut- ing actively to the spiritual life, as well as presumably to the housekeeping, of the community in Bristol.[5] A formal covenant from 1752 survives in the Methodist Archives, outlining "The Rules of an Assistant," explicitly dis- couraging itinerant preachers from marriage:

1. Be diligent never be unemployed for a moment.
2. Be serious. Let your motto be "To worship to the Lord."
3. Converse cautiously and sparingly with women.
4. Take not considerable step toward marriage without first acquaint- ing us.[6]

Peter Jaco followed the rules. He had consulted Charles Wesley about Eliza- beth Hawksworth and had been refused. He took the advice to heart and waited for two years until "a more favourable prospect," in the shape of a business opportunity, made him feel that he could generate enough income to support a wife. He explained what happened next:

> Abt [about] two years ago [1762], some of my London friends communi- cated a scheme to me under the seal of secrecy which when carried into execution would in all probability being exceedingly profitable to the pro- prietors in which I was to have a fourth part; and added to this had the advantage of preferring any person I thought fit to look after the affair with a Pension of £50 per annum.

Jaco obviously felt that with an income of £50 he would have enough to support Hawksworth on his own. As Paul Langford explains in *A Polite and Commercial People,* fifty pounds was the magic number in the mid-eighteenth century, as it was "treated as the minimum at which it was possible to aspire to membership of the middling rank."[7] There are no further specifics of the "scheme" in question, but contemporary documents suggest that a common venture entered into by preachers was to purchase a share in a ship. There is, however, a marginal note in the manuscript explaining that "several old preachers engaged in secular concerns in which most of them failed of success," and that, "They were tempted to this from the slender allowance granted for board, travelling & most of them being poor men."[8]

Jaco had no income other than the support provided by the Connexion,[9] the name for the members of the growing numbers of Methodist preachers in the mid-eighteenth century. They were literally a connected group, defined by their "connexion" to the Wesley brothers and to each other. The money raised in the individual study groups they served supported the material needs of preachers on the road. Accounts were kept and they show, for example, that the new shoes Jaco needed in 1763 cost the Connexion six shillings.[10] The glaringly unavoidable conclusion derived from extant letters and the Methodist accounts demonstrates that, as an itinerant preacher, Jaco was not a man of wealth. Eliza's claim that she was "a spoiled child of prosperity" therefore seems more wish fulfillment than fact.

With the promise of an income, Jaco felt able to move forward with his desire to marry Mrs. Hawksworth. "I now thought the way made plain," he says in the letter, "and accordingly to our agreement married Mrs. H. last May." Unfortunately, as is typically the case with get-rich-quick schemes, things didn't work out as planned. "But alas!" he proclaims, "How transitory all human prospects!" He confides that in July 1763, two months after the marriage, he "received a letter from [his] fellow adventurers," saying that there were problems and that the scheme "would never go forward." He says that: "This together with a letter from my wife that she was with child and was uneasy in her mind that she was absent from me, threw me into greater difficulty." At that point, Jaco was ready to quit the Connexion and go back to his home in Cornwall where he had been involved in his family business, a local pilchard fishery. Mr. Wesley, however, reluctant to lose one of his itinerants, decided to support the marriage of Peter Jaco and Elizabeth Hawksworth, especially as she was pregnant. Jaco concludes:

But blessed be God, Good Mr W had reclaimed me from such a desperate procedure, and roused me to my duty by shewing the dreadful consequences which (he thinks) will infallibly attend my deserting the work. I am now more satisfied in my mind, and find unspeakable serenity in my soul. My wife is on her way to me, and hope the storms I have meet with will be followed by a heartily said "Amen."

The letter indicates that the marriage took place in May 1763, as Elizabeth had written in July that she was pregnant, and if she was traveling to her husband at the end of February she would have been about to give birth.

The next surviving letter, written six months later and dated September 12, 1764, confirms that a daughter was born to them, but this child was probably not Eliza. Although I've not been able to find a birth record for her, she always claimed her birthday to be February 1, and when she identified her age, the math would put the year of her birth at 1766 (although the date carved on her gravestone is 1767). Unless Eliza consistently lied about her age, it does appear that she had one older sister, likely born in early March 1764. Given the absence of official documentation, I can only say that there are no references in any of Jaco's surviving letters to another pregnancy or another child.

In the September 1764 letter, Jaco also explains that he had been ill with St. Anthony's Fire (a painful fungal infection related to contaminated rye or wheat). He then provides a glimpse of family life:

> When I began to mend my dear little girl fell into the small pox and was soon given over by the doctor that attended her. Her affliction so affected her mother who was obliged to attend her night and day, that she had a very bad time, so that our house has been an infirmary. Blessed be the Father of Mercies we are all at present in a hopeful way, and trust that a few weeks will set us on our legs again.

A few months later, in a December 1764 letter, Jaco wrote with a brief update: "My little family are much better thro mercy." Then there is a gap. Nothing more appears about his domestic life in the extant record for several years.

It wasn't until May 14, 1771 that Peter Jaco next wrote about his family. In a letter to Charles Wesley he said he had heard that Wesley's children had survived their recent illnesses, and that he could commiserate as his own "less & little family" had experienced a similar cycle of illness and recovery, but without—as the reference to "less" suggests—the same completely happy ending. The sign-off to the letter registers loss: "My little family," he says, "& the McCownleys and the preachers join me in much affection to yourself, Mrs. Wesley and the young ones."[11] The likelihood that the child born in 1764 had died sometime before 1771 is confirmed by John Lenton, who in his detailed study of Wesley's itinerants says that "the maintenance for [only] one child appears in the (defective) London stewards accounts 1766/7 and 1774/5."[12] That information would accord with Eliza's birth on February 1, 1766 and make sense of her being the only living child of her parents by 1771.

That Eliza grew up to be the only surviving daughter of Jaco is certain and can be demonstrated through two pieces of evidence. One is a letter, dated October 24, 1779, to Richard Rodda (another preacher), in which Jaco writes first about his failing health. As the records in the Methodist archives indicate, Jaco had been based in London for some time in the late 1770s, as the rough life of an itinerant had obviously taken its toll on him physically. Despite his deteriorating health, he continued to preach: "[A]nd the assistant excepted," he says, "I labour more than any preacher in London. 'Tis happy for me that I never looked for my reward from men!" Then he alludes to what his "little family" had been doing: "Had the business that Betsy [a diminutive of Eliza or Elizabeth] & her mother are answered in according to expectations, I should perhaps have been too happy in this line." The intent of the business was apparently to supplement the allowance from the Connexion, because Jaco states first that, "it was always my ambition to preach Gospel without charge," and then concludes philosophically, "But the Lord's will be done."[13]

Although there is no indication as to what the "business" was, at his death his occupation was listed as "hosier," someone who made stockings. Jaco died in 1781 at age fifty-two just two years after the letter to Rodda was written (when Eliza was just fifteen), and his one remaining reference to Eliza is in his will, where he named her as his primary beneficiary. "To my daughter Elizabeth Jaco," he bequeathed "the sum of one hundred pounds of lawful money of Great Britain to be paid unto her at the age of twenty one years or on the day of marriage."[14] In the end, the only detail that I can verify from Eliza's 1840 letter to Reuben Moffat is that she was indeed "very young" when her father died.

In an age of electronic records, DNA testing, and ever-increasing ways of tracing genealogical records online, it is difficult to imagine that the most basic details of an eighteenth-century identity—date and place of birth, names of parents and siblings—could be so hard to confirm. Even the venerable *Oxford Dictionary of National Biography* (*ODNB*), normally the first stop for scholars in search of biographical information, did not have the correct information for Eliza in 2017. Then, the entry still read: "Fenwick [*née* Jago], Eliza [*pseud.* Revd David Blair] (1766?–1840), writer, was probably born on 1 February 1766 to Thomas and Elizabeth Jago and baptized Elizabeth on 25 June at Pelynt, Cornwall."[15] There is something fitting in the fact that the adventure romance of Eliza's life story should begin with a feature consistent in formal characterizations of the genre: the hero(ine)'s "mysterious" birth.

The one official record I have been able to find that confirms Eliza as the daughter of Peter and Elizabeth Jaco is the record of the birth in 1798 of Eliza's son, Orlando. In the register dated December 11, 1801, Orlando is clearly identified as the son of John Fenwick and "Elizabeth, Daughter of Peter and Elizabeth Jaco." Eliza's address is listed as Great Newport Street, Parish St. Ann, County of Middlesex. Mary Hays was one of the witnesses and the other was Henrietta Braddock,[16] also a family friend at the time. Because Orlando's name and date of birth (May 3, 1798) match all other documented evidence, the identification of Peter Jaco, early Methodist itinerant preacher, as Eliza's father seems demonstrably correct.

The distinction between my identification of Eliza Fenwick as the daughter of Peter Jaco, and the "*née* Jago" in the *ODNB*, is not significant as variant spellings of names were relatively common in the period. What is significant is that the identification of Eliza Fenwick as the daughter of Methodist itinerant Peter Jaco strongly indicates that neither her claim to being a "spoiled child of prosperity," nor her claim to being the only survivor of sixteen children, are likely to be true. The fact that the detail of losing her father "while very young" is true signals how easy it is to slip between what actually happened and wish fulfillment, and how hard it is to disentangle one from the other. Without resorting to outright speculation—I don't think she was deliberately lying in 1840—it looks as if she had simply settled into the role of the refined person she had become, or perhaps she had slipped so fully and completely into that role that she believed it to be true. All extant information about Eliza indicates, however, that generally she was scrupulously truthful, a woman of honor.

The point of trying to ascertain genealogical accuracy in composing a biography is really to ground a backstory for the subject, something that lends authority to the explanation of how that person's adult accomplishments were shaped. With so little verifiable information about Eliza's childhood available, the most substantive documentary evidence does come from the records related to what a Methodist childhood was like in the mideighteenth century when Charles and John Wesley were developing a distinct repertoire of religious practices and building a program of instruction to support its growth. The records of what that kind of childhood would have been like are extensive, but Eliza's relationship with her early years is more difficult to figure out. She only refers explicitly to Methodists once, and she does so in blatantly distasteful terms.

Eliza Rejects Her Methodist Roots

On January 26, 1833, writing from Niagara to Reuben Moffat's sister Mary, Eliza expresses surprise that Mary had joined the Methodists: "I am almost ready to say I am sorry for it as what I have known of Methodists has not been generally in their favor." Eliza then qualifies her disapproval: "but you Mary are too gentle to become a bigot & I have too much judgment not to discern the difference between purity of heart & purity of words merely." That's the only time the word Methodist turns up in any of Eliza's extant letters, and there is nothing in her clear distaste for the practice that hints at her own childhood as the daughter of a Methodist preacher who had been chosen and inducted into the ministry by John Wesley himself. There is also something deeply unsettling in the one comment Eliza does make about the distinction between "purity of heart" and "purity of words." Is that an allusion to her suspicion of an underlying hypocrisy in Methodist practice? Her condemnation of Methodists as potential bigots only suggests that her dislike was more than casual.

The lives of the Methodist men in Eliza's life, beginning with her father's life as an itinerant, were characterized by absence. The two men who precipitated the events that led to both she and her daughter having to take sole responsibility for their respective children—her husband John Fenwick and her son-in-law William Rutherford—were also the sons of Wesley's itinerant

Adeline and Mary Moffat
by John Wesley Jarvis.
(Courtesy of the Frick Art
Reference Library)

preachers. Both men, like Eliza, appear to have abandoned all associations with Methodism. I can't make a case that John Fenwick and William Rutherford were bad fathers because they were the sons of itinerant Methodist preachers, but when a pattern emerges, as it does here, the coincidence is hard to ignore. In reading about the passionate commitment all the Methodist fathers had to their evangelical mission, it is hard not to notice the glaring absence of reference to their respective families.[17]

Eliza's husband, John Fenwick (1757–1823), was the son of John Fenwick Sr. (1730–87)[18] and Eliza Ann's husband was William Rutherford (1783–1829), the son of Thomas Rutherford (1752–1806). By all accounts, John Fenwick Jr. and William Rutherford, though a generation apart in age, were at least initially charismatic, great storytellers, and active in journalism (writing and editing newspapers) and the theater (John Fenwick wrote plays and William Rutherford was an actor). Both were also given to the very un-Methodist-like vices of excessive drinking and gambling. There are hints that William was also physically abusive to Eliza Ann.

Eliza first announced her decision to separate from John when her children were just eleven and two. "But never, never," she says in a letter to Mary dated July 4 and 5, 1800, "will I again, if the means are to be had by my industry of supporting my children, involve myself in such miseries & perplexities as I have endured." Almost two decades later, on January 20, 1819, Eliza wrote again to Mary, with the horrible news that her own history had repeated itself and that Eliza Ann's separation from William had taken place six months earlier (eighteen years after the announcement of her own separation), "exactly one hour after she had been put to Bed of her fourth child," on July 16, 1818, the date Orlando (Roland) Rutherford was born. "An insatiable love of Company & late hours," she explains, "seduced Mr. R into a habit of constant intoxication." Although I will not dwell on the point here, the "habit of constant intoxication" among the men in Eliza's life does track through her story.

From a distance of more than two hundred years, one fact stands out: Eliza, her husband, and son-in-law were all the disaffected children of Wesley's original itinerant preachers. All three fathers—Peter Jaco, John Fenwick Sr., and Thomas Rutherford—were, in the mid-eighteenth century, committed to the evangelical Methodist mission of John and Charles Wesley. As itinerant preachers all three were members of the Connexion, and were deeply connected with each other through their shared commitment to the growing Methodist movement. As the records in the Methodist archive show, those early preachers regarded themselves as part of an extended family, sharing a commitment to their roles as preachers, and to their mission to bring people to a holy state. Their faith was characterized as "enthusiasm" (though the word was used as a term of derision in the eighteenth century)[19] and it manifested itself in what we might regard as an overemotional response (crying, fainting) of the kind we recognize in people who are moved by their experiences at revivalist rallies and rock concerts. The intensity of their religious experiences preaching to thousands on muddy fields or on stony beaches reads, in their own accounts, as something akin to the reports of being at Woodstock in 1969 or at Glastonbury in 1970, reflecting a shared feeling of community and of participating in something of historic importance, and a sense of pure joy.[20]

The centrality of Methodist practice, study, and preaching in the day-to-day lives of Peter Jaco and Thomas Rutherford is evident in the records they left.[21] As an example, there is an account of how deeply Rutherford was moved by hearing John Wesley preach. The anecdote survives in a slightly roundabout way in Wesley's records. He copied part of a letter from Rutherford describing the experience of hearing Wesley preach in 1770:

> His apostolic and angelic experience struck me exceedingly. He appeared like one come down from heaven to teach men the way thither. His text was Heb 8:10–12. He opened the words in a concise and easy manner, and spoke from them with such perspicuity and simplicity, and, at the same time, with such wisdom and authority, as I had never heard before. To me he seemed like one of the apostles going about confirming the churches.[22]

Thomas Rutherford's genuine belief reverberates through the passage as he really does perceive Wesley as a living angel sent from God. Mountains of similar testimonials in the Methodist archives make it abundantly clear that John and Charles Wesley profoundly galvanized the support of people they recruited: Methodism became the focus of their lives and the lives of their families. That must have been the world into which Eliza Jaco, John Fenwick, and William Rutherford were born. Yet, in all of the surviving records related to (writings by and/or descriptions of) Eliza, John, and William, mentions of God in particular or of religion in general are very rare.[23] In attempting to reconcile all three with their respective fathers, tensions surface between connection and separation, between fathers committed to their religious beliefs and children who rejected those beliefs.

In a literal way, all three Methodist fathers were on the road a lot, though of the three only Thomas Rutherford left substantive accounts of his children. And because Methodism was still in its formative phase in the mid-eighteenth century, it was both embraced by those with early adopter enthusiasm and dismissed by those suspicious of new ways of practicing

Christianity. Eliza and John Fenwick seem to have channeled the religious zeal of their fathers into secular commitments: John to political reform, Eliza to social reform, especially to the rights of women to be educated. The familial and religious ties that bound them initially had to be broken in order for them to forge new ties grounded in political and social freedom.

It's tempting to assume that John and Eliza came to know each other through their respective fathers, but there is no explicit evidence of that. The fact that Eliza and John's daughter should also decide to marry the son of one of Wesley's preachers does appear to be a particularly strange and unhappy coincidence. When Eliza Ann and William Rutherford met, as actors in Barbados in 1812, they were both far away in time, distance, and ethos from the eighteenth-century Methodism of their respective grand-fathers and fathers. There is, however, a letter from Eliza written to Mary, on September 25, 1812, explicitly acknowledging the connection between her father and the father of her future son-in-law. The letter dates from when Eliza Ann first announced her interest in William. Eliza's focus was on her daughter's happiness, so the letter reads as a response to rumors of William's (implicitly bad) behavior, and reassurance that whatever gossip Mary was hearing in Britain may have been overstated. Eliza writes that William's father Thomas was a "sort of ward" of her father's and "*That he was a truly good man*" (emphasis in original).[24] It is here that Eliza makes the only explicit link to the community of preachers who informed her Meth-odist childhood. She notes that she knew William's mother and sisters. She must also have known that Thomas Rutherford had recently died (in 1806). In what is perhaps an allusion to her own early loss of her father (and bely-ing her later claim to being a "spoiled child of prosperity"), she writes that "Clergymen's widows and orphans are seldom too well provided for." The remark was in the context of information that her future son-in-law had "resigned some property that came to him to increase the comforts of his mother & sisters." Finally, Eliza explains that she had become privy to this information, despite her "total separation from all [her] father's friends," through a chance encounter with a "Mrs. Bruce," who reconnected her with her Methodist roots.

The Roots of Methodism

In keeping with the chronological structure implicit in the genre of biog-raphy, this chapter is called "Daughter of Methodism" because a subject's childhood is supposed to reveal something about who that person has be-come. Because Eliza's husband and son-in-law had childhoods formed like hers in a common pool of religious ideas, the roots of Methodism formed a significant part of all their lives. Although information about Eliza's childhood is minimal, extensive records of the ideas John and Charles Wesley had about educating children survive. Both had an intense practical interest in what a Methodist childhood should look like and established schools (eventually Kingswood for boys and Mrs. Owen's school for girls) in order to raise the children of their community into the religious observance in which they so fervently believed.

In the days when John and Charles Wesley were alive, the people who joined them found something exciting and adventurous, a spirit of reform and commitment in the newly forming Methodist societies, something that is still audible in the accounts of the preachers who worked directly with the Wesley brothers. Something of that spirit grew in both the young Eliza Jaco and the young John Fenwick, though they rechanneled the religious reform that had characterized their fathers' lives into social and political reform.

The Methodist church to which Eliza's young friend Mary Moffat was aligning herself in 1833 New York (probably the First Methodist Church at 44 John Street in what is now Lower Manhattan) would have been anathema to Eliza's father Peter in the 1750s, when he joined the Methodists. In the formative phases of the movement, Methodists were members of the Church of England who met in societies or study groups led not necessarily by ordained ministers but by class leaders, like Eliza's mother, or by lay preachers, both men and women, who in the early stages of the movement were selected by John or Charles Wesley personally. The mission of the movement was to take Christianity to the people rather than wait for people to come to it, or have it delivered by formally ordained priests.

The Methodist movement had originated, as its name suggests, in a "method" of religious devotion founded on practices developed by John Wesley (1703–91) while at Oxford in the late 1720s. With his brother Charles (1707–88), he formed what was essentially a bible study group, called "the Holy Club," in 1729. It grew into a loose association of similar study groups focused on close bible study, self-examination, and strict discipline. The group was initially the butt of jokes and the subject of scorn. They were nicknamed Methodists first in 1732, and though it was at first regarded as a term of derision the name stuck and the number of converts attracted to the movement grew exponentially. In 1755, Samuel Johnson gave a kind of credibility to the upstart movement by including it in his 1755 *Dictionary of the English Language*, defining a Methodist as "one of a new kind of puritan lately arisen, so called from their profession to live by rules and in constant method."[25] John Wesley himself, however, was reluctant to acknowledge that his movement had become a thing unto itself. In fact, he wrote a treatise in 1758, titled "Reasons Against Separation from the Church of England," explaining why "so-called Methodists"—as he referred to his own group throughout the document—should remain faithful to the Established Church.[26] Methodists were faithful to the Church of England, at least until John and Charles Wesley died, when they formally recognized their group as separate, distinct from the Church of England.

The Wesley brothers were not alone in their dissatisfaction with the Church of England. As V. H. H. Green explains in his study of Wesley, "the years following the accession of George I [were] a hot-bed of high Tory, if not Jacobite, politics as well as theological obscurantism."[27] Other splinter groups, Baptists and Quakers for instance, collectively known as "Dissenters," were actively setting themselves up as distinct from the Church of England, but for different reasons. While Methodists were reacting to their perception that the Established Church had become overly insular (expecting people to come to it, instead of taking faith to the people), Dissenters objected to the state interfering with the church. There were unfortunate consequences for religious groups who strayed from the Church of England party line. They were banned from schools and from holding official positions.[28] The positive side of the exclusion was that it did nurture some of the pedagogical reforms that provided the ground for a modern rational and useful education, including the induction of science, history, and modern languages into the curriculum.[29]

For twenty-first-century secular readers without scholarly investment, the religious debates that had been so central to Anglo-European life in the long eighteenth century now seem arcane. The details of those debates have drifted, at best, to the peripheries of historical knowledge. Only when noticing the large number of solid, imposing churches—Baptist or Unitarian (both modern descendants of the Dissenters), Catholic and Methodist—there are in contrast to relatively small populations in countless little towns in Europe and North America does the sense of how central each denomination was to its community become manifest, how important specific Christian practices and philosophies were in the day-to-day lives of the people who attended those churches. The intense religious debates and the commitments that generated those imposing and expensive structures have long been defused, and many of the buildings themselves have long settled into their repurposed lives as restaurants, art galleries, and other secular spaces.

Though John and Charles Wesley were ordained priests, they believed early on that their spiritual needs were not being met by the Church of

England. They rejected what V. H. H. Green describes as the "growth of seeming unbelief and infidelity" in the Established Church and a sense that it had entered into a period of stasis; that it was boring and complacent (5). They were also uneasy about the fact that the parish structure rewarded the rich and provided incomes for only the privileged few. The Wesley brothers yearned for something more, something Green defines as a kind of "sacrificial ardor," something of the religious zeal that had characterized Jesus and the beginnings of Christianity (25).

Even before their movement had a name, John and Charles were trying to bring to life a form of religious observance that was at once more rigorous and more egalitarian than what they experienced in the Church of England. They wanted a religious community that was, to quote Abraham Lincoln anachronistically, "of the people, by the people, for the people."[30] Unlike the clergymen of the time, who, as John Lenton says, "defined themselves as a closed calling to which it became more difficult to gain access without the right qualifications,"[31] John and Charles encouraged people from all walks of life, rich and poor, tradespeople and people running small businesses, to take charge of their own spiritual health. As a result, Methodists quickly attracted all kinds of people, including: Peter Jaco, whose family ran a small pilchard business; Stephen Nichols, a tinner; John Fenwick Sr., "a man of property";[32] and women such as Mary Bosanquet Fletcher (1739–1815). All became leaders in Methodist societies. Although there is no evidence that Eliza was at all influenced by the early Methodist ethos that supported the viability, integrity, and autonomy of women as preachers and teachers in the late eighteenth and early nineteenth centuries, they were present in her world. Her own mother (as noted by Peter Jaco, citing Charles Wesley) had been recognized as a "class leader." More broadly, as Lenton explains in "Support Groups for Methodist Women Preachers 1803–1851," Methodist women collectively created a network to provide mutual assistance and "spiritual companionship." They engaged in the work of "writing letters, visiting, passing on news, publishing, travelling and preaching together."[33] Except for preaching, Eliza did all of those things.

In "She Offered Them Christ," Paul Wesley Chilcote describes a day in the life of one of Wesley's relentlessly energetic female preachers, Grace Murray. After the death of her husband in 1742, she was appointed one of the original class leaders in Newcastle, and like Eliza's mother Elizabeth Hawksworth, was designated as a "housekeeper." She had "full a hundred classes" that "met in two separate meetings and a band for each day of the week" and she also "visited the sick and backsliders." That sounds like a lot of work for one woman each week, but it does provide a sense of just how committed the early adopters must have been and how organized the whole movement was at the beginning.[34]

John and Charles Wesley, and the third founder of Methodism, George Whitefield (1714–70)—or Whitfield as it is sometimes spelled—together worked out ways of making Christian practice more inclusive and more democratic. They organized their evangelical campaign with military precision. Taking their cues from the Moravians (another Protestant evangelical denomination) in Germany, they developed not Methodist churches but Methodist "societies" in which people could examine each other on their faith and engage with a class leader in an intense kind of bible study and self-examination of one's commitment to God. Society members became a kind of family, united in their newfound devotion to a more egalitarian, more participatory form of worship. In contrast to the practices of the Church of England, Methodism was proudly evangelical, and thanks to John and Charles Wesley, was hugely successful in recruiting converts.

After the formation of the first Methodist society in Bristol in 1739, the movement expanded rapidly and new societies began springing up. By 1740, John Wesley knew that he needed help if he was going to keep all of his converts focused, so he began to recruit lay preachers (assistants, as he called them) to assist. In 1746, there were just seven circuits of societies to be visited, but by 1765 there were thirty-nine. John Lenton explains: "the basic organization of travelling preachers" worked a circuit of societies for six weeks at a time, so that "every society would be visited once a fortnight." Wesley met with his preachers in "conference" in order "to discuss their practice and doctrine, provide training and report on their successes and discover where Wesley would send them next."[35] By moving the preachers around and making sure that they were repeating their message, but doing so differently each time, he could keep everyone engaged and focused. Thousands flocked to open-air fields and beaches to hear sermons by Wesley's army of preachers.

The life of an itinerant preacher on the road was physically hard. Travel between towns was usually on horseback, and accommodations were limited. Peter Jaco wrote that his own life consisted of "preaching three or four times a day and riding thirty or forty miles thankful for a little clean straw with a canvas sheet to lie on." And like many of Wesley's initial itinerants, he could not be assured of a warm welcome from his hosts.

It was the on-the-ground, patient, personal efforts of the Wesley brothers and their assistant preachers that eventually paid off and contributed to making conversion to Methodism so popular. Thomas Rutherford provided an intimate account of exactly how that personal approach worked.

He remembered riding on horseback with John Wesley on May 10, 1776, and described it as "one of the highest treats" he had ever enjoyed. Because Wesley "could not read or write as he did when travelling in his carriage," he explained, "he gave himself up to conversation, which was at once replete with information and entertainment." The occasion also gave him some insight into how Wesley's attention to the details of individual communities contributed to the steady success of the Methodist movement. On their ride together they had "passed a gentleman's seat," which Rutherford said he could not name despite that fact that he "had passed it repeatedly." Wesley responded: "When I can learn nothing else," he said, "I like to learn the names of houses and villages as I pass them." Rutherford learned his lesson, explaining that Wesley's words "carried reproof."[36]

I've cited the incidents recorded by both Rutherford and Jaco because they are so telling about the kind of life that William Rutherford's father and Eliza's father lived. Their stories speak to the degree of commitment and networking Wesley required of his itinerants in order to spread the Methodist message of the value of an educated, dedicated religious life. There is no direct evidence that Eliza learned how to make cold calls from the Methodist playbook when she began recruiting for the schools she established in Bridgetown, New Haven, New York, or Niagara, but she did have the same drive, attention to detail, and awareness of the nuances of the social life and hierarchy in each new community in which she settled.

Wesley's itinerant preachers were not just foot soldiers in an expanding Methodist army; they were the rock stars of their day, performers committed to the thrill and the pain of being on the road all the time as they were building an audience of faithful converts. Hundreds, even thousands of fans often stood in the mud or on the beach, in the cold or wind, listening intently to their words. Adored by new converts, the preachers were also reviled by those who felt their way of life threatened the status quo. Yet at the heart of the early Methodist mission was the constant reaffirmation that the sinful would be forgiven and redeemed. This is where Eliza's father, Peter Jaco, comes in. Converted by John Wesley in 1746 and inducted as an itinerant preacher on May 8, 1754, he served until his death in 1781. He was a convert dedicated to the cause of converting others in the Methodist way of redemption. The account he gave of his conversion was the stuff of Methodist legend.

The story Jaco wrote of his own conversion in a letter to John Wesley is significant as it was the first in a series of "Lives" of Methodist preachers, printed in the first issue of *The Arminian Magazine* in 1778, a periodical Wesley created to promote his doctrine of universal redemption as a counternarrative to the Calvinist doctrine of predestination. As one of the magazine's central tenets was to provide "accounts and letters containing the experience of pious persons," Jaco's telling of his own experience of redemption had an immediacy and truth that could not be conveyed in abstract doctrinal terms.[37] The fact that the essay was then reprinted at the start of the six-volume *The Lives of Early Methodist Preachers* in 1865 testifies that Jaco's story endured, as does the fact that it was also reprinted in the *Weekly Wesley* of Monday September 6, 2010. The pattern of the story is familiar and follows the traditional trajectory of "I was a hopeless sinner but found the truth and now I am saved." Because the story provides a glimpse of the kind of atmosphere in which Eliza must have been immersed as a child, it is worth sketching.

Jaco says he was born "in 1729 of serious parents," and grew into an adolescent "of a gay, lively disposition," though indifferent at school because he couldn't stand his teacher, whom he described as "given to drink to excess"[38] At fourteen he joined his father in a pilchard-fishery business (pilchards are small sardines) in Newlyn, near Penzance in Cornwall. Jaco's father was not a pilchard fisherman but rather a small businessman involved in fish processing. The pilchards were salted, pressed, and exported. By the mid-eighteenth century in Newlyn, the pilchard-processing business was thriving. In a Christian context, there is obviously something symbolically right in the idea that someone involved with fishing should become a fisher of men.

Peter Jaco heard John Wesley preach for the first time on Sunday July 12, 1747, still very early in the evangelical mission of the movement (again, the first Methodist society had been founded just a few years earlier, in 1739). Wesley was preaching on a beach and there was a love/hate relationship with the novelty of the experience. People turned out in droves and Wesley himself described the occasion:

> At five I walked to a rising ground, near the sea-shore, where was a smooth white sand to stand on; an immense multitude of people was gathered together; but their voice was as the roaring of the sea. I began to speak, and the noise died away: But before I had ended my prayer, some poor wretches of Penzance began cursing and swearing, and thrusting the people off the bank. In two minutes I was thrown into the midst of them; when one of Newlin [sic], a bitter opposer till then, turned about, and swore, "None shall meddle with the man: I will lose my life first." Many others were of his mind: so I walked an hundred yards forward, and finished my sermon without any interruption.[39]

Jaco was a witness to the event, but not a participant. In his own retro-spective account he says that at the time he stayed apart though watched as Wesley was rescued from the "wicked mob." Only later, after hearing an-other of Wesley's first recruits, Stephen Nichols, described as "a plain hon-est tinner," did Jaco recognize himself as a sinner who potentially could be saved. That's when he found his calling: "I felt no guilt, not distress of any kind," recalled Jaco; "[m]y soul was filled with light and love."[40] As I read Eliza's letters and her fiction, the same pattern of what she herself describes as "sinning and repenting" kept turning up.

The kind of religious awakening Peter Jaco outlined is not unfamiliar. It is exactly the kind of redemption typically proclaimed by fundamental-ists of all religious persuasions. But it was Jaco's spiritual awakening that primed him, in 1751, to accept John Wesley's invitation to take up preach-ing as a full-time job and become a member of the Connexion. Another of Wesley's original preachers, Charles Atmore, named the attributes Jaco pos-sessed, attributes that made him a particularly good candidate for Wesley's evangelical mission: "Remarkably comely in his person, tall and handsome, and possessed an amiable natural temper. His understanding was strong and clear: and he had acquired much useful knowledge, which rendered him an agreeable companion. His talents for the Christian ministry were very con-siderable; and he was a scribe well instructed in the things of God."[41] That is, Jaco, like most successful religious and political evangelicals through the ages, was charismatic. He was also attractive. In 1802, Eliza, writing from Penzance, where she had relocated temporarily to work with her brother-in-law Thomas Fenwick, encountered again some of her father's family. She was pleased to see that her son Orlando (then about four) had inherited some of their best genetic traits: "They are," she says, referring to the Jacos, "the handsomest set of people I have ever seen." She also notes their "fine & bold beauty."[42]

The Methodist archives contain one other tiny bit of information about Jaco's Cornwall relations. In a letter to Mr. Merryweather, dated March 7, 1763, Jaco refers to the "cross" he has to bear in the context of his family "as a kind of 'Bedlam.'" He elaborates:

> An aged and afflicted Father (the Fondest of parents) & brothers have long flourish'd in the most prosperous manner, now thro' a variety of Losses and disappointments and the vanity of mankind, are on the brink of Ruin and Dissolution! This has not a little affected me lately. I am sent for to come home as soon as possible to see whether I can settle affairs which are now in Distraction.[43]

The passage speaks to tensions between devotion to vocation—in Jaco's case, to preaching—and family responsibilities. As Eliza's life played out, she had to cope with the same tensions, in her case between her vocation as a writer and her responsibilities as a mother. Gender obviously contributed to the ways in which father and daughter negotiated potential turning points in their respective futures. Eliza had to put novel writing on hold in order to support her family, but Jaco did not have to return to the family pilchard fishery business.

In March 1763, when Jaco had to make the choice between continuing as an itinerant preacher and returning home to Cornwall, he was still a relatively young man, and on the verge of marriage. Just two months later, in May 1763, he married Elizabeth Hawksworth and so the family into which Eliza was born was not one concentrated on the financial concerns of running a family business in a small coastal town, but rather one marked by constant motion, and a commitment to spiritual life and to education.

Two linked commitments were part of the defining features that John and Charles Wesley were embedding into their evolving Methodist ethos: making preaching a lay activity, and making it open to men and women of all classes and educational backgrounds. The very fact that Methodist preaching could be a non-specialist activity, practiced by tinners or women or shoemakers or pilchard fisherman, made it attractive. By becoming "lifelong learners" as we might say today, untrained people could potentially obtain the kind of education that they otherwise missed by chance, class, or circumstance. John and Charles Wesley actively encouraged all the preachers they enlisted to read, especially, as John Lenton notes, "Cicero, Virgil, Horace, Terence, Homer, Greek epigrams, Pascal, Spenser and Milton."[44] Peter Jaco, like all of Wesley's itinerants, was urged to engage in the repertoire of an "Oxbridge" classical education.

As a mark of faith in Jaco's abilities as a preacher, even without formal education, John Wesley inducted him into the Connexion. After a brief stint in local preaching societies, Jaco was admitted as an itinerant on May 8, 1754. On that day, he along with six other young men bound themselves formally to each other, to John Wesley, and to the Methodist evangelical cause of taking religion to the people. At the John Rylands Library in Manchester there is a copy of the original covenant in which all seven swear that:

> In order to prevent all jealousies of each other, and to increase that mutual confidence which is highly desirable we whose names are here underwritten freely and willingly declare that it is our full and deliberate purpose never to depart from the Church of England or from each other, or to act

independently of each other, till we have first obtained the full covenant of the rest of the brethren at the conference.[45]

The document is signed by John Wesley, John Creigthon, Christopher Hopper, E. Perronet, John Jouncie, James Roequet, John Finwick (sic), and Peter Jacco (sic). At the time, neither John Fenwick nor Peter Jaco could have known that their as yet unimagined children (Eliza's husband John was born in 1757) would unite in marriage and reject the practices of their Methodist fathers. In 1754, all the signatories of the covenant were still relatively young, healthy, strong, and perfectly poised for their adventurous lives as evangelical Methodist preachers.

John Fenwick (1730–87) was slightly unusual as an early itinerant. Unlike the majority who, like Jaco, were from the lower end of the middling classes, owners of small businesses or tradesmen, Fenwick was described as a "man of property, a wealthy merchant."[46] John Wesley, in a 1758 note, comments on how much he trusted Fenwick. In another note, to Joseph Benson, on December 3, 1769, Wesley wrote, "What preacher now deals so plainly with me as John Fenwick? And whom do I love and trust more?" The late 1760s do seem to have been a time when Fenwick was very active in Wesley's service. Another note, dated November 27, 1766, from John Wesley to Christopher Hopper, says that, "John Fenwick will set out tomorrow morning, which is as soon as he could be spared from hence." This looks like an ordinary administrative note, but it ends oddly, with a request to "cure" John "of his coxcomicality" so that "he may do good." "Coxcomb," or "cockscomb" as it is sometimes spelled, hints at something undermining or contradicting the serious trust that Wesley had placed in him. The Methodist Minutes of 1785[47] provide clarification: John Wesley expelled John Fenwick for "drunkenness" and relegated him to "supernumerary" status; that is, as extraneous. Fenwick died in 1787. In a memorial tribute, another preacher, Charles Atmore—damning with faint praise—said that John Fenwick's "ministerial gifts were small, yet he had a considerable degree of zeal," though "not always tempered with Christian knowledge," and that his end "was not glorious or triumphant."[48]

In fulfilling their oaths to take the Methodist message to the people, both Peter Jaco and John Fenwick faced rejection and violence, especially in the early years of the movement. Jaco, in fact, recalling his experience when the work of Methodism was "in its infancy," remembered that new preachers on the road "had hardly the necessaries of life." Attacks by the locals of the kind that John Wesley himself had experienced in Newlyn a few years earlier were still likely. Jaco described a couple of such frightening encounters.

He said that, in one of his early visits to Warrington, he was "struck so violently with a brick on the breast, that blood gushed out through his mouth, nose and ears."[49] And on another occasion:

> At Grampound I was pressed [pressganged] for a soldier kept under a strong guard for several days, without meat or drink, but what I was obliged to produce at large expense; and threatened to have my feet tied under the horse's belly, while I was carried eight miles before the commissioners; and though I was honourably acquitted by them, yet it cost me a pretty large sum of money, as well as much trouble.[50]

Even without the violence, life was hard. When the Wesley brothers gathered the itinerant preachers together for their annual conference, the money that had been raised within each Methodist society was then distributed to cover the living expenses of each preacher preparing to go on the road again. An account, for February 1763, exists and gives a breakdown:

> Feb. 6. The Preacher's horse, 11 nights 16/6; corn and hay for 2 preacher's horses 1/
> March 12 the Preacher's horse 7 nights 10/6.[51]

The idea of taking religion to the people was a relatively novel innovation, and by figuring out how to make it a viable option financially and logistically, Wesley demonstrated his ability to attract and retain talent. His quasi-military gift for organizing an army of religious workers meant that he was able to realize his vision of a revitalized mode of Christian practice. As John Lenton explains, the lay preachers "became the foundation of Wesley's success"[52] primarily by dint of focused, intensive religious practice in individual communities throughout the British Isles and then abroad.

The Wesley brothers and their army of lay preachers made religious practice at once theatrical and intimate. Robert Southey (Romantic poet and later Poet Laureate) explains in his *Life of Wesley; and the Rise and Progress of Methodism* that, "[F]ield preaching was a great novelty; it attracted greater multitudes and brought him [John Wesley] more immediately among the lower and ruder classes of society, whom he might otherwise in vain have wished to address."[53] With an army of charismatic and articulate assistants to help in his mission, Wesley was attracting and retaining the attention of "multitudes" of the "lower and ruder classes of society." One particularly useful technique Wesley used to keep the crowds coming was—to use an anachronistic phrase—"changing-up" the preachers; that is, by moving the preachers around, Wesley knew that the novelty of new voices coming regularly to individual communities would keep audiences returning for more.

There is, as it happens, a note John Wesley himself wrote as part of a prog-ress report on Peter Jaco and another itinerant with whom Jaco was part-nered on the advantages of putting preachers into circulation rather than assigning them to single locations:

> Be their talents ever so great, they will ere long, grow dead themselves, and so will most of those who hear them. I know, were I to preach one whole year in one place, I should preach both myself and most of my congrega-tion asleep. Nor can I ever believe, it was ever the will of our Lord that one congregation should have one teacher only. We have found by long and constant experience, that a frequent change of teachers is best. This preacher has one talent, that another. No one whom I ever know, has all the talents which are needful for beginning, continuing, and perfecting the work of grace in a whole congregation. (*LJW* 3:194–95)

For a twenty-first-century reader, Wesley's descriptions of his preachers on their circuits feel uncannily like descriptions of rock stars on road trips, keeping their fans faithful to their work by changing up their playlists. But there are also similarities between finding a preacher to inspire a congrega-tion of people and finding a teacher to inspire a classroom full of students. When Eliza looked for teachers to staff her schools, she was as rigorous as John Wesley in her desire for people able to galvanize attention.

As the Connexion records show, all of Wesley's preachers were on the road a lot. Scattered references to the impact Peter Jaco made on others remain. Fellow preacher J. Hanby wrote, "I love Peter Jaco."[54] Another preacher, Mr. Thomas Tennant, in 1769, described the "affection and ten-derness" he felt for his "good friend Mr. Jaco."[55] Others talked about the various sermons he preached and the lessons he gave, all indicating that he was well liked by his fellow itinerants, and that he was good at his work. There is something almost magical about still being able to touch the warm testaments to the living presence of Eliza's father as a young man, something energizing about imagining what he must have been like, some-thing that speaks to the courage it must have taken to be a field preacher in the "infancy," as Jaco himself described it, of Methodism.[56]

One more touching reference to Jaco surfaced in the late nineteenth cen-tury, almost a century after he had been preaching in fields around Britain. Eliza's granddaughter Elizabeth, as a very old woman, wrote to her own son Thomas in response to his requests for family history, saying that she re-membered Eliza describing her father as "a man of learning" and saying that "he would have been a dignified clergyman had he lived longer."[57] That is ex-actly the kind of scrap of recorded memory that should constitute a tangible link to the past: Eliza herself providing a memory of her father, which she conveys to her granddaughter, who conveys it to her son. But it just misses the mark. Does the reference to a "dignified" clergyman hint at recognition of the fact that Wesley's itinerants were "undignified"? Or was it Elizabeth's own projection of what she would have liked to imagine as her own history, given the fact that she was herself the wife of a "dignified" American clergyman and the mother and mother-in-law of two more, although by that time they were a family of Episcopalians rather than Methodists. Or perhaps Elizabeth did not even fully appreciate that her great-grandfather had not been a conventional well-educated, "dignified clergyman" sitting in a parish church, but rather an itinerant, riding around Britain on horseback, preaching in muddy fields, being loved and loathed by the locals. When I asked John Lenton about the likelihood of Peter Jaco having been a "dignified" clergyman, he responded by saying that though "many of John Wesley's preachers hoped to be ordained in the Church of England," even the few who did "rarely became 'dignified.'" Rather, Lenton says, "It was something however their descendants might well remember as a dream they had had."[58]

Through the 1760s and the early 1770s, Peter Jaco did continue to maintain his rigorous road schedule, though after his marriage his was likely not quite the rough-and-tumble life of his first years in the ministry. In 1766 (the year Eliza was born), he was in Sheffield, and then in Lancashire in 1770, Newcastle in 1772, and Dublin in 1773. There is a curious comment in one of John Wesley's letters from 1770 (*LJW* 6:49) that appears to be some kind of joke about Jaco and his wife, but it is hard to understand exactly what it means. Because preachers traveled on horseback, Wesley had been trying to procure a horse that would accommodate both Peter and Elizabeth Jaco. He writes, "Can you help us to a horse that will carry him and his wife?" Then, "What a pity we could not procure a camel or an elephant."[59] It is an odd comment that sticks precisely because it looks straightforward enough but doesn't seem to contain quite enough information to make the meaning clear. It must have made perfect sense if Wesley had expressed his concerns in conversation, but it is just beyond the reach of readers 250 years later. Maybe it does speak to Elizabeth Jaco being pregnant, or maybe both Peter and Elizabeth were physically large and two horses would have been better than one to carry them, or maybe they had a lot of luggage or household goods to transport.

As the original itinerant preachers began to marry and have families, aged, and became infirm, and as Methodist societies multiplied, the Wesley brothers were faced with the problem of how to manage these demographic changes. It is a tribute to their prescience that they worked out a way of

upscaling their movement successfully. The Minutes of the Methodist conference held on August 7, 1770 indicate major changes. That is when John
Wesley asked all preachers to stop engaging in trade, though he did continue
to allow them to have a share in a ship. That is the year he also set up allowances for preachers' wives and children. In 1772, for instance, the Minutes
of the Methodist conference indicate that forty-three preachers' wives were
provided for, and the next year, forty-four. A note from August 1774 de-
creed that "every preacher's wife have £12 a year." As John Lenton explains
in *John Wesley's Preachers*, at first Wesley stipulated that four pounds would
be the allowance for each child per quarter, and twenty-four pounds per
annum the allowance for each preacher's wife.[60] Eliza's mother benefited
from the change in policy, especially as Peter Jaco became increasingly infirm. The Minutes of the Methodist conference on August 4, 1778, for
instance, state that forty-four wives were provided for, "including sister
Jaco in London."

Boys received allowances until they were eight and girls were supported
until they were fourteen. By 1780, six pounds was made available for the
education of each girl.[61] The Minutes of the August 9, 1774 conference record that a question was asked about the "education of daughters" and the
answer was given: "If any of them were sent to Mrs. Owen's school (perhaps
the best boarding-school in Great Britain) they would keep them at as small
an expense as possible." Although, as Paul Langford says, "education was
kept well within the financial range of the modestly comfortable middle
class," it still looks as if it was a stretch for the children of the itinerants unless they were students at Kingswood, in which case the tuition was free.[62]
Otherwise, the tuition in the mid-eighteenth century was between sixteen
and twenty pounds per annum. It was twelve pounds per annum at Warrington, a famous dissenting academy, and fifty pounds at Eton.[63] By way
of contrast, when Eliza was running her first school in Barbados, she was
charging up to forty guineas per annum for day school pupils, depending on
what they studied. Schools were still private and unregulated in the period.
They would rise and fall with the success or failure of the people who owned
and ran them.

Eliza would have been eight in 1774, but there is no record of whether or
not she went to Mrs. Owen's Methodist school for girls. Two years later, in
1776, the Methodist Minutes record that Peter Jaco was stationed in London,
and because of declining health, was no longer on the road. That is where
he remained until his death in 1781. No record of funds for Eliza's education turned up in any of the Methodist Minutes, but John Lenton explains
that, as Jaco was stationed in London, it is likely that Eliza simply attended

a local school for girls. Lenton also explains that the Minutes were sketchy, so not everything was recorded.[64] Despite the lack of evidence about Eliza's education, it is clear that the education of Methodist preachers' children was important.

A Methodist Education: "Train Up
a Child in the Way He Should Go"

On Midsummer's Day, June 24, 1748, John and Charles Wesley opened the first Methodist school at Kingswood (originally King's Wood), near Bristol. The location was significant, as it was where John Wesley first preached in the open air to colliers in the district, and it became the school to which the children of itinerant preachers—both boys and girls initially—could go to be educated. Wesley himself preached at the opening, developing his sermon from Proverbs 22:6: "Train up a child in the way he should go, and when he is old he will not depart from it." The Jesuits took up the same theory in developing their schools. A modern test of the validity of this approach is famously in progress through director Michael Apted's *Up* series of documentary films. Apted wanted to see how the training "up" of children from various backgrounds in Britain would "go" through the years. He began with a group of seven-year-olds in 1964 and filmed them every seven years. His subjects did turn out for the most part as their gender, education, and class predicted they would "go" in their lives.[65] As Eliza Jaco, John Fenwick, and William Rutherford were all born to deeply committed preachers, I was looking for distinguishing features as I searched the archives, ones that would have formed their characters and contributed to their decisions to distance themselves from the Methodism of their fathers. My readings of the historical Methodist records provided clues, in that I could see how devoted, committed, and passionate the Methodist fathers were to their religious callings, and I could also see that the spartan educational regimes the Wesley brothers mandated could engender rebellion rather than obedience.

The "old boys" who authored the *History of Kingswood School* to mark the occasion of its 150th anniversary in 1898 began by observing that John Wesley's original pedagogical scheme involved "total elimination of everything from their lives which could in any way militate against the success" of the "perfect control of children" (14–15). The plan Wesley attempted to impose on the children at Kingswood mirrored his own rigorous routine and his commitment to not wasting any time. As he rose at four in the morning, winter and summer, he expected the children of the school to do the same. At five, the children were to meet together and work (in the garden or the house depending on the weather, or some were allowed to use the time to study music or philosophy) until breakfast at six. School began at seven, with languages until nine, then writing until eleven. At eleven, the children could walk or work. Dinner was at twelve, with singing until one. Languages were practiced again from one until four, then prayer at five, and bed at eight.

According to Mary Clare Martin in "Marketing Religious Identity: Female Educators, Methodist Culture and Eighteenth-Century Childhood," Methodist education for girls, like the education Wesley devised for boys, focused on developing "habits of industry," though that was not exclusive to the Methodists in the period. Martin, citing the manuscript material related to a school run by the prominent Methodist female preacher Mary Bosanquet Fletcher (1739–1815), sets out the school regime: "Rising at four or five, the children attended school from eight to twelve and two to five, interspersed with time for prayer, and some recreation, and were in bed by eight."[66] Even though I could not find any trace of Eliza's or John's specific educational history, the records of the pedagogical programs recommended by John and Charles Wesley suggest that both Eliza and John, who would have been school-aged children in the 1770s, would have been exposed to those programs. The description of life at Kingswood provides a sense of both the day-to-day scheduling and the curriculum. Though not all students took all subjects, the eighteenth-century program of study included, as it did in other progressive (especially Dissenting) institutions, "reading, writing, arithmetic, English, French, Latin, Greek, Hebrew, history, geography, chronology, rhetoric, logic, ethics, geometry, algebra, natural philosophy and metaphysics."[67] John Wesley also specified what the children were to eat and when:

> Breakfast: Milk porridge and water gruel, by turns
> Supper: Bread and butter or cheese, and milk by turns
> Dinner: Sunday cold roast beef
> Monday: Hashed meat and apple dumplings
> Tuesday: Boiled mutton
> Wednesday: Vegetables and dumplings
> Thursday: Boiled mutton or beef
> Friday: Vegetables and dumplings. And so in Lent
> Saturday: Bacon and greens, apple dumplings

Water was the only drink allowed. There was to be no food between meals, and children were also given the option, if they so desired, to fast until three in the afternoon on Fridays.[68]

Wesley's educational and dietary program sounds draconian and impossible to modern readers, but applying twenty-first-century assumptions to eighteenth-century conventions is rarely a good idea, so I was grateful for confirmation from someone closer to the time period under discussion, Robert Southey. In his *The Life of Wesley*, he wonders "that any parents should have suffered their children to be bred up in a manner which would inevitably in ninety-nine cases out of an hundred, either disgust them with religion or make them hypocrites" (47).

Southey's comment about children "bred up" according to Wesley's plan, turning out to feel "disgust" with religion or to become "hypocrites," resonated instantly. Eliza knew Southey.[69] His statement about the likelihood of Methodist children growing up to be hypocrites is in exactly the same register as Eliza's January 1833 concern for her young friend Mary Moffat's decision to join the movement. Despite taking the edge off her comments by saying that Mary was "too gentle to become a bigot" and had "too much judgment not to discern the difference between purity of heart & purity of words merely" (that is, not to become a hypocrite), Eliza was making her suspicion of Methodist practices completely clear.

Southey did find it surprising that "any children other than the sons of preachers would have remained" and did note that in the two years after Kingswood was established, only eighteen of the original twenty-eight scholars remained. To be fair, Southey was writing about the earliest days of the school, so the "two years" would have been between 1748 and 1750. Four years later, in 1754, when John Wesley tried to send Peter Jaco (who had left school at thirteen)[70] to Kingswood before taking him on formally as an itinerant, the school was full. By 1783, however, Kingswood was seriously running amok again. In the Methodist Minutes of July 29, 1783, there is an explicit comment saying that "the children are not religious, they have not the power, and hardly the form of religion." The school had its ups and downs, and it looks as if Eliza's son-in-law William Rutherford arrived there during one of its down periods.

There is a record of Rutherford's admission to Kingswood at age nine in 1792,[71] though from early on it appears that he was not going to be "trained up" according to the expectations of his father, Thomas Rutherford, or of John Wesley. The report on the dismal state of affairs at Kingswood came from John Pawson, another of Wesley's original itinerants. He was so disillusioned with the school that he said he would rather his own child be "an honest shoemaker than that he should be exalted so far above his parents with contempt and despise the whole Methodist Connexion." He then offered "terrible examples" as "proof" of the deplorable situation at the school.

"Did not young Cownley" (one of the sons of Joseph Cownley [1723–92]), he asked, "tell his blessed father to his face, 'I am ashamed to be seen walking the streets with you'?" Pawson concluded his disparaging remarks of the state of the school by alluding to William Rutherford: "What is to become of poor Rutherford?" he asked, before answering rhetorically, "I know not, the son of such an excellent father."[72] Thomas Rutherford was appointed to a committee in the 1790s to investigate the problems at Kingswood, but nothing else seems to have been recorded. William Rutherford left the school and went to America to try his hand at acting before moving to Barbados, which is where he met Eliza's daughter in 1812.

John Wesley had designed his ambitious pedagogical plan so that the minds of the pupils at Kingswood would be inclined toward "wisdom and holiness." He assumed that "by instilling the principles of true religion, speculative and practical, and training them up in the ancient way" children would emerge as "rational scriptural Christians."[73] The plan does not seem to have worked for William Rutherford, who grew up, as will become clear, to lack both the discipline and faith that Wesley had hoped to instill. Eliza and John Fenwick, however, seem to have absorbed the lessons about passion, industry, commitment, and dedication, but then to have redirected those characteristics toward political and social rather than religious reform. John and Eliza were also certainly fluent in French, and Eliza was accomplished in music too, and as they fit easily into the intellectual life of 1790s London, they both must have acquired the academic competence necessary to fit in with those who had received formal, classical educations.

As Eliza and John Fenwick and William Rutherford all had connections with the theater in the early nineteenth century,[74] I wondered if anything in their childhood experiences might account for their shared interests, especially given the explicit Methodist disapproval of games, including sport, dancing, folk pleasures, and other popular entertainments. As David Hempton explains in *Methodism and Politics in British Society 1750–1850*, Methodists did find outlets for their creativity. "The Love Feasts, watch-nights, hymn singing, providential interventions and colourful local versions of the cosmic drama, between God and the Devil," says Hempton, functioned as alternatives to the "holy war" that had been declared "on drink, hurling [an early version of field hockey], wrestling, bull-baiting, cock-fighting, and folk superstition."[75] Hempton's basic point is that secular drama, like religious drama, is based on tensions between opposing forces, great storytelling, and the ability to generate passionate emotional responses such as love, hate, anger, sorrow, joy, and remorse. Charismatic, dramatic preaching was, by all accounts, essential for the brotherhood of Wesley's original band of itinerant preachers, all of whom were required to galvanize listeners in their evangelical missions. Their sermons had to be strong enough to keep new converts riveted and committed. As firsthand accounts of Eliza and John Fenwick and William Rutherford indicate, all three seem to have absorbed the charismatic qualities of their fathers.

Part of the narrative drive of Methodist preaching was the promise of redemption, especially for those who had sinned and repented. The promise of eternal life as a way of triumphing over the inevitability of death is, of course, profoundly compelling, which is why accounts of people facing their deaths are so moving. A glimpse of what Methodist childhood was like appeared in the accounts of the deaths of two of the children of Thomas Rutherford. Rutherford was unusual as a Methodist itinerant because he and his wife Isabella had a large family. They had thirteen children, though just five survived, and the accounts of the final days of two of their young children as they succumbed to their final illnesses are arrestingly poignant and memorable. Drama, storytelling, and redemption intensely fused as Thomas Rutherford told the story of his daughter Elizabeth, "snatched away by a fever in the fourteenth year of her age," and Isabella Rutherford told the story of the death of their younger son, Henry, who was just four.[76] In contrast to the unholy life their older brother William led, Elizabeth and Henry both lived, and died, grounded in the Methodism of their parents. The stories of their lives and deaths belong to a specific genre of such stories beginning with James Janeway's famous *A Token for Children, Being an Exact Account of the Conversion, Holy and Exemplary Lives, and Joyful Deaths of Several Young Children,* a bestseller about the good Christian deaths of children published a century earlier in 1671 and 1672.

Fourteen-year-old Elizabeth Rutherford was a perfect Methodist daughter to the end. Her father wrote that despite "incessant pain" in her head, she "was patient and quiet as a lamb; pleased with everything that was done for her, and grateful to all who attended her, constantly thanking them for every thing they gave her, even for the bitterest potion." He focuses on her pure Christian faith: "Her steady and cheerful resignation to the divine Will, her lamblike meekness and composure of mind and countenance, her love and gratitude, and above all, her humble devotion," he concludes, "were truly exemplary." The description of her piety goes on for a couple of pages and includes her "most affectionate account of the whole family." She even asks about her (black sheep) "brother William who sailed for the West Indies a short time before she was taken ill."[77] Thomas Rutherford also wrote a separate account of his daughter's impending death. In it, he begins by saying that his daughter Betsy is "altered exceedingly for the worse":

She is a sweet child, and is in a sweet state of mind. She has repeatedly told us, that she wants rather to die than live, because she is afraid she should become careless. Her mind is much taken up in prayer, and frequently she calls her mother and I to pray with her. Such a pattern of patience and resignation I hardly can behold, contentment on her countenance and expressions of gratitude to the Lord for her great goodness and to all about her for everything they do for her, flow from her lips. But her care and tenderness for her dear distressed Mother exceed all experiences—she says nothing makes death painful to her, but the thoughts of what others will suffer.[78]

Although sad, Betsy had a perfect Christian death, a model death. That, however, was not the case for her younger brother.

In Thomas Rutherford's *Methodist Magazine* memoir of 1808, there is a macabre and unforgettable story, as told by Thomas's wife Isabella, about the last illness and death of Betsy's four-year-old brother Henry. As will become clear, the account is moving partly because it is so uncensored, the voice of the four-year-old not yet smothered in Methodist doctrine. Isabella explains his initial "greatest unwillingness to die," especially as "he could not bear the thought of that ugly hole where they had put his sister; and if there were no other road to heaven, he should not like to go there, though he much desired to see Betsy again." Isabella's account of her son's response to his impending death then goes off the Christian script. Instead of young Elizabeth's stoic acceptance, what comes across is the story of a tired mother struggling with the ordinary incessant demands of a four-year-old while trying to prepare him for the incomprehensible approach of his death. Isabella writes:

He yet wanted some months of being five years old. About a month before his death, being one day very importunate to be measured for a suit of new clothes, that he might ride out with his father, when he got better, in the spring; after trying to divert his mind from it, by a variety of means, I at length told him there was now no hope of his being better in this world, and that his next suit would be like Betsy's. Soon after, he desired to lie down on the sofa, first telling his sisters, they were to put by his hat and other articles, which he should not want. As I sat by him, thinking he was asleep, he hastily raised himself, and said, 'Mother, I am not afraid to die now, and I don't care about the grave: they may put me in, I shall be with Betsy, so you know it cannot hurt me. I wish my coffin to be just like hers only it need not be so large; but I suppose Mr. W— will measure me for it as he did her. My father and sisters will go to see me put there; you mother, are not able.[79]

The whole sequence is unbearably compelling, especially Isabella's experience of trying to distract a four-year-old from something on which he has fixed (being measured for a new suit). Anyone who has ever attempted to distract a four-year-old from something on which that child is fixated knows how difficult that task is, and how it requires enormous inventiveness, patience, and persistence.

Isabella Rutherford's exhaustion is almost palpable as she explains how she attempted to "divert his mind from it, by a variety of means," but ultimately failed. That is why the unexpected finality of her last attempt comes as such a shock. She just has to tell him that he can't have a suit because he is going to die. That truth eventually does the trick, and Isabella records Henry's assimilation of the unalterable fact of his impending end. His pragmatic discussion about the disposal of his worldly goods to his sisters, the practicalities of being measured for a coffin, and the fact that he appreciates that his death will be too much for his mother to bear are heart-wrenching. What is most devastating—though nothing is said on this in the narrative—is that Henry had worked out, on his own, how to reframe his desire to be measured for a suit, so he could get his own way in the end: he understands that he will be measured, but for a coffin, as was his sister, rather than for a suit. If Isabella understood that Henry had managed to find a way of accomplishing his "importunate" demands, she did not say so. The story is left to speak for itself.

At the end of this chapter, I appreciate that it has been more about the lives of eighteenth-century Methodist preachers and their families than specifically about Eliza's childhood. Yet because the lives of Eliza, her husband, and son-in-law were all shaped by the commitment of their respective fathers to the evolving practice of Methodism, it does provide core clues to their entwined adult lives. As soldiers in the army of Wesley's itinerant preachers, Peter Jaco, John Fenwick, Sr., and Thomas Rutherford were necessarily redefining family life, as all had to balance commitment to the Connexion against commitment to their families, and their lives on the road with their domestic lives. The fact that Eliza and John Fenwick and William Rutherford all abandoned their Methodist connections seems simultaneously significant and opaque. The fact that none of them could sustain stable family lives seems an obvious sign that something was somehow missing in all of them. Famous, though anachronistic, literary assessments of families come to mind. From the late nineteenth century, Leo Tolstoy's comment (from *Anna Karenina*, originally published in Russian in serial form between 1873 and 1877) is the first that sticks: "all happy families are alike; each unhappy family is unhappy in its own way."[80]

As I will show more explicitly, Eliza does write about family dynamics—about good, happy parents begetting good, happy children, and bad, unhappy parents begetting bad, unhappy children—in *Lessons for Children: Or Rudiments of Good Manners, Morals and Humanity* (first published in William Godwin's Juvenile Library in 1809). Stories about family dynamics are the core of our literary inheritance and they play out across genres from Greek myth to reality television, so Eliza's stories fit the model we believe to be true. Philip Larkin famously makes the point about parents "fucking up" their children in his 1974 poem, "This Be the Verse":

> But they were fucked up in their turn
> By fools in old-style hats and coats,
> Who half the time were soppy-stern
> And half at one another's throats.[81]

The evidence on whether or not the "soppy-stern" early Methodist lives of Peter Jaco, John Fenwick, and Thomas Rutherford "fucked up" the lives of their respective children is difficult to prove. Only the fact that all three rejected the Methodist practices of their respective fathers is demonstrably clear.

Yet when I read Eliza's 1795 novel *Secresy*, which is at least partly about a father who "fucks up" the life of his ward, Sibella, the novel's condemnation of what look like critiques of "soppy-stern" Methodist child-reading attitudes suddenly comes into relief. Sibella levels the charge: "Mr. Valmont calls himself my father; and *calling* himself such, he there rests satisfied. Cold in his temperament, stern from his education, he imagines kindness would be indulgence and indulgence folly. Ever on the watch for faults, the accent of reproof mingles with his best commendations" (*Secresy* 73). There is no actual proof that the dysfunctional father-daughter relationship Eliza sets up in *Secresy* is an account of her real relationship with her father Peter Jaco. Yet at the heart of the novel is the outrage, and the harm, that comes because Valmont denies Sibella agency: "I have chosen a part for her," he says, "and nothing is required of you but obedience" (59). That is the passage that Isobel Grundy helpfully glosses in the introduction to her edition of the novel, citing Rousseau's assertion from *Emile* (1762) that "dependence is a condition natural to women, and these girls feel themselves made to obey."[82] *Secresy* is essentially a pointed critique of the denial of education and rational thought to daughters. The novel ends tragically primarily because

Sibella, denied agency, is denied the capacity to think through a future of her own. Unlike sons, who are defined by their futures, as heirs for instance, daughters are defined by their pasts. Even the *OED* gives the definition of a daughter as a "woman considered as the product of a particular person, influence or environment, as in she was a daughter of the vicarage in manner and appearance."[83]

Eliza Jaco, unlike her fictional character, Sibella, did manage to reject her past as a "product" of a Methodist childhood and move toward a future as what Mary Wollstonecraft described as a "new genus" of woman.[84] Peter Jaco died in 1781 and in John Wesley's letters there exists a long account of his final illness and his good death. About a week before he died, Wesley reported that Peter Jaco said to his wife Elizabeth: "I know I am accepted of God: I have not a shadow of a doubt. O, what a blessing it is that the enemy is not permitted to come near me!"[85] It looks as if Eliza's life as a Methodist daughter ended with the death of her father at the beginning of the 1780s. She left just one retroactive glimpse of a moment that marked the transition from one phase of her life to the other.

In a letter dated January 26, 1833, written from Niagara, Eliza wrote to the Moffat family in New York with a memory of her first visit to the theater in London. If she dated the event correctly, the year would have been 1780, so just before her father died. As Methodists would have shunned the pleasures of the theater, her account of the occasion is particularly telling:

> I well remember the first time I ever entered the theatre—it was to see the opera Artaxerxes, & we entered a front box just as the curtain was rising to the exquisite symphony of the beautiful duet between Mandane & the young Prince—the splendid scenery, the Persian dresses—the crowded & brilliant audience & the music, altogether made such an impression on my nerves that I burst into tears. I was but 14 & that is 53 years ago & yet the recollection is far more vivid than those of more valuable and important events.

Eliza was with someone on that occasion but she doesn't name her companion. She just says "we entered a front box." Was she with John? There is no way of knowing. As he was born in 1757 he would have been nine years older than she was, so twenty-three in 1780, an adult when she was an adolescent. The only thing that reads clearly in the account is that it was the "first time" she had been to the theater. That moment in 1780 would have marked the ending of her life as a Methodist daughter and, it appears, the beginning of the life that comes into focus in the 1790s, as an author, wife, mother, and member of the radical literary and intellectual community circling Mary Wollstonecraft and William Godwin.

2

Mother and Author

Biographers are explorers scanning oceans of history for sightings of their subjects. My last glimpse of Eliza was on the shore of her girlhood at fourteen, around 1780, vividly remembering being moved to tears by her first encounter with an opera, *Artaxerxes*. I also have a refracted sighting, evidence of Eliza's presence, in Peter Jaco's 1781 bequest to his daughter in his will. There she was, in London, in her mid-teens, around the time of the death of her Methodist father. Then she disappears completely for seven years. When she does turn up again in London in November 1788, she is married to John and the two of them are meeting regularly with William Godwin (1756–1836) and Thomas Holcroft (1745–1809)—writers, avowed atheists, and advocates of social and political reform.[1] In the late 1780s both Godwin and Holcroft were not yet the contentious public figures they would become a few years later: Godwin for the publication of *An Enquiry Concerning Political Justice* in 1793, and Thomas Holcroft as a playwright, translator (from French), and as one of the people indicted for high treason in the infamous Treason Trials of 1794.[2]

Where was Eliza in the seven critical years between 1781 and 1788? And what happened between the time her childhood self was bounded by the Methodist piety of her parents and her twenty-two year old self emerged on the far shore in 1788, married, surrounded by atheists and political activists? At the end of the 1780s, I can see her coming into focus on the brink of her active engagement in the life of radical London literature, politics, journalism, education, and theater. That would be her milieu for the following two decades, and in all practical ways it was completely antithetical to the religious life her parents had lived. As no records at all turned up to explain what Eliza was doing in the missing years between 1781 and 1788, a Tristram-Shandyish empty page—signaling a blank space in the biographical record of Eliza's life—seemed a viable option.[3] I decided against it when I realized that navigating the complicated waters of Eliza and John's reinvention of themselves in Britain in the late 1780s through the 1790s provided the biographical material needed to set the course for Eliza's continuing

William Godwin and Thomas
Holcroft by Sir Thomas Lawrence.
(Courtesy of the National Portrait
Gallery, London)

reinvention of herself through her nineteenth-century colonial adventures.
The elements that would ultimately combine to forge her new independent
self were clearly there, in plain sight, in letters political, fictional, and personal. All three kinds of letters are at the heart of the first part of this chapter about Eliza as a writer. In the second part, I demonstrate her ongoing
determination to negotiate what quickly became single motherhood and
her writing life.

Political letters, albeit not ones written by Eliza, are the first ones to address, as they date from the late 1780s and early 1790s in the wake of the start
of the French Revolution. By and about people who were close to Eliza (including her husband John Fenwick), I foreground the letters pertaining to
the "corresponding" societies, groups of people who came together to advocate for parliamentary reform in the 1790s. I then demonstrate how Eliza's
1795 novel of fictional letters, *Secresy,* conveys an explicit radical agenda
ultimately informing her pedagogical and social ethos. And finally I turn to
a personal letter Eliza wrote as an old woman to her friend John Moffat, as
that is where she outlines the history of her writing life.

Political Letters

When Eliza showed up in London in 1788, the world was at a tipping point,
as Malcolm Gladwell might say,[4] of radical change. The French Revolution was around the corner, and the drive toward it had been gathering

momentum through the 1780s. Both John and Eliza were fluent in French. Had they been in France in the mid-1780s? Independently? Or not? The details surrounding their first sighting as a couple in London shed some light on the possibility of French connections.

The first record of John and Eliza together is on November 9, 1788. They were hosting dinner at their house for William Godwin, Thomas Holcroft, and Charles André Mercier (1741–1823). The editorial notes in the Godwin Diary project helpfully explain that Mercier was an engraver, art dealer, and newspaper editor, and that he "was running a hotel in Paris in 1783,"[5] which is where Holcroft had met him. Was it possible that John and Eliza had met him there too? There is a clue: in September 1784, Holcroft, Mercier, and Nicolas de Bonneville (1760–1828) were together in Paris translating the hit play *The Marriage of Figaro* by Pierre Beaumarchais, first performed that year. Bonneville later turns up as a character, a revered tutor, in *Secresy*. There is one further Anglo-French connection: Mercier's niece Louisa became Holcroft's fourth wife in 1799.

Godwin and the Fenwicks met frequently through the fall of 1788 and often a few times a month through much of 1789. The first surviving letter from William Godwin to John Fenwick dates from this period. On November 18, 1789, Godwin wrote to John with the tragic news of the suicide of Thomas Holcroft's son, William.[6] There is one more detail about Eliza in the first months that she was known to be in the company of Holcroft and Godwin that is irrefutable: she was pregnant. The baptism of Eliza Ann, daughter of John and Eliza Fenwick, was recorded on June 28, 1789 at the Parish of St. Dunstan and All Saints, Stepney. Thus began the confluence of Eliza's life as both a writer and a mother, as well her struggle to balance political activism with maternal duties of care.

In the years around 1790, Eliza was embarking on motherhood and living in the company of atheists, dramatists, and political reformers. Around her, signal events—some of which now serve as markers on timelines of transition into the modern world—were unfolding. In Britain, William Pitt the Younger (1759–1806), in his first stint as Prime Minister (the youngest in history, elected at age twenty-four in 1783) was watching the gathering revolutionary storm and dealing both with the madness of King George III and with what became known as "The Regency Crisis" of 1788–1789. Charles Wesley died in March 1788, marking the beginning of the end of the founding period of Methodism. *The Times of London* began publishing in 1788. The storming of the Bastille took place on July 14, 1789, marking the beginning of the French Revolution. William Blake started printing the first plates for *Songs of Innocence* in 1789. On April 29, 1789, Olaudah Equiano published his slave memoir in Britain and became an important figure in the movement toward the abolition of the slave trade.[7] John Wesley died in 1791, making way for the formal separation of Methodists from the Church of England in 1795 and completing the shift of the movement from its origins as a radical reconfiguration of worship into something more conventionally settled into the spectrum of Christian denominations. William Wilberforce first tried, and failed, in 1791 to pass a bill in Parliament to abolish the slave trade. Thomas Paine published *The Rights of Man* in 1791. Mary Wollstonecraft published *A Vindication of the Rights of Woman* in 1792.

The London Corresponding Society (LCS), a kind of populist pressure group promoting universal suffrage and parliamentary reform, was created in 1792, and John Fenwick was among its earliest members. In retrospect, the LCS was something like the "Occupy" movement of its day, exposing the injustice of the ninety-nine percent majority being controlled by the one percent with power and money. Its significance in the mid-1790s will feature later in this chapter as there are direct connections between the LCS, the Treason Trials of 1794, and the publication of Eliza's novel *Secresy* in 1795. Even from a distance of over two hundred years, the shivering thrill of change running up the spine of history through the first half of the 1790s remains palpable.

In the turbulent few years between 1788 and 1792, as the world was tipping, John and Eliza were inventing (or reinventing) themselves, though they covered their tracks well. John's backstory in particular is rife with contradictions. The documented trace on John shows that he was baptized in St. Mary Newington, Surrey, in 1757, just three years after his father, John Fenwick Sr., and Eliza's father, Peter Jaco, were inducted as itinerant preachers. Yet none of the extant references to John by people who knew him in the 1790s and early 1800s link him in any way with the Methodism of his father or his father-in-law. When John's London friends characterized his past, they described him as Irish, as having been in the army, and as having inherited and lost money.

Henry Crabb Robinson (1775–1867),[8] famous for his memoirs of the Romantic poets, especially Coleridge and Wordsworth, was repeatedly explicit in his character sketch of John's backstory. In a December 1807 letter to his brother, explaining why he is asking for money to help Eliza (who couldn't afford a room of her own at the time), Robinson describes her as "the wife of a very honest but very improvident man, an Irishman by birth & some years since an officer in the army." He adds that John "has all the virtues & failings of his countrymen." He also says that John had inherited and lost "£14,000."[9] And in an 1829 annotation to an 1808 letter written to him by

Eliza, Robinson says again that Eliza had an "unhappy marriage to a wild Irishman of good heart but no conduct" who "reduced her to poverty from affluence."[10] As far as the actual historical records go, there are no indications that John was born or raised in Ireland. Evidence of having been "an officer in the army" has proved equally elusive. Despite several searches of the British Army "lists" (names, ranks, and regiments of people who served), I could not find evidence of the John Fenwick I was looking for (so no John Fenwick whose dates would have put him in the army in the early 1780s) in any of them.

Although John wasn't Irish or an officer in the army, there is compelling evidence that he was charming, intelligent, well liked, and committed to political justice and equity. The most eloquent portrait of him is by Charles Lamb (1775–1834), who confirms John's attractiveness as a person, as well as his laissez-faire attitude toward money and his reputation as a prodigious drinker. In "The Two Races of Men," from *Essays of Elia,* Lamb presents his friend as the fictional character "Ralph Bigod," a cleverly suggestive name, as it could be pronounced either as "be good" or, more likely, as "by God," perhaps a catchphrase John Fenwick might have used at the time. Lamb even gives us a description of what John was like and what he looked like, beginning with the statement that he had "an undeniable way about him," and that "he had a cheerful, open exterior, a quick jovial eye, a bald forehead, just touched with grey (*cana fides*)."[11] In the essay, the "two races of men" of Lamb's title are identified as "borrowers and lenders." Bigod was both: "Borrowing money when he didn't have any and lending or giving or throwing it away the rest of the time." Lamb also offers a memorable aphorism that he attributes to John: that "money kept longer than three days stinks." Which is why, Lamb explains, John/Bigod "made use of it while it was fresh." Then Lamb writes, in detail, about what John did with the fresh money:

> A good part he drank away (for he was an excellent toss-pot), some he gave away, the rest he threw away, literally tossing and hurling it violently from him—as boys do burrs, or as if it had been infectious—into ponds or ditches, or deep holes—inscrutable cavities of the earth;—or he would bury it (where he would never see it again) by a river's side under some bank, which (he would facetiously observe) paid no interest—but out away from him it must go peremptorily, as Hagar's offspring into the wilderness, while it was sweet.

Lamb obviously loved John as a friend and companion and eloquently eulogizes him:

He anticipated no excuse and found none. And of his character. When I think of this man; his fiery glow of heart; his swell of feeling; how magnificent, how *ideal* he was; how great at the midnight hour; and when I compare him with the companions with whom I have associated since, I grudge the saving of a few idle ducats, and think that I am fallen into the society of *lenders,* and *little men.* (35–36)

Lamb's affectionate larger-than-life portrait of Bigod/Fenwick generates a feeling for the charming and compelling measure of the man, balancing subsequent characterizations of him as a drunken deadbeat. Even though no images of John have surfaced, Ernest Shepard—later best known as the illustrator of A. A. Milne's *Winnie-the-Pooh* stories—in a collection titled *Everybody's Lamb* has drawn Bigod/Fenwick, smiling, tall, imposing, huge tankard in hand, as an "excellent toss-pot."[12] Shepard has also drawn Lamb into the picture, slight, younger, with curly hair and a more modest-sized glass in hand.[13]

Because John Fenwick's actual history has been so hard to verify, Lamb's compelling verbal portrait of him is all the more intriguing. Lamb clearly knew John intimately and probably had the answers to questions that now

Ernest Shepard's illustration of Fenwick/Bigod "as an excellent toss-pot." (From *Everybody's Lamb*, ed. A. C, Ward. London: G. Bell and Sons, 1933)

stand unresolved. Did Lamb know anything about John's claim to being Irish, or possible connections with the army? Did he know how John and Eliza met, or when and if they married? One of the reasons Lamb's presence lingers as a source of answers to those questions is because a large, serious portrait of him by John Opie (1761–1807), an artist who was also a friend of people in the Wollstonecraft/Godwin circle, hangs outside the door of the Rare Books Reading Room at the British Library in London. Every time I go into the library in search of John or Eliza or their London friends, the portrait of Lamb, smiling with knowing assurance, serves as a kind of teasing reminder of what he knew and I don't.

Lamb's account of John's "easy come, easy go" relationship with money seems to confirm that there were periods when John had money and periods when he didn't. Where any of that money came from isn't clear, but there are hints that some of it might have had dubious origins. The evidence suggests, however, that at least some of it may have been inherited. John's father was described as "a man of property,"[14] and he died in 1787, just before John and Eliza turned up in London. The only will that exists for him (in the London Metropolitan Archives) says that John's share in the property bequeathed to him was just £450. That's a far cry from Robinson's comment in his 1807 letter that John had "inherited £14,000 from his grandfather." Yet Lamb also says in his memorial essay that John claimed Fenwick/Bigod had inherited money and that he was "a descendant of mighty ancestors."[15] Lamb goes on in the essay to explain that his thinly disguised friend had also conveyed a "noble disinterestedness" in money, and that when he had any "he took almost immediate measures entirely to dissipate and bring to nothing" (34). Lamb, Robinson, and Mary Hays also intimate that John was dabbling in risky investments on a regular basis. In the 1807 letter to his brother, for instance, Robinson says that John, "with a most astonishing imprudence" had "indorsed [sic] Bills for a scoundrel-friend a London Merchant." Nevertheless, John was obviously well liked both for his easy-going happiness, and because he was also a serious, dedicated political reformer, active in several media: translation, journalism, literary non-fiction (as we might term the genre now), and theater. In the period leading up to the publication of *Secrecy*, through the early 1790s, both John and Eliza were part of the community of people in London beginning to define the social, cultural, and political changes taking place around them.

When John and Eliza were in London in the 1790s, the books that still resonate as signal contributions to the rise of parliamentary reform and modern democratic societies were being published: Thomas Paine's *The Rights of Man* in 1791, Mary Wollstonecraft's *A Vindication of the Rights of Woman* in 1792, and William Godwin's *Political Justice* in 1793 all stand at the top of the list. It was on February 15, 1793, soon after the publication of *Political Justice,* that Godwin entrusted John Fenwick with his new book to take to France to give "to General Miranda," who was at the time a general in the French Revolutionary Army.[16] It was a dangerous assignment, as people in power in both France and Britain were worried about threats to their authority. Fenwick, Godwin, and their radical friends, including Thomas Holcroft, were also worried about the possible backlash, the threat of being accused of treason.[17] Godwin's letter is deliberately coded in order to avoid being read as inflammatory. He reminds John to "be cautious in your expressions, that you may not bring your friend into trouble."[18] The timing could not have been more delicate. The "Traitorous Correspondence Act," passed by the British government in 1793, "made it an offence to aid or travel to France or to correspond with French citizens."[19] That is, by asking John to take *Political Justice* to General Miranda, Godwin was asking his friend to undertake a potentially treasonous act. The punishment for treason was death. The urgent need to galvanize public support in the context of so much revolutionary change in France speaks to the commitment exhibited by both Fenwick and Godwin.

On May 12, 1794, Fenwick's English translation of *Memoirs of General Dumouriez* (Dublin: J. Milliken) was published.[20] As it happens, Godwin notes in his diary of July 11, 1795, that he had just read four volumes (of what was ultimately a six-volume work) of *Memoires du général Dumouriez écrits par lui-même,* suggesting not just that Dumouriez's work was important to both of them, but also that they understood its political implications, and in John's case, actively disseminated the work to a wider—English—audience.[21] Although no explicit evidence that John held a position in the British Army has turned up, he did, as Pamela Clemit notes, express "his wish to serve in the French Revolutionary Army . . . as one of his [General Miranda's] aides de camp."[22]

Despite the lack of evidence that John was in either the British Army or the French Revolutionary Army, he was a supporter of the ideals of the Revolution: "liberté, égalité, fraternité." Although the phrase has now become the familiar, conventional slogan for French nationalism, it was new in the period, having been first used in a speech delivered by Maximilien Robespierre (1758–94) on December 5, 1790. In France, the fallout after the storming of the Bastille in 1789 was getting bloodier as the dominant political factions, the Girondins and the Montagnards, vied for overall power.

In Britain, the move for political reform and a more egalitarian society was being championed by what we might now call "grassroots" organizations. Foremost among them was the LCS,[23] founded in 1792, as an ad hoc group, devoted, as explained in their mandate, to promoting "Universal Suffrage, Equal Representation and Annual Parliaments."[24] Fenwick, Holcroft, and John Horne Tooke (1736–1812) were all active participants, and all were caught up in the events of the early 1790s. The letters, pamphlets, and handbills generated by the members of the society, outlining the shape of potential parliamentary reform, were regarded as seditious. Another of the important members of the LCS was Jeremiah Joyce (1763–1816). A radical Dissenter, Joyce was also the secretary to the Earl of Stanhope, and so, as John Issitt says, "a vital link between metropolitan radicals and a highly supportive Whig aristocrat."[25] Like Eliza, Joyce was also one of the authors writing under generic pseudonyms for the educational books published by Richard Phillips. Olaudah Equiano (1745–97), author of the allegedly autobiographical slave narrative *The Interesting Narrative of the Life of Olaudah Equiano, or Gustavus Vassa, the African* (1789), was also a member of the LCS.[26]

Mary Thale, in her edition of selections from the LCS's papers, explains the rationale for the odd name of the group. It was to be a "committee of secrecy in part," she says, "to prevent spies from being able to name the author of any letter or address issued by the Society." The notion of secrecy was immediately attacked and the committee became known as the correspondence committee and then the executive committee. It consisted of six members whose principal duty was to reply to letters, and write notices, addresses or petitions sent out in the name of the LCS.[27] As an epistolary novel, *Secresy* mimics in the private sphere, the public letter-writing political activities of the LCS. And in both the real public and the fictional private spheres, the consequences of secrecy, subterfuge, and protest against patriarchal authority have lethal consequences.

In its manifesto, the LCS stated that its purpose was "to fulfill two interlocking aims of the Society, first, to publish the correspondence, and second to provide other reforms and reform societies with inexpensive works of enlightenment." John Fenwick sustained his involvement, and his name pops up periodically.[28] For twenty-first-century readers, the reform agenda of the LCS looks admirable in its attempt to breathe democratic rights into life, but that is not the way it looked to the British government in the early 1790s. In his introduction to his six-volume edition of the works of the LCS, Michael T. Davis says the government saw the organization's activities as potentially dangerous portents of "insurrection," and so took action accordingly. Given the "Reign of Terror" and the bloodbath raging in France (the worst years of which were 1793–94), William Pitt's government passed a series of acts in order to prevent the kind of what we might now call "terrorism" in France from taking place in Britain. "Through an intricate network of spies and informers," writes Davis, "the government kept a close watch on the LCS and instituted what has arguably been described as a 'reign of terror' to check sedition and subversion in Britain."[29]

In the mid-1790s, the LCS was at the forefront of promoting what we would call freedom of speech at a time when the British government, nervous about the revolutionary aftermath in France fueling dissent in Britain, was trying to keep the voices of opposition in check. To that end, a committee made up of government appointees including Edmund Burke (1729–1797)[30] was instructed to report on the potentially seditious activities of the LCS and other related English and Scottish societies. On May 17, 1794, "The First report from the Committee of Secrecy of the House of Commons Respecting Seditious Practices" was published. Citing Thomas Paine's *Rights of Man*, intercourse with French societies, and "approbation of the French system," the committee decided that the societies constituted "a traitorous conspiracy for the subversion of the established Laws and constitution, and the introduction of that system of anarchy and confusion which has fatally prevailed in France."[31] The message was clear: the activities of the LCS were considered, in and of themselves, treasonous. It was one of those moments in time when the tension between the rule of law and the need to fight for freedom was held in a fine balance. In the end, only one person was hung for high treason in Britain, James Coigley, though not until 1798. It was John Fenwick who wrote a chilling account of his trial; tellingly, the charges against Coigley were made on the strength of a letter.

John's book is titled *On the Trial of James Coigley for High Treason Together with an account of his death including his address to the spectators to which is added an appendix containing an interesting correspondence relative to the Trial, between Mr. Coigley's solicitor and the duke of Portland* (1798). Coigley (or Quigley sometimes) was the only one of six men accused of treason who was actually executed after his conviction following his trial in April 1798. The initial indictment claimed that Coigley and five other men had conspired to "maliciously and traitorously . . . conceal and keep, a certain paper-writing, which was deemed threatening to King and country." In his account, John points out that accusation of treason was based solely on "the *possession* (emphasis mine) of a treasonable paper, with an intention of being the bearer of it to the government of France."[32] He describes the events that led up to poor Coigley being in possession of the ostensibly treasonous documents in a way that makes the charges look like they had been trumped up by an eighteenth-century version of the Keystone Cops. Nevertheless, as John had carried potentially treasonous letters to France on William Godwin's behalf in 1793, Coigley's trial must have been personally resonant for him. Particularly unsettling is John Fenwick's account of the execution: "on 6 June 1798, Coigley, aged thirty-six: on the gallows he eats an orange which has been quartered for him." For readers at the time, the metaphoric significance of the quartered orange would have been obvious: persons convicted of treason would have been hung, then cut down from the gallows while still alive, then had their entrails cut out and burned. Then their heads would have been cut off and their bodies divided into quarters.

Fictional Letters

As Eliza Fenwick's novel *Secresy: or The Ruin on the Rock* was published in 1795, not long after the "First Report from the Committee of Secrecy," the coincidence in timing between John's involvement with the LCS and Eliza's novel about conspiracy designed to keep women obedient seems hard to ignore.[33] It is also worth noting that the spies reporting on the activities of the LCS sent their findings to what was known as the "Castle." Although foreboding castles, as Eliza calls the gloomy prison in which her story's heroine Sibella is locked up, are standard tropes of Gothic fiction, the political resonance of calling the prison the "Castle" would have been understood. It is also hard to ignore the coincidence between Eliza's subtitle, *The Ruin on the Rock,* and Holcroft's 1792 play, *The Road to Ruin: A Comedy in Five Acts,* which, like *Secresy,* is also partly about the consequences of a young man marrying a rich widow for her money.

Because *Secresy* is an epistolary novel, it grounds my argument that in the absence of subsequent novels, Eliza's letters became her literary life. Taken together, Eliza's extant letters from 1797 to her death in 1840 become her epistolary autobiography. There is a touching irony in the dedication to the first edition of her novel, to an "Eliza B—." Although there is no documentary evidence on the identity of "Eliza B—," there is evidence that Eliza Fenwick had entertained Mary Wollstonecraft's estranged sister, Eliza [Elizabeth] Bishop in November 1793.[34] In the dedication, Eliza privileges the survival of the novel over the letter: "What does the world care about either you or me? Nothing. But we care for each other, and I grasp at every opportunity of telling it. A letter, they may say, would do as well for that purpose as a dedication. I say no; for a letter is a sort of corruptible substance, and these volumes *may* be IMMORTAL."[35]

The Gothic plot of *Secresy* looks familiar enough. There are star-crossed lovers: Sibella, orphaned at six, had been raised by her uncle, George Valmont, within the confines of his gloomy castle. For company, she had Clement Montgomery, who joined her as her uncle's ward when he was nine years old. They were educated in the castle together and played together, until George Valmont found them innocently sleeping together under a tree when they were sixteen. At that point, Valmont banished Clement so that he should learn to be morally strong and useful in the world. Valmont, incidentally, is the name of the villainous character in *Les Liaisons dangereuses,* the 1792 novel by Pierre Choderlos de Laclos, who enjoys making his victims miserable. Eliza's Valmont seems to have the same predilections.[36]

Clement, however, quickly finds the dissipated life of the idle rich more attractive and soon adapts. Sibella and Clement have a pair of "seconds," characters who in a contemporary "rom com" would be the BFFs (best friends forever): Caroline Ashburn, who is Sibella's friend, and Arthur Murden, who is Clement's. As Sibella is a child of nature (in a Rousseauian way), Caroline is her foil, in that she has been raised in an environment of excess by her status-conscious mother. Sibella and Caroline both stand for truth, though they keep secrets. During the course of the novel, Murden and Clement switch places with regard to their relationship to deceit. Clement, afraid of being without an income, sneaks back into Valmont's castle and enters into a "natural" (without benefit of clergy) marriage with Sibella, and then makes her promise not to tell. When it becomes obvious that Sibella is pregnant, the secret is out and Valmont cuts off Clement. When faced with the prospect of a life without an income, Clement marries Caroline's middle-aged widowed mother. Murden, who initially recommended dissipation, falls in love with Sibella but can't have her as she is in love with Clement. Everyone is doomed, of course: Sibella dies soon after delivering a stillborn son, Murden dies of a broken heart, and secrets are revealed. Valmont, whose egotistical desire to have his niece and his illegitimate son conform to his version of the social order, loses everything when Sibella dies.

Another pair of characters in the novel, Lord Filmar and Sir Walter Boyer, read as a couple of almost Shakespearean clowns. Like Rosencrantz and Guildenstern or slapstick comedians, they fumble around, disguised in the dark, revealing secrets and failing in their attempts to carry out a nefarious plot to kidnap Sibella so that Walter Boyer can marry her for her money. Even here, however, Eliza has included a small insider's satiric attack on patriarchal authority by playing on Filmar's name. Robert Filmer (1588–1653),[37] as it happens, is the name of the author of the well-known treatise *Patriarcha: Or the Natural Power of Kings* (published posthumously in 1680) defending patriarchal authority and the divine right of kings. *Secresy* is, of course, about the failure of patriarchal authority and divine right. As Sarah Emsley points out in "Radical Marriage," the unhappy ending of *Secresy*, in which a rigid social structure literally kills off freedom, is characteristic of the Jacobin novel, a genre of fiction specific to the political events clustered around the French Revolution.[38] For John and Eliza, the evils caused by a rigid social structure killing off individual rights were up close and personal. A chronological list of some of the events that directly concerned Eliza, John, and their immediate circle of friends in the early 1790s conveys just how closely the personal and the political were entwined:

1789   The baptism of Eliza Ann Fenwick on June 28.

The storming of the Bastille in Paris a few days later on July 14, marking the start of the French Revolution.

1791   Thomas Paine publishes *The Rights of Man*.

1792   Mary Wollstonecraft publishes *A Vindication of the Rights of Woman*.

The establishment of The London Corresponding Society (LCS).
Thomas Holcroft joins the Society for Constitutional Information (SCI).
The staging of Holcroft's *The Road to Ruin* at Covent Garden.

1793   William Godwin publishes *An Enquiry Concerning Political Justice*.

Godwin entrusts John Fenwick with a copy of *Political Justice* for General Miranda in France, a potentially treasonous act.
The Traitorous Correspondence Act is passed by Parliament.

1794   John Fenwick publishes the English translation of the first two volumes of *The Memoirs of General Dumouriez*.

Thomas Holcroft becomes responsible for developing a liaison between the LCS and the SCI.
The arrest of Holcroft for treason in the fall of that year.
The publication of "The Second Report from the Committee of Secrecy," based on reports from spies who had infiltrated the LCS and SCI and were acting as double agents.
The arrest of Thomas Hardy, John Thelwell, and John Horne Tooke (of the LCS) on May 12.
The acquittal of Hardy, Thelwell, Horne Tooke, and Holcroft in November.

As the chronological list of events demonstrates, Eliza was in the thick of debates about freedom of speech, reform, revolution, and treason in the years leading up to the publication of *Secrecy*, debates that swirled around her in letters, newspapers, and corresponding societies (not only the one based in London),[39] as well as in fiction, on stage, and in popular philosophical treatises. Given the level of political intrigue, the fact that she cloaked her polemical protest against patriarchal authority—personal, political, and religious—in the guise of a Gothic novel makes perfect sense. The "secret" story in the novel is that letters, especially those between Sibella and Caroline, serve to demonstrate that all the defenses of patriarchal authority (the rules, the walls, the wealth) could be brought down by freedom of thought. As Miriam Wallace notes in "Constructing Treason, Narrating the Truth," Eliza's novel was just one of several in the period featuring "tyrannical, volatile and self-interested gentry, patriarchs, judges or members of parliament" (such as George Valmont in *Secrecy*) set in contrast to "sensitive but-self-contained heroines" (like Sibella Valmont and Caroline Ashburn).[40]

Although the fictional critique of patriarchal authority takes place, as the brief chronology indicates, in the midst of real game-changing political events and fictional commentaries on those events, Eliza's critique is personal as well as political: *Secrecy* is also a successful escape story for Eliza from the unthinking obedience of the Methodism of her childhood, and by extension from literal obedience to the Methodism of her father. There is a particularly telling passage, quoted by Clement in a letter to Murden, in which Valmont arrogantly assumes the success of his strict educational methods and authority, and his ward's unquestioning obedience: "'Fully assured, Clement,' says Mr. Valmont in his letter, 'that you cannot have departed from the *rule of conduct* [italics mine] I desired you to pursue, I do not doubt but that you will joyfully quit the haunts of treacherous sordid men, to enjoy with me the pleasant solitude of Valmont castle, &c &c'" (116). The rule of conduct, as it happens, refers to a sermon John Wesley gave in 1778 and is reported to be the origin of the phrase about cleanliness being next to godliness.[41]

In *Romantic Correspondence: Women, Politics and the Fiction of Letters*, Mary Favret provides an analysis of the political use of the letter in women's fiction that is uncannily close to Eliza's use in *Secrecy*. "The letter had," she writes, "in fact become a phenomenally useful political tool, available to anyone with a pen." Although Favret does not at any point discuss *Secrecy*, she does make a direct connection with the LCS and an indirect connection with *Les Liaisons dangereuses*. Favret explains that:

> Political activity was the cause and effect of the letters of the London Correspondence[sic] Society, founded in 1792 as the first working-man's

political organization in England, and outlawed by 1794 [*sic*] as a treasonous conspiracy. When letters carry the seeds of organized rebellion or "conspiracy," we discover *les liaisons dangereuses* inside and outside the realm
of sentimental romance.[42]

In the two years prior to the publication of *Secresy*, also among the bloodi-
est in the Revolutionary period in France, two people close to Eliza, her
husband John Fenwick and her friend Mary Wollstonecraft, had both been
involved in potentially treasonous cross-border activities.[43]

Not only was John's taking the letter and the copy of *Political Justice* to
General Miranda in France in 1793 a treasonous act, as Favret explains,
citing the actual Traitorous Correspondence Act, which stated that the
government had the right to "scrutinize, appropriate or restrict any written material circulating in and out of England."[44] In the same period, John
was also translating the work of General Dumouriez, of the French Revolutionary Army, though Dumouriez was apparently involved in duplicitous
correspondence with General Miranda.[45] This was exactly the time when
Mary Wollstonecraft embarked on her trip to Scandinavia. Favret's citation
of the Traitorous Correspondence Act is in the context of Wollstonecraft's
journey on behalf of her traitorous lover Gibert Imlay, who was also the
father of her child Fanny. As Favret argues in "Mary Wollstonecraft and
the Business of Letters," Imlay had "recruited Mary Wollstonecraft as an
agent and possibly as his safe 'cover'" for his dubious business dealings in
Scandinavia.[46] Mary eventually used the occasion for the composition of the
volume of letters that ultimately secured her independence and autonomy.
The book was a commercial success when it was published and it was the
last work she saw in print during her lifetime.

In *Secresy*, the walls imprisoning Sibella in her uncle Valmont's castle
are breached by the letters she receives from Caroline. The novel begins in
fact with Caroline seeking permission from Valmont to communicate with
Sibella, by reassuring him (disingenuously as it turns out) of the harmless-
ness of a friendly letter: "A letter, Sir," she says, "cannot waft down your
drawbridges; the spirit of my affection breathed therein cannot disenchant
her from the all-powerful spell of your authority" (39). That is exactly what
Caroline's letters do, of course; they are powerful enough to break the spell
that keeps Sibella trapped. And, in the end, in Caroline's last letter to Valmont, as Sibella lies dying after the death of her child, and after Clement has
married Caroline's mother for her money, it is Caroline herself who delivers the moral on the folly of blind obedience. So "whenever the commands
of parents are contrary to the justice due from being to being," she writes,

"I hold to be vice." She then extends the message so that it is personal as well as political: "The perpetual hue and cry after obedience and obedience has almost driven virtue out of the world, for be it unlimited unexamined obedience to a sovereign, to a parent, or husband, the mind, yielding itself to implicit unexamined obedience, loses its individual dignity, and you can expect no more of a man than of a brute" (349).

If the events related to "traitorous" correspondence were the immediate context for acts of political resistance to "unexamined obedience," then the other secret acts of resistance in *Secresy* were in the context of Eliza's Methodist past. Isobel Grundy spots the connection brilliantly, though almost casually, when she first notes that Eliza (in one of Caroline's letters) "likens the pursuit of pleasure to a religion by mentioning votaries, or worshipers," and then comments that, "it is a technique she [Eliza] favours" (*Secresy* 64, n.3). Grundy makes the reference with respect to Caroline's assessment of Valmont's wife (who had been a friend of Caroline's own dissipated mother) "who loved crouds [sic], detested solitude, and was a votary of dissipation" (64). As Eliza equates excess pleasure and spectacle with religious experience in the novel, the over-the-top excesses of wealth stand as a metaphor for the over-the-top Methodist practices of her childhood, the ones that she rejected as hypocritical. In a scene near the beginning of the novel, for example, Caroline recounts the meeting between her mother and Mrs. Valmont: "Can you not imagine my mother secretly urging her triumphs over the immured Mrs. Valmont, by lamenting the slavery of pleasure to which she herself is perpetually compelled? And can you not see your disappointed, disgusted Caroline Ashburn viewing caresses without warmth, hearkening to professions without sincerity?" (53). In Mrs. Ashburn "lamenting the slavery of pleasure," Eliza alludes clearly to Mary Wollstonecraft's warning line in the *Vindication,* in which she asserts that if women are "kept in ignorance," then they will become "in the same proportion the *slaves of pleasure* [emphasis mine] as they are the slaves of man."[47] The words Eliza uses in describing Mrs. Ashburn's hypocritical "caresses without warmth" and "professions without sincerity" as a kind of prostitution are in exactly the same vein as the words she would then use almost forty years later in her personal letter to explain her abhorrence of Methodists. Both are grounded in her observations of an inability to "discern the difference between purity of heart & purity of words merely" (EF to Mary Moffat, 26 January 1833).

The entire long discussion on the personal and political context of *Secresy* is only possible because of its inclusion—albeit still peripheral—in the canon of eighteenth-century literature. And the only reason that the novel is the subject of so much scholarly work is because second-wave feminist scholars interested in recovering the writing of otherwise lost, forgotten, or neglected women authors and making their books accessible in new scholarly editions make sustained modern exegesis a viable option.[48] Gina Luria Walker's 1974 edition of *Secresy* for Garland, Janet Todd's 1989 edition for the "Mothers of the Novel" series published by Pandora Press, and Grundy's two editions (the first in 1994 and the second in 1998) for Broadview all made the novel accessible to scholars and students alike. As the work of a recovered author, *Secresy* was soon being taught and discussed in university courses and set into the political and social contexts of other major books published in the period. Eliza's novel suddenly became interesting in relation to, for example, Wollstonecraft's *Mary: A Fiction* (1788), *A Vindication of the Rights of Woman* (1792), *Letters Written in Sweden, Norway, and Denmark* (1796), and the posthumous *Maria: Or The Wrongs of Woman;* Elizabeth Inchbald's *A Simple Story* (1791); Charlotte Smith's *Celestina* (1791); William Godwin's *Enquiry Concerning Political Justice* (1793) and *Things as They Are; or, The Adventures of Caleb Williams* (1794); and *Memoirs of Emma Courtney* (1796) by Mary Hays. Modern scholarly articles began situating Eliza's *Secresy* in contexts of, for example, eighteenth-century ideas about marriage, motherhood, madness, father/daughter relationships, epistolary communities, Gothic novels, Jacobin novels, and pedagogical reform.[49] Grundy, at the end of her comprehensive introduction to the novel, marvels at its strengths. Her sense of respect is audible as she writes: "Fenwick retains her grandeur of imagination and her capacity to surprise. The plangent succinctness of her conclusion is classical rather than romantic in tone. None of the available labels—epistolary, gothic, sentimental, radical, novel of manners, or novel of social conscience—can package this stunning single work."[50]

Despite the nuanced interpretive possibilities available in the novel, the reason that *Secresy* remains on the fringes of the canon is that it is the only known work of fiction unmarked as being for children that Eliza published. Without an acknowledged body of work with which to contextualize critical discussions of her status as a literary figure, *Secresy* stands alone as a kind of awkward only child. In a more typical literary biography, *Secresy* would have been situated as an accomplished first novel, published when Eliza was just twenty-nine. It would then be read in the context of Eliza's evolution as an author. If Eliza did write other fiction as successful as *Secresy* it has either not survived or is not clearly identifiable as having been written by her. Her other extant published writing—the children's books and the 1798–1828 letters to Mary Hays[51]—if referenced at all in discussions about *Secresy,* are treated as peripheral or as sources of incidental information.

When scholars in disciplines other than eighteenth- or nineteenth-century literary studies (those working in children's literary studies or Caribbean studies) mention Eliza's writing at all, it is in isolation, separate from *Secresy*'s success. In F. J. Harvey Darton's *Children's Books in England,* first published in 1932, Eliza is just one of the hack Georgian writers, all of whom happen to be female, that he passes over "with the mere mention of their names."[52] And for Caribbean scholars, most notably Hilary Beckles, Pedro Welch, and Evelyn O'Callaghan,[53] their interest in Eliza is in the context of her years in Barbados between late 1814 and 1822. Only her sketches of life on the island are discussed, particularly her accounts of enslaved people. Few, if any, references are made to her literary life in Britain.[54]

In each field—eighteenth-century literary studies, children's literature studies, and Caribbean studies—Eliza's writing is interesting enough to earn a space in the discussion, but as she makes only a brief appearance in each context, there is no scholarship connecting the links between them. And as the letters Eliza wrote in North America between 1829 and her death in 1840 were unreferenced and otherwise unknown until I found them in 2008, the entire period of her writing from Upper Canada, Upper New York State, and Rhode Island is absent from the scholarly record.

Given that *Secresy* is the first surviving example of Eliza's writing, it provides a solid foundation for the discussion about what makes the rest of her writing, her children's books and her letters, worth reading. Even in sticking strictly to the technical literary merits of *Secresy,* Eliza's eye for selecting telling details in her description of scenes, her ear for conversation, and her ability to play with the tropes of genre fiction all stand out. *Secresy* has all the usual elements of Gothic fiction: the gloomy castle, the imprisoned maiden, and the hermit and "ruin on the rock" of the subtitle. Because the novel is so nuanced, however, so elusive as well as allusive, the appearance of the Gothic, like so many other features in the book, reads as a kind of disguise for the in-depth discussions of gender, class, and social, educational, and cultural politics played out in the story. Despite attempts to lock *Secresy* up into a definable category—Gothic, Jacobin, or feminist—aspects of the novel refuse to fit neatly, demanding their own space. The irony of trying to lock the novel into a neat category became obvious only gradually: *Secresy* is, after all, a cautionary tale about the harm caused by locking out access to freedom of information. In its synthesis of the personal and the political, of private letter and public protest, *Secresy* grounds all of Eliza's subsequent extant writing. Her first novel holds the key to treating her body of personal letters as extensions of her literary accomplishments and her capacity for reinvention.

Personal Letters

As a sixty-six-year-old woman, in 1832, thirty-seven years after the publication of *Secresy*, Eliza provided a thumbnail sketch of her history of authorship. I found the fragment in the New-York Historical Society archive. It had been cut apart and separated from the letter with which it had originally been composed, and was in a folder marked "unpublished," but as when fitting a jigsaw puzzle piece into place, I eventually found the manuscript letter from which it had been removed. The letter, dated June 10, 1832, was to John Moffat, and when I fit the fragment to the letter, I could see that all elements matched perfectly. The fragment slid neatly into place, matched to the shape of the cut, the color of the paper, and the context, though part of the page on which it had been composed must have been discarded.

The fragment itself begins modestly enough, almost as an apology, and the beginning of the first sentence is missing: ". . . such a troublesome business," Eliza says, "when I read of your hunting for Mrs. Fenwick's writings." She then provides a context for the publishing world of her young adult life, when she was a promising writer in the 1790s. She explains: "In London, writing, I will not say literature is as much a trade to live by as making Vests & Pantaloons." There is something eloquently touching in her deprecating construction of hack writing as a very feminine kind of piecework, just an edge of sorrow or regret that feels almost audible in the background. As Eliza continues her account, she allows herself the luxury of reminiscing about her long-ago life in the radical, literary London of the 1790s:

> It is true when I was very young & my brain a little turned by the reading Godwins Political Justice & Mrs. Wollstonecrafts Rights of Woman, I wrote a work of fiction, wild enough & under an odd title. I will not name the title, for I once stumbled on it in a New York library after the memory of the transgression was almost obliterated. The reviews blamed the principles but commended the Style & imagination of the novel & I began another, but being then independent & sharing the dissipation of fashionable life, I thought no more of Authorship till wealth had vanished.

About the people who were her friends in the period, she says nothing, only that she "had acquaintance with most of the writers of the day," which even then must have been a very modest way of describing her literary circle of friends. When I read the passage, at first I was a little puzzled. Eliza does not say, for instance, that William Godwin and Mary Wollstonecraft were her friends, or that in 1797 she had been present at the birth of the newborn Mary Shelley, who was, by 1832 when Eliza wrote her account of herself, the famous author of *Frankenstein*. And she does not name other illustrious authors with whom she was well acquainted, including Elizabeth Benger, Mary Hays, Charlotte Smith, Samuel Taylor Coleridge, Mary Robinson, Charles and Mary Lamb, Jane Porter, Percy Shelley, and William Hazlitt. So to say that she "had acquaintance with most of the writers of the day" seems strangely self-effacing.

Eliza also doesn't say that she knew several of the publishers of the day, including Joseph Johnson, who published Anna Barbauld, Maria Edgeworth, Thomas Paine, William Blake, Mary Hays, and Mary Wollstonecraft. And she doesn't say that one of the original publishers of *Secresy* was John Whitaker (1746–1840), a music publisher who remained her friend. The one material possession linking Eliza to her literary life is, in fact, John Whitaker's *The Seraph: A Collection of Sacred Songs*, published in 1818 with a drawing by "the late William Blake" engraved on the title page. A leather-bound copy with Eliza's name embossed in gold, a gift from the composer, turned up in the Archives of American Art at the Smithsonian in Washington. The fact that it was later owned by Eliza's granddaughter, Elizabeth Savage, is noted in pencil on a blank page.

Eliza concludes her account of her literary life by naming the publisher who paid the ready cash she needed so much in the early nineteenth century, but at a cost:

> & chance making me known to Sir Richard Phillips he engaged my assistance in his many enterprises and translations from the French, & compilations, chiefly of school books. A Chapbook bearing in the title page the Name of Rev d David Blair, Sir Richard, then Mr. Phillips paid me 150 guineas for compiling & many others under the same & other important names enabled me largely to assist in giving a finished & most expensive education to the Son I lost by yellow fever in the West Indies.

The last line, Eliza's acknowledgement of her son Orlando—for whom she worked to procure "a finished and most expensive education," the son then "lost by yellow fever in the West Indies"—is the key to foregrounding her conflicting identities as writer, mother, breadwinner, and career woman.

Mother

After the publication of *Secresy* in 1795, the possibility of a literary life had become a reality for Eliza. Her successful transition from aspiring to published novelist was complete. The reviews were positive and within the first year of the book's life, Eliza had switched from the conger of publishers she

Title page of *The Seraph,* with the engraving drawn by William Blake. (Courtesy of the Thomas Casilear Cole papers, 1750–1976, Archives of American Art, Smithsonian Institution)

had originally used, when initially gambling on the success of her work, to a new one, a Fleet Street publisher, G. Kearsley.[55] On the political front, Eliza soon found that the fictional world of her novel, about the harm caused by an authoritarian denial of freedom of speech, freedom of thought, and freedom of meetings between "friends," was being played out in her real world. The government of William Pitt had, as a response to protests against the government's resistance to political reform, introduced a series of measures, gagging orders, that led to the passage of the Seditious Meetings and Treasonable Practices Acts in 1795. Those laws, targeting groups such as the London Corresponding Society (LCS), were passed at the same time as John Fenwick decided to become increasingly active in the organization. On February 5, 1795, he was elected to the executive committee,[56] and later that year, *The Moral and Political Magazine* of the LCS was established. No editor was named on the masthead, perhaps, as Mary Thale suggests, as form of protection against possible arrest or prosecution for "seditious words" (362), but the minutes of the LCS do indicate that John Fenwick edited part of the magazine for at least two months, "gratis" (364).

It was within the context of the increasingly repressive and restrictive measures introduced during the mid-1790s that the number of fictional works identifying and protesting against the restricted lives of women was growing. In 1796, two novels both explicitly influenced by Mary Wollstonecraft and William Godwin were published: the *Memoirs of Emma Courtney* by Mary Hays and *Nature and Art* by Elizabeth Inchbald. This also was the year that Wollstonecraft published *Letters Written During a Short Residence in Sweden, Norway, and Denmark*, which was received as a commercial and critical success. And it was also in 1796, at the home of Mary Hays, that Wollstonecraft and Godwin reconnected. Although their first meeting, at the home of the publisher Joseph Johnson in 1792, had not gone well, they hit it off in January 1796 and quickly became lovers. By late fall, Mary Wollstonecraft was pregnant.

The fact that Mary and William were happily anticipating the birth of their child in a period marked by the development of new theories of parenting and education, some of which they had written, others of which were written by their friends, heightened the anticipation of a brighter future for the rising generation. Mary had already produced *Thoughts on the Education of Daughters* (1787) and *Original Stories from Real Life* (1788) with her publisher, Joseph Johnson. In the same period, Johnson was publishing other important works on education, including Anna Barbauld's *Lessons for Children* (1778) and *Evenings at Home* (1792–96), co-written with her brother John Aikin. Johnson had also published Maria Edgeworth's *Letters for Literary Ladies* (1795) and the first part of *The Parent's Assistant* in 1796. Wollstonecraft, Maria Reveley, and Eliza would also have been reading their own mothering practices in the context of Lady Ellenor Fenn's *Cobwebs to Catch Flies* (1783), published by J. Marshall (another London children's book publisher and friend of Eliza's), and of works by the French educational philosopher Stéphanie Félicité du Crest de Saint-Aubin, Comtesse de Genlis, referred to as Mme de Genlis (1746–1830), whose *Les veillées du chateau* (1784) was translated as *Tales of the Castle* by Thomas Holcroft in 1785. Parents listened attentively to the new educational treatises that were being promoted and enthusiastically adopted the enlightened social change they promised.

There's a lovely albeit anachronistic line by the late twentieth-century poet Ted Hughes (1930–98) that speaks to the feeling of new parenthood alive in that late eighteenth-century moment: "Every new child," says Ted Hughes, "is nature's chance to correct culture's error."[57] In 1796 and 1797, Eliza, a recognized writer working on her second novel, was also in that wonderful phase of motherhood between a child's infancy and formal schooling when there is a window of time for shared exploration and play. Eliza's seven-year-old Eliza Ann would play with Wollstonecraft's three-year-old daughter Fanny, and another friend, a little boy, eight-year-old Henry Reveley. Fanny was the (illegitimate) daughter of Wollstonecraft and Gilbert Imlay,[58] and Henry the son of Maria and Willey Reveley.[59] Wollstonecraft was in the late stages of pregnancy in the summer of 1797 with the daughter who would become Mary Shelley.

Feelings of sunshine, warmth, play, and hope for the future still linger in the glimpses left by Wollstonecraft and Godwin as they awaited the birth of their child. Their letters are infused with the spirit of the dawn of a new, warmer, more egalitarian age (what would become the Romantic period) counterpointing the seismic political events of the day. The playful register of a surviving note from Wollstonecraft to Reveley, reminding Reveley about what we would call a play date to which her son, Henry, had been invited with Eliza Ann and Fanny, still conveys the happiness of the moment: "Little Eliza has been here two or three hours; and appears so horrified at not seeing her playmates, that I send to remind you of your promise. The day is so fine it would be a pity to deprive them of the expected pleasure; nay, we hope to see Henry return with the messenger, though you should have chanced to misunderstand me."[60] A glimpse of the play in which the three children were engaged and the pedagogical theories that informed the interactions between the adults and children of their charmed circle is found in another note from Wollstonecraft to Reveley. It is written in the voice of Fanny to Henry:

Little Fanny would be very glad to have the promised Rake, in the course of a day or two, because she wishes to make Hay in the fields opposite to her house. If Henry will bring it she shall like to have a tumble with him on the Hay. The Pitchfork has been used every day. Fanny sends her love to Henry and wishes him to direct his next letter to herself, and she will put it up with her books, in her own closet.

Polygon Wednesday morning.

Mama hopes to see Mrs. Reveley on Saturday (half after four) if not before.—She sent a note yesterday by the Post.[61]

The idea that a child would delight in receiving a letter ostensibly from a peer is one that had been advocated more than a decade earlier by Lady Ellenor Fenn (1743–1813), in *Juvenile Correspondence or Letters Suited to Children from Four to Above Ten Years of Age*, published in 1783 by the innovative children's book publisher John Marshall. Lady Fenn writes that: "The receiving of a letter is such a joy, that there needs little spur to answering it: the sight of such letters as young folk of their own age are feigned to have written has a great effect—this I have experienced."[62]

Wollstonecraft feigning to be three-year-old Fanny speaks to the kind of affectionate, engaged parenting that was being put into everyday practice by young mothers in that late eighteenth-century period, into the early nineteenth century. Ellenor Fenn was among the cluster of women—Anna Barbauld and Maria Edgeworth were others—promoting a new kind of maternal pedagogy, one premised on the idea of children wanting to learn and mothers playing an active role in cultivating a desire for knowledge in their children. Eliza alludes to Lady Fenn's most popular book, *Cobwebs to Catch Flies* (1783), in *Secresy* when she wants to demonstrate Valmont's arrogance in rejecting the validity of educating women. "Cobwebs to catch eagles!" says Valmont sarcastically, mocking the kind of pedagogy promoted by the affectionate, informed Caroline in the novel.[63] Valmont persists in insisting that he has a lock on the truth, which, of course, he doesn't.

Wollstonecraft, by way of contrast, writing in the voice of her daughter, engages actively in the new principles of maternal teaching that she promotes in her own parenting advice books. The co-educational physical outdoor play is present in the invitation to Henry to tumble in the hay (before sexual connotations would have been associated with the invitation), and is exactly the kind of active play she explicitly advocates in the *Vindication of the Rights of Woman*.[64] The fact that the game she refers to involves raking hay with a real rake prefigures the idea that Maria Montessori (1870–1952) developed a century later on play as the work of the child.

The intimacy between the Reveleys, the Godwins, and the Fenwicks during that spring and summer of 1797 is at least suggested by the fact that Godwin's diary has them all dining together frequently. Although there are no extant letters between John and Eliza on their views on raising and educating their daughter, the letters between Godwin and Wollstonecraft reveal the kinds of practical education[65] they were developing for Fanny and their expected child. In a letter to Godwin, Wollstonecraft revels in their shared pleasure in seeing a child—Fanny in this case—actively learning to think. Mary tells a funny anecdote about what happened one day when she was having tea with Mrs. Reveley: "Fanny often talks of you [William Godwin] and made Mrs. Reveley laugh by telling her, when she could not find the monkey to shew it to Henry, 'that it was gone into the country.'"[66] The cute-things-kids-say story about Fanny's assumption that the misplaced toy monkey had "gone into the country" is exactly the kind of story that parents still love to relate, as it demonstrates how a child processes adult conversations and phrases and figures out how to apply them to new situations. In the terms that Mary Wollstonecraft herself uses in the *Vindication*, Fanny was already developing a capacity to "think," that is, to develop an "active mind."[67] When Fanny couldn't find her toy monkey to show her friend, she simply provided the answer that adults convey for absence: it must have "gone to the country."

There is another letter, not long after, from William to Mary in which he shows that he continues the game. "Kiss Fanny for me," he writes at the end, "remember William [the name they had used for the child Mary was carrying], but (most of all), take care of yourself." He also asks that Fanny be informed that he had "safely arrived in the land of the mugs." He was referring to the fact that Etruria, where he was traveling, was where Wedgewood potteries were made, so he had arrived in "the land of the mugs."[68] William made a point of saying that he would bring a mug home for Fanny and for one of her playmates. And on June 12, 1797, William also asked Mary to let Fanny know that "the monkey has not come to Etruria" (Godwin 220). The entire exchange speaks to the level of conversation occurring in that happy summer of 1797, a summer in which the promises of love, education, and play were so tangible.

While pregnant that summer, Wollstonecraft was also working on a series of *Lessons for Children* that she had started two years earlier, in 1795, when she was contemplating suicide after Gilbert Imlay had left her. She had intended the work partly as a series of personal letters to Fanny, and partly as pedagogical texts that would be useful to mothers of young children. She was writing in the genre of Anna Barbauld's *Lessons for Children*, first published in 1778 by Joseph Johnson, the publisher they shared, so in an affectionate tone and keyed to the domestic environment of the child.

Because childbearing was risky at the time, pregnant women would sometimes write letters to their existing children in case they didn't make it through the process of giving birth. Mary had started her *Lessons* at a time when she thought that her suicide would leave Fanny an orphan, so the dedication, written in 1795 reads: "The first book of a series which I intended to have written for my unfortunate girl." But by the time she was pregnant with her second child, Mary fully expected to be there, especially as Fanny's birth had been so relatively easy. The unfinished lessons are of the kind intended to be useful in preparing a child to be an older sibling. As William Godwin's letter from Etruria indicates, he and Mary were calling her unborn baby "William," so the lessons intended for Fanny anticipated her big sister status within the family. The warmth is there in the establishment of the new family unit, with Godwin clearly cast as the father, and Fanny as the affectionate toddler. "Lesson VIII," for instance, begins with Fanny's own babyhood:

> You were then on the carpet, for you could not walk well. So when you were in a hurry, you used to run / quick, quick, quick, on your hands and feet, like the dog.
>
> Away you ran to papa, and putting both your arms round his leg, for your hands were not big enough, you looked up at him, and laughed. What did this laugh say, when you could not speak? Cannot you guess by what you now say to papa?—Ah! it was, Play with me, papa!—play with me! (Wollstonecraft 4: 470)

It's a lovely scene, tracing exactly the lived experience of a toddler needing both hands to hug the leg of a parent.

Mary then gently moves the scene to cast Fanny as the older child at play with her father, while the projected infant, "William," watches the imagined scene: "Papa began to smile, and you knew that the smile was always—Yes. So you got a ball, and papa threw it along the floor—Roll—roll—roll; and you ran after it again—and again. How pleased you were. Look at William, he smiles; but you could laugh loud—Ha! ha! ha!—Papa laughed louder than the little girl, and rolled the ball still faster" (Wollstonecraft 4: 470). The sequence of lessons evolves in exactly the kind of developmental way that Wollstonecraft and Godwin were working out at the time. In the *Vindication*, Mary advocates for the education of women and their children to be focused on "[a] cultivated understanding, and an affectionate heart" (Wollstonecraft 5: 167). William would later echo this phrase eloquently when explaining that the goal of education should be to generate "an active mind and a warm heart."[69] I've cited the intimate exchanges between William and Mary because they are the antithesis of the kind of education Valmont provides for Sibella in *Secresy*. His pedagogical plan is to keep Sibella from both thinking and feeling: "I tell you, child," Valmont says to Sibella, doubling the point, "you cannot, you shall not reason." And then he repeats the injunction, again twice, saying, "Child, you are not born to think; you were not made to think" (*Secresy* 43). The formal rhetorical structure known as anaphora, the parallel repetition of phrases, conveys the sense that words are true because they have been repeated, as in the patriarchal voice of biblical authority.[70]

In *Lessons for Children*, Mary focuses not only on encouraging thinking in her young daughter but also on enabling her to understand that she has the capacity to think, to feel, and to understand the value of empathy. Lesson X is a case in point. The scene begins with a description of Fanny being unthinkingly noisy until told by "papa" that the noise makes her mother's headache worse. Mary then inserts two little parallel scenarios in the narrative about having a stomach ache. She explains that when papa had one, he knew he couldn't eat fruit and was wise enough to know that he had to drink chamomile tea, but when Fanny had one, she was not yet wise enough to know to do the same. And then Mary gets to the point of the lesson, that Fanny has learned both thinking and feeling:

> You say that you do not know how to think. Yes; you do a little. The other day papa was tired; he had been walking about all the morning. After dinner he fell asleep on the sopha. I did not bid you be quiet; but you thought of what papa said to you, when my head ached. This made you think that you ought not to make a noise, when papa was resting himself. So you came to me, and said to me, very softly, Pray reach me my ball, and / I will go and play in the garden, till papa wakes.
>
> You were going out; but thinking again, you came back to me on your tip-toes. Whisper—whisper. Pray mama, call me, when papa wakes; for I shall be afraid to open the door to see, lest I should disturb him.
>
> Away you went—Creep—Creep—and shut the door as softly as I could have done myself.
>
> That was thinking. When a child does wrong at first, she does not know any better. But, after she has been told that she must not disturb mama, when poor mama is unwell, she thinks herself that she must not wake papa when he is tired.
>
> Another day we will see if you can think about any thing else. (Wollstonecraft 4: 474)

In the summer of 1797, when Mary was pregnant—not with a son of course, but with a daughter—all three mothers, Mary Wollstonecraft, Maria Reveley, and Eliza Fenwick, were living with their own young children. The enlightened pedagogical theories that were coming to the fore informed their maternal practices. Mary was enacting the scenarios of her as yet un-published *Lessons for Children*. Eliza, with *Secresy* in print, was also acting according to the principles she advocated in the novel. All three women were in their prime. They had it all, in that they were intelligent and were married to intelligent men who loved and respected their intelligence. Mary was a celebrity author and Eliza, though not an author of Mary's stature, was accomplished in her own right. Though they were living in difficult times, they were changing their world, and were in the company of people who were working to make Britain a freer, more egalitarian place.

It was at the very end of that summer, on August 30, 1797, that Mary Wollstonecraft Godwin was born. Janet Todd, in her biography, *Mary Woll-stonecraft: A Revolutionary Life,* describes first the pain and the boredom that preceded the birth, the long eighteen-hour labor, and the assurances of the midwife, Mrs. Blenkinsop, that all was slow but well. Eliza and John Fenwick were there on the night the baby was born at 11:20. The baby was small and weak but fine. Both mother and child had come through and the only thing they were waiting for was for the placenta to be expelled. They waited for three hours and it didn't come, and that's when everything began to unravel. Todd writes a compelling hour-by-hour account of what happened next, including the details of the disastrous intervention by Dr. Louis Poignand, who literally reached into Wollstonecraft's womb in an attempt to wrench the placenta out of her. It broke, and that was the beginning of the end. Other doctors came and went, tried and failed, offered opinions and left. Eliza moved in to care for Wollstonecraft. William Godwin described her as "the best nurse ever." Once Wollstonecraft developed septicemia, there was nothing to be done except mark the painful hours until she died, which she did on September 10, 1797, just ten days after giving birth.

Although the details of the birth of the baby and the death of her mother are familiar, it doesn't make the story any less heart-wrenching. Godwin had, as Todd writes, "recorded the time in his journal, then drew three wordless lines."[71] The detail is frequently recorded in accounts of Mary's death, but the physical journal itself, in the Abinger Collection in the Bodleian in Oxford, communicates something more: the physical sense of Godwin's grief is visible in the three shakily-drawn lines, the three lives—the husband and two daughters—left to deal with Mary's absence. Twenty-first-century readers can't help but also impose the "flatline" image of a modern heart monitor, and hear the beeping blips replaced with a single flat note signaling the end.

When John and Eliza had arrived for dinner with Godwin on the day the baby was born, it must have been a companionable occasion; friends keeping each other company at a time of tension but one that held the promise of a happy outcome. Over the next few days as Mary's condition worsened, the friends who had come to celebrate came to share in grief. In the letters they wrote after Mary died, they recorded the details of the tragic turn of events. Mary Hays wrote that, "Mrs Fenwick attended her from the beginning of her confinement with scarcely any intermission."[72] In writing of Mary's death to Mrs. Cotton on September 14, 1797, Godwin wrote:

> Mrs Fenwick, author of Secrecy, a novel, was her principal nurse, & mr Carlisle said, the best nurse he ever saw. Four of my male friends staid night & day in the house, to be sent at a moment's warning any where that should be necessary. I spent the principal part of my time in her chamber.
>
> I will desire mrs Fenwick to write to you. (Godwin 244–45)

It was Eliza who was entrusted with the task of informing Everina Wollstonecraft of her sister's death. On September 12, 1797 Eliza wrote with reassurance and comfort:

> Mrs Godwin died on Sunday, Sept. 10th, about eight in the morning. I was with her at the time of her delivery, and with very little intermission until the moment of her death. Every skilful effort that medical knowledge of the highest class could make was exerted to save her. It is not possible to describe the unremitting & devoted attentions of her husband. Nor is it easy to give you an adequate idea of the affectionate zeal of many of her friends who were on the watch night & day to seize on an opportunity of contributing towards her recovery & to lessen her sufferings.
>
> No woman was ever more happy in marriage than Mrs. Godwin—Who ever endured more anguish than Mr. Godwin endures? Her description of him in the very last moments of her recollection was, "He is the kindest best man in the world."
>
> I know of no consolations for myself but in remembering how happy she had lately been & how much she was admired & almost idolized, by some of the most eminent & best of human beings.
>
> The Children are both well—the Infant in particular. It is the finest baby I ever saw.
>
> Wishing you peace & prosperity
I remain your humble servant
Eliza Fenwick[73]

I've quoted the entire letter because it conveys so much about Eliza's sensitivity and compassion, her acute awareness of the feelings of others. Despite delivering the devastating news of her sister's death to Everina, she conveys comfort and consolation by focusing on the strengths of Mary's last days: on the care she received, on the fact that she was never alone, on the degree to which she had been loved, "admired, and almost idolized" by so many important people, on the complete happiness of her marriage—including the last words about William Godwin as "the kindest, best man in the world"—and finally on the children, saying that both were "well" and that the newborn Mary was "the finest infant" she had ever seen. The last note of consolation on the newborn's condition was likely comforting exaggeration. In her biography of Mary Wollstonecraft, Todd describes the newborn Mary as "puny and weak" and says that "[n]o one really expected her to survive."[74] As Wollstonecraft was becoming increasingly weak in the days after her daughter's birth, she couldn't nurse, so both the baby and Fanny were sent to stay with Maria Reveley. Eliza did not convey that information to Everina.

The whole horrible process of watching her friend die in the aftermath of childbirth was likely intensified for Eliza, as she must have simultaneously started to realize that she was in the early stages of another pregnancy. Although her son Orlando was ultimately born safely on May 3, 1798, the ten-year gap between her first and second pregnancies suggests that there may have been miscarriages and/or stillbirths in between. On March 22, 1831, more than thirty years after Orlando was born, Eliza wrote a note of consolation to her New York friends, the Moffats, after the news of another miscarriage or loss of an infant: "Poor Mrs. Moffat has all the suffering without the sweet reward of rearing her infants. This I think is the third she has lost successively. I partook of the same misfortune—May she never know what it is to lose those who have grown up into friends & companions!" (EF to JM, 22 March 1831). Eliza did know all too well about the pain of losing adult children when she wrote that note. By 1831, it had been fifteen years since the death of her son and just three since the death of her daughter.

Two years later, after her note of consolation to the Moffats on the loss of another infant, Eliza wrote again on January 26, 1833, this time, in a congratulatory vein: "Does this babe make 11 or 12 in Number of your young family?" But then Eliza shifts her tone, and quickly plunges into a dark meditation on mothering:

I do not envy you while I sincerely rejoice in the safe arrival of the little stranger—that is not true—I do envy you, heartily & devoutly envy you

Hannah Moffat by John Wesley Jarvis.
(Courtesy of the Museum of the City
of New York)

those delicious feelings which my sad case have turned to bitterness and
gall—I cannot *but* lament that I ever became a Mother—And could I now
form a wish with the certainty of its success it would be that I might be left
alone, childless, to linger out in cheerless certainty that they *were gone,* my
little lamps of life. Yes, even my bonnie Bessy [Bessie] would I resign to the
grave rather than think she might one day be doomed to such suffering as
I have undergone.

In the spring of 1798, Eliza's losses were still in the unimaginable future.
That year she was coping with her new baby, Orlando, and her ten-year-
old daughter, Eliza Ann. She was also witness to Godwin's struggles with
his grief, his attempts to manage the day-to-day demands of the motherless infant Mary and the bereft toddler Fanny. If Eliza did write about giving birth or being a nursing mother, her impressions have not surfaced. As
her experiences coincided with Mary Wollstonecraft's written accounts of
young motherhood, they must have been still fresh and present for her despite being inevitably tangled with her friend's absence. It is through Wollstonecraft's work that the experience of late eighteenth-century motherhood
comes into focus.

Unfinished at the time of her death, in *Maria: Or the Wrongs of Woman,*
Mary had written a perfectly realized moment of nursing a newborn: of a
mother experiencing her baby, "half speaking half cooing," and feeling "little
twinkling fingers on her burning bosom" (Wollstonecraft 1: 85). And in *Letters Written During a Short Residence in Sweden, Norway, and Denmark*
(the last book published during her lifetime), Mary wrote, slightly chillingly,

about the private experience of young motherhood in the context of the state of the society into which her daughter had been born:

> My child was sleeping with equal calmness—innocent and sweet as the closing flowers.—Some recollections, attached to the idea of home, mingled with reflections respecting the state of society I had been con-templating that evening, made a tear drop on the rosy cheek I had just kissed; and emotions that trembled on the brink of ecstasy and agony gave a poignancy to my sensations, which made me feel more alive than usual. (6: 248)

Whether or not Eliza was thinking about her late friend's comments in the fall of 1798, Mary's lines about observing her sleeping child "innocent and sweet as the closing flowers" while thinking about the "state of society," and feeling "on the brink of ecstasy and agony," reflected perfectly Eliza's life at that moment. Because the surviving letters Eliza wrote to Mary Hays begin in October 1798, that is exactly the moment when Eliza's personal life comes into view, and when it becomes clear that both financial and political insecurity in the world posed serious personal threats to her and to her young family.

3

Children's Book Writer and Friend

The word *friend* in the twenty-first century has become a verb, as in "to friend." In Eliza's world, *friend* was still a noun, but it had personal and political connotations that we have largely lost. To be a friend of the London Corresponding Society—or any of the other hundred or so "radical societies established in England between 1790 and 1797"—was to signal affiliation with "societies, associations and committees committed to parliamentary reform."[1] Mary Wollstonecraft, in her advocacy for equity in marital relationships, invoked "friendship" as "the most holy band of society."[2] In *Secresy,* Eliza has Sibella echo Wollstonecraft's sentiments: "To be the companion," writes Sibella to Caroline, "I must be equal—To be the friend, I must have comprehension and judgment: must be able to assist, or willing to be taught."[3] Eliza aspired to all of those ideals and, as the eighteenth century faded into the nineteenth, she needed all the friends she could get, especially as John descended increasingly into political and financial difficulty.

In 1798, on the English political front, paranoia about the threat of treason was increasing. Just before Orlando was born in April, two of John Fenwick's friends, John Binns[4] and James Coigley, had been among a group of five men arrested for treason.[5] On May 22, Coigley was convicted—the only one of the five found guilty—and on June 7, he was hung for treason. John's pamphlet on the trial was published soon after Thomas Holcroft, as he wrote in his diary of August 7, had "walked to Godwin," and had then given him "a favourable account of Fenwick's pamphlet on Coigley."[6]

With Eliza's first extant letter to Mary Hays on October 22, 1798, the themes of social and economic insecurity that persisted throughout her life are introduced. A. F. Wedd, in her published collection of Eliza's letters, omits the beginning of the first letter and its gritty statement that Eliza, John, and their young children are stuck for another week in their "miserable dwelling," and that John's (presumably bad) leg "obliges him to sit still." A little farther on in the letter, Eliza confesses that she is so poor that she does not have any underwear. She quotes a line she knows will resonate with Mary: "As Dame Quickly says (vide Mr. White) 'a modest change next to the skin . . . is . . . necessary to give people a good opinion of one.'"[7] That is the kind of oblique reference usually relegated to a footnote, but because it is exactly the kind of detail that speaks to Eliza's intimacy with eighteenth-century literature, the reference will receive a paragraph of its own here.

For Eliza and Mary, the Dame Quickly reference to "a modest change next to the skin" was a shared inside joke from a popular little book that had been recently published, *Falstaff's Letters* (1796), a spoof consisting of letters by James White (1775–1820) pretending to be Falstaff.[8] The reference demonstrates both Eliza's comfort level at being in the thick of London literary life and the fact that in the final two years of the eighteenth century, she had become so financially insecure that adequate clothes as well as adequate shelter were becoming difficult to sustain. Although John and Eliza were still together and trying to make their lives work for themselves and their young family, they were also relying on their friends to cover their shortfalls. There is, for instance, a little note from Holcroft on November 2, 1798, saying that he "advanced Fenwick 3£ to support his wife with necessaries."[9] And it looks as if their hardship continued into the new century. Godwin, in a note to his old friend James Marshall (dated August 2, 1800), writes that he too has "seen Mrs. Fenwick dressed out of poverty with a grey gown and no linen visible" (Godwin 2: 157).

Between Orlando's birth in May 1798 and when she first announced, on July 4, 1800, her intention to separate from John's "good and bad fortunes," Eliza was trying hard to maintain her integrity, to write, and to hold their young family together. But it does look as if their family fortunes had been in decline since at least 1795, and that Eliza was struggling to find time to write. "I am persevering," she wrote to Hays in November 1798, "to do that which had I done three years since I might have done well but now I have not even a hope to console me."[10] Eliza was apparently referring to a second novel, the one she ultimately abandoned, but the comment foregrounds her growing realization that she was going to be the one responsible for supporting her children.

In the early 1800s, as a young mother facing this realization, Eliza was still trying to figure out how to fulfill both her promise as a writer and her maternal responsibilities. Late eighteenth-century author Charlotte Smith wrote to Mary Hays about Eliza's situation in the context of her own:

> Of several new acquaintance, I know none for whom I am more interested than Mrs. Fenwick. She always appears to me to be not only a Woman of talents but of great sweetness of temper, & an excellent heart, & it grieves

me when I hear she is not as fortunate, as I am sure she deserves to be—I have really felt afraid of knowing more of her because I am sure I should love her enough to feel an additional source of concern in knowing so excellent a woman to be unhappy from causes which might be relieved without having the power to relieve those causes. I have known so much of pecuniary distress myself & feel so acutely what it is to have children for whose future fate the mothers heart is always oppressed, while their immediate wants claim every hour of the passing day, that it makes me feel acutely for our friend in whose pleasing countenance I imagine I see all those sensations. I wish I had the house & the income I ought to have; less for any other reason (for I am become indifferent to almost all the World calls good) than because I could then sometimes receive my friends & sometimes ask proofs of their friendship, but I am—married—! (Charlotte Smith to Mary Hays, 26 July 1800)[11]

Smith clearly captured the elements that would become the refrain of Eliza's life: her "talents," her "sweetness of temper," her "pleasing countenance," and the fact that she was in dire straits as she tried to secure a future for her children. The other point that comes across in the letter is the desire to help, something that seems directly related to Eliza's gift for friendship and her later flair for networking.

Though John and Eliza were gradually descending more deeply into poverty in the final years of the eighteenth century, John certainly remained enthusiastically involved in the literary and theatrical communities. While Eliza was struggling to care for their young children, John seemed to be maintaining his active social and political public life. In 1798, a play titled *He's Much to Blame, A Comedy*—which according to the British Library catalogue is attributed both to John Fenwick and Thomas Holcroft—was performed at the Theatre Royal, Covent Garden.[12] In 1799, John published the one literary work for which he is remembered: the first biography of William Godwin. In a genre today described as literary non-fiction, John's biography of Godwin originated as one of a series of essays published by Richard Phillips in his *Monthly Magazine*.[13] A short essay really, John's account reads as a tribute to a close friend, yet it also provides a prophetic sketch of the major themes that resonate in later scholarly retrospectives. Although ostensibly an account of Godwin's break from his Dissenting roots, it also reads as analogous to John Fenwick's own distance from his Methodist roots. Fenwick concludes with his assessment of his friend as "foremost among those who approach that rule, of making the happiness of society the object of moral conduct."[14] There is a kind of sad irony in that this essay was written while John's own "moral conduct" was deteriorating as his ties to and responsibility for his own family were weakening.

While John continued his public activities in the opening years of the nineteenth century, Eliza found herself scrambling to determine how to provide for herself and her children. In reading A. F. Wedd's account of that period in Eliza's life, just as she was trying to figure out how to earn an income of her own, it is hard not to be struck by her exasperated disapproval:

> Had she but stuck to one occupation, or known how to make the best use of such funds as come into her hands, she might have fared better. She is always moving from one lodging to another and from place to place. She tries in turn writing, school-keeping, helping in her brother-in-law's shop, translating, and coloring prints, previous to acting as resident governess in the Mocatta and Honner families. For her to declare any scheme has been abandoned invariably ensures the subsequent announcement of its having been put into execution. A chance piece of advice, the casual suggestion of an acquaintance, is enough the change the mind of this weathercock woman. So soon is she settled in one employment than she is off to another.[15]

From her early twentieth-century perspective, Wedd couldn't appreciate that Eliza was serving an apprenticeship of a kind, trying various options to see which one would enable her to find financial and social security for her family. With a little help from her friends, Eliza was building the repertoire of skills she needed to succeed.

Eliza Moves Toward Self-Sufficiency

In the years around 1800, Eliza found herself in an on-again, off-again situation with John. Should she stay or should she go? By all accounts he was still his charming, politically committed self, and he remained the life of the party among all the friends they still shared. Eliza wasn't exactly contemplating marital breakup; instead, she was beginning to recognize that she would have to take full, uncompromising responsibility for raising and educating their two children if John continued to be such a *bon vivant*. In many ways, the separation agreement between John and Eliza reads as a very modern arrangement. Their lives were separate but not disconnected. They still saw their friends. William Godwin's diary records many occasions after 1800 when they were in his company as a couple. Eliza also records in her letters to Mary periods when they were together. As the nineteenth century took hold, those times became fewer and more fraught and the periods when he was with their children more difficult.

Eliza knew that she would have to be the one to ensure that the children were equipped to earn their own livings. That meant figuring out what kind of work she could do to provide enough money to fund their education and imbue them with the self-confidence to feel comfortable holding their own in all social situations. Eliza's own employment options were basically limited to teaching, writing, and shopkeeping. She tried them all, gradually building the repertoire of knowledge and skill she would need to succeed.

My views of Eliza's career decisions are, however, at odds with the critical judgment of A. F. (Annie) Wedd, who, in the introduction to *The Fate of the Fenwicks*—her 1927 edition of letters to Mary Hays—scolds Eliza for being "recklessly impulsive and as unpractical as her miserable husband." She describes Eliza as a "weather-cock woman" and insists that "[h]ad she but stuck to one occupation, or known how to make the best use of such funds as come into her hands, she might have fared better."[16] As it happens, one of Wedd's nieces, Imogen Wedd, actually remembered her aunt and explained that "Aunt Nancy" (as she was known in the family) viewed the world from an upper-class perspective of entitled authority.[17] What Annie Wedd didn't appreciate was that Eliza was learning from her mistakes, and, piece-by-piece, was putting together the knowledge she needed to succeed socially and financially at a time when the odds were stacked against women attempting to do so on their own. In reading Eliza's rationale for each of her ventures, her unfailing sense that she really could succeed in the face of opposition is profoundly moving, as is her repeated commitment to putting in the hard work and dogged persistence she would need to make her dreams come true.

At first, through the late 1790s, Eliza struggled to work with John—as a friend, co-worker, and companion—to provide enough income to support their young family. In January 1799, she was running a school, working six hours a day with six children, aged two to five, and bringing in "£8 a quarter." She was also working with John on his translations from French, acting as his "amanuensis," as she says, writing to his dictation. Eight hours of work, however, only brought in £2.10, but without her assistance, she explains to Mary, he would only have been able to manage about half the amount of work. By February, John was on the run, escaping from both creditors and the political pressures of his potentially treasonous defense of James Coigley. Eliza was on her own with the children when she received first from Chester a "scrap" of assurance that he was en route, then the confirmation that he was finally "safe in Dublin."[18]

As the century turned, the world was also a much less friendly place than it had been for the three young children (Eliza Ann, Fanny, and Henry) who had played together with their energetic young mothers in the happy, sunny, optimistic summer of 1797. With John fleeing from the potential consequences of his unpaid debts and treasonous writing (prison or worse), there was certainly less time for Eliza to play with Eliza Ann and her baby brother Orlando. Mary Wollstonecraft's daughters, Fanny and her baby sister Mary, were motherless in 1800, as William Godwin struggled with his own grief after Mary's passing, his work, and the demands of his girls. Young Henry Reveley was also suddenly bereft. His father, Willey Reveley, died of an apparent brain aneurism on July 30, 1799. Eliza, by chance, had arrived just as he was collapsing and provided nursing care as she had for the dying Mary Wollstonecraft. A month after Willey Reveley's death, Eliza wrote to Mary Hays about the grieving widow: "Mrs Reveley," she writes, "still sacrifices to a tight drawn etiquette. She receives no one, she visits no one" (30 August 1799). The newly fatherless Henry, with his mother in deep mourning and not receiving or visiting friends, was not likely to be having much fun either.

Amidst the grief and loss, Eliza was consolidating her resources: friendship mattered. Extant evidence suggests that Eliza and Mary Hays had met around 1796 or 1797 through their shared friendship with Mary Wollstonecraft.[19] In her dying days, both Mary and Eliza had been there, and it is not a stretch to imagine how the experience must have brought them closer. After the death of Wollstonecraft, their friendship strengthened. They focused on their lives as literary women, and as women who had been unlucky in love. Their friendship was important, but not without its tensions. As is still very much the case, once women become mothers of young children, relationships with their unmarried, childless friends can become awkward. In January 1799, Eliza wrote to Mary, "I cannot understand why you have not written to me & I have sometimes thought of it with excessive pain." In May of 1799, Eliza, doing the best she could to make ends meet, was feeling both hurt in some way by Mary and afraid that she had accidentally caused offense:

> Gratified as I am by this new proof of your attention to our liking yet the manner in which you conveyed our tickets has given me exceeding pain. Are you, dear Mary, are you offended with me? Do you cease to call me your *dear friend?* Do you restrain your pen & suffer it no longer to convey to my heart the feelings of yours because you no longer deem me worthy of that beloved title, of that endearing elevated confidence? Is this so? Alas,

amidst a multitude of torturing anxieties the remembrance of your affection has never been effaced from mine. (EF to MH, 31 May 1799)

Without the other side of the correspondence, it is difficult to know exactly what happened, but the tone indicates that Eliza was trying hard to reassure Mary that whatever offense had been taken was not intended. The rest of the letter suggests that Mary had assumed Eliza was coming for a visit, but when Eliza didn't—because she was working and because her shoes had been soaked through, so she couldn't walk—Mary was miffed.

There was more to the friendship between Eliza and Mary than just maintaining their scheduled tea-drinking dates. They connected as literary women, novelists specifically, and their friendship engaged not just the intimacies of their personal lives but also their public work. But it was only by comparing Eliza's original manuscript letters to Mary against the 1927 published collection by Annie Wedd that it became possible to see how much of their shared literary lives had been edited out by Wedd. In early 1799, for example, Eliza acknowledged receipt of a new book by Mary. Though she doesn't name it, the date and its feminist themes of injustice and discrimination suggest that it is *The Victim of Prejudice*, originally published anonymously in 1798. In an unpublished fragment of a letter, Eliza begins with an apology: "I have not read your book through," she confesses, "& therefore will not *criticise* till I have finished it." Ever the diplomat, Eliza continues: "so far as I have gone I find it very eloquent." Then there is a beautifully deflected comment, as Eliza reports, obliquely, on the review by her precocious ten-year-old daughter who has read the book: "Eliza [Ann] says it reminds her of Caleb Williams [the 1794 novel by William Godwin] because he was so persecuted & driven about the world & though she likes it a great deal she does prefer Caleb Williams" (EF to MH, 15 February 1799).

It doesn't appear that Eliza had much time to read or write as the century turned. On October 9, 1799, Eliza wrote to say that her family would be moving in with writer Ralph Fell at Christmas. William Godwin records a meeting on December 9, 1799, at the home of Ralph Fell that John, Eliza, and a few of their other friends also attended. Yet, despite valiant attempts to keep things together for her family, by July 1800, Eliza seems to have had enough. She did what countless other desperate women do when they find the security of their young children threatened: she fled, with the children, in search of sanctuary.

Eliza's first stop was about 150 miles from London, to the estate of J. H. Pierce, called New Park, just east of Axminster in Devon, a place Eliza apparently knew well. Unfortunately she arrived at a time when the Pierce family was also in crisis. The second oldest daughter, Fanny—who had been a close friend of young Eliza Ann, a "most beloved friend and companion"— had just died at age fourteen. Fanny's mother, Mrs. Pierce, was "lying in" with her twelfth child (whom she also named Fanny), and Orlando had the "chicken pochs." In the midst of the chaos, Eliza made explicit her resolve to make it on her own, to take full responsibility for supporting, raising, and educating her children:

> I have once heard from Mr F. since I have been here. I do not suppose you have seen him. For he intended to keep very close to avoid danger. I am determined Mary, if it be possible, to consider myself & children totally separated from his bad or good fortunes. If I should be able to contribute to his repose & comfort I shall rejoice, but never, never, will I again, if the means are to be had by my industry of supporting my children, involve myself in such miseries & perplexities as I have endured. (EF to MH, 4 July 1800)

The visit to the home of J. H. Pierce in Axminster must have been an initial stopgap, a familiar place where she knew that she and her children would be welcome, but she clearly regarded the move as temporary.

By August 1800, Eliza and the children had moved to Englefield Cottage, the home of poet and actress Mary Robinson (1758–1800), in Egham Surrey, about twenty miles from London. At that point, Eliza must have been desperately poor, and again, as she'd said in 1789, without something to wear next to her skin. It is unclear when Eliza first met Mary Robinson, but William Godwin first lists a dinner with her on March 5, 1800, a dinner also attended by John Fenwick and Eliza. That spring, Robinson dined several times with John, Eliza, and Godwin, and once on April 25 with John Philip Kemble, the actor, director, and stage manager of Drury Lane and Covent Garden, as well.

Although Mary Robinson's name might not be as familiar to twenty-first-century general readers as the names of Marie Antoinette or Britain's Duchess of Devonshire (i.e., Georgina Cavendish, née Spencer, a direct ancestor of the late Diana, Princess of Wales), she was famous, even infamous, in the eighteenth century—first as an actress and mistress of the Prince of Wales (later George IV), and then as a poet. By 1800, however, Robinson was very frail, badly crippled, and reportedly had to be carried even across very short distances. The May 3–6, 1800 issue of the *Whitehall Evening Post* contains both a report of a new play at Drury Lane, "The Indian," written by Mr. Fenwick, and a note on Mrs. Robinson, saying that her health had been "gradually declining" for a year, and that her illness had "entirely originated in mental inquietude."[20]

Mary Robinson provided sanctuary for Eliza and her children, and enough leisure so that Eliza could focus her novelist's eye on her surroundings. Modern biographers still use Eliza's descriptions to Mary Hays of Robinson's home to explain what it was like.[21] Eliza begins her depiction of Mary Robinson's surroundings with what would, in a film, be described as a situation shot, a long shot, indicating how the cottage sits in its landscape. She describes it as "singularly beautiful," and located "on the summit of a high hill," with the views opening onto "an astonishing prospect of richly wooded & cultivated country with the Thames pouring through it." There is a tender irony in Eliza's note that the cottage stands "aloof from the grander dwellings" below, a kind of veiled inversion of class dynamics played out in the landscape. When Eliza moves to the description of the interior, however, her conflicted sense of the contrast between her own chaotic existence and her peaceful surroundings filters through. With her critical eye, Eliza rates Mrs. Robinson's furniture as "perhaps more ornamental" than she should choose, but, she says, "still it is elegant & quiet—nothing gaudy nor ill placed." Once Eliza makes that observation, her own desperate situation comes crashing in: "And yet dear Mary I sigh now & then for *a home*. Ah what a charm has the idea of *a quiet home* for me who for the last six years have been tossed to & fro amidst fears & frights & perils" (EF to MH, August 1800).

On the verge of breaking down, Eliza acknowledges that it has been six years—since 1794, thus a year before the publication of *Secresy*—that she and John have been living a precarious existence. The longing for a home of her own, so poignantly expressed here, would become a leitmotif over the following three decades, although in 1800, Eliza did not yet know that. In her letter to Mary Hays, after faltering briefly, Eliza recovers her composure, counts her blessings, and looks to the future, congratulating herself "on being the guest of a woman whose powers of pleasing ever varied & graceful are united to quick feeling & generosity of temper."

Eliza's time at Englefield Cottage did provide enough respite so that she could gather her resources and begin to face the future. She was confident enough in her writing that the news of a second novel was announced in *The Monthly Magazine* 61: "Mrs. Fenwick is also writing another novel. Her elegant specimen of 'Serecy' [sic] has sufficiently proclaimed the powers of her pen."[22] The announcement was premature. If Eliza did keep a draft manuscript, no traces of it have been found, though it might have been *The Castle of Indolence*, the manuscript that would be rejected by William Godwin in 1806. There is a surviving letter to Mary Jane Godwin from Eliza, in which she explains her rationale for withdrawing the manuscript in anticipation of the rejection rather than waiting for it to be sent back: "it suits my pride better to reject myself," she writes, "than leave that for him to do." Yet Eliza also politely phrases her request for constructive criticism: "When Mr. G. has one idle hour, if he would run over the Castle of Indolence, & name the faults it has, it would be a great service to me, & with the aid of his judgment I shd be able to make a pretty book yet."[23] No evidence of the critique has been found.

The fact that Eliza had abandoned the second novel survives only in the fragment of the "hunting for Mrs. Fenwick" 1832 note to the Moffats: "I began another," she wrote, "but being then independent & sharing the dissipation of fashionable life, I thought no more of Authorship till wealth had vanished." The comment seems a little disingenuous with regard to the timing of the drafted second novel, given that her 1800 note to Mary indicates that her fortunes had been on the decline since the mid-1790s. One other important element pertaining to Eliza's hopes for the future comes out of the same 1800 note to Mary Hays: the promise she sees in her children. It was a promise confirmed, as she gently boasted, in the "charming little poem" Mary Robinson published in the *Morning Post* of Tuesday July 29, 1800, addressed to the then two-year-old Orlando who, as his proud mother noted, "improves in strength & beauty daily."

Mary Robinson's poem, entitled "Lines Addressed to a Beautiful Infant," is "inscribed to Mrs. Fenwick," and is for an adult audience in that it poignantly and eloquently sets up the contrast between the unfolding grace of infancy and the gathering dark of aging and death. It is not a cheerful poem nor is it a celebration of "infant joy."[24] Instead, the "beautiful infant" occasions a poem about growing old. Robinson opens with praise to the baby: "Orlando! when the dawn of grace, / Beams lustrous on thy cherub face!" and moves, by the stanza "to trace—/ The progress of life's weary race!" The poem concludes with a meditation on the way the darkness of life descends on the brightness, beauty, and promise of babyhood:

> Then, sweet ORLANDO! Time will see
> Full many a storm encircle thee!
> Full many a keen and poison'd dart
> Will rankle in thy beating heart;
> And ere the Summer-day has flown,
> Thy sensate breast will learn to groan;—
> And thou wilt shed the tear to find
> That mis'ry marks the feeling mind—
> That Fortune sheds its golden ray
> On dull-ey'd Folly's even way;

> While souls like thine are doom'd to trace—
> A gloomy, sad, and thorny space![25]

Besides speaking to Mary Robinson's own loss of youth and beauty, the poem occasioned by Orlando and addressed to Eliza foreshadows Wordsworth's "Intimations of Immortality," not composed until 1803, and not published until 1807. Wordsworth's famous lines still come to mind:

> Shades of the prison-house begin to close
> Upon the growing Boy,
> But He beholds the light, and whence it flows,
> He sees it in his joy;
> The Youth, who daily farther from the east
> Must travel, still is Nature's Priest,
> And by the vision splendid
> Is on his way attended;
> At length the Man perceives it die away,
> And fade into the light of common day. (*Poetical Works* 460)

The point of comparison is to indicate only that Robinson was drawing from a common pool of ideas swirling around in the circle of friends they all shared, including Samuel Taylor Coleridge, William Godwin, and Robert Southey. It was Wordsworth, of course, who caught exactly the right cadence, the one that ultimately echoed down the centuries, defining what would become known as Romantic childhood innocence. In setting Wordsworth's poem against Robinson's poem—and in the context of the maternal thinking of Eliza, Mary Wollstonecraft, and their friends, including Anna Barbauld—the point is to put a tiny chink in the historical memory celebrating masculine Romantic originality at the expense of the now-forgotten literary women in whose world the Romantic poets were nurtured.

Mary Robinson died just after Christmas, on December 26, 1800. She was only forty-three. As there is a gap between Eliza's August 1800 letter from the home of Robinson and the next letter in September 1801 (probably from Essex), there is something missing in the narrative sequence. As Eliza appears to have been with John occasionally, it looks as if they patched things up, at least temporarily. Though John was apparently still trying to escape his creditors and support political causes, he was also having another go at making it as a journalist. Godwin records twenty occasions when he was with John and Eliza together—about two or three times a month—between August 24, 1800 and September 9, 1801.

According to Winifred Courtney in *Young Charles Lamb 1775–1802*, John Fenwick bought *The Albion*, a radical newspaper at the time, after Allen [or

Allan] MacLeod, the editor, had been convicted of libel against the Prince of Wales in April 1801. The scenario was a familiar one, it seems: when the editor of one of the radical newspapers was prosecuted for "libel, blasphemy or sedition, the owner went to jail."[26] The funds to buy the newspaper, according to Courtney, came from "wealthy Radicals" who supported reform, "Lord Stanhope, the Duke of Northumberland, the Earl of Lauderdale, and probably Lord Petre, a leading Roman Catholic peer who welcomed the Albion's support of Catholic Emancipation" (311). *The Albion* ran for at least ten issues as an evening paper between June and September 1801.

In "Newspapers Thirty-Five Years Ago," Charles Lamb writes about John Fenwick's takeover of *The Albion*, describing the "humble paragraph-maker" as having expended all of his, and others', money on the "whole and sole Editorship, Proprietorship, with all the rights and titles (such as they were worth) of the Albion, . . ."[27] Joseph Ritson, another friend of both Lamb and John Fenwick who helped to fund the purchase, commented on the irritation he felt at "a swindling trick of the editor of the *Albion,* who obtained 5 guineas . . . on a false pretense and promise of punctual payment. . . ."[28] Ritson grudgingly realized that the "couple of pounds" he did get back was about all he was ever going to see of the loan.

With John "resolutely determined to pull down the Government," says Lamb, "our occupation was now to write treason" The "[r]ecollections of feelings," he says, "were all that now remained from our first boyish heats kindled by the French Revolution," partly inspired by the "right earnest fanaticism of F" (Lamb 324). The newspaper, as Lamb makes affectionately clear, was a money loser from the start, as John encouraged his friends "to write treason." According to Courtney, however, Lamb had the treason columns mostly to himself, with "one or two columns of *The Albion*'s sixteen to fill up regularly" (313). The potentially treasonous views expressed in the paper were what brought the publication to an unceremonious end. As Lamb wrote to Thomas Manning on August 31, 1801, "The Albion is dead, dead as a doornail."

John didn't give up easily. With the demise of *The Albion,* he set about trying to cobble together funding for a new venture. On October 19, 1801, Eliza was, as we'd say now, "hanging in" with John as he prepared to try again. She writes:

> Mr. Fenwick is very busy sending out the Prospectus. He finds that he shall not be ready for publishing the paper as soon quite as soon as he proposed, & if he has to make many journeys for the establishment of correspondents he probably will not commence till near the meeting of parliament. Slow

and sure is at present his maxim. If *he* grows wary & prudent what trans-
formations may we not [page is smudged, word is possibly "experience"].

Eliza sounds hopeful, obviously wanting John's best qualities to succeed
this time, betting on his ability to become "wary & prudent." The scenario
is familiar enough in the annals of marital discord: reconciliation is purchased with the promise to change, to reform, to drop bad habits—in John's
case, a recklessness with money and, presumably, excessive drinking—with
the aim of re-establishing the family on a happy and stable footing. By securing funds from the Duke of Northumberland, John was able to start a
daily newspaper, *The Plough*, in late October. Charles Lamb said, "the editor
(John) held a ball, and bought new hats for his womenfolk" (Courtney 320).
The paper failed soon after.

By 1801, four years after Mary Wollstonecraft's death, William Godwin
was beginning to put his life back together. He'd proposed to the widowed
Maria Reveley, but she rejected him.[29] Then a neighbor, Mary Jane Clairmont
(1768–1841), came into his life, and the lives of his daughters. She claimed
to be a widow though her marital status to the father of her two children
Charles (1795–1850) and Claire (1798–1879) is unclear. She was pregnant
with Godwin's child at their marriage on December 21, 1801, though sadly
had a miscarriage or a stillborn son five months later on May 8, 1802.[30] Eliza
does not write about the wedding but not long afterward, on January 2, 1802,
Godwin recorded in his diary that John and Eliza met with the newlyweds
and that then, as couples, they were together again on January 14 and 20.
From the beginning, Mary Jane was not much liked by William Godwin's
friends. She was referred to by Lamb as a "bad baby" and, on September 2,
1802, clearly not holding back, he described her as William Godwin's "pitiful
artificial wife" and a "Bitch."

Eliza seems to have left London soon after the wedding, because in
July 1802 she turns up in Penzance, Cornwall, helping her brother-in-law,
Thomas Fenwick, to run his linen-drapery shop. Despite the fact that Eliza
had announced her separation in 1800 and was determined to raise and
educate her children through her own work, wit, and determination, John
did not disappear from their lives. They continued to try to help one another
muddle through.[31] As Godwin records in his diary, they often met with him,
sometimes separately, sometimes together, in the opening years of the century. In a way completely familiar to any twenty-first-century parents trying to juggle the competing demands of work and childcare, Eliza and John
seemed alert to all possible resources and avenues of support, and also appear to have tried versions of co-parenting.[32] And although Eliza designated

Mary Hays as surrogate mother to Orlando from the earliest days of his life, she also continued to attempt to make a go of family life with John.

The attraction of life in a community where members of both her and John's extended family could offer company and potential support must have made the move to Cornwall a viable option, as it meant the provision of a secure job, even if that was shopkeeping with her brother-in-law. A linen-draper's shop was basically what we would call a fabric shop, a place that sold cloth, which could then be made into clothes or drapes for windows. The name derives from the bolts of cloth that were "draped" in the doorways for examination. Shopkeeping was not unfamiliar to Eliza, as she had tried it as a young teenager, as Peter Jaco indicated in his letter of October 24, 1779, when he wrote about the "business" his wife and daughter (Eliza would have been thirteen) had attempted and failed.

In returning to Cornwall, Eliza was returning to the community of her father's family and she seemed to be trying to integrate. She commented on the physical attractiveness of her Jaco relatives. Members of John Fenwick's family were there as well, including Miss Duckworth, the daughter of his sister. Eliza attempted to get on with everyone. She confided to Mary that her "brother"—that is, her brother-in-law—approved of her. He admired, she says, "the ease with which I bend to my new employment & accommodate the vulgar caprices of the country people." She was motivated, as she explains: "I do that certainly for I will leave nothing unassayed to promote my family welfare." She describes the work as "slavery," and the difficulty of working on "Market days" when the shop was so full that she had no respite, even though there were two other women in the shop with them. Thomas, however, was as unsuited to business as John was, and his linen-draper's shop went bankrupt, according to a report in the *London Gazette* of June 25, 1803.[33]

In the surviving letters to Mary from 1802, Eliza's accounts of the experience of trying to make a life for herself and her children in Penzance come through with aching clarity. Many of the same themes appear over and over again in her letters: her paramount concern for the welfare of her family, her lack of a home, her close observation of the landscape, her desperate desire for social stability, her love of walking in the countryside, and her desire for friendship. In 1802, she had the children with her, though, as she says, Eliza Ann had been ill. Orlando appears as sunny and winning as he had the year before as an infant in the company of Mary Robinson. John turns up occasionally with Eliza in London during 1802 though he also seems to have been working on the newspaper, *The Plough*, in Falmouth. In April 1802, Charles Lamb told his friend Manning that John Fenwick was "still in debt."

But on September 24, 1802, Lamb confirmed that all hope had faded. John Fenwick, he said, is "a ruined man," is "hiding from his creditors," and has "sent his wife and children to the country." But by 1803–1804, John was in Portsmouth, trying his hand as the editor of a country newspaper.[34]

For Eliza, the relentless demands of working in her brother-in-law's shop every day were starving her intellectual and imaginative life. In an unpublished section of the first letter from Penzance, Eliza confides her sense of loss and consoles herself with the acknowledgement of the literary life she once shared with Mary Hays, regretting that it is unfulfilled: "Here, in banishment from all that can awaken my imagination or gratify my taste," she writes, "I remember with pride & pleasure the distinguished marks of friendship you designed for me in the dedication you spoke of the last time but one we met." Although the book to which she is referring is not specified, the date would suggest that it might be *The Dictionary of Female Biography* by Mary Wollstonecraft's publisher Joseph Johnson, though it was not actually published until 1803. Mary Hays changed her mind about including the dedication, and Eliza attempted to resolve an awkward social situation:

> Do not suffer one moment's anxiety respecting the dedication. I feel my triumph in your friendship just as forcibly without it. I confess I was most highly gratified by your intention & could not forbear naming it to one or two persons yet I was not so vain, but I perceived it was a distinction I had no way merited with the world & that the enquiring of, Who is this Mrs. Fenwick? might produce answers not quite pleasing to my pride. To the persons who had heard from me of this testimony of your regard I must explain it as I cannot endure they should suppose I am less to you than I was or than I believed myself to be. I depend on your promise of sending me your work by the first wagon after its publication. (EF to MH, 17 December 1802)

Eliza was clearly struggling, attempting to be generous about her friend's success, while keenly aware that the possibilities of a literary life of her own were dwindling: "When I think of it I can have but one thing to regret—that you are so ill paid for your talent & labour." Eliza reiterated that her "barren imagination & still more barren situation" rendered the possibility of a "second work" even more remote. And she couldn't help but regret that their mutual "good friend Mrs. Plumptre"[35] had been successful despite the fact that she had "not more talent" than Eliza saw in herself.

Eliza's attempt at shopkeeping in Penzance must have come to an end around the time when Thomas went bankrupt in 1803. The news of what

John and Eliza were doing comes in a gossipy letter from Mary Lamb to Dorothy Wordsworth on July 11, 1803:

> You saw Fenwick when you was with us—perhaps you remember his wife and children were with his brother, a tradesman at Penzance. He (the brother) was supposed to be in a great way of business, has become a bankrupt; they are now at Penzance without a home and without money; and poor Fenwick, who has been Editor of a country newspaper lately, is likely soon to be quite out of employ; I am distressed for them, for I have a great affection for Mrs. Fenwick.[36]

As Eliza and John turn up frequently together in Godwin's diary through 1803, it looks as if they returned to London, and Eliza began to make her living in a more intellectually hospitable environment than running a linen-draper's shop could afford. Sometime that year must be when she took up writing for children.

Writing for Children, 1804–1813

The immediate cost-benefit analysis of writing for children was obvious. Unlike her 1795 novel *Secresy*—or any long novel unmarked as being for children—Eliza's children's books would necessarily be short and would appeal to a rapidly expanding market, especially in London. For Eliza at that point, the need to "make writing profitable," as she'd said in 1798, was more urgent than ever.[37] Fortunately, many of the publishers, including the children's book publishers, were conveniently clustered around St. Paul's Cathedral, as the churchyard was the hub of the book trade. Joseph Johnson, the publisher of Mary Wollstonecraft, Maria Edgeworth, and Anna Barbauld, had his shop at 72 St. Paul's Churchyard. Johnson would have been a neighbor of Richard Phillips at 71. A few doors away, at 65 St. Paul's Churchyard, was the publishing house regarded as the best known and most innovative: John Newbery's shop, under the sign of the Bible. Sun. John Marshall, who had just begun selling wonderful miniature wooden bookcases, filled with tiny books for children, was more or less around the corner at 4 Aldermary Churchyard. And a little farther west was the firm of Darton and Harvey at 35 Gracechurch Street.

It was with the move into the thriving children's book market that Eliza began in earnest to recognize her capacity to earn an income of her own and to chart a life of her own, separate from her husband, but devoted to her children. And it is here that she began building the skills that enabled her to succeed—eventually—as a businesswoman, teacher, and school owner in the Caribbean and North America. The period in which Eliza wrote for children was relatively short, about ten years, between 1804 with the publication of her first book *Little Mary and her Cat,* for Benjamin Tabart's Juvenile Library, and 1813 with the publication of her last known book *Lessons for Children,* published for William Godwin's Juvenile Library. Even though she was living under the competing demands of caring for her children while writing enough to support her small family, the books themselves testify to Eliza's literary gifts and her contributions to the development of children's literature in the period.

As the years between 1804 (when Eliza's first books for children were published) and 1814 (when she left for Barbados) covered such profound transitions for all the members of the family, it makes better narrative sense here to concentrate on how Eliza built up her educational credentials as a writer and governess, and her business acumen, rather than to adhere to a strict chronological account of who was doing what in any given year. In that ten-year period as Eliza developed her independence, John fades from the scene and her children mature and receive—thanks to her—educations that prepare them to become self-supporting. The capacity for friendship that characterized Eliza's life in the 1790s developed in the nineteenth century into a capacity for networking.

When Eliza retrospectively sketched her literary career to the Moffat family in 1832, she was clear that her foray into the children's book business was driven by a need for ready cash rather than by a desire to produce great literature, and that the milieu in which she was working in London was compatible with her purposes. "In London," she explains, "writing, I will not say literature, is as much a trade to live by as making Vests & Pantaloons." Although the distinction she makes between being a (hack) writer and a (literary) author now reads as a prescient foreshadowing of Roland Barthes's famous distinction between a writer and an author,[38] Eliza regarded the kind of writing she was doing as low-status piecework, akin to sewing clothing. That is why, as she clarifies almost apologetically, she never put her "name to any publication except to some tales for young Children & that was done by the Bookseller," she says, "without my knowledge when I was absent from London." Eliza wrote this account from Niagara, Upper Canada (now Ontario), when she was thousands of miles and twenty years removed from the literary London she had known. Despite her self-deprecating take on her work (and a long period after that of being regarded as out of fashion), Eliza's contributions to children's literature were more valuable than she thought.

In 1932, one hundred years after Eliza's note from Niagara, F. J. Harvey Darton, a descendant of a publishing dynasty that had flourished in London from the mid-1750s, published his pioneering history of children's literature, *Children's Books in England*. In it, he takes a dim view of women, the "lady moralists," as he calls them, who wrote for children between 1790 and 1820. His general tone suggests that he is rolling his eyes disapprovingly as he grudgingly grants that the books of the period were recognized as "a semi-artistic literary form, with philosophic purpose subordinated to the story."[39] Eliza barely rates a mention in *Children's Books in England*. In his generic dismissal of the books largely written by women in the early nineteenth century, Darton condescendingly states that "unless one reads very closely, their books cannot but give a certain impression of rigidity, of inhuman excellence, of making life not worth living in the attempt to live it worthily" (174). It is hard not to think that he must have been pleased with himself for writing such a pithily clever sentence, one that solidified his own superior value judgment. Darton was writing from a position designed to trace a narrative arc moving from what we retroactively call eighteenth-century "Rationalism" to nineteenth-century "Romanticism." He did that by demeaning the old in order to celebrate the new "Golden Age" of imaginative literature for children characterized most famously by Lewis Carroll's *Alice in Wonderland* (1865) and *Alice Through the Looking Glass* (1871). As is typical with historical accounts, the "truth" of the story of the past is shaped by the conditions of the present.[40]

For Darton, writing in the 1930s, children were perceived as Romantic innocents, separate from the social, political, and economic spheres of adults. In the early nineteenth century, however, that was not the case. Children were constructed as people, encouraged to take responsibility for their own actions and to become socially engaged and responsible. In that way, children of the early nineteenth century are more like the children of the early twenty-first century; that is, the thinking, knowing, socially engaged and connected children of the digital age have more in common with the ones Darton dismissed as attempting to live life "worthily" than with the closed-off, separated Romantic innocents he valorized. In light of the way that perceptions of children have changed, Eliza's books look different than they did in the early twentieth century when Darton dismissed them, or in the early nineteenth century when Eliza was in the midst of making something new, something celebrating parental involvement with the education of children. Despite the fact that Eliza's children's books have long been out of circulation, they provide evidence of her literary credibility, partly because they demonstrate her narrative gifts and partly because they speak to a construction of children and childhood that feels very real for twenty-first-century readers.

It was in 1804 that Eliza emerged, already fully formed, onto the children's book scene in London. That is the year she had three titles (*Little Mary and her Cat, The Life of Carlo,* and *Presents for Good Girls*) on the list of new books published for Benjamin Tabart's Juvenile Library, the upmarket children's book arm of Richard Phillips's educational publishing enterprise. The chronological list of publications, as organized by Marjorie Moon in her meticulous 1990 bibliography, *Benjamin Tabart's Juvenile Library,* demonstrates that only in 1804 did the list begin to distinguish itself as appealing to a new, pedagogically informed upmarket demographic. Prior to that, between 1801—when Tabart's shop first opened at 157 New Bond Street—and 1803, the list of titles bearing the Tabart imprint looked thin, dominated by conventional books such as David Irving's *The Elements of English Composition* (1801) and W. F. Mavor's *The British Nepos* (1802) and *The English Spelling Book* (1802). To be fair, there were innovative and original books on the first three lists too, such as Lucy Aikin's *Poetry for Children* (1801), Jane Porter's *The Two Princes of Persia* (1801), and William Godwin's *Bible Stories* (1802), published under the pseudonym William Scolfield. In 1804, however, the list suddenly more than doubled its offerings (from seventeen to forty) and exploded with vital, imaginative titles, and a clear acknowledgement of the influence of the French fairy tales. Offerings on the list include tales by Mme d'Aulnoy, *The History of Fortunio,* and by Charles Perrault (*Blue Beard,* the French *Cendrillon* and the English *Cinderella, Hop o' my Thumb, Puss in Boots and Diamonds and Toads, Riquet with the Tuft,* and *Sleeping Beauty*). The 1804 list also includes *Tabart's Collection of Popular Stories,* compiled and retold by Mary Jane Clairmont Godwin. That collection contains some of the stories that became standards in children's literature, including "Whittington and his Cat," "The Children in the Wood," "Peronella," "Fortunatus," "Griselda," "The White Cat," and "Robin Hood."[41]

In 1804, both Eliza Fenwick and Mary Jane Clairmont Godwin were publishing under Benjamin Tabart's imprint, as was William Godwin. It wasn't until the following year that William and Mary Jane Godwin opened their own rival "Juvenile Library," but it is easy to see why writing for children must have appealed to them as well as to Eliza: they were all writers, all with young children, and all in need of quick cash to meet their needs. Although Eliza Ann was fifteen in 1804 and no longer in need of constant care, Orlando was just seven. William and Mary Jane in 1804 had five children to care for: Fanny (Imlay) was ten, Mary (Wollstonecraft Godwin) was eight, Charles (Clairmont) was nine, Claire (Clairmont) seven, and William (Clairmont Godwin) just two.

While Eliza was turning herself into an income earner, John was sinking inexorably into debt, though the unalterable consequences wouldn't become fully evident until a little later. On January 15, 1806, Charles Lamb wrote to William Hazlitt: "Fenwick is coming to town on Monday (if no kind angel intervene) to surrender himself to [debtors'] prison." Nineteen months later, on November 5, 1807, Eliza wrote to Mary Hays: "I have now the boy [Orlando] on my hands to maintain—Mr F is gone to Prison." Eliza had not waited until John had completely imploded. Between 1804, when Eliza's first book for children appeared, and 1806, when John first went to prison, Eliza had been working at speed and under pressure, writing, compiling, and translating books for children; first for Benjamin Tabart and Richard Phillips, then for William and Mary Jane Godwin.

The exact number of books Eliza published is difficult to confirm, as some were anonymous and some were composed under the generic pseudonyms that Richard Phillips had adopted for his textbook publishing enterprise.[42] Although Eliza claimed to have written "many" books commissioned by Phillips and published under one of the generic pseudonyms, only one—*The Class Book,* published in 1806 under the name of Rev'd David Blair—can be clearly identified as having been compiled by Eliza. The list of Tabart's publications not explicitly designated as schoolbooks consisted of volumes with named and anonymous authors. Eliza seems to have contributed both to the list. In 1805, she was responsible for three books, two under her own name (*Presents for Good Boys* and *Visits to the Juvenile Library*) and one anonymously, *Songs for the Nursery.* In 1810, *Infantine Stories* was published under her own name, and *Six Stories in English and French*[43] anonymously. That year, when Eliza began working as a governess in London, she also published (under her own name) *Rays from the Rainbow* for Godwin's Juvenile Library. Finally, in 1813, she published *Lessons for Children* (also under her own name), which as far as I know was her last published children's book in Britain. The gaps suggest that some of the anonymous books published by Tabart and/or Phillips during that period were by Eliza, but without corroboration from another source, it is only possible to name the books that are clearly identified. The books Eliza compiled and/or edited were innovative and provided evidence of an original mind at work; a mind tuned to plot, characterization, and a novelist's nose for story, ear for conversation, and eye for telling detail. Marjorie Moon, in fact, notes that when Eliza became one of Benjamin Tabart's authors, "a real catch had swum into his net."[44]

In writing her first stories for children in 1804 and 1805, Eliza drew on her keen awareness of her immediate environment and her understanding of its potential for fiction. *The Life of Carlo*,[45] for example, is the backstory of Carlo the performing dog who, in a play titled *The Caravan*, "leapt into a stream of real water and saved a child, received nightly the most tumultuous applause." A playbill from December 9, 1803 announces that the play, which had been "produced for the third time on Wednesday evening was again received throughout with rapturous applause, by the most brilliant and overflowing audience and will be repeated every Evening after tonight, till further notice."[46] The theater manager at the time, incidentally, was Richard Brinsley Sheridan (1751–1816), famous author of, among other enduring plays, *The School for Scandal*. *The Caravan* was a hit and there were funny cartoons in the papers crediting Carlo the dog with saving the fortunes of the theater. One says, "DRURY LANE THEATRE SAVED FROM RUIN BY THE DOG CARLO IN CARAVAN." Another, reproduced below, says, "The Driver and his Dog or Sherry brought into Port." Eliza took the news of the day and quickly fashioned a variation on a "Lassie-come-home" adventure story/celebrity biography, more or less on the spot, capitalizing on Carlo's transient fame while gauging the buzz about the dog. The hit stage play would generate a market for *The Life of Carlo*, a kind of prequel to the play.

"The Driver and His Dog or Sherry Brought into Port." (©Trustees of the British Museum)

All of the stories Eliza wrote so very quickly in 1804 and 1805 testify to her narrative skill, her flair for the dramatic, and her ability to move a plot along swiftly with the emotional highs and lows paced perfectly to keep readers (unmarked by age range) turning the pages. Though every book of hers is different, Eliza demonstrates an uncanny ability to tune in to the cultural desires of devoted parents in her particular moment in history. She does it, for example, in writing about the "presents" in *Presents for Good Girls,* which "encourage the habits of regularity and industry," as she says in the introduction to the volume, while still encouraging little girls to engage with "the more active exercises of their brothers." The book itself is cleverly constructed: the six gifts that form the subjects of each of the six stories are contained in the framing story of a large box of presents that the mother has prepared for her two daughters, containing three gifts for each. And they are wondrous gifts, including a beautiful doll, an equally beautiful tea set for the doll, and a fully fitted doll's dressing table. As Eliza was struggling to support herself and her children during those early years of the nineteenth century, the words in the stories become substitutes for the material gifts she couldn't possibly afford.

Eliza tapped again into her cultural moment when she foregrounded empathy as a desirable quality for children both when she wrote about the inhumane conditions endured by enslaved people in *Visits to the Juvenile Library* (1805), and when she wrote about being kind to animals in *Little Mary and her Cat* (1804).[47] With the publication of *Visits to the Juvenile Library,* Eliza leveraged not only empathy but also her intimacy with Tabart's Juvenile Library and its authors. She managed to capitalize on the marketing strategy of Tabart's shop (with its appeal to an upmarket audience), maintain the narrative drive of the story, and perfectly capture the social concerns of the day: education, empathy, and abolition of the slave trade.

By focusing on the way a group of functionally illiterate orphaned white West Indian children and their enslaved nanny Nora discover liberation through literacy in the bookshop in *Visits to the Juvenile Library,* Eliza marketed the books sold in Tabart's Juvenile Library and promoted enlightened reform. Although William Wilberforce did not manage to pass the bill to abolish the slave trade until 1807 (two years after the publication of *Visits to the Juvenile Library*), the critical mass needed to support the move had been building gradually since the beginning of the nineteenth century. Eliza's publisher Richard Phillips had, in fact, been one of the founding members of the Society to Effect the Abolition of the Slave Trade in 1787.

What's unusual for the period is that in *Visits to the Juvenile Library,* Eliza upturns the conventional enslaved-person-as-hapless-victim scenario and portrays Nora's character not as a victim, but as a woman with autonomy and agency. On seeing the good effect education has had on the five young orphaned children in her care (three boys and two girls), Nora teaches herself to read. As the children are enticed into literacy via the books in Tabart's Juvenile Library, they become nicer and happier and serve as role models for the suspicious Nora who had at first regarded education as something akin to punishments meted out to enslaved people—"the terrors of rods, canes, dark closets, and stocks" (15).[48] But once Nora discovers that education frees rather than enslaves the children, she decides to teach herself to read too. And so it is that, in the story, the two eldest boys find Nora in their elegant Georgian library "with an English Spelling-Book in her hand busily employed in learning to spell the short easy words of man, can, ran &c." (71).

The fact that Nora teaches herself to read is, in itself, unusual. In conventional abolitionist stories, it is a child who teaches the enslaved person, typically portrayed as grateful but slow, how to read. That is the image sustained through the nineteenth century, and most famously stated in Harriet Beecher Stowe's *Uncle Tom's Cabin* (first published almost fifty years later in 1852) when Little Eva stands up to her mother and explains what she would "do" for the slaves: "I'd teach them to read their own Bible and write their own letters, and read letters that are written to them,' said Eva, steadily. 'I know mamma, it does come very hard on them that they can't do these things.'"[49] The usual contemporary view of enslaved people as kind

"Nora endeavoring to Read." (From *Visits to the Juvenile Library,* 1805; courtesy of the Toronto Public Library, Osborne Collection of Early Children's Books)

and affectionate but slow is one to which Eliza would have been exposed at the time.

In 1806, when Eliza, under the name of Rev'd David Blair, produced her *Class Book: or Three Hundred and Sixty-Five Reading Lessons* (so one for each day of the year), she did include abolitionist set pieces. The entry for "April the Sixth" titled "on the Slave Trade" is an excerpt from a speech given by clergyman William Paley in 1792. The other two selections, one for "August the Second" and a continuation for "August the Third," were taken from one of the standard textbooks Richard Phillips published, *Goldsmith's Geography* (1803). Goldsmith was another of the generic pseudonyms Richard Phillips created for the educational book market.[50] In order to generate sympathy for the abolitionist movement, the appeal was focused first on creating empathy and on the "cruelty" inflicted on people who were "torn away from parents, wives, children, from their friends and companions" and "transported to European settlements in America, with no other accommodation on shipboard than what is provided for brutes."[51] Then, once empathy with living creatures was established, the enslaved people were characterized as essentially harmless, as long as they were well cared for. In the entry for August 3, a child practicing reading aloud would have read the following information as a statement of fact: "When well fed, and not ill treated, they [described in the text as 'negro' people] are contented, joyous, ready for employment, and the satisfaction of their mind is painted in their countenance, but when oppressed and abused, they grow peevish, and often die of melancholy" (305). For twenty-first-century readers, the characterization is offensive, unspeakable, partly because it is so obviously akin to instructions on the proper care and feeding of pets and domestic animals, and was more closely akin to the movements at the time interested not in the abolition of slavery but the amelioration of the inhumane conditions of the enslaved.[52] That wasn't Eliza's position, but it was used by some reformers at a time when the idea of the legislated abolition of slavery seemed a remote possibility.

Eliza's atypical characterization of the enslaved nanny Nora (who demonstrates agency by choosing to pursue liberation through literacy on her own), and the more conventional characterization of enslaved people (as kind but in need of care and protection) situate her literary experience of enslaved people prior to her subsequent actual experience. In creating Nora, her primary aim was to cast oppressive pedagogical practices as analogous to the oppression of enslaved people. At the end of *Visits to the Juvenile Library,* Nora, on seeing that education has made the children in her charge nicer, kinder, more thoughtful and empathetic people, embraces as they do, liberation through literacy. When Eliza later arrived in Barbados, however, she had a difficult time reconciling constructed versions of enslaved people with the real enslaved people with whom she lived.

Throughout 1806 and 1807, Eliza was writing at speed and also actively pitching projects in order to generate income. On April 7, 1806, for example, Eliza wrote to Mary to say that she planned to see "The *forty thieves*" the next night and hoped "to get two guineas by making a little pantomimic book of it," saying that she had "done such things before." As Tabart had published a version of *The Forty Thieves* in 1805, she was either pitching a new one (a musical production at Drury Lane with a score by Michael Kelly) or pitching to another publisher. Her heartbreaking comment was that she had "never wanted two guineas more than at present." If Eliza did publish her new adaptation of the play, there is no clear record of it. In November 1807, her situation was still bleak; she told Mary that she had "proposed a Job to Wilkes" (another London publisher) and that though he encouraged her and strung her along with promises for six weeks, he ultimately retracted the offer, offering less "than half the price" she had asked. She signed that letter "Yr almost broken hearted E Fenwick."

As Eliza quickly discovered when working for Richard Phillips, she and his stable of hack writers were doing all the work while he was reaping all the profit. A telling portrait of the Richard Phillips/Benjamin Tabart business model survives in George Borrow's 1851 roman à clef *Lavengro,* a fictionalized account of his own experiences as a young writer in London. In the story, Phillips's character cries crocodile tears in a fake cover-up of his actual motives: "A losing trade, I assure you, sir," he says, "literature is a drug." The implication is, of course, that he is addicted, but doomed. In the next scene, however, the Phillips character instructs the Tabart character (called Taggart in the text) to renege on an agreement with an author of fairy tales and to dishonor the thirty pounds owing for delivery of the manuscript. The Phillips character cancels the payment, and offers a rationale: "I am dissatisfied with that fellow who wrote the fairy tales and intend to give him all the trouble in my power."[53]

The fictionalized discussion between Phillips and Tabart offers both an insight into the evolving book business model at the time[54] and a glimpse of the ways in which Eliza's story converges with children's book history. Richard Phillips was particularly successful in figuring out how to monetize the expanding textbook industry. He realized that by creating a brand-name series—"Goldsmith" for geography and "Blair" for reading—he could hire individual authors to create his generic stable of brands.[55] By buying the copyright directly from his struggling authors, he could look like a hero by providing them with much needed ready cash while building up equity in his backlist. In her June 10, 1832 letter to the Moffat family, Eliza provided a sketch of how the process worked: "A Chapbook [*The Class Book*] bearing in the title page, the Name of the *Rev'd David Blair,* Sir Richard, then Mr Phillips paid me 150 guineas for compiling & many others under the same & other important names enabled me largely to assist in giving a finished & most expensive education to the Son I lost by yellow fever in the West Indies." The comment is sad, but does not seem to convey rancor.

Richard Phillips was not much liked by Eliza's friends in the early nineteenth century. Charles Lamb in 1801 commented that "writers are his crablice and suck at him for nutriment." William Godwin didn't like him either, complaining in an 1801 letter to Mary Jane that Phillips was an impossibly dull travelling companion, "a snail in his discourse." But it was not Phillips's personality that worried Eliza. By 1807, it was clear that no matter how hard she tried, she was not going to earn enough with her freelance piece work to support herself and her children. That is when Mary Hays wrote to their mutual friend, Henry Crabb Robinson, with a suggestion that he try to solicit enough funds to tide Eliza over, at least in the short term, so that she could have a viable place to live. On December 29, 1807, Crabb Robinson wrote to his brother Thomas filling him in on the details of Eliza's situation, beginning with the fact that Eliza "has been one of Phillips drudges & has been treated by him with brutality."

Crabb Robinson then supplied a rationale for providing Eliza with money, outlining her deserving qualities. He spoke of her character and attractiveness, saying that he had known her for "some years" and had "always admired her for her sweet manners" and her ability to endure "most distressing poverty with't complaint." The money raised would be enough to get her out of the "furnished lodgings" she was in and enable her "to buy common furniture for 2 rooms & a kitchen."

By the time Crabb Robinson wrote the letter soliciting funds at the end of December, Eliza had been picking up additional employment as the manager of the bookshop William Godwin had opened up with his wife Mary Jane in 1805. Crabb Robinson continued his explanation:

> Worn out by Phillips barbarity she has been put into a shop by Godwin. Here she has no fire & Miss Hays learning that she from the want of money to buy herself flannel was really injuring her health sent her some. Miss H though herself in confined circumstances, has always been a generous friend to Mrs. F. She has imparted a project to me, which if carried into

execution will be a great relief to her friend. Mrs. F. lives in furnished lodgings where are so dear that they eat away a part of her earnings—Miss H wants to raise a sum large enough to buy common furniture for 2 rooms & a kitchen the rent of which would be so low compared to what she now pays that she would be relieved from great want by it, for she has no debts of her own & there is no thought whatever of attempting the relief of poor F who must wait for an act of grace. (Henry Crabb Robinson to his brother Thomas, 29 December 1807)

When people gave Eliza work, it often was couched in the language of charity. Crabb Robinson began the note to his brother with an appeal to pity: "An act of greater charity you were never called upon to perform," he writes, then explains that "it is on behalf of Mrs. Fenwick, the gentlewoman whom you saw in the shop where I bought the books for Thos & Betsey." Much later, in 1829, at about the time Eliza arrived in Upper Canada, Crabb Robinson appended a note to a letter Eliza had written to him in 1808 when she was, as she says, "still at Skinner Street," the address of Godwin's book shop. In reflecting on that time in Eliza's life, Crabb Robinson's note describes Eliza as "a most excellent woman of considerable talent" who had been "reduced . . . to poverty from affluence" by her husband and was "living in great poverty as an authoress."[56] The same note also contains the information that he had donated £25 to Eliza to help launch her daughter's stage career. If Eliza resented the fact that the value of her work was diminished in its characterization as charity, she did not say so. Overall, Eliza's life as a children's writer, especially in the six years between 1804 when she started and 1810 when she took on her first job as a governess (moving from writer to teacher), clearly demonstrates her prescience, her eye for innovation, and her feeling for the temper of her times. One of Eliza's most enduring contributions, which has never been credited to her, is *Songs for the Nursery: Collected from the Works of the Most Renowned Poets, and Adapted to Favourite National Melodies*, published first by Tabart in 1806. It is this volume that even F. J. Harvey Darton describes as "delectable."

Typically *Songs for the Nursery* is cited by title, with no identifying editor or compiler. The compelling evidence is that it was Eliza who successfully pitched the project to Tabart and/or Phillips, and that she'd had a particularly novel way of doing so, as the title suggests, by soliciting "from the Works of the Most Renowned Poets," as well as collecting traditional oral verse. The clue is in a letter from Charles Lamb dated June 2, 1804, to Dorothy Wordsworth. He thanks her for the "little scraps (Arthur's Bower and his brethren)" that she had sent and confirms that "the bookseller has got them and paid Mrs. Fenwick for them." His point is that the person who will benefit from the poems is Eliza: "So while some are authors for fame," he writes, "some for money, you have commenced author for charity." In characterizing the contributions to Eliza's book as acts of "charity," Lamb repeats the language employed by Henry Crabb Robinson. The fact that Lamb wrote the confirmation of receipt suggests that Eliza wanted to make sure that poems she had solicited would arrive safely in a place where she could collect them.

The first publication of Dorothy Wordsworth's "Arthur Bower" verse was in 1805, in Tabart's *Songs for the Nursery*. The poem reads:

> Arthur O'Bower has broken his band
> And he comes roaring up the land;
> The King of Scots with all his power
> Cannot stop Arthur of Bower.[57]

Because Lamb refers to Arthur Bower's "brethren" and refers to "scraps" in the plural, it is reasonable to assume that Wordsworth submitted more than one poem to the collection, but only "Arthur Bower" can be linked directly to her. The volume itself is recognized by Iona and Peter Opie, the pioneers of scholarly work on nursery verse, as being "the most important" of the collections that appeared in the early nineteenth century. In *The Oxford Dictionary of Nursery Rhymes,* they define its value in the field: "The collection, as well as being one of the corner-stones of Halliwell's work [that is James Halliwell for his comprehensive edition of *The Nursery Rhymes of England* (1842)], was the chief additional source of the American *Mother Goose's Quarto* (c. 1825), and it was reprinted a number of other times, notably in a finely illustrated edition by Darton, junior, in 1818."[58] What is achingly annoying is not knowing whether or not other poems written by Dorothy Wordsworth might be in the collection, or if there are poems by other poets solicited by Eliza. Coleridge perhaps? Or Southey? Both are likely candidates as they both were interested in traditional verse forms. Whether or not Eliza solicited "Renowned Poets" besides Dorothy Wordsworth, or if she collected traditional verses as well as those by poets, the point still stands that *Songs for the Nursery* has a significant place in the history of children's literature and that identifying Eliza as the compiler provides additional support for her ingenuity and contribution to the canon.

In outlining a few of Eliza's contributions to children's book history in the early nineteenth century, the point is to emphasize how good a writer she was, how original her work, despite F. J. Harvey Darton's view that she was only worth mentioning in passing. To be fair, Darton had not identified her as the compiler of the "delectable" *Songs for the Nursery*. And because his point was to position *Visits to the Juvenile Library* simply as an "unblushing account" of the shop, he did not value Eliza's clever inversion of the abolitionist trope of the white children teaching the black enslaved person to read. He also did not cite Eliza's *Rays from the Rainbow* (1811), a paint-by-number or parse-by-color interactive grammar book she published for William and Jane Godwin, even though Matthew Grenby in *The Child Reader, 1740–1800* praises it as the "pinnacle" among the category of books in the period designed in order to "help adults help their children, or allow children to learn even without the presence of a dependable educator."[59] Darton also did not distinguish Eliza's gift for characterization from that of the run-of-the-mill lady moralists whose "heroes and heroines . . . were no more than those brats of the moveable-head books" (165).

Darton aimed the trajectory of his history of children's books to valorize nineteenth-century Romantic versions of childhood, yet that doesn't quite explain why he failed to appreciate Eliza's dead accurate characterizations of children. Whether she was capturing the boredom of the "eldest girl" in *Visits to the Juvenile Library*, idly "pulling a window blind up and down," or the spoiled Miss Kate Smith in "The Ball Dress" from *Infantine Stories* (1810), who "cried and screamed" and threw a temper-tantrum until she got her way and wore a completely inappropriate coarse cotton cook's red gown with blue flowers to a fancy ball, Eliza demonstrated her novelist's gift for the perfectly telling detail. The children she sketched still feel real in that the quirks and behaviors she identified would sit equally well in a twenty-first-century story.

The stories Eliza wrote for children, especially the first ones between 1804 and 1807, were all written under pressure; she lacked time but needed money urgently. Perhaps that pressure contributed to her success. Ted Hughes (1930–1998) argued for writing under pressure in *Poetry in the Making* (1967). "Artificial limits," he explains, "create a crisis, which rouses the brain's resources: the compulsion towards haste overthrows the ordinary precautions, flings everything into top gear, and many things that are usually hidden find themselves rushed into the open."[60] Eliza, trying to earn enough through her writing to support herself and her children, was under exactly that kind of intense pressure. She responded by becoming acutely tuned to all the elements in her immediate environment and seeing their potential. Whether she was observing the real behaviors of real children, responding to the social buzz around theatrical performances, or recognizing the advertising potential of promoting the shop in which her books were sold, the pressures of time and money did enable her to produce original, innovative work.

Despite poverty, Eliza had managed to prepare Eliza Ann for a stage career and to send Orlando to a day school, even though she was still also trying to support John. In a letter dated January 27, 1808, Eliza wrote Mary with more bad news, just as she was to leave her salaried job at Godwin's shop:

> Poor Mr F. is ill with the gout. Lanno must go & be his nurse. I shall leave many sources of anxiety behind me & you believe me are not the least of them. I will see you after executing my commission but it will not at earliest be before Sunday. I cannot promise to dine with you for I am tied here (Skinner Street) till after Saturday.
>
> Peace be with you. Would I could restore it to you.[61]

As the end of the decade approached, Eliza was not quite as vulnerable as she had been when she made the decision to move toward independence in 1800. She had acquired business experience by working at both her brother-in-law's linen-drapers shop and at the Godwins' Juvenile Library. The children's books she had written, compiled, and translated over the previous few years had given her credentials she could use to market herself as an educator. Her career as a writer of fiction, however, seemed stalled after William Godwin's hard criticism of *The Castle of Indolence*.

On the positive side, Eliza Ann was launched as an actress, performing small parts, sometimes in private theatre companies, in England and Ireland. The famed Drury Lane actor and theater manager Stephen Kemble had asked Eliza Ann to join his touring company, though it did not work out. Committed as she was to earning her own living and to contributing to the family finances, Eliza Ann regarded acting as a job, not a vocation. In London and in provincial theaters since her debut in 1806, her name was often on the program, though she was typically cast in secondary roles. Surviving playbills tell the story. On January 12, 1811, for instance, a few months before her decision to move to Barbados, she played Ursula in *Much Ado About Nothing* at Covent Garden in London, opposite Mr. Kemble as Benedick. On January 19 and 23, she was in *Gustavus Vasa* (a popular eighteenth-century play by Henry Brooke). On March 19, she was Phoebe in *As You Like It* at the Lyceum in London, with Mrs. Kemble as Audrey.[62]

With her daughter working, Eliza only had Orlando's care and education to finance. Mary Hays helped often by looking after Orlando in Wandsworth where she lived. Eliza credited Mary as being his second mother, and she sometimes referred to Orlando as "our" boy when writing to her. From his earliest days, Eliza had been careful to nurture affection between Orlando and Mary and to have him consider her as a surrogate mother: "yet I rely on you to form & fortify him to that undeviating integrity which will shield him at least from the reproaches & stings of conscience. Do not say you regret that he is not your Son for he is yours. You are performing all the most useful, the highest, the *moral* duties of the mother" (EF to MH, [date and month unclear] 1811). With the opening of a new decade, with Eliza Ann launched on a career, and with a realization that freelance writing would not provide sufficient income or stability, Eliza too embarked on a career change.

4

Governess and Networker

On July 23, 1810, Eliza wrote a long letter to Mary Hays describing her new life as a governess for the five children of Moses Mocatta, at 33 Wyck Street in Chiswick near, as Eliza explains, "St. Clements Church." The Mocattas were a large, well-established extended family of wealthy Sephardic (Spanish) Jews whose history in banking dated from the mid-seventeenth century. The family firm of Mocatta & Goldsmid, according to *The Oxford Encyclopedia of Economic History*, had "held a privileged position as the official gold broker of the Bank of England throughout the eighteenth century."[1] Despite their wealth and influence, as Jews in early nineteenth-century Britain, they were, nevertheless, outsiders. Yet theirs was an ideal place for Eliza to develop the curriculum she would later put to good use as the proprietor of a series of colonial schools for the daughters of the rich. And it is where she confirmed both a sense of confidence in her own abilities and her independence.

Once settled into her position, Eliza confided to Mary that the Mocattas regarded her as a kind of prize catch as a governess: "The Civility & attention I receive," she says, "I have discovered to have their source in Pride. They like to make a sort of show of me and boast of keeping *a first-rate* Governess only for one little girl, whereas in fact I am governess to five." If Eliza had hoped that the regular hours of a governess—even with five children to teach—might leave her a little leisure time to write, she soon realized that this was not to be the case. "The Table groans," Eliza complained to Mary, "under the weight of Themes, exercises & translations" (EF to MH, n.d. 1811). Although twenty-first-century teachers are expected to be kindly disposed and to nurture the self-esteem of the children in their care, late Enlightenment teachers focused on results. That is why Eliza's 1811 critical assessment of the abilities of the Mocatta children reads, retrospectively, as harsh. She focuses on the abilities of each child to respond to instruction:

> The eldest boy is Dullness & frivolity personified; he wearies & humbles me in the extreme; the second boy is quick but idle, has a kind heart & not

an ungenerous temper, but requires unceasing vigilance to keep him in his proper place & prevent his extending the *mastery* he aims at. On the whole I like *him* very much. He is capable of receiving benefit. The little girl is a dull drudge who learns from want of vivacity and forgets again from want of intellect to comprehend. Tractable yet totally devoid of energy and fancy, she sticks as close to me as a burr, without engaging my affection or stimulating in any way my temper, unless indeed when I grow petulant at the nine hundred & ninety-ninth repetition of the history of her last years fit of sickness, or the dance her Mama gave last winter. The third boy is a complete dunce & the fourth a lively, promising, spoiled but good-humoured *little pickle* with an inordinate propensity to mischief and telling lies. (EF to MH, 1811)

There is something in her sharply drawn sketches of the Mocatta children that suggests she could, in fact, be portraying them as potential characters for one of her children's books, as they could easily be developed into "good" children for the "Good Family" stories or "bad" children for the "Bad Family" stories. That is, in writing about the real children she teaches, Eliza demonstrates exactly the same eye for defining detail as she does in her construction of fictional children. Her irritation at the little girl's "nine hundred & ninety-ninth repetition of the history of her last year's fit of sickness" is completely recognizable, both in the child's repetition and the adult's irritation. In describing the youngest child as a "little pickle," she alludes to a character in a popular play of the period, "The Spoiled Child." Eliza Ann, as it happens, had been playing one of the minor characters ("Maria") in the production being performed in London on Friday, February 15, 1811.

If Eliza didn't exactly soften her views of the Mocatta children during the period in which she worked for the family—between about July 1810 and April 1812—she did use the time both to encourage her own children in their interactions with them, and to hone her innovative teaching techniques. She employed, for example, what is now called "differentiated instruction," a term acknowledging that the better the match between instructional methodology and an individual child's learning style, the better the outcome.[2] Elias was the child Eliza found to be the most teachable, assessing him as "quick but idle," with a "kind heart & not an ungenerous temper." The pedagogical strategy she employed for him required "unceasing vigilance to keep him in his proper place & prevent his extending the mastery he aims at." As educators still typically appreciate, the more responsive the student, the more rewarding the teaching, and Elias seems to have been her favored pupil and the one she also preferred as a friend for her son. While still asserting the superiority of her own son above all others, Eliza was nevertheless painfully aware that without wealth and access to the kind of privilege she could not provide, Orlando would have a difficult time finding his place in the world.

Part of Eliza's rationale for fostering the relationship with the Mocatta children reads as a way of ensuring that Orlando, no matter his financial status, or his status as the child of a working mother separated from her husband, would grow up with a sense that he could feel himself the equal of those with more money, position, or power than he had. She was inculcating in her son the philosophical view toward equality that had been so much a part of her life in the 1790s. In an undated note (though probably in the same period, in 1812 or 1813), Eliza wrote to Orlando—who was in Wandsworth at the time, at school with Mr. Wilkinson but staying with Mary Hays—reminding him to write to both Elias and Abraham.[3]

When Orlando, Abraham, and Elias were in their early teens, Eliza provided a glimpse of what kind of a teacher she was, showing how she mixed warmth with encouragement. In a letter to Orlando about his education, she was both playfully affectionate and completely firm in her instruction that he was required to live up to her expectations and those of his teacher. She gave him a deadline, "73 days" (between February 9 when she wrote and his birthday on May 3), and a clear set of interim goals to improve both his penmanship and his spelling:

> Now if you write only at the rate of a line a day with care and pains you will produce 73 well written lines & become almost a confirmed good penman. I give you that time & desire you will daily think of it—for I shall be on the watch and if you don't write a tolerable hand on the day you are 14 I will give you such a trimming that you shall bless your stars there are no seven league boots to be hired for me to stride to Wandsworth in while my fury is at its height. Seriously I expect much to be done in these 73 days in *every way* for if you are not a *reasonable, patient, most industrious*—in short just such a boy as I like to love dearly I think it will break my heart on purpose to make you suffer for your neglect.[4]

The tone of her letter, at once warm and focused on results, seems to speak directly to her pedagogical agenda, but also hints, of course, to her investment in her own son. The comparison Eliza makes between Orlando and the two eldest Mocatta sons, Abraham and Elias, speaks—in a more than slightly disturbing way—to the privileging of her own son as cleverer, better, more athletic, and more *English* than the Mocatta children could ever be. "Would you believe," she writes to Mary Hays, "that Mrs M. is jealous of our boy."

Eliza takes the moment both to include Mary in the "making" of Orlando and to condemn Mrs. Mocatta:

He at 13 is much taller & more manly than her darling Abraham of 15. An old rich Bachelor whom she courts for legacies dined here on Saturday & was struck with Lanno [Orlando]. He paid me a handsome Compt [compliment] about him & Mrs M. was wounded. How weak & silly this is. She bows to my superiority over herself & is continually wishing herself like me, yet cannot endure a competition between my child & hers unless the eminence was on the latter side. She has given him no invitation to come here during the holidays, though Elias the second boy is half crazy to get him to teach him to climb to leap & c. (EF to MH, [no date] 1811)

A note in William Godwin's diary indicates that on December 11, 1811, at least one Mocatta boy met with him, Orlando, and Eliza, suggesting that she was regularly facilitating relationships between them. And Godwin, as he recorded in his diary, saw Eliza with a "Mocatta" at a lecture Coleridge gave in December 1811.

Early on in her time as a governess for the Mocatta children, Eliza also figured out how Eliza Ann (while taking her first tentative steps into the theater) might supplement her income by doing some tutoring in drawing and singing, skills acquired because Eliza had worked so hard to pay for lessons. At first, "in the ignorance & humility," Eliza says, of her "inexperience," as a governess she offered Eliza Ann, mostly as a music teacher, to the Mocatta children as a "gratuity" to Mrs. Mocatta. Though Eliza complained that Mrs. Mocatta quickly took advantage of Eliza Ann, the lessons were successful and encouraged more closeness than might otherwise be expected between employee and employer, even in the grey-zone social spheres inhabited by governesses and teachers of the children of the rich. Bracha Abigail (1795–1824) was likely the child to whom Eliza Ann taught "singing & drawing." And as Eliza later proudly told Mary Hays, Mrs. Mocatta was very pleased with her daughter's progress and credited it to Eliza Ann's teaching (EF to MH, 23 May 1811). A few months later, as a token of her appreciation, Mrs. Mocatta gave Eliza Ann "a very handsome white satin dress—a thing she very much wanted & which her funds could not have reached" (EF to MH, September 16, 1811). If Eliza and her daughter realized then that together they might make a good teaching team, there is no evidence, but it was their first experience of working together. Their division of labor in the Mocatta household in fact prefigures the way that they set up their schools in Barbados and New Haven, with Eliza teaching some music as well as the academic subjects and Eliza Ann teaching singing and, eventually, dancing, the skills she had initially acquired to facilitate her work as an actress.

With Eliza Ann able and willing to contribute to the family finances, including the education of her brother, Eliza emerged ever more strongly during the period in which she worked for the Mocatta family as someone who could function independently. As she moved forward, she became more confident in allowing John Fenwick to fade out of their lives. In a letter from early in 1811, Eliza wrote to Mary with her plans: "Secure now," she writes, "I think of remaining separate from Mr Fenwick, who invariably (even when most steady) palsied every exertion I was disposed to make, I think I shall be able to provide for my own limited wants & the expenses of my boy at any rate." A little later, in another letter to Mary, Eliza expressed regret at having waited so long to make the definitive move: "If I had had the prudence & common sense some years ago," she writes, "to exert myself independent of Mr F. I should have found friends to back me, & might now have been tolerably at ease" (EF to MH, 19 April 1812).

As Eliza was loosening her ties with John, so too was Eliza Ann. By the spring of 1811, she seems to have cut off contact with her father, partly because it appears he was making financial demands on her as well. John's brother Thomas stepped into the breach, eventually taking responsibility for him. In May 1811, Eliza wrote to Mary with the news of Thomas's promise that "he would *always* provide" for John, as "he was *now* unconvinced that his brother never would or could assist himself. . . ." And by August, Eliza reported that "Orlando says *we appear to thrive now we are away from his father*," and then confirmed her own sense of their improved life without him: "I think we do succeed better," she says, "since I burst the fetters that with him bound us down to almost every species of wretchedness." Whether conscious or unconscious, Eliza's words shadowed lines from her friend Mary Wollstonecraft's *A Vindication of the Rights of Woman* concerning the "specious slavery which chains the very soul of woman, keeping her for ever under the bondage of ignorance."[5] By the end of 1811, Eliza had secured her independence, and so too, in a different way, had Eliza Ann.

Though neither mother nor daughter could have known explicitly at the time, their newfound intellectual freedom would later become intimately bound with the lives of people living under the very legal chains of slavery, something both had understood primarily as metaphorical. It was Eliza Ann who would precipitate the change. In the five years since Eliza Ann had played her first stage part as Zorayda in 1806, she had worked more or less steadily but without particular success in London and provincial theaters. When she received the offer of a steady gig—and steady income—with a new repertory company being established in Bridgetown, Barbados, she accepted, assuming that her tenure there would be temporary. Despite her reluctance to leave, she knew that she could at last become an active contributor to the family finances and enable her mother to focus on earning enough as a governess to support herself and the last stages of the education of her younger brother Orlando.

By October 1811, Eliza had moved with the Mocatta family from Wyck Street in Chiswick to a new house at number five Tavistock Square, a more fashionable London location.[6] Modified by practical experiences both as a governess and as a parent, Eliza's attitudes toward teaching and learning were also changing through 1811 and 1812. Her passionate 1795 polemic in *Secresy* arguing for the rights of women to be educated was a long way from the practicalities of negotiating the day-to-day tedium of the classroom. Equally far away were the safe, fictional young people of the books she had written for children. Those children absorbed their lessons on cue, whether they were the orphaned rich children in *Visits to the Juvenile Library* (1805) who learned, as the subtitle of the story says, that "knowledge proved to be the source of happiness," or "John Jones," the title character in one of the *Infantine Stories* (1810), who recognized that the short-term difficulty of learning to read offset the potential for eternal boredom of not bothering to do so. Real children had to be negotiated more patiently and artfully than fictional ones. Although Eliza had been initially critical of the Mocatta children, her letters to Mary indicate that she had softened as the children made progress under her tutelage.

The give-and-take of teaching and learning, the relationship between teacher and student, increasingly came into focus for Eliza while she worked for the Mocattas, marking the beginning of a career turn from writer to teacher. Eliza seems to have been an instinctively good educator, and she also realized that by teaching the children of the rich, she could actually bridge the economic and social divide that otherwise would have kept her from attaining the social and financial security she sought. It was as a parent, however, that Eliza became better tuned to the sensitive balance in the teacher-student relationship. She was troubled when her own son's early adolescent temperament was out of sync with the expectations of his teacher. She worried that the thirteen-year-old Orlando's "mercurial spirit" was keeping his tutor "on thorns" (EF to MH, 28 August 1811). In the letter, Eliza draws back from her maternal concern and reflects philosophically on the teacher-student dyad: "How seldom Tutors think that it is necessary to be respected as well as feared, or value the love of their pupils. Which may I believe be gained without any relation to discipline. Unmerited reproof &

mortifying sarcasms may wound, but will never amend the temper or habits." Whether or not Eliza consciously applied her philosophical musings on the value of being "respected" and "loved" to her own status as a teacher of other people's children is a moot point. But something seems to have stuck. Despite her private initial critical views on the Mocatta children, she sounded a note of distinct (though reluctant) pleasure when relating the story of Mrs. Mocatta's repeated request for her to "stay to educate the baby (15 years as least)" (EF to MH, 23 May 1811). In a complicated dance of status related to intellect, money, power, and religion, Eliza used her perceived intellectual superiority, her skill as an educator, and her encouragement of friendships between her children and the Mocatta children, to suture gaps in the employer-employee divide.

As governess for the five Mocatta children Eliza must have been doing quite a lot right. By the spring of 1812, a Mrs. Hewitt of Tavistock Place (close to the Mocatta house in Tavistock Square) had scouted Eliza as a governess for her sister's family, newly relocated in Ireland. The sister, lately arrived from India where the husband, Robert Honner,[7] had been stationed with the nineteenth regiment of the British Army, had four children—three girls, the eldest almost fourteen, the younger ones ten and eight, and a boy, just eleven months younger than Orlando (about fifteen)—all born in India. Eliza initially refused the proposition. But with an offer on the table, she was again in a "should she stay or should she go" position, much like the one she had been in when she was first trying to make it on her own in the first years of the 1800s.

On the "stay" side, her job as a governess with the Mocatta family meant that she had steady employment that still left her enough time (at least in theory) to continue with her freelance writing for children. A move to Ireland would mean leaving her friends and publishing contacts who were largely based in or near London: Mary Hays in Wandsworth about six miles away, and the Lambs, Thomas Holcroft, and William Godwin all in London. In the decade since she had first stated her intention of separating from her husband, Eliza had built up enough experience and confidence to know that she could make her own way in the world. John was no longer a concern because, by September 1811, she had confirmation that he would be taken care of by his brother Thomas. But Eliza still had to consider career options for Orlando who, at fourteen, was approaching the end of his formal schooling. That decision would have implications for her next move. If she decided that it would be best for him to remain in Wandsworth or London, she would stay, but if not, then the option of leaving was viable. The military was initially a possibility for Orlando, but she knew that John, despite his potential connections, lacking "sobriety, industry & economy," could not be much help in organizing (or funding) Orlando's admission.

In reading Eliza's letters from the period between 1810 and 1812, there is a strong sense that she had developed her own, independent life; that she had succeeded in generating her own income, making decisions about the education of the children, and cultivating her own friends. William Godwin, for instance, records seeing both John and Eliza in that period, but no longer together. If she stayed in London, she had all the pieces securely in place to do so, but the offer of a move to Lee Mount, the Honners' home near Cork in Ireland, was tempting and Eliza had strong reasons for wanting to accept. First, she felt that she was a good fit with the family and with teaching responsibilities for the three girls, instead of the five children she was teaching at the Mocattas' home, she would have better working conditions. And she liked the introductory correspondence she'd had with the family; that is, she felt ideologically closer to them than she did to the Mocattas. Finally, she only had Orlando to see through to the end of his schooling, as Eliza Ann was on the verge of leaving for full-time employment in Barbados.

Eliza's account of her beloved daughter preparing to set sail for Bridgetown on November 11, 1811, with Mr. Dyke, the theater manager who had hired her, is disturbing to twenty-first century readers in its depiction of the enslaved "servant" who will accompany them on the voyage. Eliza relays the departure scene to Mary obliquely, as an encounter on the dock with Mr. Dyke's enslaved "servant," just as the ship is about to set sail: "Their black servant, a fine old Negroe, came up to me & with a tone of Natures own feeling said; *'You no grieve Maam. We take care of Missee.—I take care of Missee always, on board ship and on shore. Pray no grieve Maam. Missee shall be happy'*" (EF to MH, 13 Oct 1811).

By refracting the depth of grief through the response to it by Mr. Dyke's "black servant," she is able to convey her own sorrow at that moment more visibly than if she'd tried to do so using her own first-person perspective. But her perspective also reveals what she sees with regard to her understanding of what enslaved people are like. The person here is, of course, nameless, and described as "their black servant, a fine old Negroe." As such, he embodies the trope of the faithful, loyal (loving but not very smart) slave, a character constructed most famously not much later, in 1852, as "Uncle Tom" by Harriet Beecher Stowe. The dialect now causes a reflexive cringe, and yet the clarity of the emotional truth comes through too: "Pray no grieve Maam. Missee shall be happy." In its own time, Eliza's sketch was in perfect sync with the versions of enslaved people constructed in the abolitionist literature. What we now read as a racist trope was intended to garner empathy

and support for abolition at a time when enslaved people were typically regarded as only marginally human goods to be traded. The creation of an empathetic enslaved person characterized as capable of a full range of human
emotion was regarded, if not radical, at least as a signal that the writer was
on the side of the abolitionists. Eliza herself had, in fact, characterized enslaved people, in the "August the Third" reading for *The Class Book* she had
edited in 1806 for Richard Phillips as, "contented, joyous, ready for employment, and the satisfaction of their mind is painted in their countenance."[8]
Once Eliza Ann set sail, Eliza began to concentrate on her work as a governess, and on funding Orlando's final years of formal education. She was
also writing, as her letters show, with a novelist's eye for social commentary.

Becoming a Governess in Ireland:
Networking as an Adaptation Strategy

Prior to accepting the position as governess in Ireland, in a May 5, 1812 letter to Mary, Eliza wrote about how much she liked her initial meeting with
Mr. Honner, her potential employer. She liked "the downright, honest affection he expressed for his wife & children, the little parade about him, his
Irish description of the delight they felt in quitting a life of constant bustle &
change for a quiet home & the hope of spending the rest of their lives at one
fire side, & finding all their recreations in the society of their children." The
focus on home and family was exactly what Eliza had been yearning for in
her own life, so she concluded her musings to Mary on her rationale for
accepting by saying that "all these were recommendations at once to my
feelings and principles."

What clinched the deal for her, however, was Robert Honner's suggestion
that her son Orlando could come to Ireland too, to finish his education. His
description of what school life was like for boys in Ireland appealed to Eliza,
as it matched her own pedagogical views; she quotes Honner to Mary on the
benefits of Irish schooling: "Your English boys in schools are too knowing.
We have the luck to keep our boys out of that while they are boys. I suppose
I must not say we manage better, but I know my Robert returned home at
Christmas as pure & simple hearted as when he was but four years old. I assure you, whatever we are as men, as boys we are more moral" (EF to MH,
5 May 1812). The recommendation on schooling presented the solution to
her concerns about setting Orlando on a path to a career and a steady income. Not only did the educational atmosphere seem right, as Robert Honner described it, but Eliza must also have realized that the kind of life her
potential employer was creating for his family—what we might call private

and family-focused—was the opposite of the public, political (alcohol-infused) life John had been living. Eliza could see that the home and family she could enter in the employ of Honner would be of the kind she would have liked for herself and her children.

As an added reason for making the move, Robert Honner's son, Robert Jr., seemed an even better potential companion for Orlando than the Mocatta sons. Though Robert Jr. was clearly privileged by having, as Eliza says, the "fine horses, the dogs, the trees, bathing, fishing, riding and ranging the woods," he exhibited the kind of social ease and happiness Eliza wished to cultivate and encourage in her own son who, despite his lack of wealth and position, shared a similar sunny, athletic disposition. In considering the potential benefits of the move, Eliza understood that she would be with a family with whom she felt more at ease than the Jewish Mocattas.[9] And when she realized that she could place Orlando at school in Cork, she recognized that he would be physically close to her, just a few miles away from the estate at Lee Mount where she would be teaching. The school was run by Mr. Humphries, an enlightened master, and his name still appears in the historical record as a progressive educator. Although Eliza could not have appreciated it at the time, he did eventually take a personal interest in Orlando's progress. In the end, after Eliza accepted the position with the Honner family, things turned out even better than she had hoped when she discovered that Robert Honner Jr. would also attend the school in Cork run by Mr. Humphries.

There was another feature of Lee Mount that attracted Eliza. Despite the fact that she would be distant from her circle of friends in London, she was drawn to the beautiful rural setting and its promise of a peaceful life. Besides, at least in theory, rural Ireland was physically removed from the seemingly endless Napoleonic Wars putting European countries in conflict with each other. By 1812, the fallout from those wars had jumped the Atlantic, eventually bringing the Canadian colonies into battle against the United States.

While considering her options, Eliza wrote to Mary about being shown a painting of the Lee Mount estate, a common practice in the period when people would try to hire a governess for children whose families lived in the country.[10] She described the home in terms that still read as a setting for a romantic novel, complete with a view of a Gothic ruin—Carrigrohane Castle—in the distance: "It stands on the side of a Hill, sheltered to the North by a wood. The grounds slope down to a river, on the other side of which rises an abrupt precipice, crowned with the ruins of a fine old Castle. The background, of a range of Mountains, shuts in the whole. In the painting it is romantic and picturesque in the extreme" (EF to MH, 24 April 1812). The setting delivered on its promise. The first thing Eliza said on arrival was that Lee Mount was "indeed a Paradise" and that it was "exquisite in picturesque beauty; the house spacious & comfortable & most tastefully elegant in its accommodations & decorations" (EF to MH, 21 July 1812). The house, currently owned by the Sheriff of Cork, Martin Harvey, still stands and retains its Georgian grace and sense of proportion. The ruin of the castle is still visible in the distance and the estate is as beautiful and magical as Eliza described it, a perfect setting for a romantic novel.

Eliza paid close attention to the distinctions between surface and substance, and between authentic values and superficial manners dancing around the plot fixtures of love and money. She found time to read as well as to write while in Cork, though she complained that the available material was typically not literary enough for her tastes. Mrs. Honner, she said, subscribed to the Cork library, though she imagined it "a very bad one": "the novels of character we have sent for are never to be had & the generality of the Minerva Press compositions I cannot, however fond of a story, read" (EF to MH, 27 October 1812). The Minerva Press, incidentally, was the Mills & Boon or Harlequin, trashy romance novel imprint of its day. In a more literary vein, Eliza responded (on June 3, 1813) to Mary's apparent query about the latest Walter Scott work, a long narrative poem, *Rokeby*, which recently had been published. Although Eliza was sorry to say that she had not read

Aerial view of Lee Mount, Cork, Ireland. (Courtesy of Martin Harvey, Sheriff of Cork)

it, and that the lack of access (of the kind she would have had in London) was "a great drawback," she was pleased to report that Orlando had read it, as "his master had it soon after its publication from the Cork Institution library." Orlando, she explained, hinting perhaps at the progressive school he attended, had read it with his schoolmaster Mr. Humphries and the latter's wife. Delighted by her son's informed critical response, Eliza repeated it to Mary:

> His commendations of the poem were so much like yours as to make me stare at the coincidence. Two days after the reading he came to Lee Mount & detailed to me the whole plan of the story describing the characters & repeated some short passages. The rejected address delighted him. They fell in with his humour & with his extravagant action he often spouts lines of their Mock Heroics. (EF to MH, 3 June 1813)

Orlando was approaching the end of his formal education and Eliza was very happy with his progress. She told Mary, with pride, that he had "borne off the medal six following weeks for the greatest application & the best exercises from fifty-four boys." Eliza had also arranged for him to take drawing lessons from an artist, Grogan (probably Nathaniel Grogan the younger). By all accounts, Orlando was quite good and Eliza reportedly carried his paintings with her long after his death in 1816 and throughout her colonial journey, though they seem to have disappeared sometime after her death in 1840.[11]

As is often the case in fiction, all is not as it seems. Everything in the opening sequences of life at Lee Mount, dating from Eliza's arrival on July 13, 1812, looked perfect: peaceful, normal, and bucolic. Eliza liked Mrs. Honner a lot better than Mrs. Mocatta. She also liked the three young girls she was to instruct. And she liked that she had full reign of the curriculum, and that she was treated as a member of the family. As Eliza wrote to Mary on July 21, 1812, her new situation suited her completely:

> I have but to turn to the window & a prospect rich & varied with all the combined beauties of hill, dale, wood & water, gives me that serene pleasure which nature's chosen scenes always afford. Then our evenings, when I have been able to go to the dinner & tea table, afford me a lively & rational conversation. My Chamber is elegantly fitted up & I am requested to order any additions I may wish. God knows my humbler tastes wd never have chosen what I find.

The view that would have been Eliza's is still pretty much as she described it. A little farther on in the letter, Eliza situates herself in the room, looking out of her window, at the "charming" view with the curtains undrawn:

"The sashes [of the window]," she explained, "are low & my bed high, so I command the view as I lie." Eliza also adds a lovely, telling example of Mrs. Honner's thoughtfulness, saying that soon after she'd mentioned how fond she was "of the smell of Mignonette," she found that a box full of it had been "placed outside [her] chamber window," so that the scent could waft into the room.

In reading Eliza's accounts of her life in Cork—in that brief period between her arrival on July 12, 1812, and her departure for Barbados two years later in August 1814—her letters track what Marilyn Butler, in *Romantics, Rebels, and Reactionaries*, describes as the "rage" in the early nineteenth century for "literary *Lives*." They were, Butler explains, "part of a passion for documenting the natural world, including the human and social world."[12] That's what Eliza was doing, documenting the natural, both human and social. She was also moving from the radical to the reactionary, all the while admiring the view and smelling the flowers. As it happened, Eliza also found the real-life material that could easily have nested into a novel. In what amounts to a two-thousand-word potential plot outline, written on December 21, 1813, about eighteen months after her arrival at Lee Mount, Eliza realized that the paradise she had found wasn't all that it seemed.

It was while working at Lee Mount that Eliza discovered the plots, scenes, and conversations of the "real life" around her, which she reworked into her letters, a genre we call life writing. Almost in anticipation of Leo Tolstoy, she recognized the tension in a superficially happy family, their day-to-day happiness covering up a disturbing underbelly of dark and difficult unhappiness. There seems something uncannily prescient in that Eliza had set up a contrast between a "good" happy family and a "bad" unhappy family in stories she published first in 1809 in *Lessons for Children*. The "Good Family" in the story is characterized as being "always cheerful and happy, the children love each other, and agree together; the servants are content and eager to oblige, and visitors delight to come to the house, because they pass their time there with both pleasure and profit."[13] In "The Bad Family," the parents of the "odious children" in the stories "never look happy, nor enjoy comfort," the children "quarrel, so that the house is always in an uproar." To add insult to injury, "[t]he servants hate them, the neighbours despise them, and the house is shunned as though it had some dreadful distemper within" (98–99). At Lee Mount, it was as if Eliza found one family on the verge of morphing into the other.

When Eliza first arrived at Lee Mount, she wrote as if she had landed in a real-life "good" family. In Mrs. Honner, she found an attractive, youthful-looking, "thinking" woman, the "gentlest, most unaffected Ladylike woman"

Eliza said that she had ever met. She described Mr. Honner as "frank, hospitable, pleasant & good-humoured" with "a lively kind of blunt humour, which diverts & is always unmixed with anything that could give offence." Eliza also deeply appreciated that Robert Honner was "a kind husband & father & seems to prefer to all pleasure the evening circle of his family" (EF to MH, 21 July 1812). The unspoken comment was that he was not like John, who preferred his drinking companions and political activism to domestic comfort and stability.

The surface happiness at Lee Mount, however, disguised a darker story beneath. The reason Mr. Honner relocated his family from India was because he had been court-martialed. The details, as recorded in the *Asiatic Annual Register of 1807,* document his dismissal from the army as resulting from "behaviour unbecoming to an officer and a gentleman," in that he had been charged with giving "blows or shoves to another officer in the mess room."[14] Yet by the time Eliza met him, six years later, he was the very model of a good family man: "He is," says Eliza, "all day in his grounds, planting, draining, fencing, building & clearing his land" (EF to MH, 21 July 1812). Only later, on December 21, 1813, in the long, two-thousand-word sketch[15] (from which all the quotations below are taken) of what might have been the plot of a novel, did Eliza reveal the dark side of the purchase of Lee Mount and of Mr. Honner's home-improvement initiatives.

Eliza begins with the folly of his "unwise" purchase of the estate in 1811. Initially, it had seemed a very good deal. He had ridden the four miles from Cork "on his fine hunter" on a "lovely day" in June, and so it had seemed an easy distance—which, on a good horse, it was. Next, Eliza enumerated the ways in which Mr. Honner was blindsided by his assumptions about the value of the property:

> The trees he should cut down, the stones he should quarry, the lime he should find upon the domain wd, he schemed, pay for enlarging the house, building the stable barns, out houses &c. He forgot to look at the road & consider what it wd be in winter & indeed the greatest part of the year. Though not much or perhaps at all exceeding 4 English miles between this house & Cork it is the most impracticable road that ever was travelled & utter destruction of horses, carts, & carriages. . . . One building begot another. One after another were found to be ill-placed & pulled down for removal.

There was no limestone, he could not find laborers to cut the trees, and cultivating crops was not an option because the land was frequently flooded by the River Lee. Mr. Honner thought he might breed Arabian stallions, but they turned out to be the wrong kind of horse for the location and he lost a fortune. He tried to build a road, but ended up in legal tangles with people on whose land he trespassed. It also surfaced that he had fathered a couple of illegitimate sons when he was still in his teens. Things were not as domestically intact as Eliza had initially thought.

In her very few deft observations, Eliza, like a painter sketching the structure for a more finished work, managed to capture the heart of the tensions in the family. Robert Honner was not the only one conflicted; so was his wife. In a kind of "he said, she said" contrast between Mr. and Mrs. Honner, Eliza writes:

> She hates Ireland & most Irish people beyond all moderate & just bounds. He will, nay he must live in it. She wishes for more society as her girls grow up. She cannot have it. He says what can be necessary beyond her husband & children, but she is anxious to form these girls fashionably & elegantly as well as rationally & is fastidious & painfully conscious on little etiquettes which are in themselves nonsense.

Still, Eliza wanted to assure Mary that despite all the cracks in the perfect family facade, there was still undeniable happiness in the family circle: "Mr. Honner has natural vivacity & humour. He is very happy in caricaturing & contrasting odd incidents. Her spirits are often lively & . . . especially when Orlando is here, [we] laugh through the whole evening." Eliza's comment echoes an earlier one she made about Orlando's sunny disposition in a note where she repeated to Mary Hays words of praise about her son spoken by Mrs. Honner's lady's maid: "Well God bless him, for he seems to make happiness wherever he comes—What a comfort he must be to his Mother" (EF to MH, 24 September 1812).

Although Orlando's capacity for happiness was an important acknowledgement of Eliza's success in raising such a wonderful son, essentially on her own and under difficult circumstances, in his mid-teens he was also poised to begin to take on the responsibilities of adult life. Eliza tried to use her contacts at the time to secure a future for him, including one in the East India Company. Although that particular option came to naught, with the end of Orlando's schooling in sight and Eliza Ann fully launched in her acting career, Eliza was on the verge of a transition. At the same time, Eliza Ann was also considering new options for herself and her family— in Barbados.

Eliza Redefines Herself in Ireland, Eliza Ann Redefines Herself in Barbados: 1811–1814

It is at this point in the narrative, with Eliza in Britain separated from Eliza Ann in Barbados between 1811 and 1814, that parallel constructions of the kind natural to cinematic storytelling but awkward on the page would have been useful. The story would have individual scenes visually backing onto each other, moving the narratives of mother and daughter forward in their separate lives. Eliza Ann would be shown acting in the theater, gradually getting to know the social structure of Barbados, and reconciling herself to living and working in a world where all of the servants (enslaved people in reality) are black. The threats from ever-present natural disasters such as hurricanes and volcanic eruptions would loom ominously in the background. Meanwhile, Eliza, though still identifying with her literary life, would be shown acclimatizing to her teaching life in Cork, gradually developing confidence in her curriculum and her status as an educator to the daughters of the rich. She would be better dressed, and there would be the constant music of children playing the piano in the background at Lee Mount. The three Honner girls were each practising "2 hours per day," she says, so that the pianoforte "was regularly going 6 & often 7 hours a day" (EF to MH, 21 December 1813). That is how the professional stories of mother and daughter would unfold on screen, counterpointing the personal stories unfolding simultaneously. In Barbados, through 1812, Eliza Ann would be shown being wooed, won, and wed by William Rutherford. As Robert Honner's domestic life was winding down, Eliza Ann's would be starting up. And in the bizarre way in which coincidence and chance collide and determine the future, Rutherford's unlikely family connections with the proto-Methodist families both John and Eliza Fenwick had rejected would be revealed. Despite the odds against Eliza Ann in 1812 of meeting and marrying in Barbados the son of a man who was, like Eliza's and John's fathers, one of John Wesley's itinerant preachers in the 1770s, that is indeed what happened.

On arrival in Barbados at the end of 1811, Eliza Ann was ready for a new start, professionally and personally, acting with the new Theatre Royal in Bridgetown, scheduled to open at the beginning of January 1812.[16] Thanks to her mother's gift for networking, Eliza Ann landed in Barbados with introductions provided by Mrs. Mocatta to many of the prosperous Jewish families in Bridgetown. She also brought with her a pianoforte, a gift from the Mocattas (although Eliza complained that she had to pay for the shipping). On December 23, 1811, Eliza Ann wrote to her mother to acknowledge how well she had been received by the friends of the Mocattas: "Pray thank Mrs. Mocatta," Eliza Ann wrote, "from me & her friend who wrote these letters. She must have given me a very good character by my reception." The news of Eliza Ann's warm reception must have provided Eliza with an additional degree of reassurance about her daughter's future especially given the unspoken reasons for her leaving the British theatrical community. Besides only achieving middling success as an actress, Eliza Ann had also been in a serious relationship with the actor Henry Kemble (1789–1836), a son of actor Stephen Kemble, but had broken it off on November 11, 1809. In reflecting on the fact that her daughter's departure to Barbados coincided with the second anniversary of the split, Eliza had written to Mary Hays, confiding her concerns: "I think her quitting him was the first dawn of her prosperity, deep & bitter as was the suffering it involved. Had they not been separated they had married. She must necessarily have been miserable for life with such a Man, & might have been a forsaken Wife with children to rear in sorrow & regret for the misplaced affection that had caused their birth" (EF to MH, 13 November 1811). Mary would have recognized that Eliza was talking about her own experience as much as her daughter's, as well as their symbiotic relationship.

Not long after arriving Eliza Ann met William Rutherford (1783–1829), like her a British expat actor. Just eight months after her arrival in Bridgetown, on August 29, 1812, she married him. In Ireland, processing the news of both her daughter's abrupt marriage, Eliza struggled, in a dark-night-of-the-soul way, with the validity of the choice she had made about Eliza Ann's future. Had it been a mistake, she wondered, to put her reluctant daughter on the stage in the first place? Eliza fretted about her decision: "It was my silly earnestness to escape from the humiliations of poverty," she confessed to Mary, "that devoted her to a profession she has abhorred & which has been the source of countless miseries to her" (EF to MH, 22 September 1812). And again, a short time later: "Night and day," said, Eliza, "do I lament that I ever urged her to adopt her profession" (EF to MH, 24 November 1812). Underneath Eliza's fears about pushing her daughter into an acting career were her fears that, by doing so, she had set Eliza Ann up not for an independent life but rather for a life that would leave her vulnerable to exploitation by unscrupulous men. The awkward end of Eliza Ann's two-year relationship with actor Henry Kemble must have haunted Eliza as she expressed her deepest fear to Mary: that another actor, William Rutherford, had taken advantage of her vulnerable, lonely, homesick daughter. In March 1812, Eliza Ann started writing to her mother about her blossoming relationship with him. By the late summer or early fall of that year, gossip about his dubious character was circulating in London among their shared circle of friends in the theater community.

Mary Hays apparently wrote to Eliza reporting that Henry Crabb Robinson had intimated that Rutherford was bad news and that he had already, in his early thirties, established a questionable reputation. Eliza, trusting her daughter's judgment, asked Mary to tell Crabb Robinson not to "spread the affair & ill reports," as they would be damaging not only to Eliza's family but also to William Rutherford's mother, who might equally be alarmed at the news that her son would be marrying an actress, "a profession she looks on with horror." Yet, despite her decision not to protest the marriage, Eliza wrote one of the Cassandra-like predictions that must have come to haunt her in the following decades; if her daughter had "at last become a weak credulous dupe of an artful, wicked man," she says, "I shall pray for a lengthened life, that I may endure as I ought to do the Just punishment of my own errors" (EF to MH, 24 September 1812). That turned out to be exactly the way events unfolded.

In response to a letter received from her mother that must have cautioned—too late—against marriage, Eliza Ann wrote a poignant reply, dated October 15, 1812, from St. Croix, where her theater company had gone to perform. It was just a few months after her marriage and she was traveling for the first time as Mrs. Rutherford. Deeply troubled by the fact that her marriage might have incurred her mother's disapproval, Eliza Ann began by confirming the sanctity and of the mother-daughter bond between them. She described going for a walk, by herself, outside the town:

> Mr R went out yesterday after dinner on some business & I walked by myself up one of the mountains which lie immediately at the back of this town. When I had gained the summit, I looked back at the setting sun and thought of home—and of Orlando! I remembered how often we had wandered together up the Carlton Hill to watch the setting sun. We had seen the same moon rise and had admired it. . . . Indulging in these recollections I walked slowly,—when suddenly a voice close to me said in a tone of fondness:

> *Eliza, my dear what is the matter?* I looked over, I thought *it was you!*— Forgive me, dear Mother—it was a Negro woman, speaking to *her* child.— Had I indeed beheld you, I should have felt no surprise at that moment. I was with you in thought at the time she spoke—I burst into tears and I have cried ever since—The fear of your displeasure preys incessantly on my mind.

The passage conveys how much it meant to Eliza Ann to have her mother's approval (as the reference to the fear of her mother's displeasure preying on her mind shows), conjuring a particular instance of a mother's love, care, and concern. The experience was so intense for Eliza Ann that, even in its reconstruction, she recorded it in Standard English, not Creole.

When Eliza Ann mistakes the black woman's "tone of fondness" for exactly the tone of fondness that informs her own mother's concern for her, she makes explicit the transcendence of the mother-child bond. There is also something uncanny in the way that Eliza Ann's story parallels Eliza's story of her daughter's departure from England in 1811, when the "fine old Negroe" gave his assurance that he would "take care of Missee always," so that Eliza need not "grieve" (EF to MH, 13 October 1811). The analogous encounters—one in Britain, the other in the Caribbean—presage the unsettling relationships both mother and daughter would have with enslaved people once they were reunited in Bridgetown.

Another parallel construction that would work cinematically but not on the page would involve Mrs. Honner and Eliza Ann's pregnancies through the fall of 1812 and into the spring and summer of 1813. The progress of both pregnancies—one in Cork the other in Barbados—would register visually the passing of the nine months. Eliza attended Mrs. Honner through her difficult pregnancy and also assumed many of the responsibilities for the household. As Eliza explained on August 26, 1813, the Honner baby lived for only two days after its birth. In Barbados, Eliza Ann had kept the news of her pregnancy secret from her mother, but wrote in almost playful anticipation while in the early stages of labor on July 28, 1813, that she was about to give birth. A son, William Patrick Rutherford, was born just a few hours later, on the 29th. Eliza Ann wrote with pride and something approaching triumphant glee on the birth of her first son, the son who would drown with his younger brother in the cold waters of Lake Ontario in 1834.

With a husband and baby son making the promise of a new beginning in Barbados viable, and given that she had never much liked being an actress, when William Rutherford suggested to Eliza Ann in the spring of 1813 that they both quit the company and open a school, the virtues of the plan must have been immediately appealing. For the first time she could see a future that did not involve acting. Because she had taught singing and drawing to the Mocatta children, she could legitimately claim teaching experience. And if she could convince her mother to join the new enterprise, especially given her mother's credentials as a governess and a writer of educational books, then the school would have a very strong chance of success. Best of all, if a position could be found for Orlando too, then the whole family could be reunited, and have the opportunity to establish a secure future. Eliza Ann sketched out her proposal to her mother. Through 1813, Eliza began seriously contemplating her daughter's suggestion for reuniting the family in Barbados, and pursuing a new beginning, separate from the pain caused by John's decline and by the relentless poverty and dependency that they had endured in Britain.

Eliza began thinking about what we would call an exit strategy, a way of lining up a replacement governess at Lee Mount so that when she left for Barbados, the transition would be seamless for the Honner children. She appealed to Mary Hays, who, besides writing, was also working with her brother's children in Wandsworth. In making her pitch, Eliza both foregrounded the narrative possibilities she knew Mary would find attractive in a potential move to Cork, and sketched the pedagogical outlines for a future school for girls that was taking shape in her mind. Both aims are construed by Eliza in her assessment of Mrs. Honner's character and educational background:

> Were Mrs. Honner, her liberality of feeling, her judgment alone concerned, no obstacles would lie in the way. You would love her I know. Her little failings of pride & prejudice you would overlook or combat with that gentle firmness of manner & that eloquent and irresistible power of reasoning which you so eminently possess. It is but justice to her to say that never would she remind you of her station by the slightest failure of complete and real gentlewomanly observance. (EF to MH, 21 December 1813)[17]

Eliza was able to conclude that Mrs. Honner, in recognizing the deficiencies in her own education, was able to specify the kind of education she envisioned for her daughters. And that was the key, as Eliza told Mary: "I profited by the hints I gathered, & fortunately Mrs Honner, feeling many inconveniences which arise from her having been trained only to ornamental, [she] is anxious to blend the rational & useful with it, which suits my wish exactly" (EF to MH, 3 June 1813). As if to give Mary a sense of the kind of pedagogical ethos she would develop in a school of her own, Eliza then provided a report card-like critique of Mrs. Honner's accomplishments and shortcomings. On the plus side, Eliza rated Mrs. Honner as "an excellent French scholar & tolerably fluent, tho out of practice in Italian" (EF to MH, 21 December 1813). Eliza also praised "her language, pronunciation & manners" as "graceful & admirable," but assessed "her music only wanting in theory that a little study could give." The assessment reads as a prototype for what an actual progress report could look like for a girl attending Eliza's future school.

If Eliza's work as a governess with the Mocatta family provided her with early validation of her success as an educator, then her experience with the Honner family consolidated it. Eliza also learned, in working for the Honner family, that to be successful as an educator to the daughters of the rich, she would have to dress the part. While she had "dressed out of poverty, with a grey gown & no linen visible," as William Godwin had observed[18] in the early 1800s, when she was trying to make ends meet, the clothes she needed as a governess would have to be more explicitly suited to her position. "Every article of dress is very dear," she wrote to Mary, "& I am necessarily obliged to be more expensive than I was in London, for I wear my clothes out much faster & in conformity to Mrs. Honner's Lady refinements I dress better" (EF to MH, 26 August 1813).

As the possibility of emigrating to Barbados to start a school with her daughter began to come into focus through 1813, Eliza was consciously thinking about what such a school might look like, what kind of curriculum she would have to offer, and how she could market it to the kind of high-paying clientele she would have to attract if she wanted to become an independent businesswoman, a school owner. Eliza's letter of June 3, 1813 makes it obvious that she was consciously constructing a profile she would be able to use for her endeavor: "By conversing with Mrs Honner & Mrs Hewitt, who were certainly very highly bred," Eliza wrote, "I have managed (artfully enough you will say) to draw from them a knowledge of certain particulars of my trade which I had not before." She could see a potential curriculum that would synchronize her preference for intellectual accomplishments with the more "ornamental" accomplishments that wealthy parents would want for their marriageable daughters.

It was at Lee Mount that Eliza polished the skills she would need to plot the course of her next moves as a teacher. Cork was the pivot point, the place from which she could launch herself into a new identity in the Caribbean, presenting herself as someone whose station, education, and background would qualify her as being eminently suited to educating upper-class young ladies. In a letter dated February 1, 1813, her forty-seventh birthday, Eliza wrote to Mary with an expression of what an ideal teacher-student relationship might look like: "To be able to fix a willing delighted attention," Eliza wrote, "to communicate energy, to perceive ideas shooting expanding and maturing under your guidance & culture and to receive an intelligent need of affection & gratitude in return for your labours from yr pupils is a vision of very agreeable promise I grant you."

The passage is lovely and the elements in it would have resonated with Mary as a riff on a passage from "Spring," from *Seasons* (1730) by James

Thomson (1700–1748). The lines, frequently referenced in eighteenth-century pedagogical treatises, read:

> Delightful task! To rear the tender Thought,
> To teach the young Idea how to shoot,
> To pour the fresh instruction o'er the Mind,
> To breathe th' inspiring Spirit, and to plant
> The generous Purpose in the glowing Breast.[19]

Here, as elsewhere, Eliza adapted the conventional and shaped it to her purpose, turning the familiar lines into something sharper, clearer, more alive. While Thomson's lines capture the growth metaphor popular in eighteenth-century pedagogical treatises, Eliza's reference to "communicating energy" updates the idea, foregrounding the importance of intellectual exchange. The whole passage suddenly reads as portraying something more closely akin to a modern image of brain synapses in the act of thinking rather than something analogous to slow growth.

With a vision of ideas "shooting expanding and maturing" in the school that Eliza would run with her daughter taking shape in her mind, the viability of the move to Barbados came increasingly into focus in 1814. For Eliza, leaving Ireland would not, after all, be as awkward as she had imagined, as the cracks she had identified in Mr. Honner's situation at Lee Mount had broken open. In May 1814, Eliza wrote to Mary, both to say that her eldest student "near 17" was "old enough to quit the schoolroom" and that Mr. Honner was "advertising the sale of *Lee Mount*."[20] His other options were closing too, in much the way Eliza had predicted: "His last application to be restored to his army rank has been most decidedly rejected. Counsellors opinions says he cannot get redress in the courts of Law. His horses have been more & more unsuccessful. He is involved in two unpromising Law suits . . . & I cannot help anticipating some change in their plans of living that will part us." With life at Lee Mount falling apart, with Orlando finishing his education and facing limited employment opportunities, Eliza prepared to leave her life as a governess and begin anew with her daughter as a school owner in Barbados.

5

Colonist and Slaveholder

Upon her arrival with Orlando in Bridgetown on October 28, 1814, Eliza's focus was on the reunification of her family: "that hour," she wrote to Mary, "seemed to reward me for all previous suffering" (EF to MH, 11 December 1814). She also described Barbados as "our Land of Promise," echoing a phrase her daughter had used when she had landed three years earlier: "we arrived yesterday in Heaven," Eliza Ann had said, "this is indeed the Land of Promise." "I have been in continual transport," she enthused, "since I was swung off the side of the ship into a boat at 12 yesterday morning." She was describing her arrival in what is still called the "careenage," a shallow harbor in Bridgetown, so named because of the way arriving ships could be turned on their sides ("careened") and their bottoms scraped after their cargo had been unloaded. On entering the harbor, Eliza Ann and the other passengers would have been "swung off" the side of the ship, as she says, into small boats and rowed the short distance to shore. Eliza Ann's note, written on December 21, 1811, the morning after she landed, also contained news about a curious incident that happened soon after she settled into her lodgings in Bridgetown. "About 4 this morning," Eliza Ann wrote, "I was wakened by the oddest music & heard someone singing in the street to us. All I could make out was: 'Welcome Ladies. Welcome all—Welcome to Barbadoes Shore.'"

Like most of the white people landing for the first time on "Barbadoes Shore," Eliza Ann couldn't quite understand what was happening. The fact that she and the other new arrivals were being serenaded in the dark at four in the morning seemed odd to her, but otherwise opaque, something she couldn't interpret in the new landscape she was encountering for the very first time. She explained what she heard as a song of welcome. White newcomers to Barbados, and to other slave-dependent Caribbean islands in the period, reported analogous experiences of being greeted by black people in small boats who would sing to them as they were transferred from their ships to the shore. They too reported that though they couldn't quite understand the words being sung, they believed the black people rowing the boats were singing friendly songs of greeting. The ominous words to one such welcoming song, however, tell a different story:

> New come buckra
> He get sick
> He tak fever
> He be die
> He be die
> He be dead[1]

What neither Eliza Ann nor other new arrivals understood was that the welcome song was ironic, a grim joke telling them that about a third of their number would die "within three years of arriving."[2] "Buckra," incidentally, is Caribbean slang, an offensive term for a white man. New white immigrants were susceptible to disease, especially yellow fever, as referred to in the song. The mortality rate was high and the young were among the most vulnerable. Eliza's son Orlando would eventually become a statistic, dying in early November 1816, two years after arriving with Eliza in late October 1814. Although the serenade Eliza Ann reported had "roused the whole house" at four in the morning of her first day in Barbados, no one had seemed concerned. The landlady simply "arrived" with refreshing "green Cocoanut" to drink, then she conducted the new arrivals "to the cold bath," after which everyone "returned to Bed & slept till 8." So began the new normal in the society of enslaved and their enslavers.

Colonial Life

Three years after Eliza Ann's arrival on the "Barbadoes Shore," the promised land of Barbados was theoretically fulfilling Eliza's long-held desires for social and financial security, for a home, and for a stable life. By 1815, Eliza's family had grown to include a son-in-law and two grandsons (Tom, Eliza Ann's second son was baptized on August 3, 1815, at three months of age). Yet Eliza knew, almost from the first, that Barbados could not deliver on its promise. "I recollect perfectly," she wrote to Mary in July 1815, "that in struggles & pecuniary difficulties I used to think any place would be paradise where I could secure a living. The means are now abundant, but Barbados is not my paradise." In this contrast to her initial response to Lee Mount as "paradise," Eliza must have known that Mary would catch the comparison.

The school she established, the Seminary for Young Ladies, however did begin well for Eliza. For the first time she was an independent businesswoman. She had been beholden as a wife to John, as a writer to publishers, and as a governess to her employers. As a school owner she was in control and could move freely among the people in the top layers of the social structure. She was also faced daily with a moral dilemma; she had to reconcile her radical beliefs in equality, liberation, and freedom with the fact that her ability to succeed in a slave-dependent society required her to conform to its norms. Between 1795, when Eliza was a young novelist, married with small children, living in the company of the most influential radicals of her day, and 1815, when she was a single working grandmother running a school with her adult daughter in Barbados, the world had changed and so had her friends.

English reformers in the late 1790s and early 1800s were infused with hope inspired by the early stages of the French Revolution. That initial optimism, however, was soon replaced with prolonged, grim power struggles, death, and destruction. The bloodbaths of the "Terror" in France, the battles between the Girondins and the Montagnards, the rise of Napoleon, and the seemingly endless Napoleonic Wars all provided evidence that liberty and freedom were expensive and bloody propositions. By the summer of 1815, the Battle of Waterloo had been fought. Napoleon had lost and he was heading for Elba. In Britain, William Wilberforce's long battle to legislate the end to slavery was stalled. The euphoria following his successful campaign to end the slave trade in 1807 was long over and though it was illegal for any British companies to engage in the business of trading in slaves, it was still business as usual in other countries. The British colonies in the West Indies continued to buy enslaved people who were being "imported" by countries (Spain and Portugal, for example) not bound by the British legislation.

As Britain and its colonies had enjoyed long periods of economic prosperity built on slave trading and on slave labor, there was enormous resistance to change. A shocking statistic provided by the National Archives in the U.K. dramatically testifies to the fact that "between 1640 and 1807," Britain is estimated to have "transported 3.1 million Africans (of whom 2.7 million arrived) to the British colonies in the Caribbean, North and South America and to other countries."[3] In order to try to stem the importation of African enslaved people into British colonies, Wilberforce devised the Registration of Slaves Bill (the Registry Bill, as it was known) in 1812. In theory, the only way to stop the trade in slaves was to stop their importation. By registering enslaved people already on individual islands, anyone caught with an unregistered slave would be in violation of the laws against the slave trade. There is no evidence that Eliza initially understood the implications of the parliamentary debate about the Registry Bill on her move to Barbados.

The complicated relationship between parliamentary debate in England and life in Barbados unfolded in counterpoint to the complicated relationship Eliza and her daughter had as they negotiated their moral opposition to slavery while living and working in a slave-dependent culture. Their conflicted assessments still make uncomfortable reading: they kept trying to comprehend their new environment, but their eyes—accustomed to the liberal, intellectual world of their London lives—had a hard time making sense of what they were seeing. In some ways, the lives of the black people that would necessarily become so much a part of their world seemed incomprehensible. Eliza Ann, in March 1812 (after about three months in Barbados), for example, describing what must have been intended as a casual, gossipy note about a social occasion, visiting some of the townspeople in her employer's new carriage, suddenly catches herself in the narrative. "The black servant drives us," she says first, before correcting herself: "I see I have written the *black* servant as if we had any white ones." Eliza Ann suddenly realized that her concept of "servant" had undergone a radical shift. The "servant" category, which she had previously understood as unmarked by color (primarily because the default color was white), had become an exclusively black category. Elsewhere she noted that only one person she knew had a white servant.

Like her daughter, Eliza struggled to recalibrate a world defined predominantly by color (rather than by class or gender). The example she chose demonstrates her acute recognition of the rot that was at the base of the social structure of the community. Her visceral account still stands as arrestingly vivid testimony to what the corrupt world of Barbados was like at the time. The letter, dated March 21 and April 12, 1815, also testifies to the fact that Eliza constructed her letters with the deliberate narrative coherence of a literary text. She begins her account with an overview, tracing the social corruption inherent in the slave-dependent society of Barbados to the normalized immoral practices of the slave owners, most notably their routine rapes of enslaved women:

> It is a horrid & disgraceful System. The female Slaves are really encouraged to prostitution because their children are the property of the owner of the mothers. These children are reared by the Ladies as pets, are frequently brought from the negro houses to their chambers to feed & sleep & reared with every care & indulgence till grown up, when they are at once dismiss'd to labour & slave like treatment.

After making the generic, almost travel guide-like observation of the fact that enslaved "children are the property of the owner of the mothers," Eliza hones in precisely on the horrific fact that the mothers' "encouragement to prostitution" is perpetrated by the property owners themselves, all supposedly civilized, Christian, and law-abiding. "What is still more horrible," she says, is that "the gentlemen are greatly addicted to their women slaves & give the fruit of their licentiousness to their white children as slaves." And then, in order to make her powerful point about the way personal corruption is at the heart of social corruption, Eliza focuses on a precise moment, specific children, and an apparently ordinary morning breakfast at school: "I strongly suspect that a very fine Mulatto boy about 14 who comes here to help wait on the breakfast & luncheon of two young Ladies, our pupils, is their own brother, from the likeness he bears to their father. It is a common case & not thought of as an enormity." Eliza concludes her vignette: "It gives me disgusted antipathy & I am ready to hail the Slave & reject the Master." Yet, despite her perceptive account of the bizarre situation in her school in which the illegitimate mulatto son serves the two legitimate daughters of the same man, Eliza could not understand why the domestic servants who worked in Barbados did not behave like English servants. In the Caribbean, incidentally, the people who worked as domestic slaves (largely indoors) were described as servants. They were distinguished from the field slaves, who did the brutally difficult outdoor work required on the sugar cane plantations.

It was actually Eliza Ann, in one of her very first letters, dated January 10, 1812, who attempted to explain to her mother the new world of a servant class in the context of the old. The content is so disturbing that it is tempting to issue a warning note to readers:

> Do you expect a description of the Island, the people & the horrors of Slavery. Of the latter I have yet seen little. I think the slaves, I mean the domestic slaves, the laziest & most impertinent set of people under the Sun. They positively will do nothing but what they please. I have not seen a Negro struck since I have been here but I have seen a great many deserve it. There are always three or four to do the work of one & they laugh in their owner's face when reproved for not doing their duty. . . . They take liberties that no English servant wd [would] be allowed to do; he [Captain Soaper, the owner of the enslaved people to whom she is referring] has two who are drunk half the day & one female Negroe who waits on Mrs. S. throws herself into fits the moment she is found fault with. They will not scour the floors—that is too hard work for them & the field Negroes are sent for to do it. Bye the bye, I am told the condition of the field Negroes is deplorable enough & the only way to make the domestic slaves do as they

are bid is by threatening to send them to the Plantations. (Eliza Ann to EF, 10 January 1812)

Eliza Ann's incomprehension in 1812 of the enslaved people who would not do their assigned work was repeated by Eliza a few years later. What neither woman could really grasp was that the resistance to work was deliberate, a statement against being enslaved. Unlike servants who were paid (however poorly) for their work, enslaved people were not paid. They were treated as property, not people.

In the same 1815 letter in which Eliza described her horror at the rich white girls in her school being served by their enslaved, mulatto half-brother, she also described what a typical school day would look like in the tropics. In order to avoid the heat in the middle of the day, Eliza explained, school started at 7:00 a.m., stopped for breakfast at 8:30, then ran from 9:30 a.m. to 4:30 p.m. with an hour's break for lunch between 12:30 and 1:30. The "extraordinary sight" of the scene in the "ante room" at the school where breakfast was served each morning reads, in its uncomfortable emphasis on the exotic, like a Gauguin painting.[4] She describes the room:

> . . . lined with female black slaves, attending with the young Ladies' break-fasts, mostly attired in a picturesque costume—White Muslin petticoats, colored jackets, colored cotton or silk Handkerchiefs on their heads most fancifully put on & very frequently coral & gold Necklaces of a value & beauty that a London Belle might envy. They always attract my eye from the symmetry & beauty of their forms as well as their fantastic attire. In their manners they have a polished civility that frequently exceeds the good breeding of their owners. But except demeanor & outward form they are a detestable set of people—idle, ungrateful, dirty, dishonest & profligate in the extreme. (EF to MH, 21 March and 12 April 1815)

Eliza's frustration is audible in her account to Mary: "Nothing awes or governs them but the lash of the whip or the dread of being sent into the fields to labour. With us, therefore, they pursue a regular course of negligence lies & plunder the latter of which they carry on with a cunning & ingenuity that is surprising."

The fact that the people who worked for Eliza, people she treated, from her perspective, with "kindness & forbearance," stole from her and did not share her work ethic struck her as completely unintelligible. But it is her surprise at their "cunning and ingenuity" that really cuts to the heart of what eluded her. What Eliza couldn't understand was that enslaved people had agency, that they could think, act, and rebel with as much integrity and creativity as any of the radical people she had known in London in the 1790s who had worked toward a more democratic society. The reason why Eliza, who had been an abolitionist, a believer in equality and liberation through literacy, was completely baffled by the enslaved people in Barbados was that, up until the time she lived among them, her experience with them had been either metaphorical or hypothetical.

Eliza's metaphorical encounters were rooted in the idea of women as enslaved people, which derived from the rhetoric of the kind used by Mary Wollstonecraft, particularly in the *Vindication of the Rights of Woman*, to characterize the condition of women in a patriarchal society. It was the kind of language that had also colored some of the rhetoric of the French Revolution, and so galvanized the movement toward liberty, equality, and fraternity. Eliza's hypothetical encounters were shaped by the rhetoric of the abolitionist movements of the 1790s to abolish the slave trade. Public opposition to the slave trade had been solicited in two ways: by focusing attention on the cruelty of removing people forcibly and violently from their countries and their families; and by emphasizing the capacity of slaves to feel emotional attachment, especially to children, though the other side of that characterization was that Africans, though able to feel, were not that good at thinking.

A "slave," as defined in the *Oxford English Dictionary* (*OED*) is "a person who is excessively dependent or controlled." In Eliza's 1790s London, articulation of resistance to obedience, control, and dependency was vocal and strong. Throughout the *Vindication*, Mary Wollstonecraft makes it crystal clear that enslaving people—women, children, and Africans—is a recipe for social disaster. She exposes the false logic in the rhetoric that portrays the rule of men as beneficent and normal; that is, the patriarchal argument assigning reason and authority exclusively to men. What happens instead is that the subservient people eventually revolt, resisting either by refusing to work or by erupting into violence: "slavery will have its constant effect," Wollstonecraft says, "degrading the master and the abject dependent."[5] The *Vindication* is shot through with passionate arguments against the kind of "specious slavery which chains the very soul of woman, keeping her for ever under the bondage of ignorance" (*Works* 5: 215).

The analogy of women as slaves also exists in English literary tradition. In "Habits of Empire and Domination in Eliza Fenwick's *Secresy*" (2002), Malinda Snow traces the connection between slavery and the legal status of women in Britain to Mary Astell, who in 1700 asked: "If all Men are born free, how is it that all Women are born slaves? As they must be if being subjected to the inconstant, uncertain, unknown, arbitrary Will of Men be the perfect Condition of Slavery?"[6] Snow makes a compelling argument for *Secresy* as being about "exploitation and oppression."[7] The analogy between women and slavery is exactly the one that Eliza situates at the heart of *Secresy*, mirroring arguments shaped by the philosophies of both Astell and Wollstonecraft.

Valmont in *Secresy*, as Eliza constructs him, is the patriarchal bad guy who believes in keeping his niece locked up, enslaved, and obedient to his will under the pretext of protecting her. As Eliza had, after all, argued for the rights of women to refuse submission and blind obedience, it is hard to imagine that she didn't appreciate that irony. And yet she couldn't seem to fathom that the enslaved people working for her might equally resist their enslaved status. It is tempting to wonder if she was ever haunted by some of her own lines in *Secresy*; Valmont's "I have chosen a part for you" comes to mind, with its arrogant assumption that "nothing is required of you but obedience."[8]

Resistance to unconditional obedience was, after all, a frequent refrain in Eliza's 1790s literary London. Mary Robinson too, in her verse drama *The Sicilian Lover* (published in 1796, a year after *Secresy*), created a villain called Valmont, who, like Eliza's Valmont says,

> From the first dawn of helpless infancy
> I've taught her mild obedience to my will
> And count upon her duty more than love. (Act I, Scene I)

Eliza's and Mary Robinson's respective Valmonts were echoing, of course, Jean-Jacques Rousseau's instructions on the education of girls in *Emile*, that they were supposed to do what they were told without question. In *Secresy*, Eliza gave Sibella an eloquent speech on the value of resisting authority:

> What obedience? the grateful tribute to duty, authorized by reason, and sanctioned by the affections? No. . . . He never enlightened my understanding, nor conciliated my affections; and he demands only the obedience of a fettered slave. I am held in the bondage of slavery. And still may Mr. Valmont's power constrain the forces of this body. But where, Miss Ashburn, is the tyrant that could ever chain thought, or put fetters on the fancy? (73)

As *Secresy* is filled with lines arguing against blind obedience, I wanted to cite them here, counterpointing them with Mary Wollstonecraft's lines, also from the 1790s, on the same theme, partly because they read so ominously when set against the actual resistance to blind obedience that Eliza and her family encountered in 1816 during what the white people called a slave "insurrection."

In *Secresy*, Eliza has Carolyn Ashburn say, "I hold obedience to be vice." She continues:

> The perpetual hue and cry after obedience and obedience has almost driven virtue out of the world, for be it unlimited unexamined obedience to a sovereign, to a parent, or husband, the mind, yielding itself to implicit unexamined obedience, loses its individual dignity, and you can expect no more of a man than of a brute. What is to become of the child who is taught never to think or act for himself? (349)

The lines are a direct echo of Wollstonecraft's discussion of the problems of demanding blind obedience in children under the guise of education. In the section of the *Vindication* on parents, she writes that "unconditional obedience, is the catch-word of tyrants of every description." By way of contrast, Wollstonecraft defines education worth having as being about "cultivation of mind," something "which teaches young people how to begin to think" (Works 5: 235).

The metaphorical arguments that Eliza and other like-minded enlightened, intellectual women of her circle had marshaled against enslaving women and children still stand. As those women were not writing from a slave-dependent, majority black West Indian island, however, they were removed both physically and intellectually from an actual population of enslaved people. When Eliza and her daughter began their school in Barbados, inequity was not a metaphorical or philosophical idea; it was glaringly physical and shockingly visible. There were five times as many enslaved, imported black people on the island as there were white people. It was Olwyn M. Blouet, in "Mrs. Fenwick and Her School for Girls in Barbados, 1814–1822," who provided the startling statistics on the makeup of the population in Barbados in the period. She wrote that, "in 1816–1817 there were 77,493 blacks, 3,007 free coloureds, and just over 16,000 whites in the island." She added that at a ratio of "around 1:5," the island "had a higher proportion of whites to blacks than any other British West Indian island."[9] With the white population in the minority in slave-dependent islands, measures to keep enslaved people blindly obedient and under control were—from the perspective of the white slave owners—necessarily draconian.

As Eliza's understanding of what black people were like had been formed primarily through her exposure to abolitionist literature, she was puzzled by her experience of enslaved black people in Barbados. A common characterization from Africa was that they were affectionate and loyal, but lacking the desire for intellectual improvement. That is exactly the character

Eliza initially gave to the slave nanny Nora in 1805 in *Visits to the Juvenile Library:* an "ignorant Negro woman" who "loved the [Mortimer] children with her whole heart." Nevertheless, although "that heart was capable of great kindness towards any human being," the reader is assured, Nora's "head was weak, and she had never learned to read."[10] That is the kind of enslaved person Eliza saw in 1811 when she described the "fine old Negroe" who assured her, on recognizing her distress at watching Eliza Ann board the ship for Barbados, that he would "take care of Missee." And it was exactly the same kind-but-not-clever characterization Eliza included in the first (1806) edition of *The Class Book* she compiled for Richard Phillips.[11] The August 3 entry in particular emphasizes that, like domestic pets, Africans are affectionate and loyal: "They are naturally affectionate, and have an ardent love for their children, friends, and countrymen. The little they possess they freely distribute among the necessitous without any other motive than that of pure compassion for the indigent." The piece ends with precisely a political message: "May the time speedily arrive when the horrors of slavery shall be known only by name, and the principles by which it still exists be execrated by every being that claims the title of man!"

With only hypothetical and metaphorical understandings of enslaved people in mind, it is little wonder that Eliza found the enslaved people she actually encountered in Barbados in 1815 incomprehensible. The thing she really didn't understand was that those enslaved people were intelligent, organized, and on the brink of staging a rebellion that would shut down the island on the Easter weekend of 1816. And at that point, she didn't understand, at least not from the perspective of the white minority population, that the blame for the insurrection would be placed squarely on Wilberforce's Registry Bill.

Renting Not Owning

Despite Eliza's understanding from the first that Barbados was not her "paradise," she was, nevertheless, experiencing the realization of all her dreams: she was earning her own living, she had a home of her own, and she was with her two children, both of whom were also launched into their adult lives. Eliza Ann was married, with two lovely baby sons, and Orlando was working with a local merchant, Mr. Hozier. The Seminary for Young Ladies had attracted the daughters of the most influential members of the community and it was a family enterprise, with Eliza, Eliza Ann, and her husband William Rutherford all involved in the teaching. Eliza had finally, triumphantly recovered the social and financial status she had lost when John, sometime in the mid-1790s, had managed to take her from affluence to poverty. In Barbados she had an earned a social status of her own, alongside leading members of the community, people whose names still resonate in Barbados: Allyne, Beccles, and Da Costa.[12] The family also continued associating with the theater community and Eliza Ann still occasionally performed.

Eliza tried hard to deal with the ethical dilemma of slavery. In her first letters to Mary Hays, she describes the enslaved people who worked for her in the context of her urban life in Bridgetown as "servants" or "domestics." Though this terminology was common in Barbados—used to distinguish enslaved people who did housework from those who worked outside in the fields—Eliza also wanted Mary to know from the outset that even as her family tried to adjust to life in Barbados, they were not slave owners:

> I suppose this mental discontent will wear away as Habit inures me to new customs & manners but one thing will ever militate against my contentment,—the negro Slaves. Slaves we have none, but we hire them at high wages of their owners for Servants, & no imagination can form an idea of the unceasing turmoil & vexation their management creates. To kindness and forbearance they return insolence & contempt. (EF to MH, 21 March and 12 April 1815)

In philosophical terms, Eliza had tried what is known as the "clean hands" solution[13]; that is, she rented rather than owned slaves in order to retain a sense of moral superiority, or moral cleanliness. In theory, outsourcing "dirty work" acted as a kind of get-out-of-jail-free card. The "clean hands" tactic is what the wealthy plantation owners living in Britain practiced. By employing overseers (sometimes enslaved people, though also sometimes free people of color or poor, white descendants of Irish indentured servants) to keep the enslaved field workers in line on their Caribbean plantations, they could keep their civilized, Christian selves remote from and essentially ignorant of the oppressed lives of the enslaved people on the islands. They could keep their hands clean and their gentility intact by getting other people to be violent, brutal, and abusive for them. The fact that there were five times as many black people as white people in Barbados stood as a silent affirmation of the inability of white plantation owners to stomach the violence necessary to maintain slavery. They simply sailed away from it and reaped the profits; cities such as Liverpool and Bristol benefited and grew rich: the Codrington Library, All Souls College Oxford received a huge endowment (£10,000) in 1710 from Christopher Codrington (1668–1710), a Barbados-born, Oxford-educated son of a plantation-owning family.

Because even the idea of hiring an enslaved person as an employee reads as an oxymoron, it is hard to conceive of slave rental as a standard business model. Yet, for Eliza, it provided a viable alternative to the untenable option of buying people. In Bridgetown, the slave rental business was especially attractive to single women, particularly widows, or women who had no other source of income or support, as they could make a living and generate an income stream. Typically, enslaved people with trade skills were the ones who would be exploited by their owners for the rental market. People with navigational skills, for example, were particularly valuable in the port of Bridgetown, as were cooks and people who could do needlework, carpentry, or other domestic services. In *Slave Society in the City: Bridgetown, Barbados, 1680–1834,* Pedro Welch explains that "58 percent of slaves in Bridgetown between 1817 and 1834 could be classified as skilled slaves."[14] Welch explains how the slave rental system worked:

> Under the system, enslaver and enslaved entered into an informal arrangement in which the slave was relatively free to seek his/her employment. In some cases, enslavers would advertise the services of their property in the local newspaper. Such services could often range from that of the skilled artisan to the thinly veiled offer of prostitution services.... Under the hiring arrangement, the enslaved often provided their own housing, food and clothing. In return, a fixed payment was made to the owners. Owners could then have profits without responsibilities. (Welch 15)

From a twenty-first-century perspective, it is almost impossible to fathom just how completely normal it was for people to be regarded as property. There is a note, for instance, in the *Barbados Mercury Gazette,* explaining that a performance at the Theatre Royal in Bridgetown had to be canceled as an unfortunate accident had meant that the scenery had not been completed; it had collapsed, and a slave child who had been working on it was killed. A few weeks later, the theater held a benefit performance—for the theater owner—as she could not afford the loss of the slave she had rented to the theater. How little those enslaved lives mattered at the time still makes chilling reading, especially in the context of the "Black Lives Matter" campaigns of the twenty-first century.

The enslaved people being rented out had some advantages, in that they would have had what Pedro Welch describes as "room to maneuver," the freedom to move around the city without supervision. Outside of "working" hours, they could do what they liked. As Eliza found out, the "blurred lines of authority," as Welch describes, meant that the enslaved people who had been rented out recognized that there was a loophole they could exploit: it was unclear whether punishing disobedience was the responsibility of the slave owner or the responsibility of the slave renter.

In the slave rental system, enslaved people could keep a small portion of the rental fee, which then could be used toward manumission, a system by which they could buy their freedom. But as they only earned a fraction of the rental fee, saving money to pay for their freedom was an arduous process. For the most part, they had to work out options for survival. And as historian Sir Hilary Beckles explains, they had long figured out how to resist the system. They were practiced at "everything from feigned ignorance, malingering, sabotage, slowed down work habits, suicides and poisoning of masters and the endless invention of attitudes that reflect a general war of psychological tensions and stresses between both sides of the master-slave relationship."[15]

Although the slave rental scheme provided a "clean hands" option for Eliza, it did not work out very well and she found herself stuck, as Beckles says, in an incomprehensible "war of psychological tensions and stresses" (Beckles 67). She and Eliza Ann never could understand why the enslaved people they hired wouldn't behave like the servants she knew in Britain, especially as she was unfailingly nice to them. Eliza's observations of their "bad" behavior accords with the explanation Michael Craton provides in *Testing the Chains*. He makes the case that the white people saw enslaved people as analogous to "unruly children," in that they were "characterized by unformed intelligence and fitful moods, alternatively manic and depressed, craven and rebellious." As a result, as Craton explains, "by merely behaving like a child, a slave exposed the empty pretentions of the masters' paternalism."[16] The subtlety of this maneuver eluded Eliza and her daughter but goes a long way toward explaining how frustrating they found slave management. No matter how clearly Eliza explained to the rented domestics that she would never beat or injure them, they would not work well with her or for her. In a letter from July 1815, Eliza complained again to Mary: "the endless trouble & vexation that Black servants involve you in," she confided, "renders domestic comfort unattainable" (EF to MH, 3, 8, and 11 July 1815).

Bussa's Rebellion

Despite her continuing frustration at what she would have called (had she been in Britain) "the servant problem," Eliza expressed cautious optimism about her future in Barbados. Her report to Mary in March and April of 1815 contained the good news that the income she and her family were earning from their school fees exceeded their expenses, and that if all continued as planned she would be able to cover all of her initial startup and moving expenses and be out of debt within two years. Eliza's increasing business acumen and confidence comes across in the letter too. She had brought books and an "elegant Piano-forte" with her to Barbados and had hoped to make a profit from the resale. The books, she explained, "sold very well," but not the piano-forte, as she was being undercut by the "principal Music Master" in town. Nevertheless, Eliza contemplated for the first time the probability of a secure future for herself and her family. In an unpublished section of the letter, Eliza wrote that, despite the expenses related to buying some new furniture and to her daughter's "soon expected confinement" with her second son Thomas,[17] she could see her way forward: "I have the satisfaction to assure you that our income provides the means of living with decency & comfort & that our additional pupils will enable us in a little time fruitfully & fully to discharge every pecuniary obligation. I know how pleasing this account will be to you & therefore dwell on the detail" (EF to MH, 21 March and 12 April 1815). As part of her business strategy, Eliza positioned her school at the high end of the market. "Our prices are high very high," she confesses. The reason, she explains, is to "keep us in the higher & wealthy classes, thus securing us from bad debts." The strategy worked, she says, and the school is "*in fashion*" (emphasis in the original)—that is, it is the option for families "who do not send their daughters to England."

Besides the initial success of the school, Eliza was also able to report that Orlando was settled with a merchant, a Mr. Hozier, although she was having difficulty adjusting to seeing her son as an adult, "tall, erect manly,— thinking & acting for himself & managing the business of a considerable mercantile house with sober steadiness." "Sober" is the operative word in the sentence. Given her history with the destructiveness of John's drinking,[18] it is no wonder that Eliza would have been worried about Orlando following in his footsteps, especially because rum was the drink of choice on the island. Eliza confessed to Mary her "great uneasiness & misery lest he shd acquire a habit of drinking." She also explained that he had been advised not to drink the water because it was "accused of a tendency to create swellings of the testicles."[19]

In reading Eliza's letters from 1815 and 1816, and knowing that what is now called Bussa's Rebellion took place on Easter weekend 1816, it is tempting to imagine that she understood that the oppressed people on the island would inevitably rise up. But as her new beginning held so much promise of a financially and socially secure future, she appears to have repressed that knowledge, and was experiencing the kind of "willful blindness" Margaret Heffernan eloquently describes in her book of the same title. Although Eliza appreciated that the society in which she very much wanted to establish roots was unsustainable, she couldn't admit it because the success of her school depended on maintaining the status quo. Willful blindness requires both recognition of imminent danger and a blind faith that smothers a call to action against that danger.

Eliza was an acute observer of life in Barbados. When the rebellion started on that April weekend in 1816, she took notes. A few months later, Eliza wrote:

> I have my dear Mary, a large sheet of paper in my desk, written from April 15th, a memorable day here, to the 28th, gradually recounting all our terrors etc. in that progress of the Negroes' insurrection, & addressed to you. The news is now old, & it is useless to try to interest you about a danger which you already know has pass'd over. I quitted that sheet from illness brought on, I really believe, by terror.

As a biographer, I want to know what Eliza said. If she did send the sheet of paper to Mary at some other date, it hasn't turned up in any of the archives I have searched. Even more frustrating, however, is the fact that there was a copy of it made. In an unpublished fragment of a letter to Mary written in 1817, Eliza wrote: "Mentioning to Eliza [her daughter, Eliza Ann] that I was going to send you the letter I wrote at the time of the insurrection, Mr. R [Eliza's son-in-law] begged that he might take a copy of it. I will therefore enclose it the next opportunity & if I can write at the same time." Although both Eliza's original and a copy existed in 1817, neither exists in any of the three Fenwick archives (in New York, Chapel Hill, or Washington, D.C.) or in archives containing material related to Bussa's Rebellion (National Archives in Barbados and in the U.K.). After the insurrection, there was an official investigation into its causes, but Eliza's comments have not turned up and she is not mentioned in the 1818 published report.

Because Bussa's Rebellion represents a seminal moment in the history of Barbados, even in the absence of Eliza's account, the events are important because they speak both to her earlier life in London as a reformer and her later life in Upper Canada when she felt threatened by Mackenzie's Rebellion in 1837. Bussa's Rebellion shut down Barbados for two weeks, thus standing as evidence of the sustained resistance movement among the enslaved people of the island. In reading the 1818 official report prepared by a committee of men who were the members of the colonial government at the time, it is hard not to see "willful blindness" in action. Basically, the official report concludes that the insurrection was caused by a misunderstanding among the enslaved people, as they mistakenly believed that the Registry Bill (regarded as a tax grab by the plantation owners) was a bill granting manumission. The authors of the 1818 report were at pains to include statements from the perpetrators (primarily confessions to priests from men who were about to be executed for their participation in the insurrection) saying that they were not rebelling because of ill treatment but because they felt that the "truth" of manumission was being withheld from them. That rationale makes sense in the context of the long arguments in the *Barbados Mercury Gazette* in the weeks leading up to the rebellion in 1816, complaining, bitterly and at length, that the British government was using the Registry Bill unjustly as a way of attempting to secure "taxation without representation." The plantation owners presented detailed accounts about how well they treated their slaves, how they cared for them, and how good their "breeding" programs were. Their point was that they did not have to rely on the illegal slave trade to restock their workforce. Because they had gone to such elaborate lengths before the rebellion to blame the Registry Bill (rather than their treatment of slaves or the injustice of slavery) for any discontent on the island, it made perfect sense after the rebellion to continue the narrative. They could blame the insurrection on the Registry Bill.

In the days leading up to the slave insurrection, the newspaper was filled with the angry rhetoric generated by the House of Assembly. In the *Barbados Mercury Gazette* of Tuesday, April 9, 1816, for instance, a series of unanimous resolutions were published, including one that claimed: "His Majesty's Government is now actually in possession of positive information, derived from the highest and most authentic sources, that the Acts for the Abolition of the Slave Trade have in no single instance been infringed." The pointed resolutions were in response to the 1807 law that had made it a felony to trade in slaves at all in the British Empire. From the position of the colonial government in Barbados, the slow erosion of their right to own slaves was at issue.[20]

The *Barbados Mercury Gazette* of Tuesday, April 9, 1816, just prior to the rebellion, is filled with dense arguments on the rights of citizens of Barbados to own slaves, and anger at attempts by the British Parliament to interfere with those rights. The paper devotes page after page to the outraged opposition by the House of Assembly to the proposed Registry Bill. On Saturday, April 13, the newspaper published as usual. The rebellion started the next day, on Sunday, April 14. The paper should have published again on Tuesday, April 16, but there was nothing. There was a gap in the run. When the paper did resume publishing two weeks later on April 30, the note with the news of the rebellion and the resulting publishing gap didn't appear until the first column of the second page, under an advert for the sale "of a fine mess beef, and pork and a few firkens of second-quality butter." The notice reads:

> It is unnecessary to state to our readers in this Community, the occasion of that suspension of our labours which has taken place since 13th of this month:—it will be long and painfully impressed on their minds—but those of our Subscribers who reside in neighbouring Settlements, will no doubt be desirous of knowing the cause of it. We shall therefore endeavor to perform this unpleasant duty, although we feel considerable difficulty in the attempt.

The explanation that follows is framed, as one would expect, as good and noble soldiers versus evil and misguided slaves who threatened the community. Yet when the toll was calculated, only two white people had died in the rebellion. Michael Craton lists the consequences for the insurgents: "144 executed, 170 deported and innumerable, floggings, roaming slaves were shot, negro houses burned, captives were tortured to extract confessions to incriminate others."[21] As might be expected, the poorly armed rebels, who included enslaved and free blacks, were no match for the armed forces, although there was some confusion as some of the armed men fighting on the side of the government forces were black men who had been forced into service. Unlike Jamaica, a volcanic island that has places where people might hide in the hills, Barbados is a small coral island, lacking in mountains and other landscape features that could have provided cover. There was nowhere for the rebels to hide, no safe vantage from which they could mount an attack.

The question that puzzled the white people was why the enslaved people would rebel in the first place. The first formal answer to that question came in a letter from one of the generals in charge, Colonel Codd, written on April 25, 1816. His argument reads as a kind of "I-told-you-so" confirmation of the rhetoric that had appeared in the *Barbados Mercury Gazette* in the days just prior to the rebellion: "it is fully ascertained that the chief cause to which this unfortunate Calamity," he insists authoritatively, "is to be attributed is the general opinion, which has pervaded the minds of those misguided people, since the proposed Introduction of the Registry Bill, that their Emancipation was desired by the British Parliament." He puts the blame for the rebellion squarely on "mischievous persons, and the indiscreet conversation of Individuals on the Measure."[22] The next day, on April 26, 1816, Governor James Leith issued "An Address to the Slave Population of the Island of Barbados." It begins with a disclaimer, saying that the Africans who sold their countrymen into slavery were at the root of the problem. He blames the Registry Bill for causing the uprising and praises those who "rallied round" their owners. He encourages all the other slaves to "return with cheerfulness to their duties." And, in exactly the way that Valmont plays it in *Secresy,* Leith plays the paternalism card:

> What would be the fate of the Old, the Infirm, the Sick, the helpless Children, and a large proportion of your whole Body, who have been brought up to depend entirely upon your Masters for your subsistence, and from that circumstance, as well as from the want of knowledge as Artificers, and in other respects, would be little able to provide for your wants, if a rash measure of general Emancipation were at once to throw the Mass of the Slave Population into a new state of Society, under the flattering but fallacious name of Freedom; in reality, however, presenting only the dangers of general Disorder, and producing (except to a few) the Miseries of Confusion and Want, leading to the Commission of Crimes, and to the absolute Subversion of Public Order and Tranquility?[23]

From Leith's position, the enslaved people, the ones doing all the work, were clearly unable to look after themselves. In reading his report retrospectively, especially the assumption that the enslaved people had "misunderstood" the Registry Bill, it is possible that this misreading had been a deliberate strategy used by leaders of the rebellion to deflect attention away from the population of enslaved people who had participated, thus protecting them from punishment.

As the rebellion shut down the island for a couple of weeks, the evidence is strong that there was an organized army of resistance already in place and ready to act. One of the most telling physical hints comes from the descriptions of the homemade resistance flags that the rebels used to identify each other. In a parody of the European battlefield "colors" (as in the Queen's "Trooping of the Colour"), the rebels had their own standards. One standard-bearer identified in the 1818 report was a man named Johnny, from Bailey's plantation. The descriptions of the rebel flags indicate that the enslaved people had a sure and informed sense of irony. One flag deemed particularly offensive depicted the union of a black man and a white woman. Another was an inversion of the three lions of the British coat of arms and skewed scales of justice. If any actual flags survived, they have not been found. Only descriptions and re-creations based on the descriptions remain.[24] The sophistication of the parodies, and the acute understanding of the manipulation of ideas of justice and freedom, as the research by Hilary Beckles, Pedro Welch, and others demonstrates, evinces that a large, well-organized network of resistance was in place by the time the rebellion began in 1816.

From Eliza's position, the slave insurrection was primarily a threat to the safety of her family and the viability of her school. Yet she had recognized, even after her first few months in Barbados, that the enslaved people who worked for her displayed, as she said, surprising degrees of "cunning & ingenuity." Despite believing at some level the received view that black people lacked intelligence, Eliza seems to have understood that the enslaved people of Barbados were actively resisting their oppression. How did she react to the news that one of the rebel flags depicted the "union" of a black man and a white woman? Did she read it in the context of her own disgust at the normalized unions of free white men with enslaved black women?

And what did she think on reading, as she must have done, the "Report from A Select Committee of the House of Assembly, Appointed to Inquire into the Origin, Causes and Progress of the Late Insurrection" when it came out in 1818, two years after the insurrection had ended? Among the twenty "testimonials" included in the official report was one made by "Robert, a Slave Belonging to the Plantation called 'Simmons.'" He blamed the insurrection on Nanny Grig, describing her as "a negro woman at Simmons,' who said that she could read." He claimed that a literate slave nanny:

> was the first person who told the negroes at Simmons' so; and she said she had read it in the Newspapers, and that her Master was very uneasy at it: that she was always talking about it to the negroes, and told them that they were all damned fools to work, for that she would not, as freedom they were sure to get. That, about a fortnight after New-year's Day, she said the Negroes were to be freed on Easter Monday, and the only way to get it was to fight for it, otherwise they would not get it.

It is tempting to wonder if Eliza felt that the slave nanny Nora she had created in her 1805 *Visits to the Juvenile Library* was an eerie foreshadowing of Nanny Grig in 1816. Both Nora and Nanny Grig stand as proponents of liberation through literacy. In Barbados, however, Eliza became increasingly conservative.

Bussa's Rebellion ultimately failed at least partly because of the powerful physical and psychological measures that were in place to keep enslaved people subservient. Beatings, threats of death, branding, and labor in the fields were used to enforce obedience, but there were other, more psychological tools in play. Enslaved women who bore children for their white masters could sometimes earn privileges they could leverage to benefit their own families, even if those privileges were at the expense of other enslaved people on the island.

In examining the events surrounding Bussa's Rebellion and doing an issue-by-issue reading of the *Barbados Mercury Gazette,* the distinctions between intimate close-ups and generic historical knowledge acquired from history books come into sharp relief. Conventional historical summaries outline the general structure of the slave trade including the triangular trade route, the design of slave ships, the origin of limbo, and the Middle Passage. Wilberforce is named as the architect of the move toward abolition, and the sugar boycott of the 1790s is cited as evidence that his position was gaining public traction at that time. The abolition of the slave trade in 1807 and abolition of slavery in 1833 are regarded as the milestones to know. Information about the laws forbidding enslaved people to read or write is usually reserved for more specialist histories, as is information about laws reflecting the prevailing European perceptions that categorized "Negroes" as being closer to animals (thus as subject to brutal treatment, living conditions, and forced "breeding" practices) than to Christian "people." The day-to-day ordinary brutality of slave-dependent culture as revealed in the pages of the *Barbados Mercury Gazette* is of a completely different order than information conveyed in generalist or even specialist summaries is.[25] In Barbados, slaves who absconded and were caught were put in a cage in the center of town. Each issue of the newspaper devoted space in the classified ads to descriptions of slaves who were on the run. It was in the newspapers, especially in those classified ads, that the small events of community life were recorded in the context of big events such as the Napoleonic Wars. The shipping news was there, carrying the details of what goods were coming and going. There was furniture for sale and properties for rent, announcements about theatrical performances, and public correspondence between people who wanted to air their private grievances and disputes in public.

Eliza's lived experience of negotiating the violent shifts toward democracy sweeping through the world in the late eighteenth and early nineteenth centuries is much like that of a modern embedded journalist moving from war zone to war zone, reporting from both the home- and battlefronts. As she was born in 1766, Eliza was ten at the time of the American Revolution in 1776, and although I can't definitively place her in France between about 1781 and 1788, there are enough hints to suggest that that is where she was in the buildup to the storming of the Bastille in 1789. But by the beginning of the Revolution, she was clearly back in Britain in the thick of the debates on parliamentary reform and was in regular contract with Thomas Holcroft and William Godwin. Barbados presented a different kind of war zone, as Bussa's Rebellion happened literally on her doorstep. Even though her account of the Easter uprising in 1816 is missing, her letters to Mary Hays are filled with glimpses of her unsettling relationships with the enslaved people who worked for her.

Despite trying to keep to the moral high ground by not purchasing slaves directly, Eliza couldn't seem to win either with the enslaved people she rented from their owners or with the free people of color that she hired. In 1815, she wrote about how she felt she was being driven "almost mad" by the "dirt, disobedience & dishonesty" of the people who worked for her. Eliza complained to Mary about one rented slave in particular who had robbed them and then "boasted to her owner's other slaves that she knew [Eliza] would not suffer her to be flogged, & therefore she knew better than to work when she was not made to do it" (EF to MH, July 1815). Eliza did not fare any better with a free servant of color (who would not have had to share her wages with an owner) than she did with a rented slave: "Neglect,—idleness,—& plunder are the invariable order to the day," she wrote, before recounting the story of being robbed of forty pounds by a sixteen-year-old girl who had helped with childcare and sewing. Eliza explained the impossibility of recourse under the convoluted legal system in place in Barbados: "She was the daughter of a free colored woman by a white Gentleman, & being free herself the law could not command the flogging it would have ordered a Slave in the same circumstances. I could not bear to prosecute to death, & therefore she was turned loose by the ill-regulated Police of the Country" (EF to MH, 20 May 1820). Eliza's accounts of life in Barbados reveal that she was conflicted. She kept trying to stay true to her radical roots and do the right thing, while also sustaining her viability in a society whose values she theoretically despised. When I outlined her dilemma to a philosopher, Robert Gibbs, at the University of Toronto, he suggested that Eliza was negotiating what philosophers call "spheres of responsibility."[26] Basically, she was putting her own family first, as per Sara Ruddick's description of maternal thinking on the primacy of the "preservation, growth and social acceptability"[27] of one's own children. By refusing to trade in slaves, and refusing to beat the enslaved or free people of color she hired, she was attempting to cling to her radical, liberal ideology. Yet, she eventually caved in her attempts to maintain her moral standards by not engaging in the buying and selling of enslaved people.

Despite her refusal to beat anyone who worked for her, she eventually found that she could not sustain the losses incurred when the people she hired stole from her. In the *Barbados Mercury Gazette* of June 3, 1820, she replied to a classified advertisement with an offer to buy:

"MRS FENWICK will be glad to treat for the sale of the two female Slaves described in Saturday's paper, and requests the advertiser will do her the favour to call on her, to give a further explanation of the terms, and also permit her to see the domestics." The enslaved people Eliza purchased were part of a group advertised in the previous Saturday's paper (May 27, 1820) and, although they had been listed as slaves for rent, Eliza, fed up with her previous experiences, countered with an offer to buy them. The people in the ad were:

> Two female Negro Servants—one a good needlewoman and the ladies at-tendant, with a child three years old, and the other a good drudge. Will be hired by the year, at the interest of an appraised, valuation—to be at the risk of the person hiring, and subject to the re-appraisement when given up. They can be recommended for honesty &c. Any persons requiring them, will please leave their names at this office, which will be attended to all the next week.

The inclusion of the testimonial to the "honesty" of the enslaved people for rent seems a tacit, conventional nod toward the fact that theft was nor-mal in Barbados. Or maybe the recommendation about "honesty" was what prompted Eliza's decision to buy. In so doing, she could address the prob-lems related to thefts she had encountered when she had used the rental option. That is, she could potentially avoid the loophole in the slave rental situation in which there was no clear "master."

Given the testimonial for the "honesty" in the original advert of May 27, there is a certain irony in the fact that Eliza felt obliged, on August 5, 1820, to place the following notice in the classified ads in the *Barbados Mercury Gazette:*

> Eight silver spoons having been stolen from the subscriber's house, she re-quests that they may be stopped if offered for sale. Three tea spoons marked R engraved in German text; one table spoon with the same mark; two des-sert spoons engraved with A; and two plain ones of similar size and shape. She will liberally reward any person who can assist her to discover the thief, as she has repeatedly suffered from the like depredations.

The ad is interesting as Eliza didn't apparently think that *her* slaves were the thieves. Enslaved people were, to use Hilary Beckles's phrase, "natural rebels." In *Black Rebellion in Barbados,* Beckles explains that the enslaved people "rebelled when they could, and accommodated when they had to" (2). In the earlier stages of settlement in Barbados, and throughout the Ca-ribbean, slave traders threw together people from all over Africa. The people initially forced into slavery on small islands had to negotiate a jumble of distinct features, cultures, histories, traditions, and languages in order to communicate with each other. By the early years of the nineteenth century, however, Creoles were people—both black and white—who had been born and raised on the island.[28] The slave trade was coming to an end in the period, especially after the successful rebellion in St. Domingo (modern Haiti). As Beckles eloquently puts it, "the ebb and flow of rebellion and accommodation suggests that they [the enslaved people] understood time as a political factor in the struggle" (2). Eliza did too, but in the interim she had learned, uneasily, to adapt to colonial life in Barbados and the practices that came with it.

6

School Owner and Mourner

Though slave-dependent Barbados was ethically as well as literally a "foreign" country for Eliza and her daughter, the field of education constituted much more familiar—and less complicated—territory. The Seminary for Young Ladies in Bridgetown made its first appearance in the *Barbados Mercury Gazette* on December 28, 1813 in a "coming soon" announcement. Eliza Ann, leveraging her public profile in the community as an actress, hoped to solicit responses and test the waters for potential clientele. In that first advertisement she simply stated her intention to establish a school with her mother, Mrs. Fenwick, "on the full and extensive plan of Polite Education . . . adopted in the most approved and fashionable Seminaries at home." Even though Eliza Ann placed the ad, it was Eliza who had primed her daughter with the copy for what would become their Seminary for Young Ladies "brand."

The announcement begins with Eliza Ann elegantly stating that the "chief endeavor" of the seminary would be "to fix the attention of her Pupils by gaining their affections." She also promises "to cultivate the better feelings of the heart," while encouraging "the development of youthful understanding."[1] If the statement itself sounds familiar, it is because I have already quoted an earlier version, from a letter Eliza wrote to Mary Hays in February 1813, when she first articulated her teaching philosophy: "To be able to fix a willing delighted attention," she wrote, "to communicate energy, to perceive ideas shooting expanding and maturing under your guidance & culture and to receive an intelligent need of affection & gratitude in return for yr labours from your pupils is a vision of very agreeable promise." The fact that Eliza Ann's first 1814 advertisement so obviously echoed Eliza's 1813 sentiments suggests that mother and daughter had exchanged letters on the subject before the first announcement was placed. Though the familiar references to James Thomson's eighteenth-century lines from "Spring" linger, they have been refreshed, rephrased for the new climate and the new century. In beginning with the importance of communicating "energy," Eliza shifts late Enlightenment emphasis on a teacher cultivating the growth of children toward something more explosive, more active than the slow cultivation of plants.

If mission statements had been in vogue in the early nineteenth century, Eliza would have nailed the genre. She adapts the eighteenth-century metaphor of spring growth in her advertisement and makes education sound more like a display of fireworks. There is something wonderfully progressive in the pedagogical philosophy expressed, especially in the fact that the emphasis is not on the curriculum but on the exchange between teacher and student, and on respect for both intelligence and affection on both sides. The language does reach back first to Thomson's "Spring" (first published in 1728) then to the 1790s maternal pedagogical practices espoused by Mary Wollstonecraft and others on "thinking and feeling," and "an active mind and a warm heart."[2] For twenty-first-century readers, Eliza's sense of intellectual life as "shooting" and "expanding" conjures graphic MRI images of neurons firing in the brain.

In the creation of her school brand, Eliza also incorporated tips she had picked up in Ireland on the kind of education that would appeal to affluent parents looking for a desirable education for their daughters, something that would prepare them for the competitive marriage market. Besides inherited wealth, desirable assets included fluency in French, music, and art, and the attainment of accomplishments both "useful and ornamental." Because Eliza had hesitated when her daughter had first suggested the plan of establishing a school in Barbados, Eliza Ann opened the Seminary for Young Ladies in Beckwith Square, Bridgetown, on her own in 1814. It was with a note of relief when, in January 1815, she was able to confirm that her mother had finally arrived in Barbados and would "materially and beneficially" enable her "to extend her system of Education" to the students in the school.

The curriculum, useful and ornamental, was laid out in the announcements in the paper. As fee structures in the period were determined on a per-course basis, parents could select the subjects in which their daughters would be instructed. On the useful side, "English and French Languages, according to the most approved Grammatical constructions and the rules of composition" were offered, as were "Reading, and Reciting, with a correct and graceful enunciation." Other "useful knowledge" included "Writing and Arithmetic," as well as: "Ancient and Modern History, Chronology, Geography, Astronomy, and the uses of the Globes, together with branches of Natural History, such rudiments of the Sciences, and such objects of general knowledge as are indispensably necessary to complete the education of an intelligent, elegant and accomplished Female." On the "ornamental" side, the girls could select from "Music, Drawing, Dancing, Fancywork and other [unspecified] ornamental accomplishments."[3] By 1816, Eliza and her daughter also highlighted the bilingual education that the young women in their care would receive. Instead of referring to themselves as Mrs. Fenwick and Mrs. Rutherford, they became "Mesdames Fenwick & Rutherford."[4]

At the end of each term, Eliza and her daughter held public examinations, enabling their students to showcase their useful accomplishments, and a formal ball that allowed them to show off their most important ornamental accomplishment, dancing. The annual ball became the marquee event of their school year. The familiar rhythms and routines of school life provided structure and stability in Barbados's otherwise uncertain social and political climate, and the ball was a way for Eliza and her daughter to mark their own accomplishments as well as those of the students. It was also a good publicity tool, for in the act of making public the achievements of their pupils, they were also showcasing what they could offer to prospective parents looking for schools for their daughters.

Eliza and her daughter were aware of the marketing opportunity their balls provided. In the *Barbados Mercury Gazette* of January 2, 1819, for instance, they wrote a public thank you note to the people of the community who had supported the annual exhibition of their pupils' accomplishments:

> Mesdames Fenwick and Rutherford offer to their Friends and the Public their grateful acknowledgement for the encomiums bestowed on the general improvement of their pupils and displayed at the last Examination and Ball. Nothing short of their most assiduous care and unremitting labour could have attained equal success in the variety of accomplishments taught in their Seminary; and exertions of the same zeal and application on the part of the Teachers, for the benefit of their Pupils, will (they hope) continue to ensure the same happy effects.

The note itself reads as the fulfillment of the teaching dream Eliza proposed to Mary in 1813 and written by Eliza Ann into the first announcement for the school in 1814. Their 1819 "grateful acknowledgement for the encomiums" they received precisely recalls Eliza's desire "to receive an intelligent need of affection & gratitude in return for [her] labours," so fulfilling the "very agreeable promise" of her 1813 vision. The thank you note is significant in that it still conveys optimism in spite of what had gone wrong for Eliza and her family since their arrival on the "Barbadoes Shore."

Things Fall Apart

By the summer of 1815, Eliza was finally able to take pride in the accomplishment of achieving a home of her own in Bridgetown: "a very fine house," she explained to Mary. Although the rent was high, at "£300," the fact that she had fifty pupils and was taking in boarders justified the expense (EF to MH, 3 July 1815). In expressing her pleasure in her new home to Mary, Eliza explains that it is "not connected with any other building" and "its spacious, lofty rooms draw such a current of air through them" that she does not complain about the heat anymore. The beautiful, lofty, spacious home stood as the fulfillment of a long-held dream. Beginning with the earliest extant letters to Mary, Eliza wrote about how much a home meant to her. In 1800, while staying with Mary Robinson, Eliza wrote that she "sigh[ed] now & then for a *home*." By that time, her longing for a "quiet home" had been going on for "six years," during which she had "been tossed to & fro amidst fears & frights & perils" (EF to MH, August 1800). In 1811, she said, "How I pine for a home . . ." (EF to MH, December 1811) and in 1812, in response to a letter from Orlando: "How my heart ached when you spoke of coming home." She also confessed to envying "those happy parents who have a home wherein to receive their children" (EF to MH, 15 March 1812). In September 1816, writing about Orlando's success in his new position, Eliza must have known how much Mary would appreciate the fact that, at last, she could provide a home for him to visit. She explains that Orlando "boards and sleeps at Mr Hozier's [his employer], but he visits us every evening & spends his Sundays with us." Orlando had called it, as Eliza says, their "*delightful*" house (EF to MH, 14 November 1816). Although Eliza had finally succeeded in providing a home for her family, her pride in her accomplishment was soon to be rendered hollow.

Eliza's pride in Orlando as he matured into a self-supporting adult comes through in her description of him to Mary as "quite the Man," though "still the playful boy, with unbounded vivacity." Two months later, however, the ominous prophecy of the "New come buckra" welcome song came true. Eliza's letter of Thursday November 14, 1816 to Mary begins with the impossible news of the "heaviest Calamity" of her life, Orlando's death: "He was dancing here on Wednesday Novr. 6th, while my delighted eye dwelt on the grace & agility of his movements, & the manly symmetry of his figure. The admiration he excited gratified my vain heart, & on the following Wednesday Novr 13th, he was consigned to the grave." Orlando had contracted "yellow fever," described by the World Health Organization as "an acute viral haemorrhagic disease transmitted by infected mosquitoes."[5] Eliza wrote an eloquent memorial tribute to her son, tracing his last days, from the first severe feverish phase, to the lull when there was hope that the worst had passed and recovery was imminent, to, as she says in the letter, the moment when "the fatal black vomitings commenced and then indeed hope expired." He had fallen ill on a Thursday afternoon, had rallied on Saturday, began his final decline on Monday, and was dead by Wednesday. Eliza's eloquent words keep the bright beauty and grace of her son alive as she records his final days and hours, and his final words. After receiving Eliza's heartbreaking account of Orlando's death, Henry Crabb Robinson wrote on the back, "Mrs Fenwick's pathetic note / Her son's death."[6]

Although Eliza's moment-by-moment account of Orlando's death stands, in some sense, as a living memorial tribute to him, she had little time to grieve. The school still had to be run, there were Eliza Ann's two toddlers to take care of, and a third child on the way; a daughter, Elizabeth, was born on April 6, 1817. Eliza wrote to Mary soon after, on May 20, 1817, with an update on how she was coping with her profound loss. For the most part, she just threw herself into her work: "From five in the morning till evening, I have literally not an unoccupied moment," she wrote, "& this wretched condition is my refuge." Nevertheless, she did find consolation in literature: "For reading & writing I have no time," she tells Mary, "but what I take, as in the present case, from sleep." Yet Eliza did let Mary into her world of dark midnight hours. To characterize her grief, she quoted some lines (omitted by Annie Wedd from *The Fate of the Fenwicks*) from S. T. Coleridge's translation of Friedrich Schiller's *The Death of Wallenstein: A Tragedy in Five Acts*, published just a few years earlier in 1800:

> This anguish will be wearied down, I know;
> What pang is permanent with man? From th' highest,
> As from the vilest thing of every day
> He learns to wean himself: for the strong hours
> Conquer him. Yet I feel what I have lost
> In him. The bloom is vanish'd from my life.
> For O! he stood beside me, like my youth,
> Transform'd for me the real to a dream,
> Cloathing the palpable and the familiar
> With golden exhalations of the dawn.
> Whatever fortunes wait my future toils
> The *beautiful* is vanish'd—and returns not.[7]

Eliza's choice of consoling verse marks her acute attention to the literary currents of her time. Yet she moved seamlessly from literature to life, though retaining the cadence of poetry. "A gleam like that of a wintry sun," she wrote, "when Eliza [Ann] passed her critical hour & brought us a little girl, one of the finest babes I ever beheld." That child, Elizabeth, or Bessie, as she came to be called, did prove to be the child who would be the legitimate heir to the talent and strength of character of her mother and grandmother.

Despite the new baby, things were beginning to fall apart domestically for Eliza Ann. Through 1817–1818, her husband William Rutherford begins to fade from the newspaper records and from Eliza's letters. Although he had taught at the school when it first opened, his name soon disappeared from among the roll of teachers Eliza listed in the paper. There are a few references to the theater company he tried to run out of the Garrison, in Bridgetown, and to a newspaper he was supposed to have started called *The Times*, but no evidence of the paper seems to have survived. Nevertheless, despite the losses in their lives, Eliza and her daughter regrouped and continued in the school, the theater, and the community. An extraordinary sequence in the *Barbados Mercury Gazette* from the spring of 1818 provides a window into what their lives were like.

On April 14, 1818, an announcement appeared in the paper for a "Benefit performance" for the Seminary for Young Ladies to be held at the Theatre Royal the following Saturday, April 18. The plays to be performed were: *The Virgin of the Son*, a fairly recent five-act play, first seen in Covent Garden in 1799; *Children in the Wood*, a play and chapbook popular in the late eighteenth century, though originally a sixteenth-century ballad; and *The Register Office: Or, Who Wants a Place*, another late eighteenth-century play. There was also a note saying that "the back boxes were well lit." Things did not go well. On Saturday April 25, 1818, the week after the performance, Eliza Ann wrote a public apology, and had it printed in the *Barbados Mercury Gazette*. It must have been embarrassing at the time, but two hundred years later, her letter provides an intriguing look into cultural life in Bridgetown. At the benefit, the theater was packed. Eliza Ann expressed her "gratitude to the audience who filled the theatre on her behalf." However, the performance didn't live up to expectations, which is why Eliza Ann wrote her apology. She had engaged a Mr. Wilson who had promised to complete all the scenery to her specifications. And she had warned him, she explained in her public letter, that if he didn't come through, she would expose him. She was as good as her word, though in her explanations, there is a wonderful description of what he was supposed to have done.

Mr. Wilson had been commissioned to produce a "Room of Stars," which was supposed to display "all the signs of the zodiac and the constellations."

He substituted it with a two-dimensional painting. Eliza Ann also explained that "trees by a kind friend" were "supposed to move to and fro" in a scene, but they didn't make it onstage. In another scene, "pillars" that were supposed to be secured weren't, and Eliza Ann wrote that "she dared not pass under them." There were also supposed to be fireworks and a volcano, neither of which materialized. Eliza Ann did however acknowledge the continuing support of the community, and said she was grateful for their patronage, which she had known since her arrival on the island, from her first performance six years earlier. And finally, she thanked the audience particularly "for their approbation of the infantine efforts of [her] children," (presumably Will and Tom as adorable young children at ages five and three respectively) who had performed in the roles of the lost babes in the performance *Children in the Wood*. The benefit performance in 1818 was Eliza Ann's last, at least that year. She must have been about six months pregnant as her youngest son, Orlando (Roland), was born soon afterward, on July 6, 1818. That was the day William Rutherford left for Britain.

A few days later, on July 21, 1818, Eliza wrote to Henry Crabb Robinson, telling him the news and asking him to be discreet. She also articulated her sense that her time in Barbados was coming to an end. She writes:

> This place has not proved to me a Haven of repose and the success of my exertions has even added poignancy to other sufferings. Since the death of my beloved son, I have had to apprehend the loss of my no less beloved daughter. Her health has been in a critical state for some time & her constitution is terribly impaired that unless a very speedy renovation takes place, she must try a colder climate. If she *must* wander, I must wander with her, nor will you blame me when I add she has but me to soothe her anxieties & assist in the support & protection of her four infants.

As Crabb Robinson had been so much a part of her London circle in the 1790s, he knew all too well how John's fall into drink and debt had made Eliza's life difficult. The news that her daughter's marriage turned out equally badly must have been hard for her to convey. Eliza wrote with as much grace as she could about the situation:

> She is & has been during the whole of her married life as prudent, as estimable a woman as ever exercised the duties of wife & mother; but (I speak it in confidence) she has drawn an unhappy lot. Company & the prevalent vice of the West Indies (drinking) has detached Mr. Rutherford from his family & his duties. He had become not merely a burthen, but an injury to our affairs when happily for us he determined on going to England,

where I trust he will remain and pursue a better course of life. (EF to HCR, 21 July 1818)[8]

He didn't. When Rutherford arrived in Britain, William Godwin wrote, on September 21, to his wife Mary Jane about their unpleasant meeting. Rutherford "drank three glasses of wine," said Godwin, and "I began to be afraid would want thirteen more." Then, Godwin described Rutherford's physical decay, in that he had become "a sort of greasy, dingy, short and thick player-looking man." He concluded with the astonishing news that Rutherford next took up temporary residence with John Fenwick's brother Thomas.[9]

The School Must Go On

Eliza Ann's declining health and the recommendation that she seek a cooler climate was a source of constant anxiety. The fact that Eliza Ann had four young children by 1819 as well as students in her care and her teaching responsibilities (mostly just dancing by that time) meant that she had little chance for recovery. Eliza, though on the verge of turning fifty-three, had taken charge of most of the day-to-day responsibilities related to running the school and the house. The moral tensions of life in slave-dependent Barbados also continued to take their toll on the family and the school, especially as the slow movement to abolish slavery altogether gathered strength. In 1819, that goal was still fourteen years down the road, but the crumbling moral structure of the society (with rich white men regarding sex with enslaved black women as just one of the perks of slave ownership), the routine cruelty used to keep enslaved people from revolting, and the equally active, organized resistance tactics employed by those people, all made Barbados anything but the "promised land" or "paradise" Eliza and her family had hoped to find. Besides enduring the constant underlying threats of disease, death, crop failures, and slave uprisings, by 1819, they also had another personal crisis to negotiate: William Rutherford's departure had put yet another crack in the family's new foundations, as he had also left a trail of unpaid debts that Eliza and Eliza Ann ended up covering. With Rutherford out of their lives, and not even providing a semblance of male surety, Eliza and Eliza Ann were completely on their own. They shouldered all of the responsibility of running the school as well as raising and educating Eliza Ann's four children. As Roland, the youngest, was born the day his father left, he never knew his father at all.

Despite personal losses and setbacks, what comes across most strongly in the announcements and notes about the school that Eliza and her daughter put into the *Barbados Mercury Gazette* throughout their years on the island, between 1813 and 1822, is their sense of confidence, self-assurance, and authority. They were no longer in need of charity from their friends; instead they had a product, both desirable and profitable, for which there was a market. They had gone from struggling "author" and "actress," respectively, to the owners of intellectual property that was valuable to other people. As esteemed educators to the daughters of the rich, they had reinvented themselves, with new identities, new credentials.

If the transition to Cork constituted the first stage of Eliza's metamorphosis into a respectable, genteel woman, then Bridgetown was where she emerged. The new woman she had become was able to move across the colonial world on her own, inhabiting a social sphere that would otherwise have been closed to her in Britain. The kind of curriculum Eliza promoted is something we would now call "arts-based," heavy on modern languages, art, music, and dancing. The program she developed clearly had been influenced by French and English late Enlightenment educators, and by philosophers she either knew personally or whose work she knew. Though it is difficult to separate individual pedagogical ideas from the pool in which Eliza was immersed in the 1790s, the major figures would have been Mme de Genlis (1746–1830), Ellenor Fenn (1743–1813), Lady Finch (1725–1813), Anna Barbauld (1743–1825), and Maria Edgeworth (1768–1849).[10] The idea that children could be drawn into learning, that it would be something they wanted to do, shaped late Enlightenment pedagogical philosophy and is captured best perhaps in the title of Fenn's 1783 *Cobwebs to Catch Flies.* Or as William Godwin says in his essay "Of the Communication of Knowledge," "Study with desire is real activity: without desire it is but the semblance and mockery of activity." Then emphasizing the point, he insists that "the first object of a system of instructing, is to give the pupil a motive to learn."[11] It took more than philosophy to run a school, however, and in Barbados, Eliza had become an accomplished businesswoman, able to handle the school finances and hire teachers who could be trusted to promote her pedagogical ethos and the school brand she was developing.

Still, with the rise of Eliza's career as school owner and teacher, she was also conscious of how far she had drifted from her literary life in London. Although her correspondence with Mary Hays continued to demonstrate that she was writing her life in letters as a literary work, she does not appear to have even attempted any other kind of writing. In April 1818, though, Eliza did receive a tangible tribute to her former literary self: Hays dedicated her latest novel *Family Annals* (1817) to her. The dedication reads:

To Mrs. Fenwick,

of

Bridge Town, Barbadoes.

While the Atlantic rolls between us, allow me, dear friend, to gratify my feelings, by addressing to you this little volume, as a testimony of that friendship which nearly twenty summers have ripened; and which, founded on a parity of mind and principle, and a sympathy of feeling, neither time nor distance will, I trust, weaken or destroy.

> "Is ought so fair,
> In the bright eye of Hesper, in the morn,
> In Nature's fairest forms—Is ought so fair
> As virtuous friendship?"

The verse is from an eighteenth-century poem by Mark Akinside (1721–70). The sentiment must have been particularly significant for Eliza, especially given the weight of the concept of "friendship." It appears three times in the dedication, in the beginning as "dear friend," then acknowledging the "testimony to that friendship" over almost twenty years, and finally as the "virtuous friendship" from the line in the poem.

On April 24, 1818 Eliza responded to the receipt of *Family Annals*, expressing her delight with its warm dedication to the equity between the two women; the "parity of mind and principle" and the "sympathy of feeling." The first part of Eliza's response to Mary is, however, omitted in the published volume of Eliza's letters edited by Annie Wedd. The missing section reads:

> I yesterday received your kind letter accompanying a production of which I have reason for to be proud since its excellence is such as to confer distinction on her to whom it is dedicated. Ah my dear Mary. Had you seen how my now colourless cheeks flush when I read that dedication you would have done me justice to believe that my warmest affections are still yours though others might have deemed the glow an impulse of highly gratified vanity.

By registering the fact that she was blushing on reading the dedication, Eliza conveys a lovely physical immediacy to her "thank you" from across the ocean. Mary does not explain why she decided to put the dedication on that particular volume. It may have been an explicit way of making up for the earlier promised dedication that didn't materialize. Or perhaps it was an acknowledgement of the fact that because Eliza had entered her new life as a school owner and teacher, her writing life was, for all intents and purposes, over. It didn't matter. What did matter was that the dedication was a tangible link to their shared past, their lives as literary women, though it also marked the divide between them. Mary's new novel signaled that her life as a public, published author continued, while Eliza's writing life shrank to the world of private letters.

The omission of the first part of Eliza's thank you note from *Fate of the Fenwicks* is telling. By leaving it out, Wedd rendered the meaning of the following paragraph, the one she did include, almost incomprehensible. And by giving the letter the chapter title of "Eliza's [Eliza Ann's] Illness," the focus of the letter is shifted away from the literary lives the two women shared, to an emphasis on Eliza's failure and tragedy and Mary Hays's benevolence, which is the story Wedd wanted to tell. Although the published version of the 1818 letter does acknowledge an omission with an ellipsis, the text begins: ". . . I fear I am unworthy of you! Why do I thus continually shrink into myself & retire from communicating with a friend whose value, whose talents, acquirements I am at all times eager to contemplate & proudly to boast of? . . . I shrink from my pen with an undefinable reluctance so potent that I have not courage to contend with it." Wedd also omits the two sentences that follow: "I lament it, I believe, daily to myself yet the days & months wear away & I still have to mourn over the added folly. I bow beneath your tender reproaches when I see them & I still go on, unworthy, as I said before of such a forbearing long-suffering kindness." Given Eliza's self-flagellating response, especially her confession that she "shrink[s]" from her pen, it does sound as if Mary had been trying to urge Eliza to prepare something for publication.

Eliza actually didn't have much time to write as her waking hours were split between teaching, care for Eliza Ann and the grandchildren, and the management of the school and the household. Eliza Ann, as Wedd's chapter title "Eliza Ann's Illness," for the April 1818 letter, indicates, had been growing steadily weaker with each pregnancy and with her husband's increasing decline. On the home front, Eliza had managed to delegate a good part of her household responsibilities. She negotiated a mutually beneficial arrangement with a widowed Englishwoman who had "been left in narrow circumstances by a dissipated Barbadian husband." In exchange for taking in the woman, her two daughters, and hiring her "servants," Eliza was able to off-load all of her domestic responsibilities and concentrate on teaching and running the school.

The school was down to forty pupils by 1818 in the "large & handsome house" at New Bridge to which it had relocated when it outgrew the original school building at Beckwith Square. Eliza Ann by that time was concentrating on teaching dancing, though she was also acting part-time with the newly formed Garrison players. Rutherford, who had initially taught Geography, Writing, and Arithmetic, had been replaced by Mr. Houly, who first turned up in 1816. His qualifications were listed in an advertisement for the school on November 12, 1816: he had "passed a Mathematical examination at the Trinity House London, in September 1813," and had "taught the art of Navigation for some years in the Royal Navy." When he wasn't teaching at the Seminary for Young Ladies, he was freelancing as a private tutor teaching navigation to boys.

Throughout her time in Bridgetown, Eliza worked hard to make sure that her school for girls was the top choice for parents, but she did worry about competition eating into her market share. When another teacher from Britain set up a school for girls in Bridgetown on exactly the same "plan" as hers and had brought a "most accomplished French woman as her assistant," Eliza registered her concern to Mary in a letter from April 24, 1818: "I do not fear her taking any from me that I have, but those who were coming here may, tempted by the novelty, be sent to a newer teacher." The worried tone in Eliza's note indicates that she never lost sight of the fact that the school was a business and that she could never be complacent. In order to survive in what was becoming a competitive market, she knew that she had to evolve. As she had already dealt with competition when another teacher had "set up in opposition" the previous year, she feared that an overcrowded market would cause the whole system to implode. "We shall thus destroy each other," she wrote, "& none of us be able to do more than barely live."

The *Barbados Mercury Gazette* of April 25, 1818 contains information on the school Eliza was worried about. It was going to be opened by a woman called Miss Steeres, with the assistance of "Madame Clothilde," described as "an accomplished Lady." She was the "most accomplished French woman" Eliza alluded to in her letter to Mary, the one who was to be the "assistant" at the new school. Although there are no traces about the sequence of events that followed, by the time what amounts to a registration announcement for Eliza's Seminary for Young Ladies appeared in the *Barbados Mercury Gazette* of June 16 (two months later), Mme Clothilde had left Miss Steeres and had joined Eliza's team. In part, the note reads:

> Mrs. Fenwick has the satisfaction of announcing to her Friends and the Public that Madame Clothilde has become a member of the Family, and being an accomplished French woman, will prove a valuable assistant in the business of the Seminary. Madame Clothilde teaches French, Italian, Music (both Harp and Piano-forte), Drawing, fashionable Works, & c,

& c, Mrs. Fenwick promises herself that her engagement with Madame Clothilde will merit the approbation and support of her friends; and assures them all possible pains shall be taken, in every department of the Seminary, to further the attainments of her pupils.

Although there is something intimate about the announcement, Eliza's sharp business sense is also plainly evident. She wants to make it clear to prospective parents that the most accomplished, fashionable, and desirable teachers to be found in Bridgetown are at her school. Four days after the initial announcement about Mme Clothilde appeared, Eliza added a little more, on June 20, 1818, about her potential value. She emphasized the fact that by having daily lessons with Mme Clothilde, her students would "gain a purity of accent, and a familiarity with the idioms of the language which can only be acquired under the Tuition of an accomplished native of France."

Despite the fact that Eliza seemed to have things under control at the school, Eliza Ann continued to decline. Eliza described her daughter as having "palpitations," suggesting cardiomyopathy of some kind. As the condition was probably chronic, there would likely have been ups and downs. By 1819, Eliza Ann rallied and things at the school were looking up again. After the dip in the number of pupils enrolled, there was a recovery, and Eliza found Mme Clothilde living up to her billing as a "highly accomplished French Woman" who became, as Eliza said to Mary, a "very useful assistant."

Despite the continuing success of the school, the moral decay in the community, the constant threats of yellow fever, uprisings by enslaved people, and her daughter's ill health had all primed Eliza to plan for an exit strategy. But deciding to leave would not be easy. The success of the school had meant financial security and independence, but if the society collapsed and/or the grandchildren succumbed to moral threats, illness, or death, then all would be for naught. The persistent recommendations made by Eliza Ann's doctors that she seek a cooler climate ring as a constant undercurrent in Eliza's letters to Mary through 1819. It was another "should she stay or should she go" moment. A difficult choice.

The first extant hint of a potential exit strategy comes in a letter from August 14, 1819, when Eliza tells Mary that she is writing with a glow she had not experienced since arriving on the island, which had become, she said, "the grave of so many proud & dearly cherished expectations." The happy news she conveyed was that they would all return to England soon, and start a new school, perhaps near Clifton or Bath. Eliza had already lined up twenty students who had promised to come with her. They would be what we would call her "startup" pupils. The note bubbles with happiness as Eliza imagines what her revitalized life in Britain might be like. She didn't want to live in London again, but instead pictured in her mind "a commodious family House with a Garden etc," as she said it would "suit better, though old fashioned in its structure &c than a modern Mansion." What is charmingly clear in the note is that Eliza imagined her return would be triumphant, evidence that she had vanquished the poverty that had plagued her previous life in Britain.

By the time of the August letter, it looks as if Eliza's exit plans from Barbados had been in place for a few months. The hint is in a April 13, 1819 letter Mme Clothilde published in the *Barbados Mercury Gazette,* a denial of rumors apparently circulating about *her* imminent departure for Britain:

> Mme Clothilde is compelled to intrude on the public a positive contradiction of a report that has been circulated by some ill-designing person (evidently with a view to prevent the increase of her Pupils), namely that she is on the point of returning to England. Madame Clothilde assures the Friends who have already patronized her, and the Public in general, that the report is an unfounded falsehood, and that since she engages as Assistant with Mrs. Fenwick, she has never entertained an idea of quitting Barbados, but highly satisfied with her situation, she has not the remotest thought of removal—Mme Clothilde continues to attend private pupils in those hours when she can be spared from her duties in Mrs. Fenwick's Seminary.

As is often the case when trying to puzzle out the facts of a backstory, the question about the source of the rumor is hard to parse. Mme Clothilde's public announcement dates from mid-April, four months before Eliza's note to Mary. Did she know by that time that Eliza was planning to start a new school in England without her? Eliza's mid-August letter to Mary Hays did make point that clear: "The french assistant I have here," said Eliza, "I do not mean to take, because, though highly accomplished in French, Italian & Music, her terms are too high." Eliza asked Mary if she had any leads on the kind of teacher she would need for her new school in Britain: a "mistress of French & if possible a native of Paris and well educated," though also, Eliza insisted, "more willing to attend to subordinate matters." Was there a suggestion in the note that Mme Clothilde was not interested in "subordinate matters"? And what were those matters? Accounts? Attention to weaker students perhaps? Or was Mme Clothilde's public April announcement a way of keeping things on an even keel at the school until the end of term? In the end, the situation resolved itself. As Eliza told Mary a few months later, on her birthday, February 1, 1820, her family scrapped the move to Britain and decided to stay, even though they had booked passage and were prepared to leave.

Eliza was explicit on the reasons for staying. Eliza Ann's health had improved and the school was doing well. In fact, she described her establishment as an "excellent school." They had also "paid all the debts" resulting from "Mr R's unfortunate speculations" (a new theatrical company and possibly a newspaper, *The Times*), and, for the most part, the parents who had defaulted on student fees (when the crops had been bad) had paid up when the crops improved. On balance, as Eliza and her daughter were financially and physically secure, the "stay" side won out. By chance, a refracted image of that decision to stay survives in a description by Eliza's old friend, Maria Reveley, who, upon her remarriage became Mrs. Gisborne. In a diary entry dated Tuesday August 22, 1820, she wrote about a letter she had "received from Mrs. Fenwick" saying that "she is now satisfied with her residence at Barbadoes" and that "she is delighted to think that her plan for coming to England failed in the execution." Then, Maria Gisborne paraphrased Eliza's letter on the moment when the decision to stay rather than go became final: "She describes herself and Elisa [Eliza Ann] sitting at their window, looking at the departure of the vessel, as it moved with extreme slowness, which was to have conveyed them so far away from their happy abode, blessing themselves that they had been thwarted in their project. They had recently given a party of a hundred and fifty persons."[12] Even secondhand, Eliza's account of sitting with her daughter looking at the boat sailing off into the distance "with extreme slowness" is a perfect example of her literary skill. She chose exactly the right image to send to Maria. It reads as cinematic, with the camera behind Eliza and her daughter, capturing both of them smiling, looking out the window as the ship on which they had been booked passage sailed off into the sunset. The fact that they had hosted a goodbye party for themselves and had invited "a hundred and fifty" guests also testifies to their success in the community.

Strangely, just a few pages earlier in her diary, Gisborne had recorded a meeting in London with John Fenwick on Tuesday, August 1. She described him as looking "very old and very poor," and that "he reads nothing, remembers little and says that he has started to forget one half of his life." She then commented on how he "remembered well" a scene at Charles Lamb's house when Samuel Taylor Coleridge and William Godwin had engaged in a heated argument. Coleridge then "took pains to write a long letter on the subject to John Fenwick," she said. She also described John recounting arguments between Thomas Holcroft and Muzio Clementi[13] "in which

H [Holcroft] as usual was rude and personal." Gisborne says that she tried to get news on "the true state of Godwin's affairs from Fenwick," but said he was too far gone: "He seems to know nothing of what is going on in the world, politics excepted, and those but partially."[14]

John had long been gone from Eliza's life. The last mention of contact with him was in the context of Orlando's death in 1816. By 1820, John was, as Gisborne's remarks show, declining. He had met with Godwin only eight times between 1818 and 1822, and died a little later (on December 14, 1823) while still in the care of his brother Thomas, in Limehouse, London. In Barbados, Eliza had said, people took her to be a widow. In a letter to Mary, she said she "would not utter a falsehood if questioned, but it seemed so much a probability, or rather a certainty, that no question or hint ever came across me [to her] one way or the other." Eliza had made the comment because she was afraid that a Barbados acquaintance, a Mr. Johnstone (Lieutenant Johnstone of the 21st Regiment), might visit Mary in London and possibly have reason to speak about Eliza's former life there. That is why Eliza decided to caution Mary against saying that John was still very much alive. Eliza explained: "There is something so awkward & so humiliating in the explanations that would be necessary in stating the truth that I beg you *always* to avoid any mention of that person who has been so unjust a Husband & unfriendly a Father." Eliza confirmed that "they never hear from him or of him, & to all intents & purposes he is morally dead to us." The fact that her daughter's unhappy experience with marriage mirrored her own was not lost on Eliza. She understood the irony completely and noted "how singular" it was that her situation should be her daughter's too. "Three years have now elapsed since Mr. Rutherford left the Island," she wrote, "& we are perfect strangers to his fate" (EF to MH, 21 July 1821).

Thanks to one of Eliza's descendants, Dave Rutherford, the information survives about where William Rutherford washed up after he left Barbados. He had joined a theater company in the Isle of Man, "Mr. Munro's Company of Comedians," that performed there in 1819 and 1820. On January 26, 1820, "a team of new actors" was introduced to perform a tragedy, "Jane Shore," and a melodrama, "Ella Rosenberg." A review reported that "Mr. Rutherford's Dumont, was highly respectable, and delivered with great force and feeling." The review also contained, however, some astonishing and disturbing information: a "debutante; Mrs. Rutherford, in the character of Mrs. Flutterman, whose eccentric humour, blended with kind hospitality, proved happy support to the unfortunate Ella" in the play.[15] Did the new Mrs. Rutherford know, for instance, that her husband still had a wife who was very much alive in Barbados? With four children? Or perhaps they weren't actually married. *The Manx Advertiser* of November 16, 1820 had another bit of disturbing information. "The Gentlemen Amateur Performers," reads the ad, "have undertaken to perform a play and farce for the benefit of Mr. Rutherford, to relieve the very pressing difficulties which this respectable actor and his family labour under, from a series of domestic misfortunes." Does that mean that the new Mrs. Rutherford also had a child? Or children? There is also a strange quotation at the end of the note, from an audience member who had apparently exclaimed that "a second Kemble" had been promised, and that the performance did not disappoint. Given that Eliza Ann had been in a two-year relationship with Henry Kemble, there seems something uncanny, a hint perhaps of a family resemblance between the Kemble family actors and William Rutherford. But the November 16 performance was the last of the season as "Mr. Rutherford moved back to England and took all his scenery with him." In London, Rutherford continued to work as an actor in the 1820s and wrote a play, *Leonidas King of Sparta, Or the Fight of Termopyle.*[16] If he was in contact with Eliza's old London friends, then were they were perhaps too polite to mention it to her in letters or, if they did, no record of that communication survives.

The news of Rutherford's death a few years later did, however, reach Barbados, and was considered interesting enough to be reported in *The Barbadian* of October 2, 1829, seven years after Eliza, Eliza Ann, and the children had left Bridgetown, and two years after Eliza Ann's death in New York. The notice reads:

> In London on 21 July, Mr. William Rutherford, aged 47 years well known in this island as an Actor of some repute. He also established the Commercial Reading Rooms and was Editor and Proprietor for a short period of the Times newspaper. In a moment of mental derangement he drank a large quantity of laudanum, which occasioned his death. "Nor further seek his merits to disclose, Or draw his frailties from their dread abode."

The couplet at the end is from Thomas Gray's famous mid-eighteenth century poem "Elegy Written in a Country Church-yard." There is no mention of Eliza Ann or their children. There seems so much unspoken and opaque in the obituary. Eliza's last comment about him in her 1821 letter to Mary was: "What quarter of the world contains him, or whether he be living or dead, we know not." The cadence of Eliza's line reads as verse, and curiously seems to anticipate the lines from Gray's poem.

In 1821, however, Eliza was on the verge of making the move to leave Barbados with Eliza Ann and the children. The balance of the "should she stay or should she go" equation had changed. Although there were periods when Eliza Ann rallied and her health appeared to be improving, for the most part, it was declining. As Eliza reported to Mary, because the sugar crops in 1820 and 1821 had been bad, the parents of the girls who had regularly paid the school fees were suddenly in default. More ominously, the young of the island were routinely decimated by aggressive outbreaks of yellow fever and other diseases that attacked swiftly and without warning. Eliza wrote movingly about "a lovely & most beloved pupil" who, having left the school on a Friday "in perfect health," was "taken ill on Saturday afternoon and died on Sunday night." Though the old people of the island managed to live dissipated lives, the fact that the young and promising were taken quickly weighed heavily on Eliza. She recognized the cruel irony, writing: "We see disease, poverty & misery lingering on through long & joyless life, while the young, the blooming, the rich, the happy, are suddenly consigned to the tomb."

Despite the constant threats of disease, moral decay, and political instability in the everyday life of the island, evidence of Eliza's continuing joy in the imaginative life of literature shines through. Even as she moved ever farther away in time and distance from her literary life in London, she never lost touch with it, both as a writer and a reader. In December 1821, she wrote to Mary with her critical response to several relatively new works, some now regarded as classics:

> I have not seen Godwin's new book (not new now I suppose), nor had I heard mention of Queen Mab before your letter. I abhor its author, but infinitely more his wife, who of all human beings is the object of my sincerest detestation. I am highly pleased with your account of the answer to Malthus, & glad that he has made a votive offering at the shrine of Christianity. Let us hope it was done in sincerity & singleness of heart.

"Queen Mab" is the title of a famous poem by Percy Bysshe Shelley (1792–1822) first published in 1813, when he was just twenty, and it retains the imprint of Godwin's influence in its radical take on marriage, religion, and the possibility of a very different kind of utopian future. Janet Todd describes the young Mary Godwin as she "pored over a copy of her lover's *Queen Mab*" in her schoolroom at home on Skinner Street, with its "notes [that] were full of Godwin and the books Godwin had recommended to Shelley."[17] Although Eliza's comments appear offhand, they indicate just how attuned she was to the political, social, and literary events of the day. Her remarks require parsing now, but because they speak so eloquently to her continuing engagement with literary life, I am going to take the time here to discuss them.

William Godwin's "new book" was *Of Population. An Enquiry Concerning the Power of Increase in the Numbers of Mankind, Being an Answer to Mr. Malthus's Essay on that Subject* (1820). Robert Malthus (1766–1834) was a clergyman, and the debate he had with Godwin was basically about issues that have turned out to be critical in global politics and economics, including the relationship between population growth and sustainability.[18] Although Eliza hadn't read *Of Population* yet, as the origins of the argument are in Godwin's *Political Justice*, she had a strong sense of the philosophical ground. Mary Hays's account of Godwin's response to Malthus put Eliza back into the thick of the pleasures of philosophical debate, and she returned to the critical language characteristic of her own literary writing. The "votive offering at the shrine of Christianity" recalls her line in *Secresy* on Mrs. Valmont as a "votary of dissipation."[19] And her wish for "sincerity and singleness of heart" echoes the lines in her children's story, "Proof of Love," about the distinction between speaking "sweet kind words" and acting on them.[20] Eliza's note continues with comments and brief analyses of some of Walter Scott's recent novels, *The Heart of Mid-Lothian* (1818), *The Monastery* (1820), *The Abbot* (1820), and *Kenilworth* (1821). She disapproved of his use of "supernatural agency" but liked the "Moral Sublime" in the characters of "Jenny Deans"[21] in *The Heart of Mid-Lothian* and "Rebecca," the heroine in Scott's *The Romance of Ivanhoe*, first published in 1820, indicating that she must have read that novel too.

All of the above references to Eliza's readings are in her 1821 letter to Mary, as published in *The Fate of the Fenwicks*. There is another unpublished section of the letter containing Eliza's comments on her lack of access to recent books, including *Peter's Letters* by John Gibson Lockhart, published in 1819. Eliza then goes on to make reference to Mary's new *Memoirs of Queens*, which had just been published:

> Your life of Catherine of Medici is admirable. I prefer it I think to any other in the book though I am both surprised and pleased with the ingenuity you have used in bringing forward Catherine of Russia's talents so that to lessen our sense of her cruel ambition and sensibility. Poor Queen Caroline's memoir is very interesting and preserves the just medium between partial zeal and prudent judgment. I am glad it was written before she died. . . . Go on my dear friend, continue to exercise your pen, and let your leisure be dedicated, as it has ever been, to the support of good taste and virtue.

Caroline of Brunswick, the much-hated consort of George IV, died in August 1821, but Mary's essay in *Memoirs of Queens* (1821) must have gone to press when Caroline was still very much alive. In fact, the essay begins with Mary's disclaimer on how difficult it is "to speak impartially and dispassionately" about "characters still living."[22] As Eliza's letter to Mary is dated December 1821, she must have read the book and acknowledged the news of Caroline's death in a relatively short space of time.

The list of the books Eliza was reading in 1821 still comes across as impressive, reflecting the continuity of her critical insights and wide interests in social and political events. Given her heavy teaching load, her family obligations, and her responsibilities related to running the school, it seems astonishing that she still managed to read and respond to so many literary works. The fact that she was able to fit thoughtful reading into her demanding life also speaks to the relatively smooth and efficient way in which she had organized the operation of the school. The success of her annual school balls testifies to her own accomplishments and to those of her students. Eliza described the 1821 event for Mary:

> It took place on Friday last, & the Ball room was as numerously & elegantly filled as I remember to have seen it. A school Ball is certainly a pleasing & interesting spectacle, & ours in particular, for the children begin this branch of education early, & the little groups, all in one elegant costume of white sattin trowsers [sic], with lace, gauze or book-muslin frocks, tastefully trimmed, appear like fairies. (EF to MH, 15 April 1821)

Eliza loved the look of the girls appearing "like fairies," dancing in celebration of their achievements. The 1821 ball was both typical and special, as it was the one in which little Elizabeth at "four years & one week old made her first appearance." Eliza proudly told Mary that she had been "so well trained by her Mother" that "she went through a reel & a Quadrille without one mistake either in time or the figure."

Even during the island's economic downturns, Eliza's Seminary for Young Ladies continued to thrive. In a popular school, as all parents who do what is now called "the school run" know, drop-off and pick-up routines can result in traffic jams. Eliza had the situation under control, as her note in the *Barbados Mercury Gazette* of April 18, 1820 demonstrates. She announced a one-way system: "Carriages coming on the morning of the Examination are requested to turn from Broad-street by the house of F. Barrow Esq and to drive off by the residence of James Cummins Esq. which will prevent delays and confusion."

Toward an American Life

Despite the success of the school, with Eliza Ann's health on the decline again in 1821, Eliza deployed the exit strategy she had put into place when she had considered returning to Britain two years earlier. The first suggestion that New Haven, Connecticut, would become their destination appears in Eliza's 1821 letter with the news of the dancing success of four-year-old "little Elizabeth" at the school ball. The people Eliza Ann had known eight years earlier when she had gone to Santa Cruz with Rutherford recommended New Haven, partly because it had a long history as a port for trade with the Caribbean and partly because other West Indian expats had settled there. Some had done business in New Haven and so selected it as a safer place to live for their families. Others, it appears, who had left after the first law to abolish the slave trade had passed, chose America as an alternative in light of the British move toward abolition.[23] In order to put her exit strategy into place, Eliza convinced the parents of six girls to send their daughters with her family to New Haven to become students in the new school she would set up in town. But first, Eliza had to wind down her life in Bridgetown. Clues as to how she did that are in the *Barbados Mercury Gazette* for April 1822.

A benefit performance of Richard Brinsley Sheridan's comedy *The Rivals* at the Garrison Amateur Theatre was announced in the April 13 newspaper, stating that it would be followed by a comic opera with a special performance: "At the close of the first act of the opera, a ballet in which will be introduced A Gleaners Dance [a complicated figure dance] by some very young Ladies and Gentlemen, pupils of Mrs. Rutherford, who volunteer their services for this interesting occasion." The occasion gave Eliza Ann's pupils one last formal opportunity to demonstrate their accomplishments. The dancing school, which catered to boys and girls, had grown naturally out of the Seminary for Young Ladies. And as dance was one of Eliza Ann's most distinctive accomplishments, linked to her professional career as an actress, it was the one thing she was able to sustain as her health declined.

The same April 13 paper also contained the note that "Mr. Houly's Day School for Young Gentlemen" would be reopening the following Monday. In earlier notices about Eliza's school, Mr. Houly appears as one of the regular teachers, though he also ran advertisements indicating that he was freelancing on the side. The fact that he had his own day school by the spring of 1822 serves as another indication that Eliza's teaching staff had been making alternative arrangements for some time. Mme Clothilde disappears from the newspaper record, and she did not go with Eliza to America. Finally, on April 27, 1822, the Seminary for Young Ladies, which had opened in 1814, announced its final school ball:

> Mesdames Fenwick and Rutherford have the honour to announce their last school ball which will take place on Wednesday Evening May 6th at Mason's Hall. As the Seminary will close immediately after the Ball, Mrs. Fenwick is compelled again to request the settlement of Accounts, and to say that it is not in her power to grant further delay. She will dispose of her Furniture and the rest of her Servants in the second week of May.

Although Eliza had eventually given up on the slave rental option, her statement in the announcement that she is about to "dispose of her Furniture and the rest of her Servants" means that she was selling the enslaved people she purchased, as well as her household goods. Despite the fact that classified ads advertising enslaved people as well as household goods were common in the *Barbados Mercury Gazette* at the time, Eliza knew that Mary would not find the transaction at all normal. In her first direct admission that her "clean hands" slave rental option had not worked, Eliza wrote: "It will no doubt be repugnant to your feelings to hear me talk of *buying* Men." Then she tried to rationalize: "It was a long time revolting to mine," she wrote, "but the heavy Sums we paid for wages of hired servants, who were generally the most worthless of their kind, rendered it necessary." Of the eight enslaved people who worked at her house, Eliza owned five in the end, "2 Men, 2 boys and one woman" (EF to MH, 15 April 1821). Eliza expressed her intention of giving freedom to the woman as she was "old" and had "attentively nursed" her grandson Roland when he was a baby, but she was not the one Eliza took with her to America. The one "servant" on the ship's manifest that traveled with Eliza, her family, and the six school boarders to New Haven was listed as an eighteen-year-old female, born in Barbados. She then disappears from the record.

One last item in the *Barbados Mercury Gazette* of June 8, 1822 testifies to the fact that Eliza had achieved her goal of securing a home of her own: an advertisement for the sale of the "Furniture" and "Servants" she decided to dispose of before leaving for America. The copy reads:

> On Wednesday next, the 12th instant, will be sold at the residence of Mesdames Fenwick and Rutherford,
>
> A quantity of Household Furniture, among which are—Sets chairs with settees to match, dining room, breakfast and card tables, bedsteads, sets glass, china and earthen ware; a few articles of silver and plated ware. Also a

quantity of wines and port, a gig and harness, two well-toned piano-fortes, an excellent milch cow—and several Negroes—house servants, &c—an excellent chaise with a good chaise horse and harness, and a lady's very handsome pony.[24]

The advert is signed by H. G. Windsor, who appears to have been in the business of selling other people's household goods as there were other adverts with his name attached. The servants had been classified as just "several Negroes—house servants, &c," not even defined as being "excellent" or "good" as were the chaise and horses. Maybe Eliza was embarrassed by the fact that enslaved people were included among her household goods; maybe not. Maybe she didn't write the copy. But whether or not she did, the ad reveals just how many material possessions she had acquired since the dark days of 1807 when Henry Crabb Robinson, at the suggestion of Mary Hays, had asked his brother to contribute to raising enough funds so that Eliza could "buy common furniture for 2 rooms & a kitchen."

On Arrival in New Haven

The first letter Eliza wrote to Mary Hays "from the New World," as she said, was on September 2, 1822, but by that time she was well settled in New Haven. She had arrived with her family on July 15, and had made it her business to integrate quickly so that she could cover the expenses incurred during the move and begin teaching again in the fall. In describing the transition to Mary, Eliza's tone is upbeat, confident, and forward-looking. She writes: "But it seemed as if fortune favoured our removal, for on the day three weeks that we had eaten, rather sat, by our last melancholy dinner in Barbadoes, surrounded by weeping friends,—on that very day three weeks we dined cheerfully & heartily in Newhaven, surrounded by friends whose Joy at our arrival equalled the regret of our Well wishers across the Atlantic." Eliza loved the town of New Haven, and though she calls it neither a "paradise" nor a "promised land," it had the grace and charm that she associated with Britain. As the ability to draw a scene in words was always one of Eliza's literary gifts, she used it to sketch her new surroundings for Mary:

> Nothing can exceed the beauty of this town. The principal streets look like the fine avenues in Windsor Park, being planted with rows of lofty trees. The houses are all apart from each other, except in the streets of business, & are surrounded by Gardens & shrubberies. The houses are mostly wood, nicely painted, & are seldom above two stories, very compact &

very tasty in their papers & other decorations. It does not look at all like a City (unless you visit the Wharf of a mile long), but like a town or village of Gentlemen's houses.

Eliza's glowing description conveys a sense of renewal, of the possibility of a happy future in the beautiful New England landscape, one that clearly appealed to her:

The Country is covered with Woods & Hills & Cliffs, interspersed with beautiful small rivers, beside the noble expanse of the Sound & the prospect is bounded to the North by Mountains. I believe you know how I always doted on this sort of scenery & really my exclamations of pleasure at some of the woody, deep sunk Glens, or splendid opening of Country, in our rides, have I believe excited a smile among our party, but when I am pleased, I cannot help expressing it.

Eliza was pleased at the welcome, the landscape, and the sense that she was being supported and encouraged in the community of expatriates. On arrival, for instance, her family had been met by two carriages that had been sent by Colonel Thomas Henry Dummett (1775–1839). As Eliza says, "Children, Servant, Dog, Cat, Parrot & Macaw, were whirled away to Mr. Dummett's Country Residence." For the first three weeks of their stay, Eliza and her family were welcomed and entertained.

Despite the pleasure of the summer scenery and the company, Eliza was soon down to work. The first advertisement she placed in an American newspaper, soliciting students for her new school on State Street in New Haven— the town where Yale University (then Yale College) is located—appeared in the *American Mercury* on Monday, August 26, 1822. The entire announcement is reproduced here both because it promotes the idea that Eliza and her daughter had a desirable product to sell, and because it shows how quickly they adapted their curriculum to their new environment:

Mrs. Fenwick and Mrs. Rutherford (her daughter) English Ladies, who have resided several years in Barbadoes, and educated an extensive number of pupils to the satisfaction of their parents and friends, have lately removed, for the benefit of a healthier climate, and have opened a seminary at New-Haven, where young Ladies will be received as Boarders or day Scholars, and carefully instructed in every useful and ornamental acquirement that constitutes an accomplished female education. Gratified by the past success of their system of instruction, Mesdames Fenwick and Rutherford, devote their time unremittingly, to the care and improvement of their pupils. They give an annual examination, when the young Ladies are questioned in the presence of their friends, on the progress of their studies; and

are by this means stimulated to endeavour to excel, and merit the approbation of their connexions. Mrs. Rutherford teaches, very successfully, the
accomplishment of Dancing, and a public School Ball is also given once a
year. Boarders are treated with the utmost kindness, allowed proper recreation, and will find every possible attention paid to the preservation of their
health; while constantly in the society and under the guidance of their Governesses, their manners become formed, and their principles established.

Then there is a rundown of the standard courses offered and their costs: "English Grammar, Reading, Recitation, the Elements of Composition, Geography, use of the Globes, Map Designing, History and Chronology, Writing
and Arithmetic, with Needle Work, $12." And the extras, at $8 each, were
"French, Italian, Spanish Music (Piano-forte and harp), drawing and painting (landscape, figure, flower and velvet painting) and dancing." For boarding
students, board and washing came in at $150 per annum, with each "young
Lady" providing her own "Bed, Sheets, Towels, Spoon, Knife and Fork."

Eliza was so confident in the transferability of her skills that she did not
bother with taking time to settle in. The school was on State Street, a fashionable address, as it was on one of the "nine squares" of the original town.
Just over a year after their arrival, on Friday November 28, 1823, Eliza and
her daughter held their first school ball. Although a recognized and valuable asset in the Bridgetown school, the ball was apparently regarded with
suspicion in New Haven. An announcement of the event, in the *Connecticut Herald* of Tuesday, November 18, 1823, in advance of the ball includes a
rationale:

> Mrs. Fenwick and Mrs. Rutherford hope it will not be considered as an im-
> proper innovation on the custom at present established here, that their Ball
> is prepared for, and appropriated entirely to, the exhibition of the dancing
> of the pupils, in order that the parents and friends of the young ladies may
> have an opportunity of estimating their progress in the accomplishment,
> and in the grace and propriety of their deportment.
>
> The Ball will open with minuets, commencing at 8 o'clock, and after a
> variety of figure dances have been gone through by the pupils, the seats will
> be removed, and every facility afforded for the company to dance.

Eliza obviously felt the need to explain the hope that the ball would not be
"considered an improper innovation," and the purpose to allow "parents and
friends" to see for themselves how much the students had progressed "in
the grace and propriety of their deportment." Eliza also explained the program for the event: minuets to begin, then other "Figure Dances," and then
the floor would be opened to all assembled.

Although the people of New Haven might have been uncertain about the school ball in 1823, it did turn out to be where the orphaned Sarah Butler (1806–88)—who had become the ward of her rich, Rhode Island uncle—met a young Alexander Duncan (1805–89), who had come from Scotland to study at Yale. Eliza's granddaughter, Bessie, as a very old woman in 1890, remembered dancing with Alexander Duncan when she was "five or six," and so, it would seem, at that 1823 ball (she would have been six).[25] Butler married Duncan in 1827, and what Eliza could not have known at the time was how important the Duncan family would become for her family. A trace of that connection survived in Eliza's descendants, some of whom continued to give the name "Duncan" to their children.[26]

In the same November 1823 issue of the *Connecticut Herald* containing the announcement of the first "School Ball" in New Haven, I happened on another little notice a bit farther down on the same page regarding the retirement of Eliza's old London publisher, Richard Phillips: "Sir Richard Phillips of London is one of the few instances of the age, of men who have made a fortune by a course of literary industry. He is retiring from the business, rich—having disposed of a *third* only of his interest in the books of the Interrogative system of instruction, for £20,000."[27] The coincidence of the announcement of Eliza's first American school ball appearing in the same issue of the *Connecticut Herald* as the news that Richard Phillips was retiring "rich," seemed odd. I wondered if Eliza put the notice in herself as the irony would have seemed glaringly sad to anyone who had known them both. She was essentially starting all over again while he was retiring rich, though he'd only disposed of a third of the books in his educational publishing arm. Would anyone in New England have known or particularly cared about Richard Phillips? Whether Eliza put the notice in the newspaper herself or whether it just happened to be there, the point is that Phillips was looking forward to a comfortable retirement in England while she was in New Haven, starting all over again. As Phillips, born in 1767, was a year younger than Eliza, this must have been particularly galling. All the while Eliza had been struggling to make a living, Phillips was quietly raking in the profits from his backlist, including books that Eliza had written for him, something she had known as early as 1812. That is when she had written to Mary to say that she was pitching textbooks to other publishers, including "Law, the Bookseller," because he had been "enamoured of the extraordinary success of that Class Book" she had done "for Phillips under the name of Rev'd David Blair" (EF to MH, April 1812). Although the 150 guineas she had received from *The Class Book* financed Orlando's education, Phillips and then Longmans (who took over the copyright after Phillips retired) continued to profit from it well into the mid-nineteenth century.[28] In New Haven, as Eliza had explained to Mary, she was still faced with the daunting prospect of trying to collect money owed to her in Bridgetown. She had been compelled to leave "£872.17.10 of unsettled accounts in Barbadoes and £185 in Tortola," and had also promised a "12 per cent Commission" to the attorney she had charged with recovering the debt (EF to MH, 2 September 1822).

Eliza had never been one to dwell on past misfortunes, but despite her best efforts to integrate with her family into New Haven society, their initial efforts collapsed. When Eliza wrote to Mary in March 1825, it was with awful news that she and her daughter had suddenly become the subjects of "a string of the most atrocious calumnies" alleged by one of their former West Indian acquaintances, who "among other equally base & odious slanders asserted that Mrs. Rutherford's children were by different Fathers," and even more outrageously that Eliza "had kept a *bad house in London*." In a town as conservative as New Haven, even a hint of slander proved disastrous, and though Eliza's friends rallied and protested, and the perpetrator was charged and convicted, the rumors inevitably tarnished Eliza and her daughter's viability as respectable proprietors of an elite school for girls.

The cruel irony is that the liberal environment of the late eighteenth and early nineteenth centuries—which had nurtured Eliza and given her the intellectual skills and emotional strength she needed to become a self-supporting new genus of woman—required her to present herself to her prospective rich and conservative employers as someone who could be trusted to educate their daughters to the standards of their conservative status quo. Eliza wasn't alone in recognizing that the same intellectual accomplishments that had enabled her to make it on her own also made her suspect.

Another well-known woman in a similar position was Claire Clairmont (1798–1879), Mary Jane Clairmont's daughter. She was a child when Eliza knew her after she had become a member of the Godwin household, and she was just a few months older than her stepsister Mary Godwin. It was Claire who had joined Mary when she ran away with Percy Shelley, and she was there in Switzerland on the night "Frankenstein" was conceived in 1816. At the time, Claire was also having an unfortunate relationship with Lord Byron (1788–1824) and she bore his child, Allegra. Things did not go well. Byron kept them apart and Allegra died. In 1825,[29] Claire was reinventing herself in Moscow as a governess as Eliza was reinventing herself in America as a teacher.

By 1825, with Byron and Allegra dead, Claire was putting geographical and cultural distance between herself and her bohemian past. She wrote to her friend, Jane Williams, from Moscow, apologizing for not having been in touch, but said, "her pen would have been dipt to a black melancholy." She had been "outed." Although she had been promised a position in Moscow, the offer was rescinded, as she says in the letter, because "the charming Miss Clairmont, the model of good sense and accomplishments and good taste was brought up, issued from the very den of freethinkers."[30] If her putative employer had been concerned about Byron and Allegra, Claire didn't report it, saying only that he was worried about "the Godwinish principles she might instill." Though Eliza's connection with "Godwinish principles" on the other side of the world must have been more tenuous than Claire Clairmont's connections, no teacher to the daughters of the rich could afford even a hint of possessing radical beliefs, let alone of scandal. The sad thing is that Eliza had anticipated that when she and Eliza Ann appeared in America with the children, there might be questions about the missing men in their lives. She had copies made of the official documents attesting to the marriage of her daughter to William Rutherford, and of the baptismal records for all four of their children. They are carefully preserved in the William Rutherford Savage Papers in Chapel Hill, North Carolina, all on thin blue paper and all dated September 8, 1822, so all copied just after they left Barbados, signed and dated by the rector of St. Michael's Parish.

Marriage certificate of William Rutherford and Eliza Ann Fenwick. (Courtesy of the Southern Historical Collection, Wilson Library, University of North Carolina at Chapel Hill)

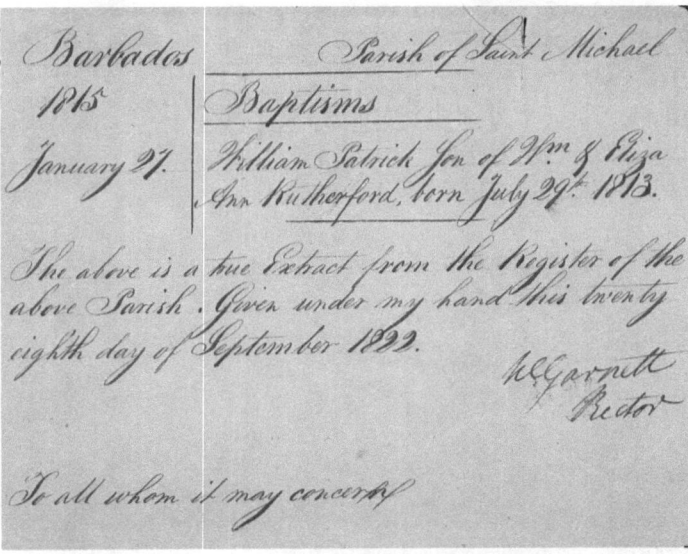

Baptismal certificate for William Patrick Rutherford. (Courtesy of the Southern Historical Collection, Wilson Library, University of North Carolina at Chapel Hill)

Baptismal certificate for Thomas Rutherford. (Courtesy of the Southern Historical Collection, Wilson Library, University of North Carolina at Chapel Hill)

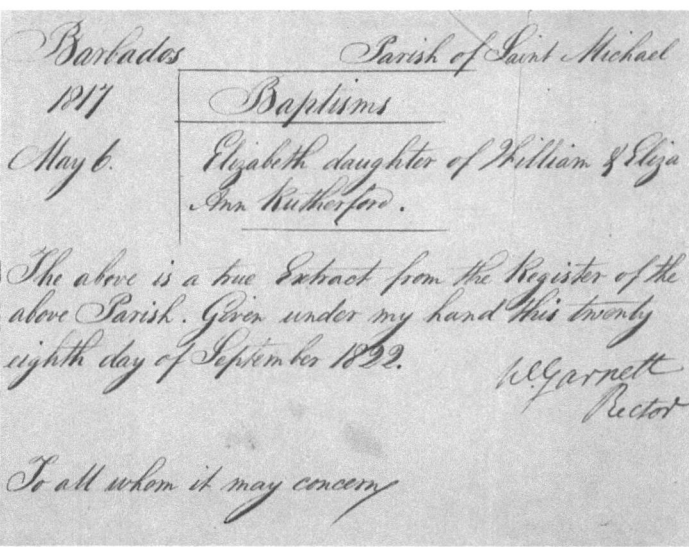

Baptismal certificate for Elizabeth Rutherford. (Courtesy of the Southern Historical Collection, Wilson Library, University of North Carolina at Chapel Hill)

Baptismal certificate for Orlando (Roland) Rutherford. (Courtesy of the Southern Historical Collection, Wilson Library, University of North Carolina at Chapel Hill)

The Chapel Hill archive contains a few other notes, including some of the letters Elizabeth wrote to her son Thomas in 1890, recalling for him memories from her childhood and her brief time in New Haven. She remembered a telling story about William, her eldest brother:

> One day in New Haven, when about ten years old—returning from school he saw boys tormenting a poor wounded bat. A string was tied to one of its legs by which they were whirling it about. William remonstrated, but finding such effort useless, offering to buy it—which he did with the whole of his weekly allowance—sixpence—and put the poor mangled creature out of its pain! (Bessie Rutherford Savage to her son Thomas, 13 May 1890)[31]

The story itself has the hallmarks of the typical eighteenth-century stories about boys torturing helpless animals. Eliza wrote a few in the genre herself, including "The Brown Linnet" (a boy decides to cage a linnet, her chicks die without her, and she dies when a cat torments her though she is in the cage), and "Bad Tricks," in which Charles kicks his dog every time he goes by. The story is also reminiscent of the beginning of Mary Wollstonecraft's *Original Stories,* when Mrs. Mason, governess, on coming across two birds wounded by a malicious boy, decides one is beyond help and puts it out of its misery; she "put her foot on the bird's head, turning her own another way."[32] Whether true or not, the noble image of William as a ten-year-old boy serves to counterbalance the sad adult he became before drowning in Lake Ontario less than ten years later.[33]

Despite the fact that Eliza's friends, especially the Dummetts, rallied in support, the scandal in New Haven was demoralizing for all of them. After a little more than three years in New Haven, Eliza and her family cut their losses and regrouped in New York City, at 663 Broadway, and started another Seminary for Young Ladies. This time Eliza quickly attracted thirteen pupils and made another connection that would remain important for her and for her grandchildren long after her death: the connection with John Moffat and his family.

It looks as if the encounter with the Moffat family was initially made in Vauxhall Gardens in New York. Named for the famed Vauxhall Gardens in London, the New York version must have resonated with Eliza and her daughter. The clue as to it being the place where the Moffats and the Fenwick-Rutherfords first met comes from Bessie, Eliza's granddaughter, on October 31, 1836. In a letter she talks about the decline of Vauxhall Gardens and comments on the moment when she met her friend, Adeline Moffat: "It was there," says Bessie, "that I first saw you Adeline." The Vauxhall Gardens were close to where Eliza lived on Broadway and where the Moffats lived on Mulberry Street. Adeline (1815–80) was just a bit older than Elizabeth, but they became friends as teenagers in New York and kept up their correspondence throughout their lives. The Vauxhall pleasure garden had long been destroyed, but the relationships between the Moffats and the Fenwick-Rutherfords endured through the nineteenth century.

Although the move to New York had given the family a fresh start, Eliza Ann's health continued to decline, and Eliza steeled herself to the inevitable end. On October 15, 1826, she wrote to Mary of her "hourly apprehension of seeing Eliza draw her last painful gasp." Eliza Ann did live a little longer. Her children were still very young. It takes no stretch of imagination to see how desperately Eliza Ann must have wanted to survive for her children, realizing that in America they would only have their aging grandmother to care for them. A tender relic from that period survives in the Chapel Hill archive, written by William Rutherford to his mother during those first dark days in New York. It is a birthday note, written on May 25, 1826 in beautiful copperplate on very thin paper. William would have been thirteen.

My Dear Mama

I am very glad that it is your birthday but I hope you will have a great many happier ones than this, and I beg you will give me a kiss.

Your affectionate son William Rutherford

It was not to be. Eliza Ann died less than two years later on March 26, 1828. By the time of Eliza's next extant letter to Mary, on April 15, 1828, there is something anti-climactic about Eliza Ann's actual death. Unlike the shock of Orlando's sudden death in the prime of his youth and health, Eliza Ann's death, as Eliza well knew, had been approaching for some time. Once Eliza Ann was gone, Eliza knew that she would be solely responsible for her four orphaned young grandchildren. "She is gone," Eliza wrote, "& I meet the cares that remain with a torpid indifference that at times even surprises me." Eliza conveys how numb she had become. The next sentence from Eliza's letter was omitted from the published correspondence: "In my misery I often go back to old times & wonder whether you also partake of that indifference to all the cares that yet may come." With the death of her daughter, the closure of her New York school, and the day-to-day needs of the four children in her care, it is no wonder that "misery" had replaced optimism. All the risks she had taken for the financial and social security of her family had come to naught. Yet Eliza was given another chance, an unexpected chance, to find solace, success, and the possibility of a future one more time.

After the death of her daughter, Eliza closed her school and moved to "a handsome house," as she described it, at 11 Bond Street in New York. It was large, accommodating, "in a Style of a genteel private family, three families who engaged to board & reside . . . for a year." Eliza had taken it over from a woman who had been unable to meet the demands of running a complex household. For Eliza, the work provided a welcome distraction, as she explained in her letter of April 15, 1828, the last of the extant letters to Mary published by Annie Wedd in *The Fate of the Fenwicks*.[34]

Across the road from the boarding house Eliza ran, at 14 Bond Street, lived John Jordan Morgan (1770–1849) and his wife Elizabeth (1782–1853).[35] Elizabeth Morgan's sister, Mary Breakenridge (1791–1871), had just been widowed. Her husband John (1791–1828), a lawyer in the Upper Canadian town of Niagara (now Niagara-on-the-Lake) had died suddenly (on April 3, 1828), leaving her pregnant with their fifth child. Elizabeth Morgan and Mary Breakenridge were both sisters of Dr. William Warren Baldwin (1775–1844), a physician, lawyer, and influential politician in York (before it became Toronto) in Upper Canada.

No correspondence has surfaced on exactly how or when the decision was made to convert the Breakenridge home at 240 Centre Street in Niagara into a school. But at some point, it must have become clear that Mary Breakenridge, with five children to support, and Eliza with four grandchildren to care for, could consolidate their respective resources in order to build a future for themselves and the bereft children in their care. Breakenridge had the house and the family connections, and Eliza had the experience and the expertise, to establish a school. They could support each other and provide a financially and emotionally stable environment for all the children, which is what they did. As the next chapter is on Eliza's life in Upper Canada and how it became the place where she achieved the kind of financial and social security she had so long sought, this chapter ends on Eliza's teaching life, in the familiar territory of school. If she had left New Haven under a cloud of scandal, and if New York had left her broken and numb after the death of her daughter, then the act of beginning a new school in Niagara revitalized her.

In an advertisement that appeared in the *Niagara Farmer's Journal* of April 22, 1829, Eliza articulates her vision for the school that she would run with Mrs. Breakenridge. She promises an educational experience she knows she can deliver. Her goal, she writes, is: "to inspire them [her students] with a zeal for exceling in their studies; and, where timidity of disposition or slowness of capacity render a child incapable of excelling others, still by noticing with approbation every step towards improvement to delight her with the consciousness of excelling her former self." The advertisement reads as reaffirmation of the vision Eliza first articulated in 1813 from Cork, then brought to life in Barbados, New Haven, and New York through the 1820s, though lingering traces of Thomson's lines from "Spring" have all but disappeared. On the cusp of a new decade, Eliza was about to bring to life her vision of what education could be one more time. Her refinement of the model of ideal teacher-student interaction is key here. The emphasis is now on the idea that children are different and so need different kinds of instructional methods in order to make good progress, although she did articulate the same idea in her initial assessment of the Mocatta children as their governess in England in the early part of the century.

To end this chapter on an upbeat note, here is a demonstration of how Eliza could take her whole history of experience and expertise, and make it something new—something that would evolve, take root, and thrive in a new environment. If Eliza's last extant letters to Mary Hays were filled with loss and resignation (she addressed her last one to Mary as her "DEAR & ALMOST ONLY FRIEND"), then her letters from Niagara to the Moffat family seem to bubble over with pleasure, hopes, and plans for the future.

240 Centre Street, Niagara-on-the-Lake. (Sketch by Robert Montgomery in P. J. Stokes, *Old Niagara on the Lake;* © University of Toronto Press, 1971)

The Niagara Seminary for Young Ladies had opened in the late summer of 1829, and by Christmas, Eliza had accomplished her first goal: to hold examinations by the end of first term. "My success *in it*," she says, "was equal to my wishes. All the first & *best* people *here*, attended, & we hear from all quarters encomiums & predictions of good fortune" (EF to John Moffat, 7 January 1830). Eliza upgraded the environment in the school, replacing the "Dreadful smoky chimneys" in the house with "five [new] stoves." She had hired "a Quaker Lady from Europe" as "an assistant in the system of school business." And when the Quaker had to leave a few months later, Eliza efficiently went about finding a replacement. A glimpse of the kind of teacher she was looking for survives in a note she wrote to John Moffat, asking if he had a line on a potentially suitable candidate:

> We require particularly Writing & arithmetic & a competent knowledge of Geography & English Grammar. If possessing other accomplishments (Drawing for instance) so much the better, and we wish to find one who had sense enough to be a steady disciplinarian and a temper patient and amiable enough to make herself loved as well as respected. We use neither whips, rods, or canes—No blows are ever struck.[36] (EF to JM, 19 April 1830)

The "teachables" Eliza required were consistent with her pedagogical agenda for a curriculum both "useful and ornamental." There was also a touching, though silent, allusion to her earlier contribution to progressive education. Her assertion that "no whips, rods or canes" are used in her school and that "no blows are ever struck" shadows her own lines from her children's book *Visits to the Juvenile Library* (1805). In the novel, Eliza depicts the enslaved nanny Nora's mistaken equation of education with punishment, with the "terrors of rods, canes, dark closets and stocks."[37]

Evidence survives from the period around 1830 demonstrating that Eliza was a successful teacher, and that her pedagogical ethos worked: "Mrs. Young of Canandaigua," Eliza says in a letter to John with only a hint of pride, "who sent Miss Havel to me as a pupil was so pleased with her improvements that after her return home she wrote me a letter saying she did not think the changes by any means equal to the labour I had bestowed on Jane, & requested my acceptance of $50 as testimony of her gratitude" (EF to JM, 7 Jan 1830). Just a few weeks shy of her sixty-fifth birthday, Eliza had earned a bonus for her teaching success.

Here is just one final image, one that demonstrates Eliza's adaptability. She had taken the old annual school ball, something that had been so much a signal event at her Barbados school, and recreated it as a "coterie." She described the event to John in 1831:

The damsels were all in plain white frocks without any ornaments. Many are very handsome & all looked well. I added 24 youths of the elite of the community—several Papas and Mamas came. They began and ended dancing punctually & I never saw better manners nor more cheerful countenances. The expenses were provided for including Fiddler & 3 shillings each to our servants for their trouble at 90 cents less than the amount of the 2 shilling subscription from members alone. . . . I am quite in fashion.

That's where I'll leave Eliza at the end of this chapter—in fashion and surrounded by young people.

7

North American Grandmother

As the deaths of Will and Tom mark the beginning of this book, the beginning of its end starts with an analysis of the extant evidence as to why Eliza wrote about the day they drowned as the *end* of her "deep, *deep* [family] tragedy." The surviving evidence represents judgments made by unseen censoring hands, long-dead hands that decided what information would be preserved into the future and what would not. Because the hole worn through the page of Eliza's letter containing the news of the deaths of her grandsons was made just at the point at which she was explaining why they had been refused a boat that fateful day, it stands as material testimony to the fact that someone was determined to excise the information. Eliza's line in the letter reads, "They applied for a boat, it appears, but was refused, the owner perceiving th. . . ." Whatever it was the owner perceived has been erased. It is tempting to supply the missing word, to make the line read, "perceiving them drunk." That would fit. Intoxication would have been visible in the way that some other intermittent disability (epilepsy perhaps) would not have been.

The extant material from the 1830s about Will and Tom says only that, when they entered their early teens, they began to suffer from what Eliza sometimes called "fits," and that those fits seem to have struck them both around the same time. In a related vein, Eliza, in writing about Roland at eighteen, said that he too had been showing "symptoms of losing health & tendency to his brothers' complaint" (EF to Dora Massa, 29 September 1839). Possibilities as to what that "complaint" might have been emerge from the medical literature of the period read in the context of the surviving scraps from letters by Eliza and her granddaughter Bessie.

In the immediate aftermath of Eliza Ann's death in 1827, all four of her children were doing well enough for Eliza to report that her "poor Orphan Children are blooming with health, & pursuing such courses as would have fulfilled their Mother's utmost wishes" (EF to MH, 15 April 1828). That news was in the last surviving letter Eliza wrote to Mary Hays. At the time, Bessie and Roland were still in school, but Eliza had turned her attention to planning Will and Tom's careers (as they were ages fourteen and twelve, respectively) in much the same way that she had done for Orlando fifteen years earlier. The news Eliza gave to Mary was that Will and Tom had both been "apprenticed in a most extensive Manufactory of Gold & Jewelry." Although Eliza did not name the concern, it was the company of John Little Moffat (1788–1865).

The New York directories from the period list John Moffat as a metallurgist or a silversmith with a business first on 84 Prince Street, and then on 68 Spring Street (the address to which Eliza sent her letters to his family). Moffat was a partner in the assaying firm of Wilmarth, Moffat, & Curtis at the time Eliza first knew him and his family, probably in 1825.[1] In Eliza's letter of April 1828, everything seemed happily settled for Will and Tom in that they would receive apprenticeship training and continue their studies, all the while under the protection of one of the partners, that is, under Mr. Moffat himself. Eliza describes him as an "excellent & talented man" who "devotes himself to the care of the boys." Later, after it was clear that the apprenticeship had gone badly, Eliza still acknowledged the fact that it had been Mr. Moffat who had been so encouraging and supportive in the aftermath of her daughter's death: "You first inspired me with hope for them," she wrote, "and still I look with perfect confidence on your friendship & protection in case of need from them, though so far removed from your immediate observation" (EF to JM, 19 April 1830).

The Lives and Deaths of Will and Tom

In 1828, however, Will and Tom were still in their early teens, on the cusp of their adult lives. As they had been young children in 1818, just three and five when their father left, the presence of a stable father figure was important enough for Eliza to emphasize John Moffat's role as a surrogate in her letter to Mary. Eliza trusted that, under his care, both boys would become well educated and well trained for secure careers. "They have also Masters to attend in the Evenings," Eliza explains, "& prosecute their usual School studies, which is very important to me, as Tom was too young to send out, but his wishes to be with his Brother were too urgent to be denied." Eliza's comment on Will and Tom as inseparable in 1828 resonates eerily with her letter to the Moffats six years later, with the news of their deaths and the poignant memorial comment that the brothers "have lived together, have suffered together and have died together" (EF to JM, 13 April 1834).

Inspired by the hope for Will and Tom that John Moffat had provided, Eliza could see, in the aftermath of her daughter's death, a way forward.

With the two eldest launched under the care and protection of the Moffat family, she could take up the teaching position in Niagara in order to provide for her two younger grandchildren. But their apprenticeships did not last. No reasons were given, but when Eliza wrote to John Moffat in January 1830, both boys were with her in Niagara and she was trying to facilitate new work options for them. Will and Tom had run away from their apprenticeships in New York, so Eliza's letter to her friend that winter reads as a model of perfectly modulated damage control, in that she gracefully puts a positive spin on what must have been a particularly awkward situation. As Moffat had invested in Will and Tom, partly as a way of helping Eliza cope with the daunting task of raising her orphaned grandchildren, the defection of her two eldest could only have been acutely embarrassing.

"Thank you my dear & ever kind friend," Eliza wrote to John Moffat, "for your wishes still to serve my deserters." She assured him that despite the flights of Will and Tom, both boys continued to speak of him and his family with "respectful & affectionate remembrances." Eliza then shifted her perspective, affirming that both were still on track for alternative careers: Tom "to York [prior to becoming Toronto] with a young man . . . who is commencing business in that city," and William "to Mr. James Crooks, the greatest Capitalist of this province [Upper Canada] who has a paper Mill—a Saw Mill—a fulling Mill, a Flour mill—Iron works & a dozen other things."[2] At the time, Mr. Crooks was a particularly valuable contact to have in Upper Canada, and the fact that Eliza had managed to develop some kind of working relationship with him so quickly is another indication of her well-honed networking skills. Even though she had only recently arrived in Niagara and was busy with the Niagara Seminary for Young Ladies, she had managed to negotiate on behalf of her grandsons with, as she says, "the greatest Capitalist" of the province. Eliza's basic message in her letter to John Moffat was that, at sixteen and fourteen, the future still held promise for Will and Tom. She even tried to put an optimistic twist on the situation by saying that "had William run away from Spring Street one night sooner," he would have been in line for "an excellent appointment" in an "Engineering department."[3]

That Will and Tom had run away from New York in a hurry and under dubious circumstances, probably in September 1829, is evidenced by the fact that they left some of their cherished possessions behind. Eliza wrote to John Moffat to ask that the items be returned from New York. Her inventory of those items provides an intimate glimpse of what Will and Tom were like, a window into their childhoods. Eliza wrote out the list of the items in a long column down one side of her letter, in the margin. A small portrait emerges of the lively, intelligent, and curious boys Will and Tom must have been when they were young. Among the items they wished to have returned were a "Bow & five Arrows belonging to Buck Indians," as well as an "Ashantee Sword & Belt," "hunting pouches," a "head ornament for Chief," a bag "woven without Seam," a "Cap with feathers," a "Jaw bone," and "pieces of back bone." There was also "a long blue box of minerals," evidently acquired during their apprenticeship in metallurgy. As for the box, Eliza simply suggests that Mr. Moffat keep it so that his "boys" could have "the privilege" of its contents, as her boys could "no longer use it" (EF to JM, 6 June 1830). Although Eliza's request for the return of the items must have been awkward, her delicate handling demonstrates again her unfailing commitment to the children in her care.

The first extant news that something was slightly amiss with Will and Tom appeared in Eliza's note to John Moffat in January 1830. Yet she was still reassuring: William "has not had any more fits," she reports, "& we miss the squirrels & wild ducks which his Gun procured us from the woods." That is the first mention of fits and in saying that Will had not "had any more," she was obviously indicating that Moffat would understand the condition to which she was referring. She continued in a resolutely positive vein on Will's industry after his arrival in Niagara: "He devoted a part of every day either to study at home or drawing in the Engineer's office. They both left Niagara on the same day Thursday the 7th Inst. I hope beginning the New Year well" (EF to JM, 7 January 1830). Although 1830 may have started on a promising note with Will and Tom fixed in new situations, the promise was short-lived. On April 19, Eliza was still hopeful. "My spirits & mind are excited by our favourable prospects," she writes, "& perhaps still more by the good success of my boys." By June, though, her optimism was fading. Eliza received the news from Mr. Crooks via a friend, Mrs. B. (Butler or Breakenridge), that William's employment was in jeopardy. In a letter to the Moffats, Eliza wrote saying that though Mr. Crooks had bestowed "gratifying praises" on William's "steadiness, intelligence, manners and principles," he had spoken "with almost paternal regret of his fits," which had "been of quick recurrence." As a kind of safety precaution, Mr. Crooks—saying that he "feared to trust him [William] among the machinery of his vast concerns lest a fatal accident might occur"—let him go. Sometime between April 1830 and March 1831, William returned to Niagara. Despite the loss of the position, Eliza, ever optimistic, wrote that William was "not depressed in spirit," that his regular letters were "written in a delightful tone of animated contentment," and that she was still hopeful that the "fits" would "leave him" (EF to JM, 6 June 1830).

One Model of an Indian House made by the South American Indians commonly called Buck Indians living near Demarara with their utensils Canoes, Hammocks, Cassada sieves &c &c.

1 Bow & five arrows belonging to Buck Indians

1 Ashantee bow — 2 Quivers one containing 20 poisoned arrows — the other 10 do

1 Ashantee Sword & Belt

3 Ashantee hunting purches

1 Ashantee head ornament for Chief

1 Bag wove without Seam

1 Cap with feathers belonged to Chief of the Buck Indians

Sharks Jaw bone & pieces of back bone

Box of Minerals

These were left at Mr Peales in April 1829 & the two boys were allowed free entrance to the rooms from that period till they left New York in Sep

List of possessions belonging to Will and Tom Rutherford, written down the side of an interior page. (Fenwick Family Correspondence, MS211, box 2, folder 1; courtesy of the New-York Historical Society)

For a modern reader, the immediate association with the word "fits" is "epilepsy." Eliza began alluding to the fact that both boys had been getting worse in some way, as the "fits" seemed to have increased in intensity and frequency. On March 3, 1831, she explained that she had declined an invitation to holiday with her close friends the Duncans in Upstate New York because of Will and Tom: their "fits," she wrote, "might create dismay in the family." She also wrote to say that though "an excellent situation" was available for William, she would not "dare allow him to go to it." On a more hopeful note, she said that if Will and Tom "were cured of their malady," Mr. Crooks [their potential employer] would "gladly receive either."

It is possible that both boys did have late-onset epilepsy, a condition that does apparently run in families. Another possibility is that they had "idiopathic" tetanus, a form of tetanus not caused by specific wound. Given the rough dating for the onset of their "malady," they would have had to have contracted it while in New York. The treatment Will received for his fits matches the early nineteenth-century protocol recommended as a remedy for tetanus. "William is now having caustic applied to the spine," wrote Eliza on October 31, 1831, "and the exemplary patience he displays under his various tortures endear him to everybody." The treatment didn't work. By October 1832, Eliza had lost the optimism that had characterized her earlier notes and referred to her eldest grandson, for the first time, as "my poor William." As hopes for a positive outcome faded, Eliza wrote that "the tide flows altogether in Bessie's favour while her brothers struggle vainly against an opposing current."

The fits from which Will and Tom suffered clearly impacted their ability to find and sustain employment, and it is possible that besides whatever medical condition caused their fits, they also—following patterns set by their father William Rutherford, and by their grandfather John Fenwick—succumbed to excessive drinking. The evidence is scant except for the fact that the man who refused them a boat on the fateful day on which they drowned must have noticed something immediately visible that informed his decision: two young men presenting as drunk, rather than as prone to fits, seems a more likely guess. How Eliza and Bessie characterized the afflictions of Will and Tom is unclear, but it is worth noting that alcohol addiction was increasingly discussed as an illness in the early nineteenth century. As Matthew Osborn explains in *Rum Maniacs,* there was suddenly a new "medical and popular conviction that heavy drinking could itself be a disease."[4] Late in life, Eliza did in fact use the word "disease" explicitly to characterize what afflicted her grandsons: "that fell disease," she explained, "not content with defacing all without, destroyed all within" (EF to Reuben Moffat, 22 February 1839).

The letters written by both Eliza and Bessie during the period have been cut apart, with only fragments, such as the line about the boat owner "perceiving" something amiss, providing hints as to what went wrong with Will and Tom. Although there is no information about who censored the letters, or when, it looks as if anything hinting at deviation from middle-class respectability was excised. By the late nineteenth century, Eliza's descendants had rooted themselves solidly in respectable North American life. Bessie had married an American physician who was also a missionary and a naturalist, Thomas Staughton Savage (1804–1880). Their four surviving children (their first child, a daughter, had died in her teens) consolidated their position: Alexander Duncan Savage (1848–1935), the eldest son, became a curator at the Metropolitan Museum of Art in New York. Thomas Rutherford Savage (1851–1918) became a physician. Their third son, William Rutherford Savage (1854–1934), was a clergyman, and their daughter Jessie (1858–1940), an artist, married a clergyman, Thomas Cole (1856–1923).

A note in the New-York Historical Society archive, written by Jessie Cole (Bessie's youngest daughter) to her brother William on the receipt of the manuscript of Annie Wedd's *Fate of the Fenwicks* suggests that preserving the upstanding reputation of the family was at stake. Although there is no date on the letter it was probably from 1926 or early 1927, just prior to the publication of Wedd's volume. Jessie on reading the manuscript was horrified to learn that her grandmother Eliza Ann Rutherford had been an actress. She writes: "I never heard before of our grandmother going on stage—possibly Mamma either didn't know it, or hid the knowledge of it, since of course our father has that old time Puritan horror and prejudice." It seems unlikely that Bessie didn't at least know that her mother had been an actress, especially as her own earliest memories, even if they were fragmentary, must have included knowledge of dancing on stage in Barbados too as a young child. By the 1920s, Eliza's American descendants were solidly conservative, and if even the knowledge that Eliza Ann had been "on the stage" had been unsettling, then the specter of a history of mental disease and/or alcohol abuse would have been beyond the pale. Jessie made it clear that she intended to protect the legacies of her mother and grandmother, but details of what that meant are absent. Only the fact that there is an entire file of letter fragments in the New-York Historical Society archive testifies to the deliberate shaping of the archival remains. The surviving fragments do, however, contain very brief traces (on the reverse sides of the pieces that were meant to be kept) of what is missing, just enough to indicate that Eliza wrote about her failures and worries as well as her successes and hopes.

Through 1832 and 1833, as news about Will and Tom faded in Eliza's letters, the news of Bessie and Roland increased. Roland had been sent to the Duncans' in Canandaigua (in Upstate New York) to apprentice in the printing business, and Bessie had been sent to study in New York. Funded by the Duncans, she was living with the Moffats and, unlike her brothers, was a model of good behavior. Eliza again affirmed her gratitude to John Moffat. "I do not forget the shelter you gave me & my cases in 1828," she wrote, "and now your parental kindness to Bessie . . . has often cheered my despondency in hours of lonely painful reflection" (EF to JM, 11 April 1833). Sarah and Alexander Duncan had remained friends of Eliza and her family from their New Haven days. In recognizing their early connection with her, they graciously functioned as patrons as their own wealth grew, helping Eliza establish her grandchildren and providing respite for Eliza as she aged.

Eliza's move to Upper Canada College, in what was still York (soon Toronto), in 1833 had been precipitated by Mary Breakenridge's declining health. Although the Niagara school had been doing well in its initial phases, Breakenridge's repeated periods of indisposition did not bode well for its survival. Eliza first described Breakenridge as being "seriously ill" in 1832, and as being cared for by her brother, Dr. William Warren Baldwin, in York. Eliza left a year later. In giving up her position at the Niagara Seminary for Young Ladies, Eliza faced the end of her quest to become a self-supporting businesswoman in a home of her own.

As Will and Tom were increasingly slipping away in 1833, milestone political events occurring on the other side of the world were not likely at the top of Eliza's concerns, but given her history, they are worth noting here, especially given the intersection of the political events in her own personal trajectory. In London on July 26, 1833, the Slavery Abolition Act was passed by the House of Commons (just three days before the death of William Wilberforce), and became law on August 28, when the bill received royal assent.

Eliza's focus in the period was still on supporting her grandchildren, especially difficult given Will and Tom's steep decline. Information on the extent of their situation comes not from Eliza, but from Bessie, in her letters to her friend Adeline Moffat. If Eliza was circumspect in her accounts, Bessie was blunt. As many of her letters were cross-written (written on one side, then turned ninety degrees so as to economize on paper), there is a sense that she felt she could be more open with her friend than she might have been otherwise, as cross-written letters were harder to read and/or share. And it is perhaps the difficulty in reading the cross-written letter that

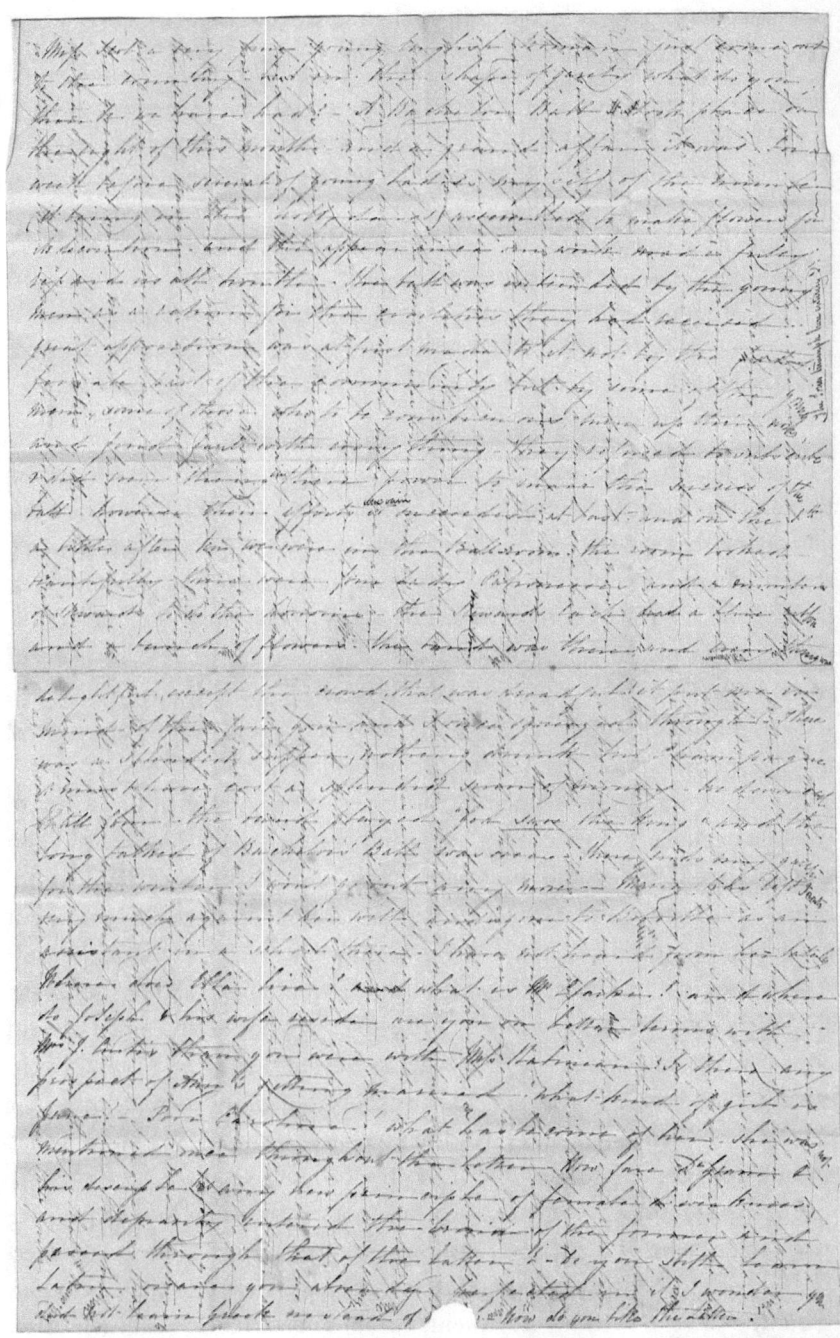

Cross-written letter from Elizabeth Rutherford to Adeline Moffat, January 1834.
(Fenwick Family Correspondence, MS211, box 2, folder 1; courtesy of the New-York
Historical Society)

facilitated its escape from later editors' hands. Bessie's letter of January 1834 has the most damning account of her brothers:

> No change for the better in William & Tom. In William I see none one way or the other but Tom I think grows worse & worse every day. Poor, poor Tom, what a dreary life he has before him cut off from all the pursuits of life in that manner. William has long ceased to feel his misfortune & talks of nothing but going back to his former occupation in New York. But Grand-mamma is the most to be pitied for Tom will soon be the same as William. She has nothing to look forward to but constant labour & I was going to say misery but I hope not. O, Adeline when I am getting ready for a party these thoughts will come to my mind and I turn sick to think I can be seeking enjoyment while *they* are so unhappy.

At the time, Eliza was actually encouraging Bessie to enjoy herself during the difficult descent of her older brothers. Eliza wrote explicitly to the Moffats saying that she wished that Bessie "was removed to some safe & happy shelter where she could not share in the distressing scenes that altered her family." Of the four grandchildren, Bessie was the most like her grandmother Eliza and her late mother Eliza Ann. "She is my pride & my solace," wrote Eliza (EF to John Moffat, 10 April 1834). In February 1834, Eliza turned sixty-eight and resolutely faced the fact that there would only be more work, more responsibility, and more disappointment in her future.

On April 6, 1834, Bessie, just before her seventeenth birthday, wrote to Adeline again, adding at the end of an otherwise cheerful note: "William and Tom are very bad, the latter particularly." A few days later, on April 10, Eliza wrote to the Moffats with overtly casual, conversational updates, but the dark undertones in the letter are unmistakable. "My first year at the College expires in a few days," Eliza says. And "I would not willingly quit," she continues, "for here I have conveniences for my poor Grandsons I should not easily get anywhere else." The other sad event that Eliza relayed was in the next sentence. The Niagara Seminary for Young Ladies was closing for good: "Mrs. Breakenridge is forced to give up the school—or rather it has given her up & her family will have to provide for her & hers."

Eliza communicated the news—of her "poor Grandsons," her continuing work, the closing of the school, and Mrs. Breakenridge's future being cared for by her family—in a series of blunt statements of fact, one after the other. It is impossible to read the statements composed starkly against each other without feeling the pain of the contrast: there was Eliza facing a future of "constant labour" in order to continue to care for her two eldest grandsons;

and there was Mary Breakenridge, with a family willing and able "to provide for her and hers."

With the demise of the Seminary for Young Ladies in Niagara, there was the end of Eliza's colonial quest for total financial independence. Like the schools she had run in Barbados, New Haven, and New York, the Niagara school had been successful, but unsustainable. A hauntingly disparaging comment made about girls' schools in Upper Canada by Charles Duncombe survives in his 1836 "Report on Education."[5] There he describes "female institutions" as "ephemeral." He explains that "in most cases every thing depends upon the character and enterprise of a single individual. A school may be at the height of prosperity one week, and the next week entirely extinct. Communities seem almost entirely dependent upon chance, both for the character and perpetuity of female schools" (39). Duncombe, as it happens, had been one of the correspondents of Robert Baldwin[6] at a time when Eliza would have been close to the Baldwin family. If Duncombe discussed the Niagara Seminary for Young Ladies with the Baldwins, nothing survives in the archive. Duncombe does, however, support an intellectual course of study in his report, and he echoes phrases that ring close to the sentiments expressed by Eliza, sentiments clearly channeling Mary Wollstonecraft. He explicitly names as the object of female education both "the physical, intellectual and moral education of children" and "the care of the health and the formation of the character of the future citizen" (41). The qualities of the women he imagines will be entrusted with the task of being companions, friends, and educators of the next generation align perfectly with Eliza's plan for educating the girls in her schools. And that was the plan she had developed in concert with Wollstonecraft, William Godwin, Mary Hays, and the other philosophers, educators, and publishers of her late Enlightenment circle in London.

The qualities Eliza identified in her ideal teacher also match the ones Duncombe sketches. He too suggests that a teacher of girls and young women should be characterized by "her warm sympathies, her lively imagination, her ready invention, her quick perception," as well as her "patient attention, calm judgment, steady efficiency and habitual self-control" (41–42). He also names "those qualities of the head and the heart" as those replacing the "weeping, vapid, pretty plaything" as the model of female loveliness (42). He champions the study of mathematics, as well as "pursuits designed to cultivate the taste and imagination, such as rhetoric, poetry, and other branches of polite literature" (44). Duncombe's report has other characteristic phrases that seem to have come from the rhetoric of the promotional materials for Eliza's schools, especially in the attention to the child-student relationship, and in regard to the capacity of all children to learn. His lines in the report read: "As the care of the intellect is the business of teachers, we find that some success always attend these efforts. However dull the child or incompetent the teacher, at the end of each year it will be found that every child has learned something, and the memory at least if no other faculty is to some extent cultivated" (47). His lines affirming that it is the job of the teacher to make sure that all children improve ring uncannily close to the lines quoted in the previous chapter from Eliza's 1829 advertisement for her school in *The Niagara Farmer's Journal,* promising that "where timidity of disposition or slowness of capacity render a child incapable of excelling others, still by noticing with approbation every step towards improvement to delight her with the consciousness of excelling her former self." Duncombe's report did not appear until 1836, but its preparation in the mid-1830s coincided exactly with the time that the Niagara school, which had opened with so much promise in 1829, was coming to the end of its viable life.

After Eliza had made so many auspicious attempts at establishing a bright future for her family, the first months of 1834 must have appeared especially bleak. At sixty-eight, Eliza was, in early nineteenth-century terms, an old woman, and she was facing the gloomy prospect of continuing damage control as Will and Tom spiraled downward. The letter of April 10, 1834 is the one that was "unsealed" and "seemingly finished" on her desk prior to the deaths of her grandsons two days later. In the context of that letter, the postscript with the news and the note that their "deep, *deep* tragedy is ended" suddenly makes sense. It is Bessie who provides the retrospective reading (in a cross-written letter) on why the deaths of Will and Tom brought an end to the tragedy of their lives. On June 15, 1834, she wrote to Adeline:

> This day eleven weeks ago I was last writing to you. It was my birthday, and the last Sunday William and Tom were with us. We weren't I can't say happy, but we were together and little thought what misery the next Sunday would bring us. I cannot realize that they are dead—that they should die & we surviving be so reconciled. I can only think how wretched it would have been had this happened Some time ago before their misfortune preparing the way warned us of what we might expect. Seven years ago we could not have borne their loss. We could not have dreamed that those bright beautiful boys would ever have been transformed into what they were lately. Their existence gave neither pleasure to themselves nor to us. They will ever live in our remembrance before we thought with pain as to what might

become of them—and now they are peacefully and happily provided for. Their death was sad but had it been otherwise it would not have been in unison with their lives.

Bessie then acknowledges the condolences she has received from Adeline, and reaffirms her recognition that the deaths of Will and Tom just marked the end of a steady seven-year decline. "Loss it cannot be called," she wrote, "For while we weep over the remembrance of their bright images in former times, late misfortune has made us resigned to the thought, that in leaving us forever they have left their dreadful malady." That Bessie specifies that the "malady" afflicting Will and Tom had started seven years earlier dates the onset explicitly to their lives in New York, just as they were entering their teens.[7]

The deaths of Will and Tom at nineteen and twenty-one changed Eliza's view of her future and the future of her grandchildren. "While they lived," Bessie explained, her grandmother "felt she was necessary to them and though her mind was in torture yet she was in health" (ER to AM, 30 March 1835). Their deaths, Bessie observed, "relieved her [Eliza's] mind," but "injured her bodily health." Eliza had done the best she could to educate Roland but he lacked what she called the "animal high spirits" of his namesake, her beloved Orlando. Although Roland ultimately escaped the affliction(s) that had so devastated his brothers, he lacked the intellectual drive that marked his late uncle Orlando, or his sister Bessie.

In an 1839 letter to her old Barbados friend, Dora Massa, Eliza provided a recap of Roland's life in Upper Canada. At twenty-one, he had settled into his adult life "as a husband & father & farmer on the wild land in the Back woods of Canada." At the time, Eliza obviously felt the need to offer an explanation of his life, and it is here that she demonstrates how her years as an educator had honed her pragmatic understanding about the relationship between individual ability and education. Although Eliza had sent Roland to apprentice with a farmer while still in Niagara, when she took the post of mistress of the boys' boarding house at Upper Canada College (still an elite school for boys in Toronto), she was able to give him "a six months renewal of useful schooling" there while he lived with her. Eliza characterizes Roland as having "an excellent temper," and she says that he was "kind, obedient & docile," but that he had no "particular ambition towards *study*." Eliza makes visible the difference between Bessie and her younger brother. She cites Bessie's "annoyance" at his lack of intellectual drive, explaining that, with her "constant desire for improvement & never failing application [Bessie] was provoked that her brother yawned over his tasks or learned them imperfectly." Eliza concludes the update with what stands as a telling character sketch for the difference between industry and idleness:

> It would have amused you as it did me to hear her [Bessie's] motherly lectures to him & see the deferential air with which he, a tall stout fellow big enough to swallow her listened to her reproaches & promised amendment. In the half year he had gone through a considerable portion of Euclid & made in Bookkeeping some progress & I thought it injurious to keep him longer from farming, particularly as the tall lads who were his associates in my house & fond of his good humoured & cheerful society were all training towards professions & abounding in *Gentlemanly notions & predilections.*
> (EF to Dora Massa, 29 September 1839)

With Roland moving toward the life of a farmer in the backwoods of Canada, Eliza and Bessie settled into their lives in the burgeoning urban hub that Toronto was becoming. Both Eliza and Bessie commented on the name change of the city from York, just before the deaths of Will and Tom. "What Adeline," wrote Bessie to her New York friend, "do you think of our change of name—Toronto is much prettier, is it not—and what do you think is the reason given by some—because it was frequently called 'little York.'" Eliza, like Bessie, thought Toronto "a prettier name," and she also liked that it reflected "the original designation."[8] Eliza, ever aware of the political climate, also noted that there had been "some opposition . . . to the change," but was "surprised to observe how readily it has been adopted."

By the mid 1830s, Toronto was fast developing into the urban center of Upper Canada. Three hundred new buildings had been erected there in 1830 alone. A lovely image of the city survives in an unpublished manuscript, *The Bonnet Box Letters,* in the Baldwin Collection in the Toronto Public Library. Although the manuscript itself was composed in the late nineteenth century, it was made up of letters between Phoebe Maria Baldwin (born February 27, 1828), the first grandchild of Eliza's friend William Warren Baldwin, and members of her family. The text begins at exactly the moment of the name change from York to Toronto: "York for all its cliques and political differences was growing up and by 1834 it had reached a population of more than ten thousand, having grown from a few hundred at the beginning of the century, and it was now time for it to be incorporated as a city while at the same time the name was changed from York to the Indian name of Toronto signifying 'a place of meeting.'"[9] The Lieutenant Governor of Upper Canada at the time was Sir John Colborne (1778–1863), 1st Baron Seton. Just a few years younger than Charles Lamb (1775–1834) and Samuel Taylor

Coleridge (1772–1834), like them he had been educated at Christ's Hospital School in London. By the time he arrived in Upper Canada, however, he had served as lieutenant governor in Guernsey. In the *Dictionary of Canadian Biography,* he is described as "Upper Canada's ablest governor."[10] Eliza and Bessie were friends of Sir John and Lady Colborne and of Lady Colborne's sister, Jane Yonge. No record survives of whether or not Eliza knew that John Colborne had tangible links, in a tangential way, to her literary London life and to people who had been close to her. Eliza and Bessie were, however, friends of the Colbornes[11] in the 1830s, a time of rapid expansion, industrialization, and the first moves toward political reform in Upper Canada.

Eliza's uncanny knack for landing in moments later characterized as defining episodes of social and cultural change followed her right to the end. In Upper Canada, she was witness to the increasing tensions of the mid 1830s that culminated in Mackenzie's Rebellion of 1837 and eventual political reform. Both John Colborne and William Warren Baldwin were instrumental in early attempts to negotiate between competing factions. Both were also involved in the establishment and support of Upper Canada College, and were influential in encouraging Eliza to take the position of mistress of the boys' boarding house in 1833.[12] There is in fact a note that Bessie, as an old woman, wrote to her son in 1890, when she was attempting to fill in the gaps of family history for him. "The school in Niagara," she wrote, "was not successful and in less than four years, my grandmother, advised by a firm friend, Mrs. Breckenridge's [sic] brother [William Warren Baldwin], to move to Toronto and took charge of the college boarding house of preparatory students."

At some level, the shift for Eliza from being mistress of her own girls' school to being employed to look after boarders at a boys' school might look like a comedown, but it was in her last working years—between 1833 when she arrived and 1838 when she retired at seventy-two to the United States with her friends the Duncans—that she finally consolidated her aims for social and financial security. She even owned property in Upper Canada.[13] After Will and Tom died, Eliza successfully shepherded her two surviving grandchildren into their adult lives, enabling them and their descendants to take root in the new world. On her own, without any male support, Eliza succeeded through a combination of her intellectual gifts, hard work, and networking, administrative, and social skills to become the "new genus" of self-supporting, thinking woman Mary Wollstonecraft had envisioned in the late eighteenth century.[14] Eliza was an early nineteenth-century immigration success story, a self-made version of Pygmalion. Only by reading Eliza's literary works and her letters chronologically and in the context of her transatlantic odyssey does the remarkable process of her metamorphosis become visible.

A few scattered images survive of what Eliza was like when she lived in Toronto in the mid-1830s. Bessie, at the end of a letter to Adeline, charmingly invokes Eliza: "Grandmamma has just taken off her spectacles and I expect every moment to hear the usual call of 'Come girls, are you not thinking of bed?'" (Bessie Rutherford to Adeline Moffat, 19 January 1834). In a letter to Dora Massa, Eliza, describing herself in August 1838, says, "I could not walk from room to room without my sticks & frequently required Bessie's arm besides" (EF to Dora Massa, 29 September 1839).[15] And in a slightly self-mocking sketch of how Roland's prospective in-laws potentially perceived her, Eliza wrote in that same letter that as she "lived in an immense & very handsome house with many servants & every appearance of comfort, they might naturally conclude me to be a wealthy old Dowager able to give my Grandson a fortune." Eliza was describing the residence at Upper Canada College in which she lived and worked as mistress to the boys of the school. Accounts of what the buildings and grounds looked like at the time include one by Thomas Rolph, someone we might now call a travel writer, who lived in Upper Canada between 1833 and 1839: "a plain, but spacious building, or rather series of buildings," he says, "with fine graveled walks and neat shrubberies in front." Rolph also credits the Lieutenant Governor, Eliza's friend John Colborne for the status and success of the new school: "This admirable institution stands a proud monument of the paternal affect which Sir John Colborne felt for the province; against every discouragement he persevered until he succeeded fully in establishing it, and it will doubtless long remain an honour to the province, and the means of diffusing the highest branches of knowledge to hundreds of her sons."[16]

Upper Canada College in 1830. (Upper Canada College Archives, Artcat 0000.3661; courtesy of Upper Canada College)

The event that prompted Eliza to leave Toronto and retire to the United States was a sequence of skirmishes that came to be known in Upper Canada as Mackenzie's Rebellion of 1837. Though apparently comfortably settled in Toronto in the late 1830s, Eliza found herself caught yet again in a battle zone. The reforming forces led by William Lyon Mackenzie (1795–1861)[17] clashed with the conservative forces (representing what was known as the Family Compact) led by the incoming Lieutenant Governor, Sir Francis Bond Head (1793–1875).[18] John Colborne, incidentally, had been appointed as the new Governor General (one level up from Bond Head). At the root of the conflict was the fact that the Family Compact—primarily composed of a small group of men, mostly British immigrants who shared close family and/or social ties (a kind of old boys' club)—held all the political power.

Eliza and Bessie knew people on both sides of the conflict, people whose names survive on Toronto streets and landmarks. The leading figures on the conservative right were Bishop John Strachan (1778–1867) and lawyer and first Attorney General of Upper Canada, John Beverley Robinson (1791–1863). William Warren Baldwin for the most part occupied a conciliatory middle position in the debates, though his son Robert (ultimately a powerful figure in shaping Upper Canada) was on the left. Leading the reform charge was Mackenzie. His name remains celebrated in Toronto, but those who stood with him during the rebellion, such as Samuel Lount (1791–1838) and Peter Matthews (1789–1838), aren't memorialized publicly. Both were tried and executed for their parts in the rebellion. Eliza, remember, had been close to scenes of others getting tried and executed for rebellious and/or treasonous actions. There was James Coigley, whose trial and execution in London were recorded in detail by her own husband John in 1798. And Eliza was in Bridgetown in 1816 when the leaders of Bussa's Rebellion were summarily tried and executed.

Although things came to a head with an armed revolt—which began officially on Monday, December 5, 1837 at Montgomery's Tavern[19]—the tensions between the reforming left and the conservative right had been simmering for some time. Eliza, ever alert to her vulnerability when caught in the shifting winds of political change, outlined some of the issues. She began in 1836, at the moment when John Colborne was leaving his position as Lieutenant Governor, and was about to be replaced by Sir Francis Bond Head:

> Our dear Governor and darling Lady Colborne are gone, left us amidst the tears & blessings of many hundreds of good people. He was the prop of the College which I fear may now totter to its foundation. We have got

a reforming parliament laboring to pull down whatever their predecessors built up. . . . Whereabouts reform & economy are first to begin or where they are to end cannot yet be stated in any definite form. (EF to JM, 10 February 1836)[20]

Eliza and Bessie both began alluding to the potential threat Mackenzie posed to peace and security. Bessie, writing to Adeline, also began with praise of Colborne, who had been promoted from Lieutenant Governor to Governor General by that time, saying that, "Even McKenzie [sic] the author of these late commotions is awed and powerless" (Bessie Rutherford to Adeline Moffat, 31 October 1836). By 1837, the House of Assembly in Upper Canada, as British author Anna Jameson (to whom I'll return) helpfully records in *Winter Studies and Summer Rambles,* was made up of "sixty-two members: forty-four are Conservative members, and eighteen are Reformers" (91).

The rebellion itself was quickly put down. It began on December 5 and was over a few days later. Susanna Moodie recorded the period (though not quite accurately), and the departure of her husband to join the government forces being marshaled to put down the rebellion, in *Roughing it in the Bush.*[21] Eliza, writing to Reuben Moffat (John's son) in New York a few months after the rebellion was suppressed, sketched the events in the context of the fact that Mackenzie had fled to the United States after the rebellion and had gathered supporters:

I fear I should have filled my sheet with invectives against certain of your Countrymen who infest . . . the frontier line opposite our Canadian shore. . . . I have read such falsehoods in print as made me shudder almost as much as when I heard of the horrible Miscreant Mackenzie with his rabble forces being on the March to burn plunder & destroy our poor city of Toronto & Massacre the leading inhabitants. Through the mistaken faith of our Governor we were on the very crisis of such an event, unarmed, unprotected by any military force, and it now seems a dream long past, to think of the extraordinary & simultaneous flocking together from all quarters of brave hearts & hands devoted to their constitution & eager to protect it & its supporters even at the hazard of their lives. I turn from the odious rebellion. . . . (EF to Reuben Moffat, 30 April 1838)

Mackenzie escaped to the United States and remained there, in exile, for the next ten years. He wrote books and continued as a journalist, eventually returning to Upper Canada in 1849, by which time the political winds had shifted to favor his views. He was pardoned, held elected office until 1858, and died in 1861.[22]

Eliza's loathing of Mackenzie's campaign for political reform marks the completion of her moves from the left of the political spectrum to the right over the course of her lifetime. What would Mary Wollstonecraft have said about Eliza's remarks on Mackenzie? Or what would William Godwin have said? Or her husband, John Fenwick? They had all fought so hard in the 1790s for reform. Yet from when she was faced first in 1816 with the slave rebellion in Barbados, and then in 1837 with Mackenzie's Rebellion in Toronto, Eliza had completed the shift—to adopt Marilyn Butler's phrase—from rebel to reactionary.[23] In Toronto as in Bridgetown, the tipping point was that the threat posed by the reformers was never only political; it was also personal. Eliza feared for the safety of her family, and in one of her last letters to Mary Hays before leaving Barbados, she said so: "I should die here with a painful impression of the various disasters that might overwhelm her [Eliza Ann] & her Children in sudden ruin,—our storms,—our hurricanes,—but above all the fatal insurrection which we constantly dread," she confessed, as they "prevent the soothing consciousness of being *at home*" (EF to MH, 21 July 1821). Faced with similar threats in Toronto, Eliza finally took the opportunity to move, one last time.

Mackenzie's Rebellion and the Beginning of the End in Upper Canada

On the scale of historical events recognized as significant enough to stick in the global cultural imagination, Mackenzie's Rebellion does not register. Yet for Eliza it must have felt like the outermost ripple emanating from the seismic world-changing events that occurred during her lifetime. As a child she would have been witness to her parents' commitment to Methodism as a new radical form of religious practice. She was ten in 1776 at the start of the American Revolution, and twenty-three when the storming of the Bastille in 1789 signaled the beginning of the French Revolution. In her twenties and thirties in London, she was living in the midst of people articulating the moves toward parliamentary democracy: Thomas Paine in *The Rights of Man* (1791), for instance, and William Godwin, of course, in *Enquiry Concerning Political Justice* (1793). Eliza's own understanding about the intellectual rights and freedoms of women came out of her close relationship with Mary Wollstonecraft, especially out of *A Vindication of the Rights of Woman*. Eliza also saw the legislated end to the slave trade in 1807, and to slavery itself in 1833. She had been witness to the dangerous and destructive consequences of the movement toward freedom, especially during the "Terror" (1793–1794) in the aftermath of the French Revolution. And in London in the 1790s, she had firsthand experience of the government's attempts to block the kinds of political reforms advocated by her husband and his friends. As Eliza began her colonial journey, the ripple effects of moves toward a more egalitarian world were in sync with her own moves: the rebellion of San Domingo (now Haiti) bought, at a price, the end of slavery and colonial rule on the island (1791–1803), and then Eliza witnessed, close up, the consequences of Bussa's Rebellion in Barbados in 1816. In Upper Canada, the brief outbreak of violence that was Mackenzie's Rebellion was actually a small blip in what was otherwise a slow legal process toward constitutional reform.

Eliza turned seventy in 1836, but despite diminished hearing, sight, and mobility, she was obviously as intellectually sharp as ever in both her reading and writing. In a letter she sent from Toronto to the Moffats, she began with a literary apology for her tardy response to a previous letter. "One of our English literati," she writes, "whose posthumous letters have been published either to show his strength or weakness says in excuse for long silence, 'You know I love you too well for it to be necessary to be punctually proving it to you, so when I have nothing new worth your knowing I repose myself upon the persuasion that you must have of my affection'" (EF to JM, 10 February 1836). Eliza had been reading the first of four volumes of the letters written by Horace Walpole (1717–1797) and quotes from his 1744 letter to Horace Mann.[24] She quotes another line from the same letter, an ironic note of regret that "letter writing is one of the first duties that the very best people let perish out of their rubric." Eliza, however, did not let that happen. An indication of how much she was valued as a correspondent is found in her response to a letter she received from John Moffat's son Reuben in 1837 requesting that they be regularly in touch. Eliza was flattered and delighted that a seventeen-year-old young man who had known her nine years earlier, when he was just a boy, should seek her out. She wrote to say that she had recently received a similar request from "one of the most gifted youth of our [Upper Canada] College." "Scarcely had the surprise of that request subsided," Eliza wrote, "(& before the correspondence commenced) when your letter arrived; you are nearly of the same age, both talented & rightly principled and proud I may well be that I am the chosen friend of both" (EF to Reuben Moffat, 18 September 1837).

By 1838, Eliza had seen enough of rebellion and its consequences. She had received an invitation from Sarah Duncan to retire to the Duncan's new home in Sodus Bay, New York, and to have Bessie come too as a governess to Sarah's young daughters, and with Eliza's youngest grandchildren almost fully grown it seemed a prudent decision to accept. It was during those final years of her life that Eliza also began alluding more explicitly to her early life and, perhaps unconsciously, to a characteristic feature of her own literary life. In a letter written to Reuben from Toronto, she again apologizes for the tardiness of her response to his previous letter, but this time, with a refracted glimpse of her childhood self and her literary history: "I remember hearing My Mother say that as a child I was at all times either sinning or repenting, being ever prompt to do wrong, as to confess it in penitence, & slowly the habit has grown with my growth & now in my old age I am sinning in the neglect of absent & dear friends & then deeply repenting my frailty" (30 April 1838). "Sinning and repenting" is the key phrase here, as it is exactly the same construction Eliza had used fourteen years earlier in one of her notes from New Haven to Mary Hays, not long after her move from Barbados: "I go on sinning & repenting," she wrote, "under the powerful imperious influence of pecuniary disappointments" (EF to MH, 24 March 1824).

Although Eliza records that her childhood predilection for "sinning and repenting" mutated as she aged, rooting it in her childhood signals that it had its origins in one of the characteristic features of the early Methodist doctrine of self-examination, promoted by John Wesley himself in the mid-eighteenth century. Eliza's father Peter Jaco was a star in that mode. In his autobiographical essay, published in the first issue of the Wesleyan magazine the *Arminian* in 1778, Jaco featured himself as "a poor, naked, helpless sinner," the "very one for whom Jesus Christ died."[25] The dramatic tension held in the crisis of sinning and repenting, as Eliza recalls her mother noting, was obviously attractive to the child who would become a novelist.

There is something quite charming in the image of the child acting out the adult game of sinning and repenting. It's a kind of playacting, a performance, as in Sigmund Freud's account of his eighteen-month-old grandson playing a "fort-da" game, by throwing out and reeling in his toy. As Freud says in "Beyond the Pleasure Principle," his grandson was experiencing the pleasure of control.[26] In a similar vein is Frances Hodgson Burnett describing how she beat her gutta-percha (black rubber) doll in order to play out the scene of Uncle Tom and the sadistic Simon Legree from Harriet Beecher Stowe's *Uncle Tom's Cabin* (1852).[27] Although Eliza had apparently abandoned her Methodist roots in her teens, as a writer of both stories and letters she took the drama of her sinning and repenting childhood and repurposed it, rescripted it. To borrow Robin Bernstein's term from *Racial Innocence,* she'd made a "scriptive thing" of her propensity for sinning and repenting.[28] At the end of the story about Eliza's life and letters, her late-in-life reference to sinning and repenting stands as a characteristic feature of all her writing, something that links her published work with her unpublished.

In her writing for children in the early part of the nineteenth century, Eliza often turned to scenes of sinning and repenting to mediate between the real and the imaginary in her books for children. Here is just one example, from a story called "Birthday Gifts" in *Lessons for Children* (1813), about good little rich boy Harvey Clayton who, because of his exemplary goodness, is to receive from his father a special present on the occasion of his tenth birthday: a pair of globes in mahogany stands, as he later finds out. Because he has been so very good, his father also offers to grant "any favour Harvey should ask of him" as an extra birthday gift. Three weeks prior to the day, however, Harvey is enticed into taking out a rowboat for what is supposed to be a harmless, pre-school spin with a few other boys. Once he gives into temptation, the sins escalate: an oar is lost, the boys have to be rescued, a hat is lost, his schoolbooks are held to ransom, he misses a lot of school, he sneaks in and out of the house, he is reprimanded for being distracted, and he has to sell some of his possessions to pay off the costs to the owner of the rowboat who wants compensation. Harvey, who is so used to being good, is horrified to find out how a moment's pleasure can get out of hand so badly. As the day of his birthday dawns, everyone is dressed up and prepared for the celebration. Harvey enters the room: ". . . his cheeks quite pale, and his eyes red and swelled with weeping. He turned his head away as he passed the globes, and dropping on his knees before his father, he said,—'Oh, Sir, you promised to grant me a favour this day, pray let it be your forgiveness! I know I do not deserve your pardon, but if you will forgive me this once, I am sure I never, never can deceive you again.'"[29] Harvey then delivers a complete written account of his transgressions. His father, though "shocked and surprised," sees that the sinner genuinely repents. The beautiful new globes are put away until the following year when Harvey has shown himself exemplary.

Eliza seems to have recognized that the sinning and repenting scenarios of her fiction were analogous to the ones that that shaped her life. Her initial decision to have her daughter trained to work in the theater, for example, and the events that followed from that decision must have haunted her, especially Eliza Ann's move to Barbados and her disastrous marriage to William Rutherford. At the time, around 1812, Eliza seems to have been uncannily prescient about the future. In a response to what must have been Mary Hays's warnings (likely filtered through rumors) about the dubious character of William Rutherford, Eliza—standing on her faith in her daughter's decision to marry him—made a vow: "I shall pray for a lengthened life," she writes, "that I may endure as I ought to do the Just punishment of my own errors" (EF to MH, 22 September 1812). Eliza did endure, and despite the deaths of her own children and two eldest grandchildren, she did live to see Bessie and Roland prepared to take on adult lives of their own and settle into their new world homes. If, as an old woman, Eliza felt that her early "errors" in life had cost her social or financial security or even a literary career to which she had aspired in the 1790s and early 1800s, she did not dwell on her losses. But as people who had connections with her literary life in London were turning up in her Upper Canadian social circles in the 1830s, it is hard not to wonder whether or not they ever met and reminisced.

Literary Life in Upper Canada

Besides John Colborne, two relatively well-known female British writers (both important in Canadian literary history) also arrived: Susanna Moodie (1803–1885) in 1832, and Anna Jameson (1794–1860) in 1836. Although there is no evidence that Eliza, Susanna, and Anna knew each other, they had friends in common, both in Britain and in Upper Canada, and their paths overlapped. In tracing the respective journeys of Eliza, Susanna, and Anna in Upper Canada through the mid-1830s, although it is possible to show where and when their paths might have crossed, all that remains is a ghost trail. What does emerge, however, is that whereas Susanna and Anna's voices were the ones that shaped the Canadian historical imagination of the 1970s soon after the centennial celebrations in 1967, Eliza's was the voice for Canada's sesquicentennial. In 2017, as Canadians began to celebrate the 150th year of confederation, a national redefinition in the context of the welcome to tens of thousands of Syrian refugees was also taking place. The enthusiasm with which Canadians embraced private sponsorship programs in particular served to consolidate a distinct identity, one defined in opposition to the increasingly xenophobic and nationalistic protectionist policies developing in other ostensibly democratic parts of the world. In contrast to Susanna and Anna, who both saw Upper Canada as a threatening, inhospitable place, Eliza—writing in exactly the same period about the same places—saw a welcoming community and place that felt like home.

Susanna Moodie, the youngest of a family of literary sisters in Britain, the Stricklands,[30] arrived in 1832 with her baby daughter and her husband John Wedderburn Dunbar Moodie, who had been "a lieutenant in the 21st Regiment of Fusiliers." As Susanna explains in the introduction to the 1871 edition of *Roughing it in the Bush*, Dunbar Moodie was "the youngest son of Major Moodie, of Mellsetter, in the Orkney Islands" and so not in line to inherit. Susanna's explanation of how they got stuck in the backwoods of Canada still reads as a warning example, a story of immigration failure.

As was typical for "younger sons of old British families," he was not "over-gifted with the good things of this world," and so took up "the grant of 400 acres of land, ceded by the Government to officers upon half-pay."[31] In a last-ditch attempt to make a life for himself and his family, Dunbar Moodie and his family arrived first to settle on a partly cleared farm in Cobourg, Hamilton Township in 1832, though they moved in the winter of 1834 to Douro Township, then a new settlement near present-day Peterborough, Ontario. "Emigration," as Susanna says emphatically, "is a matter of necessity, not of choice" (7), and *Roughing it in the Bush* stands as testimony to how miserable she was, how exploited, and how weird, primitive, and incomprehensible she found life in Upper Canada. Susanna's slightly older sister, Catherine Parr Traill (1802–1899), also emigrated in 1832 with her husband Thomas Traill, who had been Dunbar Moodie's friend, as both were in the same regiment. Like her sisters Agnes and Susanna, she too was a writer. Rather than Susanna's fictionalized account of failure to thrive in a hostile environment, however, Catherine wrote *Backwoods of Canada* (1836), a how-to guide, with a bucolic view of the endless forest around her. The land on which Catherine and Susanna settled was close to land owned by their brother, Samuel Strickland (1804–1867), who had immigrated to Upper Canada a few years earlier. Susanna, despite her protestations to the contrary, was not left to fend for herself.

Anna Jameson arrived in Upper Canada in 1836, four years after Susanna Moodie, and under different circumstances. She was a tourist—a British writer and artist—not an immigrant. Her husband, Robert Sympson Jameson, had been appointed in 1833 as the attorney general in Upper Canada. Anna and Robert married in 1825, but were apparently unhappy from the start and, by 1829, when Robert was appointed as a judge in Dominica, they had already been living separately for some time. Anna's trip to Upper Canada was not about reconciliation, it was about securing a promotion for her husband and formalizing a separation agreement.[32] If Susanna's account of life in Upper Canada reads as a whiny complaint, the story of a woman constantly wronged and out-of-sorts with her environment, Anna's *Winter Studies and Summer Rambles in Canada* (1838) reads as a pretentious, condescending account of the bumbling colonials she encounters, though she also writes, equally condescendingly, about her encounters with various indigenous people.

Because both Susanna and Anna published their versions of life in Upper Canada in the 1830s and Eliza, to my knowledge, did not, it is obviously impossible to argue that Eliza's has been neglected.[33] But with access to letters it is possible to provide an alternative historical view to Susanna and Anna's, one that feels more in tune with twenty-first-century literary and cultural sensibilities.[34] Unlike Susanna and Anna, Eliza's accounts of life in Upper Canada are filled with delight and gratitude, her appreciation of the warm welcome she received there and of the opportunities her adopted country provided for her and for her grandchildren.

Besides having a more appreciative sense of Upper Canada than either Anna or Susanna did, Eliza was also a more engaging writer—clearer, more stylistically economical, and therefore more attractive to twenty-first-century readers. Henry Crabb Robinson, in fact, was articulate in his negative assessment of Anna Jameson, condemning her "want of sincerity" in both looks and words. Particularly damning was his suggestion that her lack of sincerity was owing "to the great resemblance to the late Mrs. Godwin, whom Lamb used to call 'a liar par excellence.'"[35] He was writing in 1845 and referring to Mary Jane Clairmont Godwin (1766–1841). Eliza didn't like the second Mrs. Godwin either. But leaving personal views aside, by way of contrast, Crabb Robinson did like Eliza both as a person and a writer. In his notes to her letters, he calls her "a woman of remarkable talent."[36]

Despite periodically channeling and reimagining Susanna Moodie in her own work, contemporary Canadian author Margaret Atwood didn't like Susanna Moodie much, or her writing. She characterizes Susanna's prose style as "discursive and ornamental," old-fashioned and out of sync with contemporary readers. In the 1970s, when Margaret Atwood first began mining Moodie, it was not for her literary merit but rather for her underlying discontent, symptomatic of what she has called Canada's "national mental illness" of "paranoid schizophrenia."

More than any of the other women writing in Upper Canada in the early nineteenth century, Susanna has a place in the Canadian historical imagination, figuring in work by Canadian authors in the late twentieth and twenty-first century, most notably Margaret Atwood, but also in work by Robertson Davies and Carol Shields.[37] One of the reasons Susanna Moodie has remained such a compelling character is precisely because she reads as fictional. The slightly irritating, schizophrenic narrative voice in *Roughing it in the Bush* is at least partly a result of the fact that Susanna, born in 1803, published the book twenty years after the events she describes in the years following her arrival in 1832. As a result, Susanna's fifty-ish self provides a palimpsestic cover for her thirty-ish self. Nevertheless, the authorial persona Susanna created for herself in *Roughing it in the Bush* is the one that has stuck as the received version of pioneer life in the backwoods.[38]

If Susanna was writing as a reluctant immigrant, Anna was writing as a tourist. She arrived in Upper Canada at the end of 1836, just prior to

Mackenzie's Rebellion of 1837.[39] Her *Winter Studies and Summer Rambles,* published in 1838, soon after she arrived home in Britain, reads as a travel diary. In *Literary Culture and Female Authorship in Canada 1760–2000,* Faye Hammill helpfully explains that Anna "employs interpolated narration in her diary-letter format in order to construct multiple versions of herself at different points in her travels" (40). Unlike Anna, who wrote to provide a tourist's view, or Susanna, who wrote to provide a fictionalized warning against emigration, Eliza wrote personal letters and though she may well have had future publication in mind, those letters were primarily written to communicate news and events as they were happening. Eliza's letters are still worth reading partly because she brought all of her considerable talent as a novelist to their composition.

What Eliza has left behind is not autobiographical fiction or travel writing, but something more personal, more intimate. Her view of Canada differed from that of Anna or Susanna partly because she was older when she lived there and, by the time she arrived, had also had a longer history of attempts to remake herself than either of the other women. Anna, born in 1794, was in her early forties during her time in Canada (between the end of 1836 and the spring of 1838). Susanna, born in 1803, arrived in Upper Canada in 1832, so was in her late twenties during the period in which she lived in the backwoods with her husband. When he finally obtained a position as Sheriff of Victoria (later Hastings County) in 1839, the family relocated to Belleville, Ontario, in 1840. When Eliza, born in 1766, arrived in Niagara in 1829, at sixty-three, her writing career in the England of the 1790s and early 1800s was long over, but she had owned and operated schools in Bridgetown, New Haven, and New York. It had been thirteen years since her son Orlando had died, and two since the death of her daughter, and she was facing the responsibility of raising and educating her orphaned grandchildren. Unlike Anna or Susanna, Eliza was working at day jobs in the 1830s—first as a teacher in Niagara and later as the mistress of the boys' boarding house at Upper Canada College—and her views of society and the landscape differed from those of Susanna and Anna. What makes Eliza's perspective compelling and relevant for twenty-first-century readers is that despite the losses and setbacks in her life, she tells an immigration success story, a story of how a woman on her own, even an old woman, can establish herself and her family.

First impressions matter. For people already apprehensive about what they find on arrival at their destinations and how they are received, first contacts do make deep and lasting impressions. Susanna devotes an entire chapter in *Roughing it in the Bush,* "Our First Settlement and the Borrowing

System," to an account of how she was exploited at every turn on her arrival to Canada. A cleared farm (not a backwoods wilderness) near Cobourg, Ontario was her first destination. Her new neighbors were United Empire Loyalists who had fled to Upper Canada from the United States after the War of 1812. It was Emily, one of her family's first visitors, who introduced Susanna to the practice of "borrowing":

> Day after day I was tormented by this importunate creature; she borrowed of me tea, sugar, candles, starch, blueing, irons, pots, bowls—in short every article in common domestic use—while it was with the utmost difficulty we could get them returned. . . . This method of living upon their neighbours is a most convenient one to unprincipled people, as it does not involve the penalty of stealing; and they can keep the goods without the unpleasant necessity of returning them. (Moodie 97)

Susanna ends the chapter with an ironic narrative twist: "I overcame my scruples," she writes, and borrowed a candle from a "good neighbour." Her youngest son was ill and she needed one in order to tend to him in the night. The irony was that while she was getting a little sleep, a marauding neighborhood tomcat slipped in and stole the candle, thus providing the perfect excuse for why she would be unable to return it the next day. Without a candle, however, poor Susanna had "no light to assist" her "ill and feverish" young son. Because she wrote the episode as a book chapter, an autobiographical fiction, her last line begins poignantly with her regret that without the candle she could not, of course, "look into his sweet face." Then she breaks into a final poem, "Oh Canada! Thy Gloomy Woods." The chapter stands as a set piece, one that heralds Susanna's dark account of the social and physical gloom of her Upper Canadian life.

Susanna's account of being harassed by her new neighbors in Cobourg on the north side of Lake Ontario dates from around 1832–1833. Follow the shore of the lake west to get to the south shore, about 250 kilometers away, and you arrive at what is now Niagara-on-the-Lake, where Eliza wrote very differently and a little earlier about her reception. Writing in the late spring of 1830 from her new home in Niagara, Eliza explained to John Moffat in New York about the thoughtfulness and consideration of her new neighbors: "My Dear Friend, . . . I have been dangerously ill & am now only just able to leave my bed," she writes first and then, with a slightly comic, self-effacing simile—and riffing on a line from Pope's 1711 *Essay on Criticism*—she adds, "& crawl about my chamber like a worm dragging my slow length along."[40] Eliza, clearly feeling re-energized, celebrates the solicitous care she has received:

I cannot fail to regain my strength if the solicitude of friends can assist towards it—one sends a basin of fine Vermicelli soup—another delicate bits—another blancmange—jelly . . . in short if I were to swallow one tenth of the delicacies sent to tempt my appetite I should expire of repletion. The care I have experienced is astonishing. Three of the principal Ladies took it by turn to sit up at night with me & others aided Mrs. Breakenridge by day—I remember you once said *I shall form my opinion of the People of Canada by their treatment of you.*—And now my Dear Mr. Moffat make your estimate. (EF to JM, 29 May and 6 June 1830)

In reading Susanna and Eliza side by side, they provide diametrically different views of what Upper Canada was like in the 1830s. Susanna, in her early thirties, is miserable and complaining, naïve, clearly feeling her intellectual and social superiority to everyone around her. Eliza, in her early sixties, is grateful, cheerful, hopeful, and sincere in her acknowledgement of those who support her and her family. Both were writing women, both with histories of publication in Britain, but it was Susanna's gloomy view of life in early Upper Canada that became one of the Canada's founding national narratives.

The possibility of finding something Eliza might have published in Upper Canada in the 1830s seemed to me as her biographer, likely, but just out of reach. One potential venue for her work would have been *The Canadian Literary Magazine* of 1833. It had been edited by John Kent, the master of the prep school at Upper Canada College, and was supported by the Lieutenant Governor, John Colborne. Susanna Moodie published in its first issue, under her own name, just a year after arriving in Upper Canada. There are anonymous pieces in the same issue. It was tempting to speculate on contributions that Eliza might have authored. The magazine ran for just three issues in 1833 and the dates coincide exactly with when Eliza was preparing for her move to Upper Canada College, at a time when she knew both Kent and Colborne. A clue survives testifying to the fact that Eliza might well have been writing stories with an eye to publication in that period.

In Eliza's June 10, 1832, letter to John Moffat, sketching her "history of authorship," she confirms that she has not abandoned her literary life: "If good health, good spirits & more leisure allowed me to complete two volumes of tales" she writes, "I could sell the manuscript provided it was on examination found worthy of publication." The point that she wanted to "complete" two volumes of tales is what stood. When Eliza wrote this to Moffat, did she mean that she had been working on some tales and had intended to see if they were marketable? Had she been sending individual stories out to see if she could find an outlet for her work? Or did she just mean that she was still toying with the idea of writing for publication again? *The Canadian Literary Magazine* would have been an ideal option, especially as John Kent's opening editorial so clearly resonated with Eliza's own view of life in Upper Canada. He began, in fact, with faulting those new arrivals to Upper Canada who tried to read their new world based on gossip from the old:

> The impression which a strange land makes upon the mind, very much depends on preconceived ideas. For my own part I did not expect to find the Canadians an ignorant people, plunged in mental sloth and intellectual darkness,—senseless as the stumps around their dwellings,—or as inaccessible to light, as the buck-wheat pines of Dorchester of Galt. I find them advanced in civilization beyond my expectations. (*Canadian Literary Magazine* I: April 1833)[41]

Susanna and Anna played to the desires of their implied readers for characters conforming to preconceived ideas of Canadians as "ignorant people" wallowing in "mental sloth and intellectual darkness." Meanwhile, it cannot be proven that Eliza published in the *Canadian Literary Magazine* or any other outlet during her time in Upper Canada.

The "advanced civilization" John Kent found when he arrived, and the one he addressed in his magazine, was the one inhabited by Eliza when she took up her position at Upper Canada College in 1833. Kent himself was close at hand, and interested in keeping the intellectual and cultured company of Eliza, among others. William Warren Baldwin, his family, and the Colbornes were nearby, as were other less well-known but equally interesting members of their social group.[42] It is Bessie, in her letter of January 1834, who gives the best sense of urban life in Toronto, as it was about to be named. Over the Christmas holiday, Bessie reports the highlights of the social season: "We have had here a bazaar concert," she writes; "It was patronized as the papers said 'by her Ex-majesty' Lady Colborne & of course was crowded." Bessie liked the band, as they "Played the overture in Tancredi & several other pieces most delightfully." Bessie also reported that she and her grandmother had received "four invitations," including "two for large parties," one at the Baldwin home. Life in Toronto for Bessie and Eliza was marked by music, dancing, as well as conversations about literature and politics. It was an intellectual, urban, and urbane life especially when compared to that which they lived in Niagara. It is also Bessie who was explicit about this difference.

In an 1835 note to her friend Adeline Moffat in New York, Bessie says that Niagara "is just as it was when we first went to it [in 1829]—a deserted looking Village." It wasn't exactly deserted. By that time it had a population of about twelve hundred people.[43] If it wasn't a cosmopolitan society, it was still made up of United Empire Loyalists, Scottish Merchants, English and Irish immigrants, and people who had been enslaved in the United States and had arrived via the Underground Railroad.[44] After her life in New York, however, Bessie found what she regarded as the petty, small-town gossip of Niagara annoying, and complained that the inhabitants of the town were "busy only in scandalizing, and quarreling with their neighbors." She liked her life in "Toronto Much better," particularly the "one great attraction in it: the military band" that "plays in a beautiful spot," and though "it is not so good a band as the last we had . . . it is still delightful." She concludes happily by saying that "we are now in the prettiest of all pretty places." That note is dated February 10, 1836, during the dead of winter.

Anna Jameson arrived in Toronto just ten months later, in December 1836, by which time winter had come around again. Even allowing for Anna's anxiety being exacerbated by the fact that she was coming to negotiate a separation from her estranged husband, she really did not buy into the description of Toronto as a "pretty place." In *Winter Studies and Summer Rambles*, she writes:

> What Toronto may be in summer, I cannot tell; they say it is a pretty place. At present its appearance to me, a stranger, is more strangely mean and melancholy. A little ill-built town on low land, at the bottom of a frozen bay, with one very ugly church, without tower or steeple; some government offices, built of staring red brick, in the most tasteless, vulgar style imaginable. (15)

It is no wonder that Henry Crabb Robinson didn't like her.[45] Anna sets overwritten discussions of German literature and music against superficial accounts of the people, places, and events she encountered in her travels in 1836–1837. She seemed to write everything that came to mind.

Eliza, with less time on her hands, tended to write with more economy, thus by way of contrast her prose feels more accessible to a twenty-first-century reader. Take, for example, Eliza's depiction of her youngest grandson Roland at eleven, newly arrived in Upper Canada after seven years in the United States (he was four when Eliza landed with her family in New Haven in 1822). She writes as if capturing a happy, playful moment in time for posterity:

> Roland I assure you bounced away his canon on the 4th of July in concert with the guns of Niagara Fort & I do not believe he has yet taken into consideration whether he shall be a republican or a Monarchy man. He &

his Schoolfellows have a training day every Saturday on the Common. Their band furnishes a whistle & an old tin kettle for a Drum. Parchment & paper hats with odd pieces of red flannel, wooden swords & guns make uniforms & accouterments & being almost all Captains & Majors they look the very emblems of Glee & happiness. (EF to JM, 19 August 1829)

Even in those few lines, Roland comes to life, marching with his friends in their makeshift costumes playing at soldiers. She focuses on the details of Roland's outfit, and his pleasure in his play shows him enthusiastically and vividly in motion. And given that the War of 1812 had so recently left its mark on Niagara, Eliza's comment about how Roland would align himself, as Canadian or American, situates him immediately in a particular historical moment. Eliza, as always, was acutely aware of the political landscape around her; of the ways in which the revolutionary events shaping what was becoming the modern world inflected her life and work.

There is, as it happens, a strange symmetry in the distance she had traveled. Her own journey to find freedom and independence shadowed another kind of transatlantic political journey: the move toward the end of slavery. From being homeless in London to living in substantial homes in Bridgetown, New Haven, New York, Niagara, and York/Toronto, Eliza's colonial journey had, despite its ups and downs, resulted in a degree of financial and social independence. At almost exactly the same time as Eliza prepared to move to Upper Canada College in July 1833, the British House of Commons finally passed the bill to abolish slavery. There is no mention of the event in any of Eliza's extant letters, but given her life in Britain as an abolitionist before the law to abolish the slave trade was passed, her life as a slave owner in Barbados, and her firsthand experience of Bussa's Rebellion in 1816, she could not have been oblivious to the success of the legislation, especially as the battle for it had been so long fought and so hard won.

She also could not have been oblivious to the fact that the Niagara Seminary for Young Ladies, the school she was leaving in the early 1830s, was just a short walk away from what was called Little Africa or Negro Town.[46] Niagara-on-the-Lake, when Eliza was there, was a "terminus" for what became the Underground Railroad, a final stop for African Americans escaping from their legal enslavement in the Southern United States. It would be another thirty years before slavery was abolished in America, as the U.S. Congress did not ratify the Thirteenth Amendment until December 1865. In Niagara-on-the-Lake today, few traces of Little Africa/Negro Town remain. What was called a "slave cottage" has been preserved and is now William and Susannah Steward House. And just a few blocks away from the Centre

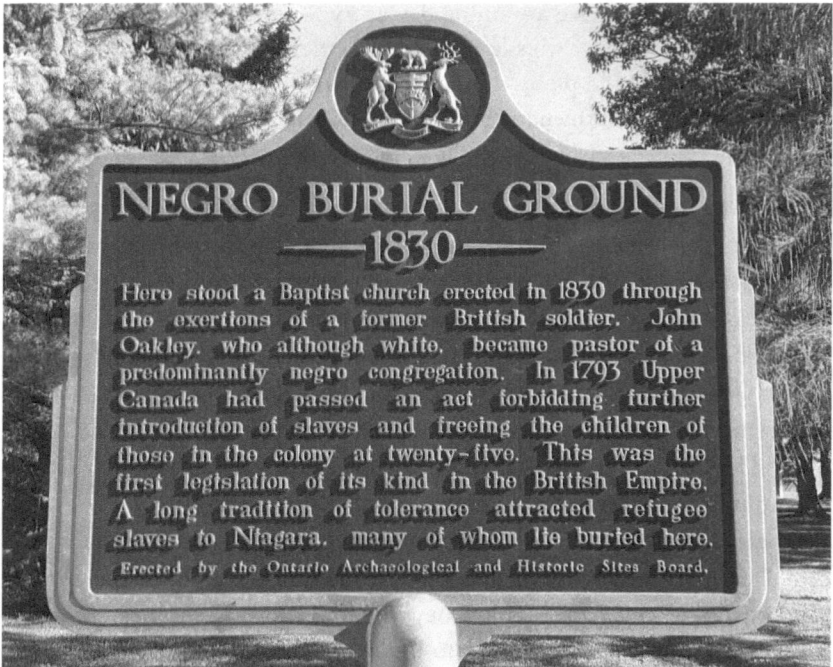

Plaque commemorating the Negro Burial Ground, Niagara-on-the-Lake. (Photograph courtesy of Murray Wilcox)

Street home of the Seminary for Young Ladies, there stands a plaque commemorating what had been the Negro Burial Ground. The inscription begins: "Here stood a Baptist church erected through the exertions of a former British soldier, John Oakley, who although white, became pastor of a predominantly Negro congregation." Besides being the pastor of the church, Oakley also taught the children of the "Negro congregation," likely children of enslaved people who had escaped to Canada or those who had managed to get to Niagara when fighting in the War of 1812 on the Loyalist side. When Eliza left the Seminary for Young Ladies in 1833 to move to Toronto it was John Oakley who took her place in the school on Centre Street. Given that Eliza had been a proponent of liberation through literacy, and given that she had created the enslaved nanny Nora, who taught herself to read in *Visits to the Juvenile Library* (1805), she could not have been unaware of the fact that just a blocks away, there was a school for black children, "in the sexton's house behind St. Andrew's church."[47]

After leaving Upper Canada with Bessie in August 1838, Eliza finally found some of the peace, leisure, and social and financial security she had

"Slave cottage" (William and Susannah Steward House), Niagara-on-the-Lake. (Photograph courtesy of Murray Wilcox)

so long sought. Alexander Duncan first took them to his home in Sodus Bay in Upstate New York. Eliza loved the serenity and beauty of the environment. It was there that she also met Martin Van Buren (1782–1862) in 1839, when he was sitting as the eighth President of the United States. That year, in October, Eliza and Bessie managed to have a wonderful trip to New York, a reunion with the Moffats. By December 1839, the new house into which the Duncans would move in Providence, Rhode Island, with Eliza and Bessie was almost ready. Eliza, preparing finally to live in a space of her own, wrote happily about choosing the furniture for it, including pieces she described as coming from the "super eminent" New York furniture-maker Mr. Phyfe (EF to Dora Massa, 17 December 1839).[48]

As Eliza prepared to furnish her own space, her own comments on the aesthetics of Mary Robinson's cottage as she had described them almost forty years earlier resonate. Robinson's home was "sheltered," she said at the time, "by the tall trees of the forest," with windows out of which she could "look over St. Ann's Hill." The furniture she classified as "more ornamental" than she would have chosen for herself, "but still . . . elegant & quiet—nothing gaudy nor ill placed" (EF to MH, August 1800). In describing to Reuben Moffat her new home in Rhode Island, also on a hill, Eliza's words oddly echo that earlier description of Mary Robinson's cottage: "In front," she wrote, "we look over the City & several miles down the river & my room windows look to a large Common bounded by a Pine Wood & the sight of a Common makes welcome another old association" (EF to Reuben Moffat, 27 January 1840).[49]

Eliza's last letters from 1839 and 1840, in her retirement with Bessie and the Duncans, sound happy and relaxed. In a letter to Dora Massa, she even wrote about her faith in the future: "I cannot calculate the amount that would tempt me to forego all my visionary pleasures of this kind," she wrote, "and I shall go on to the end of time, brushing away as hard as I can the Burrs that would fain be very tenacious & cherishing even a small bud which may by possibility grow to be a rose" (31 October 1839).

Despite her boundless intellectual energy and optimism, Eliza died on December 8, 1840, at seventy-four. Bessie, in a letter to Dora's sister Charlotte, wrote movingly about the events leading up to Eliza's death: "I wished her back," wrote Bessie, only that "I might show her how deeply I prized her." The dashes and sentence fragments read as sobs, conveying the depth of her grief and the extent of her loss:

> I have seen a gradual decay in Grandmamma even since we returned from New York, saw without—realizing it—for not until a few hours before her death—had I an idea but that she might—live for me, years to come—Saturday evening (6th) was the—last—she spent—with—the—family. She had been reading aloud to us for some time when she said, feeling tired & not—quite—well she would go to bed—the night—she passed restless & uneasily, Sunday morning, after giving her medicine, I left for Church. When I returned she was much worse, in the evening the Doctor came pronouncing it—rheumatic gout—that night went by tolerably quiet,—but—towards morning she was in such extreme agony that Dr McArnam was again sent for, he came still thinking it the same disease and that not dangerous—he called again at noon and immediately on looking at her exclaimed that it was not gout—but—the passing of Gallstones—he gave medicine accordingly still seemingly not fearing the issue—she was quieter then & remained so, apparently sleeping, till ten, when she grew Sensibly Worse, faint and fainter and so on till three when—Oh Charlotte—she died so calm, almost—sleeping her soul away. (Bessie Rutherford to Charlotte Barrell, 16 December 1840)

Although Eliza's death marked the physical end of her "visionary pleasures," the "small bud[s]" she cherished did grow into deeply rooted North American "roses," her descendants.

Coda

And Beyond . . .

Yet knowing how way leads on to way,
I doubted if I should ever come back.

I shall be telling this with a sigh
Somewhere ages and ages hence:
Two roads diverged in a wood, and I—
I took the one less traveled by,
And that has made all the difference.

       —Robert Frost, "The Road Not Taken"

If Eliza could have seen into the future, she would have been gratified to know that her grandchildren and their descendants achieved all the goals that she had traveled so far and worked so diligently to accomplish: establishing homes of their own, families, networks of connections, as well as financial and social security in both Canada and the United States. The backwoods bush farm near Tillsonburg, Ontario that Roland had labored so hard to bring into being continued to be worked by several generations of his family well into the twentieth century. Many of Roland's direct descendants stayed in the area, raising their families and giving their children names—Fenwick, Orlando, Elizabeth, William, and Thomas—that would keep Eliza's family names in living memory for generations. Roland's descendants became doctors, lawyers, academics, bankers, and accountants, worked in businesses, and contributed to the development of the social and cultural fabric of communities in Southeastern Ontario.

On the other side of the border, in Rhode Island, after Eliza's death, Bessie traveled to Liberia in Africa with Thomas Staughton Savage (1804–1880), an American physician, scientist, and missionary, where they married in 1844. He is credited with providing the first scientifically correct description of a gorilla.[1] On their return from Africa, Thomas Savage became the first rector of the Trinity Episcopalian Church in Pass Christian, Mississippi. That is where the couple raised their children. According to Bessie's son Thomas Rutherford Savage (1852–1918), a physician, a portrait of Eliza hung in their house. He asked about it in a letter he wrote to his mother on April 4, 1890, when he was trying to establish a family history: "By the way," he asked, "whatever became of the miniature of your grandfather [the miniature is of Bessie's father, William Rutherford, not her grandfather] and the painting of your grandmother."[2] No answer to the question about the painting of Eliza survives in the archives, nor is there any information about who painted it or when. Was it a portrait of Eliza when she was old or when she was young? If the portrait survives, I've not found it, though sometimes I like to imagine it is hanging anonymously in a bed and breakfast somewhere in America—a portrait of an unknown lady. Throughout my search for Eliza, despite my familiarity with her words and her handwriting on the page, the absence of her likeness remains as a huge gap in her narrative.

As Roland's descendants contributed to the development of early Canadian social and cultural life, Bessie's descendants contributed to the development of American social and cultural life. Thomas's younger brother, William Rutherford Savage (1854–1934) was, like his father, an Episcopalian priest. Alexander Duncan Savage (1848–1935) was Bessie's eldest surviving child. In giving him the name of her grandmother's friend and benefactor, Alexander Duncan, Bessie acknowledged the significant place he held in her family's integration into American society. Educated in Europe and the United States, Alexander Duncan Savage was a curator at the Metropolitan Museum of Art in New York and, for a time, the keeper of the family history. Bessie's youngest daughter Jessie Duncan Savage (1858–1940) was

William Rutherford.
(From the Fenwick Family
Correspondence, MS211,
box 3, file 11; courtesy of the
New-York Historical Society)

also named to honor the connection between the Duncan and Fenwick/Rutherford families. When Bessie moved with her grandmother in the late 1830s to live with the Duncan family (first to Sodus Bay and then to Rhode Island), she was the governess to the family's daughters. Jessie was the name of the eldest. She died, sadly, aged fourteen, when Bessie was in Africa. Bessie's daughter Jessie married a clergyman, Thomas Lafayette Cole, and their children carried on entwining family names: Elizabeth Rutherford, Thomas, and (Dorothea) Fenwick. A lovely note survives from Bessie to her son William dated January 4, 1887, announcing the birth of Jessie's new baby Elizabeth Rutherford Cole (1887–1940), reiterating the connections:

> At mid-day you became uncle of a healthy little girl with which her mother is much pleased and her father too, though I do think they both expected a little son. Had it been the latter it would have been, of course, called, Tom, as it is she is to be named I hear Bessie Rutherford. Elizabeth of course at baptism. Jessie did say she should have Rutherford and Fenwick also but I think that would be a rather long name for a little American of the middle class.[3]

I met one of that baby Elizabeth's descendants, John Cornell, at a restaurant near Central Park South in New York in the early spring of 2015. He asked me if I knew why the name "Duncan" recurred frequently in his family, and I was delighted to able to provide the answer. In the course of our conversation, however, we discovered that we had a completely unexpected "Eliza" connection. I had been talking with John about the biography I was writing about his ancestor and about the recent death of my literary agent, George Nicholson (1937–2015). In one of those moments of extraordinary synchronicity, John, it turned out, had known George well, and their families often celebrated Thanksgiving together. George would have loved the coincidence, and would have added it to his repertoire of literary tales. It also seemed right that the bulk of Eliza's manuscript letters should end up just a few blocks away at the New-York Historical Society, and that they had been deposited there by Jessie's son, portrait painter Thomas Casilear Cole (1888–1976), a great uncle of John's.

Although Eliza could not have known exactly how her descendants would fare in the new world to which she had immigrated, she did have a sense before she died of what the future in North America would look like. In an unreferenced, unindexed folder in the William Warren Baldwin papers of the Toronto Public Library, there is a letter Eliza had written to her friends Dr. and Mrs. William Warren Baldwin in Toronto on February 23, 1840. She had composed it in Rhode Island where she was securely settled with the Duncans just a few weeks after her seventy-fourth birthday and a few months before her death in December that year. Eliza begins her letter in praise of trains:

> Praised be the invention of railroads! I have been more fatigued, or as much so, in going to Spadina or Russell Hill [location of the homes of William Warren Baldwin and Robert Baldwin, about four kilometres from the original site of Upper Canada College where she lived] before Yonge Street was macadamized, than I was by whirling over 200 miles in little more than ten hours. Speed, speed, speed, is the end, & the means are sitting quiet in a commodious car, & the former comprises all the pleasure, for to watch for prospects or picturesque views is to grow giddy by the swiftly changing scene.

Given that Eliza had left England in 1814, the year George Stephenson (1781–1848) made history by building what is credited as the first viable steam engine, the fact that she was able to describe riding in a passenger steam train in 1840 indicates both how far she had come and how much technology had changed the landscape in the intervening years. Eliza reveled in the possibilities for the future: "A late traveller calls the Americans 'a loco motive people,'" she wrote, adding that "the crowds you find on the roads, & steam boats & inns," which seems to confirm that the whole population was constantly on the move. Her sentiments echo her own cross-border moves, of course, and she ends the letter from her new home with the Duncans in Providence by affirming her connections with the Baldwins in Toronto: "Elizabeth & myself continue to feel as if there was a link or connection never to be broken between us & Canada—with Toronto especially & that separation from it will ever seem like absence from home."[4]

What Eliza's note indicates is that she had graciously managed to consolidate her network of friends so that they would support her surviving grandchildren. In her will Eliza had designated William Warren Baldwin to take care of all legal matters related to Roland's life on his Upper Canadian backwoods farm. She also arranged for the Duncans to continue to take care of launching Bessie (just twenty-three at Eliza's death) into her adult life. The William Warren Baldwin files in the Toronto Public Library and the William Rutherford Savage files in Chapel Hill, North Carolina, hold some of the correspondence between Baldwin and Alexander Duncan, containing their discussions on handling Eliza's small estate in the aftermath of her death. When Bessie made the decision to become a missionary and join Thomas Staughton Savage abroad, they both worried that Eliza would not have approved.

At one level, it seems remarkable in retrospect that the Upper Canadian William Warren Baldwin and the American Alexander Duncan, both busy, influential men in their respective communities, should attend so carefully to Eliza's grandchildren. And yet, in another way, their sense of responsibility stands as affirmation of Eliza's capacity for friendship, for networking, and for creating sustaining relationships. The chance meeting in New Haven between the orphaned, teenaged Sarah Butler (1805–1889) and the Yale student Alexander Duncan (1806–1888) at a school dance Eliza had organized grew into an enduring bond between the two families. The couple married in 1827, not long before the death of Eliza's daughter, Eliza Ann Rutherford, in New York. Alexander Duncan established himself as a successful banker and businessman. The couple moved first to Canandaigua in Upstate New York in 1829, just as Eliza moved to Niagara to take up running the Seminary for Young Ladies with the recently widowed Mary Breakenridge.

In the early 1830s, Alexander and Sarah Duncan invited Eliza and Bessie to Canandaigua for summer holidays. Both loved it there and it looks as if those annual visits led to the invitation to Eliza to retire with them and for Bessie to take on the role of educating their children. Yet, as Eliza's 1840 note to the Baldwins indicates, she also regarded Toronto as "home." What is clear is that both the Baldwin and Duncan families had become entwined with her family, creating a new root system, something that would continue to develop down through several generations. The Moffat family also contributed to the new world roots Eliza established for her family, as did the descendants of the Barrell/Massa family she had first known in Barbados. The letters surviving in archives in New York, Chapel Hill, Washington, D.C., and Toronto testify to the strong bonds Eliza created with all of them.

In reflecting on how her descendants became embedded in North American life, Eliza's comments in an 1835 letter, written from Upper Canada College in Toronto to the Moffat family in New York, ring out. She had been catching them up on the news of the comings and goings of their mutual friends, concluding on a line evocative of Mary Wollstonecraft[5]: that they were all "particles" moving with the "general mass" on a "floating world" (EF to JM, 30 March 1835). Eliza herself, of course, stopped moving in Rhode Island, which is where she is buried. What survives, solidly present and alive, in addition to generations of deeply rooted formal and informal descendants, is her literary life—her published work and her letters.

Notes

Notes on the Text

1. The record of the transaction is contained in the Fenwick Family Papers in a file labeled "Correspondence." In 2011, I was contacted by Imogen Wedd, who told me that the family called Annie Frances Wedd "Aunt Nancy." Imogen also told me that the received family history indicates that the letters had been sold to Savage for £400 and that there was outrage that they had left Britain. The handwritten note says that the amount was £100.

2. The Barrell Family Papers (1751–1929) survive in the Columbia University Libraries archival collections. Traces of the links between the Fenwick, Rutherford, Barrell, and Massa families survive in the archive. Theodora Barrell (later Massa) was one of the students at the New Haven school that Eliza opened during her time there.

3. The Baldwin Collection at the Toronto Public Library includes the correspondence of Robert Baldwin and his father, Dr. William Warren Baldwin. Eliza moved to Upper Canada in 1829 in order to set up the Niagara Seminary for Young Ladies with William Baldwin's sister, Mrs. Mary Breakenridge. The families connected through Elizabeth Morgan, Eliza's friend and neighbor on Bond Street in New York, the sister of W.W. Baldwin and Mary Breakenridge.

4. Although I had ordered the boxes and found the reference to Eliza and Elizabeth in the *The Bonnet Box Letters*, it was my research assistant, Murray Wilcox, who first saw the actual letters. They are in the WW Baldwin Papers L 11 Box 106–7. 3rd folder #54.

5. John Wesley founded *The Arminian Magazine: Consisting of Extracts and Original Treatises on Universal Redemption* (London: J. Fry, 1788) partly as a way of capturing the development of Methodism as it was evolving. Eliza's father, Peter Jaco, is in the first issue of the magazine, describing his own history.

Prelude

1. As the majority of the 1829–1840 letters are from Eliza Fenwick to John Moffat and his family, they will be cited subsequently as EF to JM. Letters written by Eliza's granddaughter Elizabeth (Bessie) Rutherford will be identified as written by ER. Other letters will be identified individually.

2. With thanks to Julia Elcock, who found the reference in the *Kingston Chronicle and Gazette*: Saturday, April 19, 1834, 2.

3. See, for example, Mary Wollstonecraft's *The Education of Daughters* and *A Vindication of the Rights of Woman*. William Godwin wrote about "an active mind and a warm heart" in an 1802 letter to William Cole responding to a question about the education of daughters (MS. Abinger c.7, fols 97–98, The Bodleian Library, University of Oxford). Eliza's own 1795 novel *Secrecy* is partly about the sad consequences of preventing women from learning to think.

4. Neither mystery stories nor detective fiction really emerged as identifiable genres until later in the nineteenth century. Edgar Allan Poe is named as the "father" of the mystery story, though William Godwin's 1794 *Adventures of Caleb Williams* is cited as an early example of detective fiction.

5. See, for example, *Out of the Clear Blue Sky,* directed by Danielle Gardner (New York: Asphalt Films, 2012). See also the arresting cover of *Towers Falling* (New York: Little, Brown and Co., 2016) by Jewell Parker Rhodes. Although written for middle-school children, the Manhattan skyline depicted on the top half of the cover appears to be reflected in the sky-blue harbor on the bottom half, suggesting both the blue of the sky on September 11, 2001 and the blue of the harbor.

6. The "island" to which Eliza refers is actually a small group of islands in the Toronto harbor. Historically, the islands did not separate completely from the mainland until 1852 when a major storm washed away the connective sandy shoreline from what had been a crescent-shaped peninsula. Although the 1828 image is identified as being the view from "Gibralter" Point, it is now Gibraltar Point.

7. See, for example, *Essays on Life Writing: From Genre to Critical Practice* (Toronto: University of Toronto Press, 1992), edited by Marlene Kadar. I like her working definition of "life writing" as comprising "texts that are written by an author who does not continuously write about someone else, and who also does not pretend to be absent from the . . . text himself/herself. Life writing is a way of seeing, to use John Berger's famous phrase; it anticipates the reader's determination on the text, the reader's colour, class, and gender, and pleasure in an imperfect and always evolving hermeneutic—classical, traditional, or postmodern" (10).

8. Manuscript letter from Eliza Fenwick to her son Orlando dated only "Monday Morning." Henry Crabb Robinson made a later note on the letter, dating it as 18—. The content suggests that it was written around 1812. An additional note in Henry Crabb Robinson's hand, written sometime later, is also on the back of the letter: "An affecting letter from an unhappy mother—a person of remarkable talent." The manuscript letter survives in the Henry Crabb Robinson (1775–1867) archive in Dr. Williams's Library in London.

9. The Fenwick Family Papers do, as it happens, contain an envelope filled with carefully cut and dated reviews of *The Fate of the Fenwicks* that appeared soon after its publication. Someone in the family carefully preserved the clippings and put them into an envelope labeled "London Newspaper Reviews." The envelope is contained in Box 1, File 8, NYHS. The file is labeled "Materials re: Wedd's book."

10. F. J. Harvey Darton, *Children's Books in England: Five Centuries of Social Life,* 3rd ed. (1932; Cambridge: Cambridge University Press, 1982), 168.

11. Janet Todd, *Death and the Maidens: Fanny Wollstonecraft and the Shelley Circle* (London: Profile, 2007), 193.

12. Jürgen Habermas, *The Structural Transformation of The Public Sphere: An Inquiry into a Category of Bourgeois Society,* trans. Thomas Burger with the assistance of Frederick Lawrence (Cambridge, MA: MIT Press, 1989). See especially Chapter 7, "The Public Sphere in the World of Letters in Relation to the Public Sphere in the Political Realm," 51–56.

13. In the introduction to *Women, Sociability and Theatre in Georgian London* (Cambridge: Cambridge University Press, 2007), Gillian Russell defines "sociability" as the

"practices, behaviours and sites that enabled social interaction that was oriented towards the positive goals of pleasure, companionship or the reinforcement of family, group and professional identities" (9). For more sustained discussion on sociability, see Gillian Russell and Clara Tuite, eds., *Romantic Sociability: Social Networks and Literary Culture in Britain, 1770–1840* (Cambridge: Cambridge University Press, 2002).

14. Eliza had dinner with Aaron Burr (Thomas Jefferson's vice president between 1801 and 1805) on March 15, 1812 at William Godwin's house. Thanks to Murray Wilcox for reminding me that Eliza's granddaughter Elizabeth (Bessie) mentioned meeting the sons of Martin Van Buren, later the eighth President of the United States, in Canandaigua. She recorded the information in a discussion about political support for him (ER to Adeline Moffat, 31 October 1836).

15. Because of the wealth of information in the William Godwin Diary Project (http://godwindiary.bodleian.ox.ac.uk/search.html), it is possible to see lists of the people with whom Godwin was dining or meeting on individual dates. My list is partly generated by references from the Godwin Diary Project as they enable me to identify specific occasions on which Eliza was dining with Godwin and the names of the other people who were present at those occasions.

16. Although there were three boxes when I first looked in 2008, the New-York Historical Society repackaged the materials and now the whole collection fits into just two boxes. While working with the materials I was able to match some of the fragments in a folder marked "undated" with letters elsewhere in the archive from which they had been separated.

17. Because I promised myself that I would resist the temptation to speculate in the biography, I have not specified the conditions here that caused Eliza to regard the lives of Will and Tom as tragic, though I present the surviving evidence explicitly in Chapter Seven, "North American Grandmother."

18. The page would have been folded in half; the section with the reference to debt would have been on the bottom of the first page. The section on "hunting for Ms. Fenwick's writing" would have been at the bottom of the second page, and it marks the beginning of the sentence that continues on the third page, with the rest of the discussion on Mrs. Fenwick's writing. It is the first page, with the discussion of debt, that is missing.

19. The hints were vague, although they were noted in, for example, Isobel Grundy's 1998 introduction to *Secresy* (Peterborough, ON: Broadview Press), and the 1927 introduction to A. F. Wedd's *The Fate of the Fenwicks: Letters to Mary Hays (1798–1828)* (London: Methuen, 1927). Jill Shefrin includes similar information in her introduction to the Holp preface she wrote for the reproduction of *Rays from the Rainbow* (London, 1812).

20. In the aftermath of William Godwin's death, Mary Shelley had returned the correspondence Mary Hays had written to her father. The postscript suggests that Eliza had stopped writing sometime after the death of her daughter in 1828 and around the time of the move to Niagara. The letter is in the Abinger Collection, Bodleian Library, Oxford. c.49.

21. The New-York Historical Society apparently has no official record of the provenance of the collection. The explanatory letters are handwritten and in the boxes themselves.

22. Box 2, File 4, NYHS Fenwick Family Papers.

23. E. V. Lucas, in preparing a new edition of *The Letters of Charles Lamb, To Which are Added Those of his sister, Mary Lamb* (London: Methuen & Co., 1935), actually put a

query in *The Times of London,* searching for "certain letters that are known to have been written but which are not forthcoming, such, for instance, as those to Mrs. John Fenwick [Eliza], to her daughter Eliza [Ann] Fenwick Rutherford, and to Martin Burney." *The Times* (London), Thursday, April 26, 1934, 15. Issue 46738.

24. Janet Todd, *Feminist Literary History* (New York: Routledge, 1988). The book stands as an eloquent analysis of the state of second-wave feminist theory and criticism roughly two decades after its origins around 1970. In the introduction, Todd also writes about the persistently dismissive language used to critique feminist scholarship.

25. In *The Rhetorics of Feminism: Readings in Contemporary Cultural Theory and the Popular Press* (London: Routledge, 2004), Lynne Pearce provides a comprehensive historical account of the links between, as she says, "rhetorical innovation" and "feminist epistemology." See also Carolyn Steedman, *Dust: The Archive and Cultural History* (Manchester: Manchester University Press, 2001), for a wonderful account of the ways writing history reshapes it. And for a set of recent essays on reshaping scholarship about writing by eighteenth-century women, see *The Future of Feminist Eighteenth-Century Scholarship Beyond Recovery,* ed. Robin Runia (New York: Routledge, 2018).

26. Introduction to William Godwin, *Memoirs of the Author of the Vindication of the Rights of Woman* (1798), eds. Pamela Clemit and Gina Luria Walker (Peterborough, ON: Broadview, 1985): 13.

27. Edmund de Waal, a British ceramic artist, composed a family story in *The Hare with Amber Eyes,* tracing the history of "netsuke," Japanese sculptures that had been in his family since the late nineteenth century. His story also traces the rise and fall of the fortunes of his Jewish ancestors through the twentieth century in Europe, Japan, and America.

28. Mary Wollstonecraft, *The Works Of Mary Wollstonecraft,* eds. Marilyn Butler and Janet Todd (London: Pickering & Chatto, 1989), 6:249.

1. Daughter of Methodism

1. Peter Jaco to George Merryweather. MA 1977/487. *Copies of Original Letters and Documents collected from different sources by James Werell,* vol.2, Methodist Archives, John Rylands Library, Manchester. Letter 5, dated February 26, 1764 contains the information about the marriage of Mr. Jaco to Mrs. Hawksworth. The note in the John Rylands archive explains that Peter Jaco "was one of the earliest Methodist preachers" and that "Mr. Merryweather was an old respected Methodist at Yarm" (which was what Yarmouth was called). An additional note in the John Rylands archive, written by James Werell, explains that he made the copy of the 1764 letter from Peter Jaco to George Merryweather. The date on the note indicates the copies as having been made in 1829: "The copies were taken from the originals, in the several hands of the writers, and were lent to me by Mrs. Taylor of York, daughter of Mr. Merryweather, Manchester September 17th 1829." The spelling, punctuation, and construction of sentences all accord with the originals.

2. I wrote to John Lenton, an expert in early Methodism, especially on the itinerant preachers, and asked him to explain what a class leader was, especially in the context of John Wesley's description of Mrs. Hawksworth as "blest in her classes." On July 21, 2011, Lenton responded with the following note: "'Class' here is used in the Methodist sense. All Methodists had to be members of a class, and meet in it once a week. The class usually

met in someone's house, often the class leaders. I would understand from this that she (probably as the housekeeper at the New Room) was the class leader for several classes, some or all of which would meet at the Room and she was highly regarded as a 'class leader,' which was a significant job in early Methodism. Class leaders gave out the class tickets, which were the signs of membership for each quarter, and collected class money, which was what supported the itinerants, part of whose job it was to meet the classes at least once a quarter. The modern name is a house-group. Most wives of itinerants were class leaders, often of several different classes during the week."

3. The Bristol New Room still stands, though it is now in the middle of what is essentially a pedestrian shopping precinct, next to a Marks & Spencer. It wasn't so much a room, but rather a chapel and a series of connected rooms, which could be used as offices, study and meeting spaces, and domestic spaces used for dining and resting. The New Room remains easily accessible in Bristol and it is possible to worship in the chapel and see how the space was used when the Wesley brothers and their assistants used it as something of a central clearing house, a place to plan and stage the promotion of the Methodist message.

4. John Lenton, *John Wesley's Preachers: A Social and Statistical Analysis of the British and Irish Preachers Who Entered the Methodist Itinerancy before 1791* (Milton Keynes, UK: Paternoster, 2009), 86.

5. She was also defined as a "housekeeper." In the early Methodist societies during the lifetimes of John and Charles Wesley, women were able to participate actively in the spiritual life of the groups with which they were associated. After Wesley's death in 1803, the roles of women as spiritual leaders were restricted.

6. Methodist Archives, John Rylands, DDC 8/3 in a little Dutch paper notebook.

7. Paul Langford, *A Polite and Commercial People: England 1727–1783* (London: Clarendon Press, 1989), 62.

8. The note was probably made by James Werell when he was collecting the material from Merryweather's daughter. The date of the marginal inscription probably matches the note on the letter, so it is September 17, 1829.

9. Though "connexion" is just an old spelling of "connection," the term had a specific meaning in the formative stages of Methodism in the mid-eighteenth century. The entry in the *Dictionary of Methodism in Britain and Ireland,* accessible at http:// wesleyhistoricalsociety.org.uk/dmbi/, explains that "in the eighteenth century 'connexion' was a term used generally (e.g., in political, commercial, and religious contexts) to refer to the circle of those connected to some person or group, and to the relationship thus created." But it was the particular character of the connexion John Wesley maintained with his members, his societies, and his itinerant preachers that gave the term its technical significance in Methodism. All were connected primarily with him and thence with each other. The Connexion came to be in some senses equivalent to "denomination" and, later, to "Church," and "Connexionalism" was descriptive of a particular principle and pattern of church life that emphasized the interdependence of the constituent parts (over against independency). The World Methodist Conference of 1891 endorsed the use of the word "Church'" rather than "Connexion" and it replaced "Society" on class tickets in December 1893.

10. The information comes from the John Rylands Methodist Archives Lamplough Collection 657MA 1977/485 Location D3/26/2B. The description explains that the

materials consist of "Copies of Original Letters and other Documents from Different Sources by James Everett." The note about the shoes is contained in vol. II, 3.5: 167 of the collection and is titled "accounts." The full entry reads: "1763 Feb. 6. The Preacher's horse, 11 nights 16/6; corn and hay for 2 preacher's horses 1/ March 12 the Preacher's horse 7 nights 10/6—March 30, Mr. Jaco a pair of shoes 6/."

11. Peter Jaco to Charles Wesley, written from Durham, 14 May 1771, Wesley Family Letters 2/ (Brown Folios 1–5) DDCW2/2.

12. John Lenton, in an email letter to me on July 19, 2011, provided his personal summary of information about Peter Jaco, with the details about two records of information about payments to a single child.

13. Peter Jaco to Richard Rodda, written from London, 24 October 1779 (pencil note says 1754–1781), Item 6 in Wesley Family Letters, DDWES 1.

14. The will of Peter Jaco, hosier of St Leonard's Shoreditch (Nat Arch PROB11/1080), dated July 20, 1781. A "hosier" was a stocking-maker, so it is possible that Jaco's wife and daughter were engaged in the business while he was preaching. Because funding for Wesley's original itinerants was unstable, some did also have business interests. Ed Pope has searched for Jaco's birth record and has demonstrated that records were made under the name of "Jacka" at Paul, in Cornwall, a village near Penzance.

15. The *ODNB* error is repeated in other significant places, including the introductions to modern editions of the only book of Eliza's to remain in print, *Secresy*. See, for example, the introduction to the second Broadview edition of Eliza Fenwick, *Secresy* (Peterborough, ON: Broadview Press, 1998), in which Isobel Grundy, the editor, also tries to pin down Eliza's genealogical lines. Grundy notes that in one of the letters in A. F. Wedd's edition of letters to Mary Hays, *The Fate of the Fenwicks; Letters to Mary Hays 1798–1828* (London: Methuen, 1927), Eliza identifies herself and another "Miss Jaco" (200). Grundy also describes her unsuccessful attempt to find a Cornwall-born Elizabeth Jago, who would have been born in 1766, the birth date for Eliza that would be consistent with internal evidence in the letters she wrote to both Mary Hays and the Moffat family. Jill Shefrin, in her notes on the Osborne Collection's lovely reproduction of Eliza Fenwick's *Rays from the Rainbow* (London: Godwin, 1812), correctly identifies Eliza's maiden name as Jaco (putting a question mark against her date of birth and suggesting 1765). She incorrectly lists the date of the publication of *Secresy* as 1799 (instead of 1795) and says that the Fenwick family immigrated to Jamaica, rather than Barbados. Pamela Clemit is revising the *ODNB* entry and has done a new entry on John Fenwick.

16. Henrietta Braddock (1764–1852) appears in several of Eliza's extant letters to Mary Hays dated between 1799 and 1812. An unpublished note to Mary dated August 30, 1799 provides a little more information. Eliza writes: "Miss Braddock desired I would give her love to you. She has taken a little shop in Woodstock Street Oxford Road. I really believe it will be a comfortable position for her. She has a few friends who will interest themselves for her & she has chosen a means through which every body can if they will serve her."

17. There are the few references I've cited in Peter Jaco's letters, and, as I'll show, Thomas Rutherford did write extensively about the "good" religious deaths of two of his children.

18. The identification of John Fenwick Sr. as the father of Eliza's husband John Fenwick (Jr. as I'll call him here to distinguish him from his father) proved difficult to confirm. Fenwick is a relatively common name and Henry Crabb Robinson, on the back of letter

Eliza had written to him from Cork (undated, except for "Monday Morning," though identified as having been written in 1812), described John Fenwick as "an amicable but most improvident Irishman" (Letters of Henry Crabb Robinson, HCR Correspondence 1812.b2B, Dr. Williams's Library, London). That note was appended later, so the date reads 1812/1826. I had found references to John Fenwick Sr. in the Methodist Archives but had initially decided that he could not have been the father of Eliza's husband as he wasn't Irish. As it turned out, the Irish connection was the incorrect one. I'm grateful to Ed Pope as he found the archival records that did match internal information from the letters. In an 1802 letter written from Penzance (when Eliza tried her hand at shopkeeping with John Fenwick's brother, Thomas), Eliza says that she has received "compleat respect & attention from all Mr. F's family," and she mentions "Mrs. Duckworth's eldest daughter," a seventeen-year-old girl as someone she particularly likes. Mary Duckworth was John Fenwick's sister and both, as well as Thomas Fenwick, who is identified as John's brother, are the children of John Fenwick and Priscilla (Mackris) Fenwick. That's the confirmation I needed in order to identify Eliza's husband John Fenwick (1757–1823) as the son of John Fenwick, Methodist itinerant (1730–87).

Ed Pope also supplied the following information: In 1756, Priscilla Mackris was married at St. Mary Newington, Surrey to John Fenwick, Methodist preacher. Their first child John was baptized in 1757 at Newington, but John Fenwick retired from the work of an itinerant Methodist preacher and settled in Newcastle-on-Tyne, where he had three more children: Mary, baptized 1759 at Newcastle; Sarah, baptized 1762 at Gateshead; and Thomas James, baptized 1768 at Newcastle. His daughter Mary married John Duckworth (perhaps a relative of Methodist minister Isaac Duckworth) at Chester in 1783; his daughter Sarah married a jeweler, Peter Molyneux, at Liverpool in 1787.

19. The *Dictionary of Methodism,* accessible at http://wesleyhistoricalsociety.org.uk/dmbi/, defines "enthusiasm" as "a term of abuse" that was used to imply "rapturous self-delusion of people who believed themselves to be under the immediate inspiration of the Holy Spirit" and characterized "by cases of uncontrollable weeping or fainting."

20. Although I'm well aware that eighteenth-century studies scholars intensely dislike allusions to "presentism" as they call it, the linking of eighteenth-century experience with modern experience works for twenty-first-century non-specialist readers for whom the word "enthusiasm" conveys little of the feeling palpable in the first-hand accounts by the preachers themselves. See for example, Thomas Jackson, ed., *Lives of Early Methodist Preachers: Chiefly Written by Themselves,* Vol. 1 (London: Wesleyan Conference Office, 1865).

21. See ibid. for Peter Jaco and *Works of John Wesley, vol. 22, Journals and Diaries V, 1765–1775,* eds. W. Reginald Ward and Richard P. Heitzenrather (Nashville: Abingdon, 1993): 232.

22. The episode was reprinted in the *Methodist Magazine* 31 (1808): 437, along with a note saying that Rutherford was accepted as a preacher in 1772.

23. See, for example, EF to MH, December 1811:

I am glad that you think as I do respecting Lanno's religion. I used to be so disgusted & shocked at the blind, coarse, ignorant infidelity of Holcroft's children that I should almost have preferred making sectaries [members of religious or political sects] of mine. Unable however to teach what I did not believe, and thrown as Eliza was occasionally into the society of skeptics, she was left to herself or to chance, and she has formed for herself a religion of moral precepts & an undefined (perhaps) feeling of devotion to a sublime & supreme first cause.

Orlando has fallen more into the ordinary course, and as yet say, since youth wants every restraint of principle against the impulses of the passions, I am always glad when he is in the way of having religious feelings & impressions cultivated. That he has got over his bashfulness in not reading his Chapter in turn also pleases me.

24. Although Thomas Rutherford was younger than Peter Jaco, "ward" doesn't sound quite right, nor does protégé. Wesley did send out preachers in clusters, so they were supporting and learning from each other. The extant records indicate that Jaco and Rutherford were together in Newcastle and in Leeds. In *The Arminian Magazine* of October 1808 (vol. XXXI), Thomas Rutherford writes that, at the Conference of 1771, "Mr. Jaco, Mr. William Thomas, Mr. Thomas Simpson" and one other preacher had been appointed to the Newcastle circuit for that year, and when the last (unnamed) one didn't come, Jaco invited Rutherford "to supply his place" (440). In the November 1808 issue of the magazine, Rutherford writes that Mr. Jaco had "kindly determined" to take him "to the Conference at Leeds" and that it was a favour he had "no right to expect, and should not have presumed to ask" (482).

25. Reference is taken from the definition of "Methodism" in the *Dictionary of Methodism,* accessible at http://wesleyhistoricalsociety.org.uk/dmbi/.

26. *Reasons Against a Separation from the Church of England* is a pamphlet by John Wesley first printed in 1758. Reason seven is: "We look upon the *Methodists* (so called) in general, not as any particular Party; (This would exceedingly obstruct the Grand design, for which we conceive GOD has raised them up) but as living Witnesses in, and to every Party, of that Christianity when we preach; which is hereby demonstrated to be a real Thing, and visibly held out to all the World." Both John and Charles Wesley were ordained as Church of England ministers.

27. V. H. H. Green, *John Wesley* (London: Nelson, 1964), 5. For readers not tuned to British history, a Jacobite was a supporter of James II, who had been deposed and exiled in 1688. The name taken from the Latin for James, "Jacobus."

28. Although the "The Test Acts," as they were called (referring to the administration of "tests" of faith, that is Holy Communion), were first put into place in Scotland at the end of the Reformation in 1567, it was the Test Act of 1673 in England which made it illegal for anyone other than members of the Church of England to hold public office or to attend Oxford or Cambridge Universities.

29. The (dissenting) Warrington Academy (mostly between 1756 and 1782) was famous for its association with many of the progressive educational ideas that would ground the moves into modern pedagogical practices. John Aikin, Joseph Priestly, and Gilbert Wakefield were influential tutors. John Aikin's daughter Anna (later Barbauld) invented the primer as we know it, with large print and a lot of white space. Joseph Priestly was what we would now call a scientist (a term coined in 1833 by Samuel Taylor Coleridge). See *Religious Dissent and the Aikin-Barbauld Circle 1740–1860.* ed. Felicity James and Ian Inkster (Cambridge: Cambridge UP, 2012). See also Maurice Whitehead, "Superior to the Rudest Shocks of Adversity": English Jesuit Education and Culture in the Long Eighteenth Century, 1688–1832, in *Educating the Child in Enlightenment Britain:*

Beliefs, Cultures, Practices. Ed. Mary Hilton and Jill Shefrin (Farnham, Surry: Ashgate, 2009): 99–116. The essay contains a quotation from the prospectus of Jesuit *Académie anglais*—which was in Liege—outlining the curriculum. The prospectus is in French and I've sketched (rather than quoted) the contents. Besides the expected classes in reading, literature, philosophy, and languages (English, French, German, Latin, Greek, and Hebrew), there were lessons offered in History (sacred and secular), Geography, Algebra, Geometry, Astronomy, Mathematics, and Physics as well as music. As is still the case, students would choose from among course offerings and costs to parents would vary, depending on what was studied. Whitehead comments that the curriculum "probably exceeded the progressive curricula both of leading private institutions and of the dissenting academies" (Hilton and Shefrin 142).

30. The actual line is from the Gettysburg address of 19 November 1863 though the text is taken from what is called the Bancroft copy of 29 February 1864, as one of the published versions of the speech. The line reads: ". . . that this nation, under God, shall have a new birth of freedom, and that government of the people, by the people, for the people, shall not perish from the earth." Methodists were influential in their support of Lincoln during the Civil War. See the website developed at Cornell University, as that is where the Bancroft copy is held: http://rmc.library.cornell.edu/gettysburg150/exhibition/bancroft/index.html.

31. Lenton, *John Wesley's Preachers,* 4.

32. Lenton describes John Fenwick Sr. as "a man of property from Newcastle" who did work as an itinerant preacher between 1750 and 1758 (ibid., 341).

33. John Lenton, "Support Groups for Methodist Women Preachers 1803–1851," *Religion, Gender, and Industry: Exploring Church and Methodism in a Local Setting,* ed. Geordan Hammond and Peter S Forsaith (Eugene, Oregon: Pickwick Publications, 2011): 150.

34. See Paul Wesley Chilcote, *She Offered Them Christ: The Legacy of Women Preachers in Early Methodism* (Eugene, Oregon: Wipf and Stock, 2001): 39–40.

35. Lenton, *John Wesley's Preachers,* 9.

36. The story appears in the *Methodist Magazine* 31 (1808): 489–90, and in *The Works of John Wesley.* Ed. Richard P. Heitenrater and W. Reginald Ward. Vol. 22: 23

37. *Arminian Magazine: Consisting Of Extracts and Original Treatises on Universal Redemption* vol 1 (1778): vi.

38. "The Life of Mr. Peter Jaco Written by Himelf" that appeared in the first issue of the *Arminian Magazine,* later collected by Thomas Jackson in *The Lives of Early Methodist Preachers,* 260–68. Page references are to the Jackson edition. The text is available online. http://www.enterhisrest.org/testimonies/early1.pdf.

39. John Wesley, *The Works of the Reverend John Wesley, A. M,* First American Complete and Standard Edition in Seven Volumes, ed. John Emory (New York: J. Emory and B. Waugh for the First Methodist Episcopal Church at the Conference Office, 14 Crosby Street, 1831), 3: 402.

40. Jackson, *Lives of Early Methodist Preachers,* 161–62.

41. Ibid., 265.

42. EF to MH, n.d. 1802.

43. MA 1977/487. Location D3/26/2B, Copies of Original Letters and Documents collected from different sources by James Werell, vol.2, Methodist Archives, John Rylands Library, 2: 658c.

44. Lenton, *John Wesley's Preachers,* 65.

45. John Rylands Library, Manchester. DDPr 2/1. It is listed as a copy of the agreement made on May 8, 1754.

46. *The Letters of the Rev. John Wesley,* 8 vols., ed. John Telford (London: The Epworth Press, 1931): 3:74. Future references to this edition are cited as *LJW.*

47. All subsequent references to the "Minutes" refer to the minutes kept at the annual Connexion meetings of the Wesley brothers and their itinerant preachers. The minutes of those meetings were recorded and published as a series of pamphlets, archived in the Bristol New Room library, which is where I accessed them. I've provided dates and, as far as possible, other identifying information in the text.

48. Charles Atmore, *The Methodist Memorial, An Impartial Sketch of the Lives and Characters of the Preachers among the Methodists* (London: Hamilton, Adams, 1871), 68.

49. Jackson, *Lives of Early Methodist Preachers,* 264.

50. Ibid.

51. Note in the Merryweather letters volume directs to Mr. Jaco. See Copies of Original Letters and Documents collected from different sources by James Werell, vol.2, Methodist Archives, John Rylands Library, 3.5: 167.

52. Lenton, *John Wesley's Preachers,* 9.

53. Robert Southey, *The Life of Wesley; and the Rise and Progress of Methodism* (London: Longman, Hurst, Rees, Orme, and Brown, 1820), 248.

54. Methodist Archives Lamplough Collection 657. MA 1977/485 Location D3/26/2B.

55. Mr. Thomas Tennant, letters, Copies of Original Letters and Documents collected from different sources by James Werell, vol. 6, 239, Methodist Archives, John Rylands Library.

56. Jackson, *Lives of Early Methodist Preachers,* 261.

57. Thomas Rutherford Savage wrote a series of notes to his mother, Elizabeth (Eliza's granddaughter in the 1890s). The notes themselves do not appear to have survived, but a synthesis, written by Jessie Savage Cole (Thomas's sister and Elizabeth's youngest daughter), is in manuscript in the New-York Historical Society, Fenwick boxes.

58. John Lenton, email to author, July 19, 2011.

59. John Wesley to Christopher Hopper, 7 October 1773, in *The Letters of John Wesley,* vi: 490. Available at the Wesley Center Online, wesley.nnu.edu.

60. Lenton, *John Wesley's Preachers,* 109.

61. Ibid., 109–10.

62. For information, see Paul Langford, *A Polite and Commercial People: England 1727–1829* (Oxford: Clarendon Press, 1989): 59–123. That chapter, "The Progress of Politeness," covers schooling and the definitions of the middle class. For specific information on Kingswood, see A. H. L. Hastling, W. Addington Willis, and W. P. Workman, *The History of Kingswood School by Three Old Boys* (London: Charles H. Kelly, 1898).

63. Langford, *A Polite and Commercial People,* 86.

64. John Lenton, email to author, September 25, 2011.

65. *The UP Series:* Seven Disk Special Ed. (New York: First Run Features, 2013). The one exception was Nick Hitchen, who went from a one-room schoolhouse in Yorkshire to becoming a student and then professor at Oxford; the others were predominantly defined by their class and gender. The upper-class prep school boys went on to university and careers, the upper-class girls to upper-class marriages, the lower-class boys to

middling jobs, and the lower-class girls to marriage and jobs, though one lower-class girl did become a librarian.

66. Mary Clare Martin, "Marketing Religious Identity: Female Educators, Methodist Culture and Eighteenth-Century Childhood," *Educating the Child in Enlightenment Britain*, ed. Mary Hilton and Jill Shefrin (Farnham, UK: Ashgate, 2009), 67. The reference came from John Rylands University Library of Manchester, Fletcher-Tooth papers, manuscript biography of Mrs. Mary Fletcher, Box 23, Pt2, fol.16.

67. Hastling, et al., *The History of Kingswood School,* 295.

68. Ibid., 25.

69. In an unpublished section from a letter of December 1811 to Mary Hays, Eliza writes of hearing that Southey "domesticates but little with his family . . . because he is always engrossed by study during the day & goes to bed at eight at night." In another unpublished section of an April 4, 1813 letter to Mary Hays, apparently responding to Southey's rejection of something Mary sent, Eliza writes, "I supposed he would have been enchanted at the proposition & eager to close with it."

70. The detail about Peter Jaco's education comes from John Lenton's records. Because Jaco worked in the family pilchard fishery business after leaving school, he would not have needed much more education than he could have acquired by the age of thirteen. As John Wesley was trying to raise the intellectual range of his preachers, Kingswood school would have provided that option. According to Lenton's records, Jaco became a Methodist in 1749 when he was twenty, so he would have been twenty-five when Wesley made his unsuccessful attempt to send Jaco to Kingswood.

71. Wesley, *Works,* 10: 762.

72. John Pawson (1762–1806) was a Methodist itinerant. John C. Bowmer and John A. Vicerts, eds., *The Letters of John Pawson,* vol. 3 (closing years 1799–1806) (Peterborough: WMHS Publications, 1995), letter 256 of Joseph Benson.

73. Wesley, qtd. in Hastling, et al., *The History of Kingswood School,* 26.

74. Eliza and John were involved in the theatrical community. They knew and worked with Thomas Holcroft, for example. They also worked with the famous London theatrical family of Stephen Kemble (1758–1822), and with John Whitaker (1776–1847), organist and music publisher who wrote music for the theatre in London. Eliza also knew (and later stayed with) Mary Robinson (1757–1800), Georgian actor and mistress of the Prince of Wales. Eliza's daughter, Eliza Ann, did act at Covent Garden and was romantically involved with Henry Kemble while acting with him in Whitehaven (around 1808) and Birmingham before joining the Theatre Royal in Barbados. That's where she met William Rutherford, also an actor. Eliza's husband, John Fenwick, did write a short play, *The Indian* (1800). Although there is no evidence that Eliza wrote any plays, she was involved in the theatre. She wrote to Mary Hays in April 1806 about going to see a performance of *Forty Thieves,* which opened at Drury Lane (music by Michael Kelly), and then attempting to do a little "pantomimic" book about it, though if it was published it did not survive under her name. She did publish *The Life of The Famous Dog Carlo* (London: Tabart, 1804) for children. It is a fictional biography of a real dog, Carlo, who performed at Drury Lane in 1803.

75. David Hempton, *Methodism and Politics in British Society 1750–1850* (London: Hutchinson, 1984), 27.

76. The passages on the deaths of Elizabeth and Henry Rutherford are taken from "Biography: Memoir of Mr. Thomas Rutherford," *The Methodist Magazine: Being a*

Continuation of the Arminian Magazine for 1808 (London: Conference Office, 1808): 529–37.

77. Ibid., 531–33.

78. Although I found the information in the Wesley College Library in Bristol, that collection has been moved to the National Archives. It was in a file labeled D6/1/430a and dated 19 August 1800.

79. "Biography: Memoir of Mr. Thomas Rutherford," 536–37.

80. Leo Tolstoy, *Anna Karenina* (1873–77), trans. Constance Garnet. Available at https://www.gutenberg.org/files/1399/1399-h/1399-h.htm, accessed Aug. 22, 2016.

81. Philip Larkin, *High Windows* (London: Faber, 1974).

82. Isobel Grundy, "Introduction" to *Secresy*, 26–27, quoting *Emile, or On Education* by Jean-Jacques Rousseau, trans. Allan Bloom (New York: Basic Books. 1979), 370.

83. "Daughter," *Oxford English Dictionary OED Online*, Oxford University Press, January 2018, www.oed.com/view/Entry/47451, accessed March 23, 2018.

84. Mary Wollstonecraft to Everina Wollstonecraft, 7 November 1787, in *The Collected Letters of Mary Wollstonecraft*, ed. Janet Todd (London: Penguin, 2003), 139. The line reads, in part, "I am going to be the first of a new genus. . . ."

85. John Rylands Library, DDWes 2/85 says it is a letter containing that information of Peter Jaco's final words.

2. Mother and Author

1. See Martin Priestman, *Romantic Atheism: Poetry and Freethought 1780–1830* (Cambridge: Cambridge University Press, 2004). Priestman cites the "1794 trial for treason of Godwin's atheist friends Thomas Holcroft and John Thelwall . . . as one of the key political events of the 1790s" (29).

2. John Fenwick met with William Godwin on August 25 and December 28, 1788, as well as on November 9.

3. Laurence Sterne, *The Life and Opinions of Tristram Shandy, Gentleman,* was first published in 1795 and included print elements to indicate events. The blank page near the beginning indicates what Tristram Shandy could not know about his own birth.

4. Malcolm Gladwell, *The Tipping Point: How Little Things Can Make a Big Difference* (Boston: Little Brown, 2000).

5. *The Diary of William Godwin,* eds. Victoria Myers, David O'Shaughnessy, and Mark Philp (Oxford: Oxford Digital Library, 2010), accessible at http://godwindiary.bodleian .ox.ac.uk. See the entry for Charles André Mercier. The notes also explain that Mercier's daughter Louisa became Thomas Holcroft's fourth wife.

6. According to Pamela Clemit's notes in her edition of *The Letters of William Godwin,* Godwin had gone with Thomas Holcroft to try to stop William Holcroft from "sailing to the West Indies" with his friend Greenhill. William "had stolen £40 and a pair of pistols from his father." When Godwin and Thomas caught up with William and Greenhill in Deal (near Dover), they had already boarded the ship. William locked himself in his cabin and shot himself. Godwin reported to John Fenwick: "During the whole Mr. H. has displayed a fortitude almost more than human, but mixed with dreadful dejection & anxiety of mind" (Godwin, *Letters of William Godwin, vol. 1: 1778–1797,* ed. Pamela Clemit [Oxford: Oxford University Press, 2011]: 46–47).

7. Equiano's memoir, *The Interesting Narrative of the Life of Olaudah Equiano, or Gustavus Vasaa, Written by Himself,* was first published in 1789. John Graves Simcoe (1752–1806) was one of the original subscribers (a contributor to the publishing costs) to the book. Simcoe was the first Lieutenant Governor of Upper Canada (1791–96) and also enacted the first law (1793) toward the abolition of slavery in the British Empire.

8. See Henry Crabb Robinson, *Diary, Reminiscences, and Correspondence of Henry Crabb Robinson 1776–1867* (London: Macmillan, 1869).

9. Henry Crabb Robinson to his brother Thomas, December 1807. Letters of Henry Crabb Robinson (HCR Correspondence), Dr. Williams's Library, identified as #112: 1805–1808.

10. HCR correspondence 1808 #116: 7 January 1808 and February 1829. Eliza had written the original note to Robinson asking for funds to help her daughter prepare for the stage.

11. Charles Lamb, *Essays of Elia and Last Essays* (London: Oxford University Press, 1964), 35. "Cana fides" is from Vergil's *Aeneid* and it means "hoary faith," the point being that it was a reminder of something that we might call the "good old days," which is what Lamb is implying.

12. Charles Lamb, *Everybody's Lamb: Being a Selection from the Essays of Elia, the Letters and the Miscellaneous Prose of Charles Lamb,* ed. A C Ward, ill. E. H. Shepard (London: G. Bell and Sons, 1933), 278.

13. Shepard (1879–1976) was born long after John died, so I assume that the drawing was based on Lamb's description. The picture of Lamb, however, does match his image in portraits done when he was alive.

14. John Lenton, *John Wesley's Preachers: A Social and Statistical Analysis of the British and Irish Preachers Who Entered the Methodist Itinerancy before 1791* (Milton Keynes, UK: Paternoster, 2009), 341.

15. Lamb, *Elia,* 34. The hint is, I think, that John Fenwick was aligning his ancestry with Sir John Fenwick (1645–1697), a Northumberland baronet who had been beheaded as a Jacobite conspirator.

16. See *The Letters of William Godwin: 1778–1797, Vol. 1,* 79, n.1.

17. In a note on the letter from William Godwin to John Fenwick on February 15, 1793, Clemit helpfully explains why Godwin was so worried about sending his potentially treasonous book to France. She writes: "The risks of unguarded words, in both speech and writing, increased after the French National Convention declared war on Britain and Holland on 1 Feb., and Britain declared war on France on 11 Feb., though the Traitorous Correspondence Act did not pass into law until 7 May" (*Letters of William Godwin: 1778–1797, Vol. 1,* 80, n. 4).

18. William Godwin to John Fenwick, 15 February 1793, ibid., 79. Clemit notes that Godwin "was mindful of recent convictions for seditious language" (80, n. 4).

19. Christopher John Gibbs, "Friends and Enemies: The Underground War between Great Britain and France, 1793–1802," *Napoleon Series, Research Subject: Government and Politics: State Security and Counter-Intelligence.* Placed in February 2011 online at http://www.napoleon-series.org/research/government/british/Espionage/c_espionageintro.html.

20. Charles-François du Périer Dumouriez (1729–1823) was an important general in the Revolutionary Army in France, though his military career had developed originally in a more conventional way under Louis XVI. As the Revolution became increasingly

bloody, he became disaffected, eventually fleeing to England, and advising the British government during the Napoleonic Wars. He died in England.

21. In 1792–93, General Miranda was the commander-in-chief, and Dumouriez one of his generals. As the tensions between the Girondins in power and Dumouriez increased, General Miranda eventually supported the call to have Dumouriez accused of treason. See Richard Munthe Brace, "General Dumouriez and the Girondins 1792–1793," *The American Historical Review* 56, No. 3 (Apr., 1951): 493–509.

22. Pamela Clemit (*Letters of William Godwin: 1778–1797, Vol. 1*, 80, n.4) cites John Fenwick's letters, on February 12 and March 1, 1793 to General Miranda and gives as the reference *Archivo del General Miranda,* 25 vols. (Caracas: Editorial Sur-América, 1925–50), I, 264, 256, 258.

23. With thanks to Paul Stevens, University of Toronto, for the initial suggestion that I check for links between John Fenwick and the London Corresponding Society.

24. Michael T. Davis, ed., *London Corresponding Society 1792–99*, 6 vols. (London: Pickering and Chatto, 2002), 6:122.

25. John Issitt, *Jeremiah Joyce, Radical Dissenter and Writer* (London: Ashgate, 2006), 48. Jeremiah Joyce was also one of the people commissioned by the publisher Richard Phillips for generic instructional material, sometimes as "Goldsmith" for the Goldsmith geography books, early textbooks for Richard Phillips. Although Phillips made money, he exploited his authors, one of whom was Eliza. I will return to Phillips later in the book.

26. Although the autobiography tells the story of African birth, then capture by slave traders, the authenticity of the first part of his origin story is in doubt, as it appears that he was likely born a slave in South Carolina, so did not experience the Middle Passage. See website by Brycchan Carey: http://www.brycchancarey.com/equiano.

27. Mary Thale, *Selections from the Papers of the London Corresponding Society 1792–1799* (Cambridge: Cambridge University Press, 1983), xxv.

28. Ibid., 362. John Fenwick edited the LCS magazine between 1796 and 1797, two years after the publication of the "Committee of Secrecy" report and a year after Eliza's publication of *Secresy*. In the issues from that period, there is a long essay on education, and there is a long review (extending over several issues) of Mrs. Inchbald's novel.

29. Introduction to *The London Corresponding Society*, 1:xxxvi; note 119 (1:xlvii) offers additional sources: Clive Emsley, "The Home Office and its Sources of Information and Investigation 1791–1801," *English Historical Review* 94 (1979): 532–62; and Bernard Porter, *Plots and Paranoia: A History of Political Espionage in Britain, 1790–1988* (London: Routledge, 1989), 29–31.

30. Edmund Burke's *Reflections on the Revolution in France* (1790) prompted responses: Mary Wollstonecraft's *A Vindication of the Rights of Woman* (1791–92) and Thomas Paine's *Rights of Man* (1791).

31. From "The First Report From the Committee of Secrecy" (17 May 1794), cols 475–97. Qtd in Issitt, *Jeremiah Joyce*, 50.

32. John Fenwick, *On the Trial of James Coigley for High Treason* (London: Printed for the Author, 1798), 20.

33. At the time I was preparing this chapter in the spring of 2016, twenty-seven scholarly articles included substantive discussions on *Secresy*, though not one included a reference to the coincidence between John and Eliza's connection with the LCS or

publication of the Report on Secrecy appearing in 1794, a year before Eliza's novel *Secresy* was published.

34. Isobel Grundy suggests that Eliza B. is either Elizabeth [Eliza] Bishop (Mary Wollstonecraft's estranged sister) or author Elizabeth Benger. The evidence points to Eliza Bishop, as there is a letter she wrote to Everina Wollstonecraft, dated tentatively in the Abinger Archives at the Bodleian Library as November 5, 1793. In the letter, Bishop describes meeting "two well-bred elegant Welshmen" at Mrs. Fenwick's.

35. Eliza Fenwick, *Secresy, or The Ruin on the Rock,* ed. and intro. Isobel Grundy (Peterborough, ON: Broadview Press, 1998), 37. All future references are to this edition.

36. Although I can't confirm an explicit connection, it is worth mentioning that the poet Mary Robinson, with whom Eliza lived temporarily in 1800, sets up a scenario similar to Eliza's in *Secresy* in *The Sicilian Lover.* Act I, Scene 1, is set at "a Pavilion at Valmont," and includes the same pedagogical tyranny: "From the first dawn of helpless infancy / I've taught her mild obedience to my will / and count upon her duty more than love." The text appears in Mary Robinson, *The Poetical Works of the Late Mrs. Robinson Including Many Pieces Never Before Published,* vol. 1 (London: Richard Phillips, 1806).

37. See Robert Filmer, *Patriarcha and Other Political Works,* ed. Peter Laslett (Oxford: Blackwell, 1949).

38. Sarah Emsley, "Radical Marriage," *Eighteenth-Century Fiction* 11:4 (1999): 477–98.

39. The "corresponding societies" of the 1790s—like the pop-up protest groups of the Occupy movement in 2011—brought together a critical mass of people trying to work out a social problem (in the case of the Occupy movement, it was the increasing gap between the one percent of super-rich and the ninety-nine percent of the rest); that is, addressing the issue of the gap between those with wealth and power and those without had distinct parallels with the move toward revolution in France. The first Corresponding Society was set up in Sheffield and it was quickly joined by societies in other parts of the country, including Birmingham, Coventry, and Leeds.

40. Miriam Wallace, "Constructing Treason, Narrating Truth: The 1794 Treason Trial of Thomas Holcroft and the Fate of English Jacobinism," *Romanticism on the Net* 45 (February 2007), paragraph 11. Besides Eliza's novel, she lists Wollstonecraft's *Wrongs of Woman,* Holcroft's *Anna St. Ives,* and she names Robert Bage's *Hermsrpong or Man as he is Not* (1796), Charlotte Smith's *The Old Manor House* (1793), and Elizabeth Inchbald's *Nature and Art* (1796).

41. John Wesley, "Rule of Conduct," *Letters of John Wesley,* ed. George Eayrs (New York: George H. Doran Co., 1916), 423. The expression is an archaic proverb found in Babylonian and Hebrew religious tracts. Its debut in the English language, in a modified form, is found in the writings of philosopher and scientist Sir Francis Bacon. In *Advancement of Learning* (1605) he wrote, "Cleanness of body was ever deemed to proceed from a due reverence to God." Almost two hundred years later (1791), John Wesley made a reference to the expression in one of his sermons in the form we use it today. Wesley wrote, "Slovenliness is no part of religion. Cleanliness is indeed next to Godliness."

42. Mary A Favret, *Romantic Correspondence: Women, Politics and the Fiction of Letters* (Cambridge: Cambridge University Press, 2005), 9. It looks as if a couple of uncorrected errors appear in the paragraph: for instance, the reference to the London Corresponding (not Correspondence) Society. And the society was outlawed in 1799, not 1794.

43. Although I can demonstrate that Eliza and Mary Wollstonecraft would have had friends in common in the early 1790s, and there is internal evidence in *Secresy* that Eliza had read Wollstonecraft's *Vindication,* I can't place them together in 1793–94.

44. Favret, *Romantic Correspondence,* 39. Favret also quotes from *Public General Acts* (London: Charles Eyre & Andrew Strahan, 1793), LXII: 68.

45. The discussion on the Dumouriez/Miranda correspondence is in Favret's chapter on Helen Maria Williams (1759–1827). See especially the discussion on the relationship between official and friendly letters (*Romantic Correspondence,* 87).

46. Ibid., 97. Favret's chapter focuses on Wollstonecraft's *Letters Written During a Short Residence in Sweden, Norway, and Denmark,* first published in 1796.

47. Mary Wollstonecraft, *The Works of Mary Wollstonecraft,* 7 vols., eds. Janet Todd and Marilyn Butler (London: Pickering, 1989), 5: 245. References to Wollstonecraft's *Works* will be cited parenthetically in text throughout the rest of the chapter.

48. Elaine Showalter is credited with coining the term "gynocriticism" in *A Literature of Their Own: British Women Novelists from Bronte to Lessing* (Princeton, NJ: Princeton University Press, 1977), a scholarly apparatus and infrastructure developed largely because of work by early feminist scholars such as Showalter, Sandra Gilbert, and Susan Gubar (authors of *The Madwoman in the Attic*). Through the establishment of publishing houses such as Virago, otherwise inaccessible novels by women from the eighteenth and nineteenth centuries began to appear in modern paperback editions and become accessible.

49. For a discussion on *Secresy* in the context of marriage, see for example, Sarah Emsley, "Radical Marriage," *Eighteenth-Century Fiction* 11.4 (1999): 477–98. Emsley's essay also contains a helpful discussion (via Marilyn Butler's 1975 *Jane Austen and the War of Ideas*) on *Secresy* as a Jacobin novel (where the hero/victim is oppressed by society) and *Pride and Prejudice* as anti-Jacobin (where the hero/victim learns to accommodate to society); see also Jennifer Golightly's *The Family, Marriage and Radicalism in British Women's Novels of the 1790s* (Lewisburg, PA: Bucknell University Press, 2012). For a discussion on *Secrecy* in the context of: motherhood, see for example, Mercy Cannon, "Hygienic Motherhood: Domestic Medicine and Eliza Fenwick's *Secresy,*" *Eighteenth-Century Fiction* 20.4 (2008): 535–61; madness, see for example, Patricia Cove, "'The Walls of Her Prison': Madness, Gender, and Discursive Agency in Eliza Fenwick's *Secresy* and Mary Wollstonecraft's *The Wrongs Of Woman,*" *European Romantic Review* 23.6 (2012): 671–87; father/daughter relationships, see for example, Frances Chiu, "From Nobodaddies to Noble Daddies: Writing Political and Paternal Authority," *Eighteenth-Century Life* 26.2 (2002): 1–22; epistolary communities, see for example, Christopher Bundock, "The (Inoperative) Epistolary Community in Eliza Fenwick's *Secresy,*" *European Romantic Review* 20.5 (2009): 709–20; Gothic novels, see for example, Angela Wright, "'To Live the Life of Hopeless Recollection': Mourning and Melancholia in Female Gothic, 1780–1800," *Gothic Studies* 6.1 (2004): 19–29, and Ellen Malenas Ledoux, "Gothic Space and Female Agency in *Emmeline, The Mysteries of Udolpho* and *Secresy*" in *Women's Writing* 18: 3 (August 2011): 331–47; Jacobin novels, see for example, the 1996 PhD thesis (New York University) by Elizabeth Denlinger (curator of the Pforzheimer Collection of Shelley and His Circle at the New York Public library), "The Gratification of Demons: The Fallen Woman Narrative in Novels of Five English Jacobin Women Writers"; and pedagogy, see for example, Lissa Paul, *The Children's Book Business: Lessons from the Long Eighteenth Century* (London: Routledge, 2011).

50. Isobel Grundy, introduction to *Secresy,* 30.

51. The one other published letter is to Jane Porter (20 August 1832) from Canandaigua. Grundy includes it in her edition of *Secresy* (375–76), and it is in the Pforzheimer Collection at the New York Public Library.

52. F. J. Harvey Darton, *Children's Books in England: Five Centuries of Social Life,* 3rd ed., rev. Brian Alderson (Cambridge: Cambridge University Press, 1982), 168.

53. See, for example, Hilary Beckles, *A History of Barbados: From Amerindian Settlement to Nation-State* (Cambridge: Cambridge University Press, 1990). He cites Eliza's discussion (in a letter dated April 12, 1815) of the way that color effectively leaves the wealthy Creole population excluded from white privilege (67). Pedro Welch, in *Slave Society in the City: Bridgetown, Barbados 1680–1834* (Jamaica: Ian Reade, 2003), categorizes Eliza as a "female operating in a system in which the norms of slave behavior were markedly different from those of the rural patriarchal system" (16). Because Welch does not seem to be aware of Eliza's abolitionist status when she was in Britain in the 1790s, he only reads her in the context of plantation-based slave owners.

54. Although Evelyn O'Callaghan recognizes Eliza in *Women Writing the West Indies 1804–1939: A Hot Place, Belonging to Us* (London: Routledge, 2003), in the context of the radical London Godwin/Wollstonecraft 1790s community, she incorrectly names Mary Hays as the author of *Secresy.* In context, it looks like an error that was accidentally overlooked before publication.

55. For a comprehensive analysis of the publishing history of *Secresy,* see Isobel Grundy's introduction to her Broadview edition (Peterborough, ON: 1998). Grundy explains that Eliza was originally publishing on commission for the six booksellers who made up the original conger, with "Lane, the first name on the list," taking responsibility for the production costs: "He would reimburse himself by a 10% levy on copies sold, and pay the rest of the proceeds to the author." Grundy says that this was "an unusual way to publish fiction," and was a gamble. If not enough copies were sold, then Eliza would have risked paying off the publishing costs. One of the publishers in the initial conger, John Whitaker, remained her friend (8–10).

56. Mary Thale, *Selections from the Papers of the London Corresponding Society 1792–1799* (Cambridge: Cambridge University Press, 1983), 342. Further references to Thale made in text.

57. Ted Hughes, "Myth and Education," *Winter Pollen: Occasional Prose,* ed. William Scammell (London: Faber, 1994), 149.

58. The story is well known. Gilbert Imlay (1754–1828), an American (described sometimes as a businessman, and sometimes as a speculator), met Mary Wollstonecraft while in France. Although he apparently regarded their affair as casual, he did father Fanny. When he left in 1795 for another woman, Mary tried to commit suicide. As a way of keeping Mary distant, but useful, he sent her to Scandinavia to attend to dubious business on his behalf. Mary's letters to him ultimately became her *Letters from Sweden, Norway, and Denmark,* published in 1796.

59. Willey Reveley (1760–99) was an architect, and is known for working on Jeremy Bentham's "Panopticon." He died at age thirty-nine, apparently of a brain aneurysm. Eliza was there when he was suddenly taken ill.

60. Mary Wollstonecraft, *The Collected Letters of Mary Wollstonecraft,* ed. Janet Todd (New York: Columbia University Press, 203): 436.

61. The note is tucked inside a first edition of Mary Wollstonecraft's *Mary: A Fiction* (1788) at the Huntington Library in Los Angeles, California.

62. Mrs. Fenn, *Juvenile Correspondence or Letters Suited to Children from Four to Above Ten Years of Age* (London: Marshall, 1783).

63. Fenwick, *Secresy,* 304. Eliza writes about going to see Marshall in an unpublished line in the first extant letter to Mary Hays on October 22, 1798. She says: "I intend writing today to Mr Marshall, he is very active & has a good heart, he may be able to do something."

64. In the *Vindication,* Mary Wollstonecraft argues for co-education, suggesting that schools "ought to be surrounded by a large piece of ground, in which the children might be usefully exercised, for at this age they should not be confined to any sedentary employment for more than an hour at a time" (*The Works of Mary Wollstonecraft. 7 vols.,* eds. Janet Todd and Marilyn Butler [London: Pickering, 1989], 173). Although there is no explicit connection, Anna Barbauld also makes reference, in part two of *Lessons* (1778), to Charles playing with a pitchfork and a rake. As William McCarthy explains in "Mother of All Discourses: Anna Barbauld's *Lessons for Children,*" in *Culturing the Child: 1640–1914: Essays in Memory of Mitzi Myers,* ed. Donelle Ruwe (Lanham, MD: Scarecrow, 2005), 95, the play/work game is a literal enactment of the proverb about making hay while the sun shines.

65. Maria Edgeworth and her father Richard Lovell Edgeworth had published a two-volume work called *Practical Education* in 1788.

66. Mary Wollstonecraft to William Godwin, 10 June 1797, in *The Collected Letters of Mary Wollstonecraft,* 420.

67. See, for example, Wollstonecraft, in the *Vindication* explaining that "only education [which] deserves emphatically to be termed cultivation of the mind," will be viable as it "teaches young people how to begin to think" (*Works* 5: 234–5). See also, "An active mind embraces the whole circle of its duties, and finds time enough for / all" (*Works* 5: 241).

68. William Godwin to Mary Wollstonecraft, 7 June 1797, in William Godwin, *The Letters of William Godwin: 1778–1805, 2 Vols.,* ed. Pamela Clemit (Oxford: Oxford University Press, 2011), 214. All excerpts in the text from Godwin's letters are from this volume unless otherwise indicated.

69. William Godwin to William Cole, 2 March 1802, MS. Abinger c. 7, fols. 97–98, The Bodleian Library, University of Oxford.

70. Eliza's invocation of the rhetorical structure typically used by preachers in sermons is perhaps another slant allusion to her proto-Methodist childhood.

71. Janet Todd, *Mary Wollstonecraft: A Revolutionary Life* (London: Bloomsbury, 2014), 456.

72. Charles Kegan Paul, *William Godwin: His Friends and Contemporaries* (London: Henry S. King, 1876), 282.

73. Eliza Fenwick to Everina Wollstonecraft, 12 September 1797, MS. Abinger b. 4, fols. 101.

74. Todd, *Mary Wollstonecraft,* 450, 453.

3. Children's Book Writer and Friend

1. Mary A. Favret, *Romantic Correspondence: Women, Politics and the Fiction of Letters* (Cambridge: Cambridge University Press, 2005), 27.

2. Mary Wollstonecraft, *The Works of Mary Wollstonecraft*, 7 vols., eds. Janet Todd and Marilyn Butler (London: Pickering, 1989), 5:98. Future references are to this edition.

3. Eliza Fenwick, *Secresy, Or the Ruin on the Rock*, edited with an Introduction by Isobel Grundy (1795; Peterborough, ON: Broadview Press, 1998), I: 57. Future references are to this edition.

4. In *Recollections of the Life of John Binns* (Philadelphia: Printed and for Sale by the Author and by Parry and McMillan, 1854), 46. There is a terrific little story about John Fenwick and John Binns walking along Holborn in London late one night, when they came about a "sad spectacle" of a man being taken into custody charged with "having stolen a public house pewter pint measure." Fenwick and Binns "became interested, and accompanied the accused, one on each side of him, to the watch house." When the man was searched, nothing was found and the man left. Fenwick and Binns "congratulated themselves on having in some measure contributed to the liberation of an innocent person," when Fenwick found the stolen pewter pot in his pocket, and guessed that the accused had slipped it in while the three men were walking together.

5. The full account of the "Trial for High Treason" in Maidstone, Kent in April 1798 is available at: http://freepages.genealogy.rootsweb.ancestry.com/~mrawson/treason.html.

6. Thomas Holcroft, *Memoirs of the Late Thomas Holcroft, Written by Himself and Continued to the Time of His Death from His Diary, Notes and other Papers*, ed. William Hazlitt (London: Longman, Brown, Green: 1852), II: 174.

7. A. F. Wedd, *The Fate of the Fenwicks: Letters to Mary Hays (1798–1828)* (London: Methuen, 1927), 2.

8. *Falstaff's Letters* by James White, originally published 1796. White was one of Charles Lamb's oldest friends as both had been to Christ's Hospital School together. White loved Shakespeare and apparently frequently used lines from Shakespeare as quips in conversation.

9. Holcroft, *Memoirs* II: 193.

10. A. F. Wedd edited out the comment in her 1927 edition of *The Fate of the Fenwicks*. By comparing the manuscript letters with the published volume, I found that Wedd had routinely omitted references that confirmed Eliza's continuing participation in London literary life and her relationship with Mary Hays as literary, novel-writing women.

11. *Letters of Charlotte Smith*, ed. Judith Phillips Stanton (Bloomington: Indiana University Press, 2003): 350. At the end of the letter, Smith writes that she is "impatient for the Novel promis'd in the papers" (351), though the footnote comment is that "Fenwick did not publish another novel" (352). Smith had found herself impoverished because, as laws dictated, she had transferred her property to her husband on their marriage. He proceeded to dissipate it all and left her to fend for herself.

12. *He's Much to Blame: A Comedy: in Five Acts*. As performed at the Theatre Royal, Covent Garden by Thomas Holcroft, 1745–1809, available at http://ota.ox.ac.uk/id/3992 via http://writersinspire.org/content/hes-much-blame-comedy-five-acts-performed -theatre-royal-covent-garden. Accessed on Saturday, March 12, 2016. It turns out that Holcroft wrote the play but, wanting to deflect attention away from himself, produced

it with the attribution to John Fenwick. Later, Holcroft confessed gleefully, it seems, to William Godwin on August 1, 1799, his pride in his accomplishment of the deception: "Met Mr. G—whom I informed that the comedy, 'He's much to Blame' was written by me. He testified great satisfaction at the shame its success brought on my persecutors, and that the king, not knowing the author had commanded it twice." The information is in Holcroft, *Memoirs*, 213.

13. The essays later came out as a separate volume, titled *Public Characters of 1799–1800* (London: Phillips, 1799). What distinguishes John Fenwick's portrait of William Godwin from those in scholarly retrospective accounts is how fresh and personal it is. Richard Phillips (1767–1840) was an important publisher in his day. Although Godwin didn't like him particularly, and neither did Eliza, he is credited with figuring out how to make money on textbooks. By hiring hack writers, buying the copyright, and publishing their texts under generic names, he could increase the profits on his backlist. See John Issitt, "The Natural History of a Textbook," *Publishing History* 47 (2000): 5–30. Eliza was one of his hack writers.

14. Fenwick, "William Godwin," *Public Characters of 1799–1800*, 384.

15. *Fate of the Fenwicks*, x.

16. A. F. Wedd, *The Fate of the Fenwicks; Letters to Mary Hays (1798–1828)* (London: Methuen, 1927), ii. Future references are to this edition.

17. Imogen Wedd, email to author, September 19, 2011: "For what it is worth," Imogen says, "I think Aunt Nancy had the prejudices of her time (and of 'new money' at that). She was very contemptuous of the very thing I think most interesting about the Wedds, Dunkins & Hays, their religious dissent, and she had the lack of sympathy for those with financial struggles which only those with a private income who have never had to work can have!"

18. Eliza doesn't say where or with whom, but his friend John Philpot Curran (1750–1817) seems an option, as John Fenwick introduced him to William Godwin a few months later. John Curran invited William Godwin to Ireland a short time after that.

19. Eliza and Mary had friends in common through the mid-1790s, so they may well have met and perhaps even exchanged letters prior to the first 1798 letter that appears in *The Fate of the Fenwicks*. William Godwin records his first meeting with Mary Hays as being on November 15, 1794. By that date, both John and Eliza Fenwick had been meeting regularly with Godwin too.

20. Burney Collection of 17th and 18th Century Newspapers, British Library.

21. See Hester Davenport, *The Prince's Mistress: A Life of Mary Robinson* (Stroud, UK: Sutton, 2004), or Paula Byrne, *Perdita: The Life of Mary Robinson* (London: Harper Collins, 2004).

22. *The Monthly Magazine or, British Register* Vol. X, Part II (August-December 1800), August 1, 1800: 48. The notices on forthcoming publications announce that Miss Plumptre, a friend of Eliza's, is also "preparing a novel for the press."

23. Eliza Fenwick to William and Mary Jane Godwin, 17 November 1808, Abinger Collection c.10 (Dep. C 527), Bodleian Libraries, University of Oxford.

24. William Blake's "Infant Joy" had been first published in *Songs of Innocence and of Experience, Shewing the Two Contrary States of the Human Soul* (London: W. Blake, 1789).

25. "Lines Addressed to a Beautiful Infant," *Morning Post and Gazateer,* July 29, 1800, in *The Works of Mary Robinson,* vol. 2, ed. Daniel Robinson, series ed. William D. Brewer (London: Pickering & Chatto, 2009): 108–9.

26. Winifred Courtney, in *The Young Charles Lamb 1775–1802* (London: Henry S. King, 1876), 281, explains that "wealthy Radicals" funded the transitory radical newspapers such as Fenwick's *The Albion.* Future references are to this edition.

27. Charles Lamb, *Essays of Elia and Last Essays,* The World's Classics (London: Oxford University Press, 1964), 324. Future references are to this edition.

28. Charles Kegan Paul, *William Godwin: His Friends and Contemporaries* (London: Henry S. King, 1876), II: 62.

29. Then, as now, powerful, intelligent men were regarded as sexually attractive. Godwin and Holcroft were both desirable. In a letter of June 1795, Amelia Alderson says, "You have no idea how gallant he [Godwin] is become; but indeed, he is much more amiable than ever he was. Mrs Inchbald says, the report of the world is that Mr Holcroft is in love with her, *she* with Mr Godwin, Mr Godwin with *me,* and I am in love with Mr Holcroft! A pretty story indeed! This report Godwin brings to me, and he says Mrs I. always tells him that when she praises *him* I praise Holcroft. This is not fair in Mrs I. She appears to me jealous of G's attention to me, so she makes him believe I prefer H to him. She often says to me, 'Now you are come, Mr Godwin does not come near me.' Is not this very womanish." See William St. Clair, *The Godwins and the Shelleys: The Biography of a Family* (London: Faber, 1989), 153.

30. The dating is from a note in *The Diary of William Godwin,* eds. Victoria Myers, David O'Shaughnessy, and Mark Philp (Oxford. Oxford Digital Library, 2010), available at the Godwin Diary Project, http://godwindiary.bodleian.ox.ac.uk. The stillborn son was called William and is identified as the William Godwin who was born, possibly as the note suggests, on 8 May 1802, and died. The details are unclear.

31. As late as 1807, publisher John Wilkes proposed to Eliza to enlist Mr. F's assistance to complete a job for "speed's sake." One of the clearest signs of their ongoing familial association comes from the Godwin diary, where John and Eliza Fenwick are recorded meeting together with Godwin (and others) on eighty-nine occasions (between 1800 and 1812), that is, in the period after Eliza decided to pursue her own life. The practical end of the marriage came in 1812, when Eliza took up a position as governess in Ireland. With thanks to Murray Wilcox for reminding me of the timelines.

32. Eliza later expresses regret, in a note from August 1811, that Charles and Mary Lamb were "of the opinion that her [Eliza Ann's] father by one sort of imprudence will always frustrate her hopes here [in England]."

33. The *London Gazette,* June 25, 1803, notes that "Thomas James Fenwick, of Penzance, in the county of Cornwall, Linen-Draper and Shopkeeper, Dealer, and Chapman, and he being declared a Bankrupt, is hereby required to surrender himself to the Commissioners in the said Commission named, or the major in the Forenoon and on the 9th of August following, at Ten in the Forenoon, at Guildhall in London, and make a full Discovery and Disclosure of his Estate and Effects" (764).

34. Charles Lamb to John Rickman, 16 July 1803, in *Letters of Charles Lamb,* ed. Alfred Ainger (London: Macmillan and Co., 1904) 1: 252.

35. Anne Plumptre's novel, *Something New; Or Adventures at Campbell-Park* (London: T. N. Longman and O. Reese) was published in 1801.

36. Mary Lamb to Dorothy Wordsworth, 11 July 1803, letter 108, in Charles Lamb, *The Letters of Charles and Mary Lamb*, ed. E. V. Lucas (London: Methuen, 1912), 286.

37. In the first extant letter to Mary Hays, from October 22, 1798, Eliza acknowledges the demands of her young family (Eliza Ann would have been nine years old and Orlando just five months). She says: "I cannot write, perpetually surrounded with my family even were I assured that I have talents to make writing profitable & I possess no such confidence."

38. Roland Barthes, "Authors and Writers," *A Barthes Reader*, ed. Susan Sontag (New York: Hill and Wang, 1960).

39. F. J. Harvey Darton, *Children's Books in England: Five Centuries of Social Life*, 3rd ed. (1932; Cambridge: Cambridge University Press, 1982), 156. Future references are to this edition.

40. The credit for providing the earliest critical re-evaluation of Darton's views of the "lady moralists" goes initially to Mitzi Myers. See particularly her groundbreaking essay, "Impeccable Governesses, Rational Dames, and Moral Mothers: Mary Wollstonecraft and the Female Tradition in Georgian Children's Books," *Children's Literature* 14 (1986): 31–58. For other works on re-evaluating late Enlightenment writing by women for children, see, for example, Lynne Vallone, *Disciplines of Virtue: Girls Culture in the Eighteenth and Nineteenth Centuries* (New Haven, CT: Yale University Press, 1995); *Culturing the Child: 1690–1914: Essays in Memory of Mitzi Myers*, ed. Donelle Ruwe (Lanham, MD: Scarecrow, 2005); and *Opening the Nursery Door: Reading Writing and Childhood 1600–1900*, eds. Mary Hilton, Victor Watson, and Morag Styles (London: Routledge, 1997).

41. Marjorie Moon suggests that evidence in William Godwin's journal is that "he helped her" in the composition (Marjorie Moon, *Benjamin Tabart's Juvenile Library. A Bibliography of Books for Children Published, Written, Edited and Sold by Mr. Tabart, 1801–1820* [London: St. Paul's Bibliographies, 1990], 43).

42. See John Issitt, "The Natural History of a Textbook," *Publishing History* 47 (January 2000): 5–30, and Issitt, *Jeremiah Joyce: Radical Dissenter and Writer* (Aldershot, UK: Ashgate, 2006). In both the essay and the book, Issitt discusses the way in which Richard Phillips hired writers to produce the copy that would be published under a generic pseudonym. Like Eliza, Jeremiah Joyce (1763–1816) was one of the writers regularly used by Phillips.

43. With thanks To Anne Markey for the identification on *Six Stories in English and French*, later republished by M. J. Godwin as *Six Stories for the Nursery*. In an email to me dated September 1, 2014, Markey identified the trace for Eliza's authorship as coming through "an ad in *The Morning Chronicle* of 22 December 1822," in which *Six Stories for the Nursery* is identified as the *sequel* [italics mine] to "*The Mouse-Trap. For Children from Two to Five Years of Age. By Mrs Fenwick*, printed for M. J. Godwin and Co., Juvenile Library for Schools and Families, French and English, No. 195, (St Clement's Strand)." To my knowledge, no copy of *The Mouse-Trap* has been found, but Marjorie Moon points out that *Six Stories in English and French*, published by Tabart in 1810, was republished as *Six Stories for the Nursery* by Mary Jane Godwin in 1824. As *Six Stories in English and French* consists of the same stories as those in *Six Stories for the Nursery*, *Six Stories in English and French* can be attributed to Eliza.

44. Moon, *Benjamin Tabart's Juvenile Library*, 7.

45. Marjorie Moon singles out *The Life of Carlo* for praise, noting that though Eliza's writing for children was inspired by "sheer necessity," what "sprang [was] not a hack, but a composer of interesting tales like her dog story, *The life of Carlo* (1804) . . ." (ibid.).

46. All playbills referenced are from the Theatre Archives, Blythe House, Victoria and Albert Museum, London. The Drury Lane and Covent Garden playbills are held in files organized by date. I went through the extant bills, year by year, finding those in which Eliza Ann's name appeared. I also found the playbills related to the performance of the dog Carlo in *The Caravan* at Drury Lane.

47. With thanks to Anne Markey for supplying the information about Maria Edgeworth's praise for *Little Mary and her Cat,* as seen in a letter she wrote to her friend Mrs. Bannatyne dated December 1811: "Have you seen a little book called 'Mary and her Cat'? It is not new, I believe it is almost out of print, but my sister Beddoes brought it to my youngest sister Lucy, who has actually learned to read well from the pleasure and curiosity it excited." Frances Anne Edgeworth, ed. *A Memoir of Maria Edgeworth: With a Selection of Her Letters* (London: Joseph Master, 1867), 284. Lucy Edgeworth's copy of *Little Mary and her Cat* is in the Morgan Library in New York.

48. In his argument in *An Enquiry Concerning Political Justice* (1793), ed. Mark Philp (Oxford: Oxford Worlds Classics, 2013), on the way the threat of punishment is used to maintain social order, William Godwin writes: "Whips, axes and gibbets, dungeons, chains and racks are the most approved and established methods of persuading men to obedience, . . ." (15). Eliza seems to have echoed the content and the cadence of Godwin's line in her creation of Nora's understanding of how the threat of punishment is what keeps enslaved people obedient. See Eliza Fenwick, *Visits to the Juvenile Library, or, Knowledge Proved to be the Source of Happiness* (London: Tabart, 1805), 15. Future references are to this edition.

49. Harriet Beecher Stowe, *Uncle Tom's Cabin; or Life Among the Lowly,* Vol. II (Boston: John P. Jewett & Company, 1852), 69.

50. Only the 1806 edition of *The Class Book* has the entries on opposition to the slave trade, as the law bringing about the abolition of the trade was passed the following year. The April 6 entry is from a speech by William Paley, reprinted in his collected works. See William Paley, *The Collected Works of William Paley* (London: William Smith, 1838), 552–53. The August 2 and 3 entries on the slave trade were taken from the first edition of what became known generically among schoolchildren as *Goldsmith's Geography*; Rev J. Goldsmith [pseudonym for Richard Phillips], *Geography for the Use of Schools, And Young Persons in General* (London: Richard Phillips, 1803): 51–53. The entries disappear with no explanation.

51. Eliza Fenwick (pseudonym Rev'd David Blair) *The Class Book: or Three Hundred and Sixty-Five Reading Lessons, Adapted to the Use of Schools; For Every Day in the Year* (London: Tabart, 1806), 117. The quotations are all from the 1806 edition; after the slave trade was abolished, Richard Phillips replaced the selections from April 6 and from August 2 and 3 with alternative readings.

52. The slip between showing empathy for animals and empathy for people is also at the heart of Eliza's *Little Mary and her Cat* (1804). The copy at the Pierpont Morgan Library, incidentally, was owned by Lucy Edgeworth (1805–1898). She wrote her name in it, and dated it 1811, when she would have been about six. In contrast to Darton's assertion that books in the period were heavy on "opposing cruelty to animals" (*Children's*

Books in England, 156), Eliza, in the spirit of Mary Wollstonecraft's unfinished *Lessons for Children*, took the positive position. The pedagogical point was not that it was bad to be cruel, but that being kind to animals and people was a way of showing empathy. In *Little Mary and her Cat*, Eliza sets into motion a little plot on the difference between the title character (Mary) saying the right words (that she loves her mother) and showing that she means them (behaving appropriately). The distinction is exactly the one Eliza makes almost thirty years later about her concern that Methodists can't distinguish between "purity of heart" and "purity of words" (Eliza Fenwick to Moffat family, 26 January 1833). In the space of a few pages, Nurse Brown becomes ill and, in a very affecting death scene, dies. She charges Mary with both care of the cat, and a duty for empathy, though as the story is limited to words of one and two syllables (for beginning readers), the word empathy is not used. By way of comparison, Lesson XIII of Mary Wollstonecraft's *Lessons for Children* offers a parallel lesson on empathy. The story begins with an observation of a "poor puppy" who "has tumbled off the stool." Mary instructs her daughter "to comfort" the puppy, to give him "a little milk in a saucer," and to pet him. Then she makes the child/pet comparison with the mother-daughter relationship: "You are wiser than the dog, you must help him. The dog will love you for it, and run after you. I feed you and take care of you: you love me and follow me for it" (Mary Wollstonecraft, *The Works of Mary Wollstonecraft*, eds. Janet Todd and Marilyn Butler [London: Pickering, 1989], 4: 473).

The gap between moves toward the abolition of slavery and the amelioration of the brutal conditions to which enslaved people were subjected in the period is not really at issue here. When Eliza was writing for Richard Phillips in the early 1800s, just the move toward the abolition of the slave trade in 1807 was regarded as a hugely progressive one, and even that only finally happened sixteen years after William Wilberforce had first attempted to pass such a bill in 1791. Eliza's views were aligned with the views of human rights expressed by the people in her circle, including William Godwin in *Political Justice*, Mary Wollstonecraft in the *A Vindication of the Rights of Woman*, and Thomas Paine in *The Rights of Man*. Because Eliza was writing for Tabart/Phillips in *Visits to the Juvenile Library*, she uses indirect discourse in reference to Nora to create the analogy between the corrosive effects of cruel tutors and such effects of cruel slavemasters. For a discussion on eighteenth-century arguments in support of the amelioration of the conditions of the enslaved people—as opposed to the arguments in support of abolition—see George Boulukos, *The Grateful Slave: The Emergence of Race in Eighteenth-Century British and American Culture* (Cambridge, Cambridge University Press, 2008).

53. George Borrow, *Lavengro* (London, 1861), 182.

54. In *The Children's Book Business* (New York: Routledge, 2011): 55–57, I wrote extensively about Phillips's business practices including references to how unpleasant a man he apparently was. Godwin, for instance, in a letter dated October 9, 1801, to Mary Jane, complains that he is a "snail in his discourse, so pompous, so empty."

55. As John Issitt explains in *Jeremiah Joyce: Radical Dissenter*, Joyce had been one of the radical dissenters caught in the Treason Trials of 1794. Phillips, partly to offer employment to some of the people who were struggling because of their political views, gave Joyce work, though as Issitt explains, as a "jobbing writer." Working for Phillips, he likely had to "forego any sense of moral purpose in his concern to secure sufficient income" (175).

56. In February 1829, Henry Crabb Robinson appended his note to a letter Eliza Fenwick had written to him on January 7, 1808. Letters of Henry Crabb Robinson (HRC Correspondence 1808 #116), Dr. Williams's Library.

57. In *The Oxford Dictionary of Nursery Rhymes* (Oxford: Oxford University Press, 1997), Iona and Peter Opie say that the rhyme Dorothy Wordsworth sent to Lamb reads, "Arthur's bower has broke his band, He comes riding up the land, The King of Scots with all his power Cannot build up Arthur's bower," 64–65.

58. Ibid., 35.

59. M. O. Grenby, *The Child Reader, 1700–1840* (Cambridge: Cambridge University Press, 2011), 231.

60. Ted Hughes, *Poetry in the Making* (London: Faber and Faber, 1967), 23.

61. Although Wedd includes the beginning of the passage in *Fate of the Fenwicks,* she omits most of the words after "anxiety behind me."

62. The playbills are held in the Theatre Archives, at the Blythe House location of the Victoria and Albert Museum. There are separate files of playbills for Covent Garden and Drury Lane, organized by year, and those are the ones I accessed. The March performance in which Eliza Ann appeared took place at the Lyceum Theater, which was being used at the time by the Drury Lane Theatre Company. The files containing the information about her performances here were in the Covent Garden files for 1811 and the Drury Lane files for the same year.

4. Governess and Networker

1. Dario Gaggio, "Gold and Silver Industry," *The Oxford Encyclopedia of Economic History,* ed. Joel Mokyr (Oxford: Oxford University Press, 2003).

2. See for example, G. Gregory and C. Chapman, *Differentiated Instructional Strategies* (Thousand Oaks, CA: Corwin Press, 2002).

3. The letter is in Dr. Williams's library, in the HCR correspondence, vol. 2, 15. The date is uncertain. Eliza Ann was established in Barbados, but Eliza has not yet left for Ireland, suggesting an 1812 or 1813 date.

4. Although Isobel Grundy has an edited copy of the letter, I have included a little more of the text. The date written by a later hand on the copy in Dr. Williams's Library says Thursday, 9 February [1810] and is in the 1725–99 (66) file of the HCR correspondence. There is a problem with the date. Grundy suggests 1812 as the year the letter was written (as that is the year Orlando would turn fourteen), and suggests that the date reads as 17 February, but the calendar for that year identifies February 17 as a Sunday (Eliza Fenwick, *Secrecy,* ed. Isobel Grundy [Peterborough, ON: Broadview Press, 1998], 366).

5. Mary Wollstonecraft, *The Works of Mary Wollstonecraft,* 7 vols, eds. Janet Todd and Marilyn Butler (London: Pickering, 1989), 5:215. Future references are to this edition.

6. There is a Mocatta Library at University College London. The banking firm was originally Mocatta and Goldsmid and they were involved with the development of the institution. The block on which the Tavistock house was located now belongs to the University of London.

7. In *The Fate of the Fenwicks,* A. F. Wedd has incorrectly transcribed the family name as Honnor. Both the archival records in Cork and the military records confirm that the correct spelling is Honner.

8. Eliza Fenwick (Rev'd Daid Blair), entry for August 3, *The Class Book: or Three Hundred and Sixty-Five Reading Lessons, Adapted to the Use of Schools; For Every Day in the Year* (London: Tabart, 1806), 117.

9. The specter of latent anti-Semitism is disquieting for twenty-first-century readers. Eliza had complained about the fact that Mrs. Mocatta had wanted a rigorous program of study for her children, and that there were hints that she should appear in the schoolroom at six in the morning. "Mrs. M. cannot endure to see the children have any relaxation," she wrote in a letter to Mary Hays in 1811. As there is no date on the letter, the context provides the approximate dating. Eliza also wrote about how uncomfortable she was when she was expected to be there when the Mocattas had company. She complained in the same letter that she had been represented as something "extraordinarily clever," and that made her very uneasy: "But unknown to them, unacquainted with their connections & their sources of small talk, I cannot utter a single word & feel myself wretchedly isolated and humbled in their circle." The undercurrent suggests discomfort with their culturally influenced social network. The Honner family, as she describes them from the first, seem more English. The suggestion that athleticism and play are regarded as being of value hints at the cultural differences between the two families.

10. In *Irish Watercolours and Drawings* (New York: Harry N. Abrams, 1995), Anne Crookshank and a man who romantically calls himself the Knight of Glin, include Eliza's account of the picture she was given of Lee Mount in the context of the fact that "[p]rospective governesses as well as prospective wives were sometimes sent views." Crookshank and Glin situate Eliza's account as similar to one in Jane Austen's *Emma* (1815), in which Mr. Dixon "was wooing Miss Campbell" by sending her his drawings of "Ballycraig, which the chattering Miss Bates described as a beautiful place."

11. Eliza's granddaughter Elizabeth confirmed that the paintings had traveled with her grandmother throughout all of her moves. After Eliza died in 1840, Elizabeth left them for safekeeping with her friends the Duncans, but they seem to have subsequently disappeared.

12. For a more complete account of the interest in literary lives at the beginning of the nineteenth century, see Butler, *Romantics, Rebels and Reactionaries: English Literature and its Background, 1760–1830*, 2. Although Eliza does not say so explicitly, the success of Mary Wollstonecraft's 1796 *Letters from Sweden, Norway, and Denmark* was also partly because of the way the personal and the political are entwined. From the time Eliza arrived in Cork in 1812, her letter writing increasingly incorporated literary and political notes, as well as skillful accounts of her physical environment.

13. Eliza Fenwick, *Lessons for Children* (London: Godwin, 1813), 100.

14. See *Asiatic Annual Register, or A View of the History of Hindustan, and the Politics, Commerce, and Literature of Asia, Volume IX—for the year 1807* (London: T. Cadell and W. Davies [Booksellers to the Asiatic Society in the Strand]; and Black Parry and Kingsbury [Booksellers to the Honourable the East India Company] in Leadenhall-Street, 1809), 202–4.

Wedd does include a section of the letter in *Fate of the Fenwicks*, but lacking the context of what happened, it feels one-sided. The published lines (from the same December 21, 1813 letter) read: "She [Mrs. Honner] has told me, & he in fact corroborated it, that from the time of his fracas with General Maitland, his Court Martial & his dismissal, they have been living on their Capital. His coming to England to lay the statement of his wrongs before the King etc. etc. must have been very expensive. The King's madness rendered his memorials useless—The Prince would not interfere because his father might recover, the Commander-in Chief was the personal friend & adherent of General Maitland & Mr H could not get a step forwarder." Eliza's analysis of the situation is significant in indicating her acute awareness of the political nuances of her employer's situation.

15. In *The Fate of the Fenwicks*, A. F. Wedd only includes a fraction of the sketch that appears in the unpublished manuscript letter.

16. In "A Tradition of the Theatre, Part 1," *Bajan and South Caribbean Magazine*, August 1981, Warren Alleyne writes that on "1 January 1812, the Theatre Royal, at a cost of £10,000 opened with a performance of 'The West Indian,' staged by a cast of fourteen [including Eliza Ann] and a farce called 'The Spoiled Child.'" He also explains that performances were held on Mondays and Thursdays, and that the theater declined by 1819, went up for auction in 1821, and was destroyed by fire in 1831 (17).

17. If Eliza had read Jane Austen at the time, she did not say so in any of the extant letters. But given the date, the fact that she was writing to Mary as one literary woman to another, and the reference to Mrs. Honner's "little failings of pride & prejudice," it is hard to ignore the coincidence. *Pride and Prejudice* was published in 1813 (the same year as Eliza's letter), and *Sense and Sensibility* in 1811. As a writer, Eliza was also a critical and thoughtful reader, attentive to literary trends and nuances, so the possibility of Austen's influence remains viable but unknowable.

18. William Godwin, *The Letters of William Godwin: 1778–1805*. 2 Vols. Ed. Pamela Clemit (Oxford: Oxford University Press, 2011), 2, 157. Godwin uses the description of what Eliza looks like when dressed "in poverty" as the basis of his comparison with Lady Margaret Mountcashel's clothiers. Margaret Mountcashel had been Mary Wollstonecraft's charge in the 1780s. Mary had been employed by Margaret's mother, Lady Kingsborough.

19. James Thomson, *Poems, Viz. Spring. Summer. Autumn, Winter. A Hymn to the Seasons. To the Memory of Isaac Newton* (Dublin: Printed by S. Powell, for George Risk, at the Shakespear's Head, George Ewing, at the Angel and Bible, and William Smith, at the Hercules, Booksellers, 1730), 56–57. For discussions on the phrase in eighteenth-century studies, see for example, Julia Briggs, "'Delightful Talk!' Women, Children and Reading in the Mid-Eighteenth Century," *Culturing the Child: 1640–1914*, ed. Donelle Ruwe (Lanham: Scarecrow, 2005), 67–82.

20. By May 1814, Eliza wrote to Mary to say that Mr. Honner had put Lee Mount up for sale. In the Cork archives, on a folded sheet dated June 27, 1820, there is a "Surrender and Conveyance" document identified as U196A/0848 Box 20. In it, Robert Honner asks to be released from and sells back "the house, dwelling house, out offices, garden, wood, demesne [the land attached to the manor], and removes the rent of 340 pounds half yearly and the River Awbeg and the school."

5. Colonist and Slaveholder

1. The example is cited by Karina Williams, *Contrary Voices: Representations of West India Slavery, 1657–1834* (Kingston, Jamaica: University of West Indies Press, 2008), 424. See also Vincent Brown, *The Reaper's Garden: Death and Power in the World of Atlantic Slavery* (Cambridge: Harvard University Press, 2010).

2. Matthew Parker, *The Sugar Barons: Family, Corruption, Empire and War in the West Indies* (New York: Walker, Bloomsbury, 2011), 46. All future references are to this edition.

3. "Britain and the Slave Trade," National Archives, U.K., available at http://www.nationalarchives.gov.uk/slavery/pdf/britain-and-the-trade.pdf.

4. I had the painting "Ta Matete Aka The Market" in mind as the women in it are graceful and beautifully dressed, though Paul Gauguin (1848–1903) was not born until long after Eliza had died.

5. Mary Wollstonecraft, *The Works of Mary Wollstonecraft*, 7 vols., eds. Janet Todd and Marilyn Butler (London: Pickering, 1989), 5: 68. Future references are to this edition.

6. Mary Astell, *Some Reflections upon Marriage, in Political Writings*, ed. Patricia Springborg (Cambridge: Cambridge University Press, 1966), 18–19, qtd. in Malinda Snow, "Habits of Empire and Domination in Eliza Fenwick's *Secresy*," *Eighteenth-Century Fiction* 14.2 (2002): 166. Future references to Snow are to this edition.

7. Snow, "Habits of Empire and Domination," 160. For a comprehensive discussion on *Secresy* as being about the politics of oppression, Malinda Snow's essay provides a compelling argument. She cites, for instance, Ronald Paulson's *Representations of Revolutions 1789–1820* (New Haven, CT: Yale University Press, 1983), 228, in which he argues that by 1789, with the opening stages of the French Revolution in play, "women's experience, like that of the black slave, was a model waiting for use. . . ." (228, qtd in Snow, "Habits of Empire and Domination," 166). Paulson then continues and develops the nuances of the analogy by explaining that "the experience of the female chattel, of oppression with no recourse to law, or sexual pursuit and assault upon body and mind, all provided the woman novelist (who had read *Clarissa* and *Otranto*) with the experience and point of view for a proto revolutionary novel that could be adapted by Holcroft and Godwin" (Paulson, 228, qtd in Snow, 166). Eliza was one of those novelists and in *Secresy,* she exploits the woman/slave analogy repeatedly to address Sibella's exploited status.

8. Eliza Fenwick, *Secresy,* ed. Isobel Grundy (Peterborough, ON: Broadview Press, 1998), 59. All future references are to this edition.

9. Olwyn M. Blouet has the school closing in 1822. See Blouet, "Mrs. Fenwick and Her School for Girls in Barbados, 1814–1822," *Journal of Caribbean History* 34, 1–3 (2000): 1.

10. Eliza Fenwick, *Visits to the Juvenile Library* (London: Tabart, 1805), 11.

11. The first edition of *The Class Book,* edited by Eliza Fenwick, using the pseudonym Rev'd David Blair (London: Tabart, 1806), published a year before Wilberforce's bill was passed, contained two readings in support of the abolition of the slave trade: one on April 6, the other on August 3. Both were called "On the Slave Trade" and both were removed from the 1807 editions of the book. The April 6 entry is by William Paley from his 1792 speech, and the August 3 entry is attributed to "Goldsmith." The April 6 "On the Slave Trade" emphasizes the cruelty of removing people from their homes and families, as that is where "the wickedness begins: the slaves, torn away from parents, wives, children, from their friends and companions, their fields and flocks, their home and country, are transported to the European settlements in America, with no other accommodation on shipboard than what is provided for brutes" (117).

12. As Matthew Parker points out at the end of *The Sugar Barons,* the white names that dominated in the eighteenth and nineteenth century as plantation owners are now found in the twenty-first century as names of black people. Parker gives the example of the once powerful and influential (white British) Beckford family in Jamaica. As Parker

explains, Beckford "is now indisputably a black Jamaican name" (363). In Barbados, the same pattern is repeated. Judge Beccles was a well-respected (white) man in the community in Eliza's time. Sir Hilary Beckles (the current spelling of Beccles) is now a famous historian in Barbados and the president of the University of West Indies. In the same vein, the surname Cumberbatch is associated with the white actor Benedict in the U.K., though the surname survives among black people living and working in Barbados.

13. See, for example, the entry on Simone de Beauvoir in the *Oxford Encyclopedia of Human Rights* by Sonia Kruks, "Simone de Beauvoir" (Oxford: Oxford University Press, 2009). In synthesizing de Beauvoir's argument from *The Ethics of Ambiguity* (1947), Kruks says that by "dishonestly claiming to be constrained in one's decisions by 'objectively existing' duties and values, such a person may unleash carnage on others while claiming to have a clear conscience and 'clean hands'" (150). As an updated example, she identifies "those who murder workers at abortion clinics [who] easily justify their actions in the name of the 'rights of the unborn child'" (ibid.).

14. Pedro Welch, *Slave Society in the City: Bridgetown Barbados 1680–1834* (Kingston, Jamaica: Ian Randle Press, 2003), 15. All future references are to this edition.

15. Hilary Beckles, *Black Rebellion in Barbados: The Struggle Against Slavery, 1627–1838* (Bridgetown: Antilles Publications, 1984), 67.

16. Michael Craton, *Testing the Chains: Resistance to Slavery in the British West Indies* (Ithaca, NY: Cornell University Press, 1982), 35.

17. Thomas's baptismal certificate (see illustration on p. 189) indicates that he was three months old when baptized on August 3, 1815.

18. A tendency toward alcoholism can apparently be genetic. I don't know whether or not Eliza knew that John's father, John Fenwick, had been temporarily expelled from the Methodist Connexion for his excessive drinking.

19. In *The Fate of the Fenwicks,* Annie Wedd left out the detail about "swelling of the testicles." I'd originally thought it was a prurient early twentieth-century omission, but that was not the case. In early nineteenth-century Barbados, rum drinking had been characterized as a health benefit (as we might characterize the intake of red wine or cannabis) in order to justify all-day drinking among men. The health advisory did not apply to women, of course, as they didn't have testicles, and so they could drink the water. With thanks to Tara Inniss, specialist in Caribbean history and medicine at the University of West Indies, Cave Hill, for explaining that there was a parasite in the water that did cause swelling of the lower body, a kind of elephantiasis.

20. At some level, they were, of course, right. Wilberforce was, incrementally, moving toward the abolition of slavery. The first move had been to make the slave trade illegal in 1807, then the 1811 bill to make it illegal to trade in slaves from other countries. The Registry Bill first proposed in 1812 was a way of attempting to enforce the legislation. Historically, slavery was not legislated out of existence in the British Empire for another two decades, in 1833. Although the legislation initially went into effect in 1834, there was a transitional phasing-out period that ended in 1838. The deal included financial compensation for the plantation owners.

Because the rhetoric used by the members of the House of Assembly makes such strange reading, I am including some of the arguments they used to claim that the British government was violating their rights: "Resolved unanimously, That it is contrary to the principles of British Jurisprudence, the birth-rights of Englishmen, and the natural privileges of free-born subjects, to suffer penalty either in person, character, or estate, but for the offences legally charged or strictly proved." And the coup de grace: "Resolved unanimously, That the proposed Bill is evidently viewed by the colonists, not only as oppressive in itself and in direct violation of the unalterable principles laid down in the preceding resolution, but as introductory to a more extended system of interference with their municipal regulations and domestic concerns, and in breach of the pledge held out to the colonists by the Act of Parliament."

21. Michael Craton, "Proto-Peasant Revolts: The Late Slave Rebellions in the British West Indies 1816–1832," *Past & Present* 85 (1979): 102.

22. Colonel Codd to James Leith, 25 April 1816, CO 28/85, National Archives, U.K. Handwritten copy. It seems that Leith used it for the basis of his proclamation, as it appeared in the published version the next day.

23. A copy of "An Address to the Slave Population of the Island of Barbados, dated 16 April 1816" survives in the National Archives, U.K., in the CO28/85 file. That is the copy I used.

24. For comprehensive accounts of Bussa's Rebellion, see especially, Beckles, *Black Rebellion in Barbados*; Craton, *Testing the Chains*; Karl Watson, *The Civilized Island of Barbados: A Social History 1750–1816* (Ellerton, Barbados: Caribbean Graphic Production, 1979); Welch, *Slave Society in the City*; and Steven A. Knowlton, "Contested Symbolism in the Flags of New World Slave Risings," *Raven* 21 (2014): 71–94. I also worked with original source material in the National Archives in the U.K., including the CO 28/85 government documents. The April 30, 1816 copy of the *Barbados Mercury Gazette* is there. Two documents from the period of the rebellion are helpful: *Remarks on the Insurrection in Barbados and the Bill for the Registration of Slaves* (Ellerton and Henderson, 1816) is an argument on how ludicrous it was to blame typically illiterate slaves for misunderstanding the Registry Bill; and the official *Report from a Select Committee of the House of Assembly appointed to inquire into the Origin, Causes and Progress of the Late Insurrection* (*Mercury and Gazette,* 1818) was the official report on the rebellion. I am grateful to Hilary Beckles, Evelyn O'Callaghan, Karl Watson, and Pedro Welch for their patient explanations as I tried, slowly, to understand how the slave system in Barbados worked.

25. See, for example, Gad Heuman, "Runaway Slaves in Nineteenth-Century Barbados," *Slavery & Abolition* 6, no. 3 (1985): 96–111.

26. Simon Blackburn, in the *Oxford Dictionary of Philosophy,* 3rd ed. (Oxford: Oxford University Press, 2016), in the online entry on morality, suggests that Kantian ethics "based on notions such as duty, obligation, and principles of conduct" potentially trump Aristotelian notions of virtue.

27. Sarah Ruddick, *Maternal Thinking: Toward a Politics of Peace* (New York: Ballantine, 1989), 17.

28. The *OED* gives 1604 as the first appearance of the word "Creole," defined as a "Negro born in Brazil, home-born save formerly of animals reared at home." Later, it was defined as someone "born and naturalized in the West Indies, etc. but of European (or negro) descent."

6. School Owner and Mourner

1. *Barbados Mercury Gazette,* December 28, 1813.

2. 1802 letter from William Godwin to William Cole responding to a question about the education of daughters (MS. Abinger c. 42. fols 97–98).

3. *Barbados Mercury and Bridgetown Gazette* (conventionally referenced as *The Barbados Mercury Gazette,* or just *The Gazette*), December 28, 1813. All future references to the paper are cited in the text by date. The first reference I found to Eliza and Eliza Ann referring to themselves as "Mesdames Fenwick & Rutherford," was on August 10, 1816. I was only able to piece together the information about the school (teachers, curriculum, life in the community) by reading crumbling microfilm copies I was able to access first at The National Library in Barbados, then, before it closed, the Colindale Newspaper branch of the British Library in London. Those were the only sets listed as more or less complete (all copies indicate gaps). The physical papers were inaccessible in the National Archives in Barbados. Because the microfilms were made on diazo, they were disintegrating. With thanks to a British Library Endangered Archives Programme Grant awarded in the fall of 2017, digitization of the surviving papers will be complete by 2019.

4. In December 1813, Eliza had written an account for Mary of what the school day looked like for the Honner children she was teaching in Cork. As it appears that she used a variation of this schedule in Bridgetown, I've copied in the entire account. Although the heat in Barbados required a slightly different schedule, the content and organization were probably similar. Here is Eliza's outline of the school day at Lee Mount:

Monday,—(allow always for a walk before breakfast when weather allows. In summer we breakfast at 8, but now at ½ past). In School at nine (prayers before breakfast), Mary Anne at the instrument till 10; then begin the English by rote lessons, consisting of spelling, grammar, Geography, sections of Blair's Preceptor on the arts & sciences, & sections of History, together with prose reading from all; overlooking & attending to the progress of a small & large hand copy from Helen & Fanny, and one large hand from Henry, with revising a Sum from each fully occupying me till one & sometimes longer. While they write, Mary Anne is preparing her french [sic] translation for next day.—From that till half-past one I sometimes walk, sometimes play at Battledore & sometimes lounge & chat with Mrs H. At ½ past one the Children dine & are ready by 2 or ½ past two to return to the schoolroom. I then sit down to the Piano forte. While I give one her lesson, the other hears Henry & Charles read etc., & works. The Playing & singing occupies me till 5, or if I take an hour out of doors from 2 till 3, then I can only leave myself a ¼ of an hour to dress before dinner, which is fixed for 6, but most generally begins at ½ past. . . .

Tuesday Morning,—French lessons. Mary Anne is translating Charles 12th on paper, beside which she reads & translates from some other French book & illustrates some grammatical rule or parses. Helen translates a fable, reads & does French exercises on construction. Fanny learns dialogue & repeats a verb & is just beginning her fables.—The writing & Cyphering as the day before, only I give Mary but ½ an hour at the instrument & so I have more leisure on french days.

Wednesday pretty nearly like Monday only I make them read the maps & answer desultory questions in Geography, which taking up more time I cut off the afternoon singing lesson in part, confining it to the Sol Fa.

Thursday,—the same course as Tuesday.

Friday,—Poetical or prose recitation, & general questions, with writing & music as usual. Saturday Morning they do no Sums, write only a copy of figures &, in addition to their french lessons, question each other on all the arithmetical tables. Once a month I give some time on Saturday to questions on the Major & Minor scales of Music. (I forgot to say that on the Wednesday, Monday & Friday they each write an English exercise.) Each now practices 2 hours per day, including the time I am giving their lessons on the instrument. Saturday afternoon I generally take to myself. They take it by turns to practice one hour before breakfast & one hour in the evening, so that theinstrument is regularly going 6 & often 7 hours a day.

5. "Yellow Fever" factsheet available at the World Health Organization website, http://www.who.int/mediacentre/factsheets/fs100/en/. It was updated in May 2016. The symptoms outlined are exactly as Eliza describes them in her letter: initial flu-like symptoms, then a high fever, a lull, and then with the kidneys and liver under attack, "black vomiting," and ultimately death. Although modern vaccines keep yellow fever relatively rare today, it was a killer in the early nineteenth century.

6. Letters of Henry Crabb Robinson, HCR Correspondence file for 1816 (131 also in the manuscript copy), in Dr. Williams's Library, London.

7. Eliza was quoting from S. T. Coleridge's translation of *The Death of Wallenstein: A Tragedy in Five Acts* from the German of Frederick Schiller (London: G Woodfell, 1800), 130.

8. In the HCR correspondence files for 1818, Dr. Williams's Library.

9. Charles Kegan Paul, *William Godwin: His Friends and Contemporaries* II (London: Henry S. King, 1876), 255–56.

10. For information about these influential educators, including discussions of their work, see, for instance: essays in Andrea Immel and Michael Whitmore, *Childhood and Children's Books in Early Modern Europe* (New York: Routledge, 2006); Andrea Immel, "'Mistress of Infantine Language': Lady Ellenor Fenn, Her *Set of Toys,* and the 'Education of Each Moment,'" *Children's Literature* 25 (1997): 215–28; Jill Shefrin, *Such Constant Affectionate Care: Lady Charlotte Finch, Royal Governess, and the Children of George III* (Los Angeles: Cotsen Occasional Press, 2003); Michèle Cohen, "Gender and 'Method' in Eighteenth-Century English Education," *History of Education* 33.5 (September 2004): 585–95; Adrian O'Connor, "Nature, Nurture and the Social Order: Imagining Lessons and Lives for Women in Ancien Régime France," *French Culture, Politics and Society* 30.1 (Spring 2012): 1–22; Marilyn Butler, *Maria Edgeworth: A Literary Biography* (Oxford: Clarendon, 1972); and William McCarthy, *Anna Letitia Barbauld: Voice of the Enlightenment* (Baltimore: Johns Hopkins University Press, 2012).

11. William Godwin, "Of the Communication of Knowledge," *The Enquirer. Reflections on Education, Manners and Literature: In a Series of Essays* (London: Simpkin and Marshall, 1823), 70, 71.

12. Frederick E. Jones, ed., *Maria Gisborne & Edward E Williams: Shelley's Friends, Their Journals and Letters* (Norman: University of Oklahoma Press, 1951), 46.

13. That would have been Muzio Clementi (1752–1832), a composer. His second wife, Emma, was the sister of Maria (Reveley) Gisborne's husband, so it makes sense that Maria would have recorded the incident.

14. Jones, *Maria Gisborne*, 43.

15. With thanks to Dave Rutherford for providing the reference to Bill Kelly, *Chrononhotonthologos, Phantasmagoria, Cotillions and Supper Entertainment in the Isle of Man 1793–1820*, chapter 11, accessible at Theatre and Variety Acts, http://www.isle-of-man.com/manxnotebook/history/theatre/1800s/chap11.htm.

16. The *Public Ledger and Daily Advertiser*, London, on October 5, 1829, identifies that play as coming from William Rutherford, "who committed suicide during a fit of insanity, produced by want and a series of misfortunes." The piece was produced at the Adelphi Theatre, according to the London *Morning Advertiser* of October 6, 1829.

17. Janet Todd, *Death and the Maidens: Fanny Wollstonecraft and the Shelley Circle* (Berkeley, CA: Counterpoint, 2007): 133. By 1821, however, Shelley had revised the poem, his first wife Harriet had long since drowned herself in 1816.

18. In the introduction to *On the Origin of Species*, first published in 1859, Charles Darwin credits Malthus and his discussion on population growth and "the recurrent struggle for existence" with his own development of his ideas about natural selection. See Darwin, *On the Origin of Species* (New York: F. F. Collier & Sons, 1872): xxxi.

19. Eliza Fenwick, *Secresy*, ed. Isobel Grundy (Peterborough, ON: Broadview, 1998).

20. Eliza Fenwick, *Lessons for Children* (London: Godwin, 1813).

21. I've kept Eliza's spellings. The print version of the novel uses "Jennie" rather than "Jenny" Deans.

22. Mary Hays, *Memoirs of Queens: Illustrious and Celebrated* (London: T and J Allman, 1821): 93–94.

23. A quirky newspaper article by Wayne Chandler turned up in the *Daytona Beach Morning Journal* of April 20, 1958, titled "War, Romance, Scandal." The Dummett family eventually ran a sugar plantation near Daytona Beach. The article contends that the family of Thomas Henry Dummett, when confronted with having to obey "the British Abolition Act of 1807" (the act to abolish the slave trade), "herded" all their slaves into a ship and sailed off into the night "while the British officer who was supposed to issue the decree was sleeping off the effects of too much liquor." The article does say that the Dummetts settled in New Haven in the 1820s, as the son, Douglas, attended Yale for six years.

24. With thanks to Murray Wilcox for the following information. The annual income to support a household of comparable size in England at the time would have been between £1,000 and £1,500. He found the information in Edward Copeland, *Women Writing About Money: Women's Fiction in England, 1790–1820* (Cambridge: Cambridge University Press, 2005): 4.

25. The information is in a letter Elizabeth Rutherford Savage wrote to her son Thomas in April 1890 in response to his questions about the family history. I want to credit Murray Wilcox here for putting together some of the information for me on the Butler-Duncan meeting in New Haven.

26. John Cornell, one of Elizabeth Rutherford Savage's descendants, asked me, in 2014, if I knew why the name Duncan had persisted in his family. I was delighted to have

been able to supply the answer about the connections between the Fenwick/Rutherford and Duncan families.

27. Both announcements appeared in the *Connecticut Herald* of November 18, 1823. I read print copies of the newspaper in the New Haven Historical Society.

28. The ledger accounts for the Phillips publications taken over by Longmans are at the University of Reading Publishing Library.

29. The letter from Claire Clairmont to Jane Williams is dated October 27, 1825. Marion Kingston Stocking, ed. *The Claire Clairmont Correspondence: Letters of Claire Clairmont, Charles Clairmont, and Fanny Imlay Godwin* (Baltimore: Johns Hopkins University Press, 1995), 225.

30. Claire Clairmont to Jane Williams, December 1826, ibid., 240.

31. The letter is part of a group in the William Rutherford Savage Papers, Wilson Library, Chapel Hill, North Carolina.

32. See, for example, Eliza Fenwick, "The Brown Linnet," *Lessons for Children* (London: Baldwin and Craddock, 1828), 39–44, and "Bad Tricks," *Infantine Stories* (London: John Souter, 1820), 34–48; and Mary Wollstonecraft, *Original Stories From Real Life* (*The Works of Mary Wollstonecraft. 7 vols. Eds. Janet Todd and Marilyn Butler* [London: Pickering, 1989], IV: 369). In *Children's Books in England: Five Centuries of Social Life* (1932; Cambridge: Cambridge University Press, 1982) , F. J. Harvey Darton notes, sardonically, the frequency of the cruelty to animals genre: "It is almost inconceivable," he writes, "that so many small boys spent so much time as is alleged in pulling the wings of flies, throwing at tethered cocks, and tormenting puppies and kittens" (156). Elizabeth's story is so classic that it is tempting to doubt its veracity as it was recalled so many years later.

33. In another story, Elizabeth remembered William and his pet parakeet on the ship to New Haven.

34. As the letter from Mary Hays to Mary Shelley—dated November 30, 1836, asking about the "fate" of her friend—indicates, it looks as if the move to Niagara marked the end of Eliza's letters to Mary. As Mary says in her note (MS Abinger c. 49), she had tried to find Eliza, but her attempts had "proved fruitless." Though Eliza continued to write long, engaging letters to her "new world" friends, there are no surviving letters (to my knowledge) of letters to her British friends.

35. With thanks to Murray Wilcox for working out the links between Eliza and the Morgan family. On June 1, 1826, Eliza had sent a letter to Mary in England with "Major Dix," as she says in the letter. John Adam Dix (1798–1879), who had been a major in the Civil War, was a lawyer and later a politician in New York (he was eventually Secretary of the United States Treasury). He married Catherine Morgan on May 29, 1826.

36. All transcriptions are mine, made from the letters I found in the New-York Historical Society. A. F. Wedd edited a volume of Eliza's letters to her ancestor, Mary Hays, published as *The Fate of the Fenwicks: 1798–1828* (London: Methuen, 1927). There were errors in her transcriptions (especially in some of the identifications of people). As I explain in the introductory note to the text, I made new transcriptions of all the letters, comparing the print edition with the manuscript originals.

37. For the first three weeks of their stay, Eliza and her family were welcomed and entertained.

7. North American Grandmother

1. The place and time of the meeting of the two families comes from a note from Bessie Rutherford to Adeline Moffat in October 1836. Bessie complains about what she calls "that Corporation": "I have never forgotten," she writes, "its destroying our pretty walks in dear Vauxhall, it was there I first saw you Adeline." John Jacob Astor cut up what had been the Vauxhall Gardens (named for the one in London) in 1826, created Lafayette Street, and built what might now be called luxury homes. With thanks to Murray Wilcox for the information.

2. James Crooks (1778–1860) was a major industrialist in Upper Canada. He had come to Fort Niagara in 1791 where his half-brother, Francis, was operating as a merchant supplying goods to the military, though they were largely destroyed in the War of 1812. After the war, he relocated in 1814 to West Flamborough Township. According to the article in the *Dictionary of Canadian Biography* written by David Ouellette (Toronto: University of Toronto/Université Laval, 1985), available at http://www.biographi .ca/en/bio/crooks_james_8E.html, between 1814 and 1818, "in a remarkable display of energy and resilience, he had constructed there along Spencer Creek a grist-mill, saw-mill, carding-mill, general store, cooperage, and blacksmith's shop." And by 1834, "he had built mills on the Speed River, in the region west of Dundas, and his complex on Spencer Creek had been enlarged to include, among other manufactories, a tannery, distillery, potashery, agricultural implement factory, woollen-mill, and oil-mill."

3. With thanks to Murray Wilcox for explaining that the "Engineering department" would have been with the British detachment at Fort George.

4. Matthew Warren Osborn, *Rum Maniacs: Alcoholic Insanity in the Early American Republic* (Chicago: University of Chicago Press, 2014). 4.

5. Charles Duncombe, *Doctor Charles Duncombe's Report Upon the Subject of Education, made to the Parliament of Upper Canada, 25th February 1836. Through the Commissioners Doctors Morrison and Bruce, appointed by a Resolution of the House of Assembly, 1835 to Obtain information on the subject of Education* (Toronto: M. Reynolds, 1836).

6. Baldwin Family Papers, Toronto Public Library, L12 1801–1843. See September 15, 1836: A 42 number 171.

7. With thanks to Dr. Jo Ann Majerovich, physician and epidemiologist. We did discuss the difficulty of trying to make a retroactive diagnosis based on fragmentary evidence and discussed options including tetanus and epilepsy. If it was tetanus, the timing, the fact that they would have both had it, and the symptoms suggest a possible link with their apprenticeships in metallurgy. With thanks to Murray Wilcox for identifying "caustic applied to the spine" as a treatment for tetanus in the period.

8. The conventional wisdom at the time was that the original designation of Toronto was "meeting place," but that does not seem to be historically accurate. The City of Toronto website, in its page on the origin of the name, claims that it was called "lac de Taranteau" on a map of Southern Ontario produced in 1670 by Father René de Bréhant de Galinée. See https://www.toronto.ca.

9. *Bonnet Box Letters,* unpublished manuscript. Baldwin Family Papers, Toronto Public Library.

10. Alan Wilson, "Colborne, John, Baron Seaton," *Dictionary of Canadian Biography* IX, 1861–1870, University of Toronto/Université Laval, accessible at http://www.biographi .ca/en/bio/colborne_john_9E.html.

11. Bessie, as an old woman, in an 1890 letter to her son, told him that Lady Colborne's sister Miss Jane Yonge (Yonge Street in Toronto is named after a cousin of hers) visited Eliza regularly and corresponded with her until she died. Introductions to the Colbornes were probably made through Col. George Phillpotts, who was John Colborne's aide de camp and Eliza's friend from the time of their arrival in Upper Canada.

12. Bessie provided the information to her son Thomas Rutherford Savage in a letter written in 1890. She explained that Eliza, "advised by a firm friend, Mrs. Breckeridge's [sic] brother [William Warren Baldwin], moved to Toronto and took charge of the college boarding house of preparatory students."

13. She owned two hundred acres in what she describes as the London District (in modern Tillsonburg), and had taken it as payment for the cost of educating Rebecca Connoly. (EF to Reuben Moffat, 20 April 1838).

14. In a November 7, 1787 letter to her sister Everina, Mary Wollstonecraft describes the support she had received from the publisher, Joseph Johnson: he "assures me," she writes, "that if I exert my talents in writing I may support myself in a comfortable way." She then adds the famous prophecy: "I am then going to be the first of a new genus. . . ." (Mary Wollstonecraft, *The Collected Letters of Mary Wollstonecraft*, ed. Janet Todd [London: Allen Lane The Penguin Press, 2005], 139).

15. Dora Massa was the daughter of Theodore Barrell (1771–1846). The Barrell Family Papers (1751–1829) are held at Columbia University Libraries in New York. The information about Dora's marriage to Ferdinand Massa is in that archive, as well as the information that Eliza and Eliza Ann attended their wedding in 1826. An early translation of John Locke's 1767 *Thoughts Concerning Education*, published in 1708 in French as *De L'Education des enfans Traduit de l'Anglois*, is also in the archive.

16. Thomas Rolph, *A Brief Account together with Observations made during a visit in the West Indies and through a Tour through the United States of American in parts of the years 1832–3 Together with a statistical Account of Upper Canada* (Dundas, ON: Heyworth, Hackstaff, 1836). He praises the teaching and the educational standards at Upper Canada College: "There are several teachers belonging to it," he writes, "distinguished for their attainments, and at the annual examinations several of the scholars by their merit and talent have reflected high honor on the establishment" (174).

17. Eliza and Bessie used variant spellings I have regularized to "Mackenzie."

18. Francis Bond Head is recognized as the leader who managed to quell the rebellion. A town called Bond Head, not far from Toronto, commemorates his place in Upper Canadian history.

19. Although not related officially to my story, my first encounter with the Mackenzie Rebellion came when, as a young child, no more than seven, the Jewish Sunday school I attended in Toronto was housed in Montgomery's Tavern (it had long ceased being a tavern, but was protected as a historical site). There was a historical plaque there and I remember reading it.

20. In her note, Eliza has written "King's College" as her location. King's College, incidentally, was the precursor to the University of Toronto and, in the 1830s, King's College (intended as a post-secondary institution) and Upper Canada College (intended as a prep school) were merged while the details of the institution's religious affiliation were being debated. Basically, Bishop Strachan wanted it to be a strictly Church of England institution, and John Colborne did not. Although the charter for King's College had

been granted in 1827, while Colborne and Strachan wrangled about its religious affiliation Upper Canada College served as a kind of placeholder. Colborne, Strachan, and Baldwin are names still to be found in Toronto. There is a Colborne Street, Bishop Strachan is the name of an elite school for girls, and the Baldwin Steps climb up to a the top of a hill where the Baldwin estate once stood.

In *Winter Studies and Summer Rambles,* Anna Jameson in fact records a discussion about Upper Canada College in the House of Assembly, quoting "the governor at the opening of the session," commenting "that 'no useful result had hitherto attended the beneficent intentions of his majesty in granting a charter to King's College, and their hope that the province would shortly possess the means within itself of bestowing upon the young a *refined* and *liberal* education.'" See Anna Jameson, *Winter Studies and Summer Rambles in Canada,* afterword by Clara Thomas (Toronto: McClelland & Stewart, 2009), 95.

21. See Carl Ballstadt, "Secure in Conscious Worth: Susanna Moodie and the Rebellion of 1837," available at http://canadianpoetry.org/volumes/vol18/ballstadt.html. He cites the patriotic poem she sets at the end of the chapter in which she is apparently recording the events around the report of the rebellion and the call to arms. Ballstadt argues, convincingly, that she has the dates slightly wrong and suggests that she has telescoped the events in order to concentrate the tensions between the reformers and the government in both Upper and Lower Canada at the time.

22. This is not the place for a long discussion on Mackenzie, but he was active as a political reformer at Queenston in the Niagara region, where he ran a radical newspaper, *The Colonial Advocate,* between 1825 and 1826 (just before Eliza arrived). For visitors in the area today, the site has been converted to a house museum, the Mackenzie Printery and Newspaper Museum. There are several working printing presses on site and wonderful interpretive staff. Visitors are invited to participate in printmaking demonstrations. In Toronto, Mackenzie House at 82 Bond Street is the house in which Mackenzie lived when he returned from exile in 1849.

23. Marilyn Butler, *Romantics, Rebels and Reactionaries: English Literature and its Background, 1760–1830* (Oxford: Oxford University Press, 1982).

24. Eliza quoted from letter 144, to Sir Horace Mann, written on July 22, 1744, in *The Letters of Horace Walpole, Earl of Orford, Including Numerous Letters Now First Published from the Original Manuscripts, Vol. 1, 1735–1745* (London: Richard Bentley, 1846), 359. Available in the HathiTrust Digital Library, https://hdl.handle.net/2027/njp .32101017568088.

25. In his memoir for the *Arminian Magazine* in 1778, Peter Jaco wrote his "sinning and repenting" story: "I had not walked far, before it was strongly suggested to my mind, that Jesus Christ died for the vilest sinner; I immediately replied, Then I am the wretch for whom He died!"

26. Sigmund Freud, "Beyond the Pleasure Principle," *A General Selection from the Works of Sigmund Freud,* ed. John Rickman (New York: Doubleday Anchor, 1957), 141–68.

27. Frances Hodgson Burnett (1849–1924), author of *The Secret Garden,* among other well-known books for children, writes about the scene in her autobiography, *From the One I Knew Best of All: A Memory of the Mind of a Child* (New York: Charles Scribner's Sons, 1893). The young Frances is recreating a scene from Uncle Tom's Cabin. She

writes about herself in the third person, being discovered by her mother "apparently furious with insensate rage, muttering to herself as she brutally lashed, with one of her brother's toy whips, a cheerfully hideous black gutta–percha doll who was tied to the candelabra stand and appeared to be enjoying the situation" (55–56). Available at the *Internet Archive,* https://archive.org/details/oneiknewbestofalooburn.

28. See the "Scriptive Things" chapter of Robin Bernstein's *Racial Innocence: Performing American Childhood and Race from Slavery to Civil Rights* (New York: New York University Press, 2011), 69–91. See especially the "Dances with Things" section (72–74) of the chapter.

29. Because there is an edition of this story on the Internet, I am going to reference that version. See Eliza Fenwick, *Lessons for Children* (London: Baldwin & Craddock, 1828), 141–42.

30. Susanna Moodie (writing under her maiden name Susanna Strickland), before coming to Upper Canada, published a number of children's books in England, including: *Hugh Latimer, or, The School Boy's Friendship* (London: Dean and Munday 1828); a volume of *Patriotic Songs,* with her sister, Agnes Strickland (London: R. Green, 1830); and *The History of Mary Prince* (London: Westley, and Davis, 1831). Agnes Strickland (1796–1874) was the most famous of the Strickland sisters, especially for her twelve-volume *Lives of the Queens of England* (London: Colburn, 1840–1848).

31. Susanna Moodie, *Roughing it in the Bush: Forest Life in Canada,* rev. ed. (Toronto: Hunter, Rose and Company, 1871), 7. All future page references are to this edition.

32. In *Anna Jameson: Victorian, Feminist, Woman of Letters* (London: Scolar Press, 1997), Judith Johnston says that Anna's trip to Canada was "strictly a matter of business." She describes the end of Anna's marriage to Robert in a sentence: "He needed her presence to earn a promotion, and she needed a formal ratification of their separation and an undertaking from him for some form of financial support" (2). Robert had been appointed as Attorney General to Upper Canada in 1833. In 1837, he was appointed as Vice-Chancellor to the new Court of Chancery. Johnston also adds that Robert didn't mention Anna at all in his will. He died in 1854.

33. Both Susanna and Anna were prolific writers. Susanna began writing in 1822 (she was nineteen and using her maiden name, Strickland) and published eleven books prior to 1831 (just before leaving for Upper Canada), as well as another seven as Susanna Moodie. She was also a regular contributor to periodicals in Britain, the United States, and Canada. Anna had her first poem published in Britain in 1822, and then, by my count, another twenty-five books, the last published posthumously in 1864, four years after she died. Anna too was a prolific contributor to periodicals.

34. A complete volume of Eliza's letters will follow, funded by a grant from the Social Sciences and Humanities Research Council of Canada.

35. Henry Crabb Robinson to "My Dear Madam" (unidentified), 16 July 1845, Letters of Henry Crabb Robinson, HCR Correspondence, Dr. Williams's Library, London.

36. Undated annotation on a letter Eliza Fenwick wrote to Henry Crabb Robinson. Eliza has dated it "Monday Morning." A note in pencil on the letter says 18—. Letters of Henry Crabb Robinson, HCR Correspondence, Dr. Williams's Library, London.

37. Faye Hammill provides a full list in an appendix to *Literary Culture and Female Authorship in Canada: 1760–2000* (New York: Rodopi, 2003). She includes a play by Robertson Davies, *At My Heart's Core* (Toronto: Clarke-Irwin, 1950), Margaret Atwood's

poem sequence, *The Journals of Susanna Moodie* (Toronto: Oxford, 1970), and a novel by Carol Shields, *Small Ceremonies* (London: Fourth Estate, 1995). I'm adding *The Illustrated Journals of Susanna Moodie* (Toronto: Cormorant, 2014), Margaret Atwood's collaboration with artist Charles Pachter.

38. For an American equivalent, though in a more cheerful vein, and written for children, see *The Little House on the Prairie* series of nine books by Laura Ingalls Wilder (1867–1957).

39. There were rebellions in both Upper and Lower Canada. Mackenzie's Rebellion of December 1837 was short-lived and was quickly put down. The rebellion in Lower Canada did continue through 1838.

40. Eliza has adapted the line from Part II of Pope's *Essay on Criticism,* originally published in 1711. The original couplet reads: "A needless Alexandrine ends the song, / That, like a wounded snake, drags its slow length along." Pope's line is, incidentally, an Alexandrine (a twelve-syllable verse form). Pope was writing about writing (the good, the bad, and the ugly). Eliza's allusion is a playful critique of her own writing. Alexander Pope, *Essay on Criticism* (London: T. Daniel and J. Steele in Paternoster Row, 1758), 16.

41. I did go through *The Canadian Literary Magazine,* and many issues of other periodicals in which Eliza might have published in the period, including *The Albion, or British, Colonial, and Foreign Weekly Gazette,* which published between 1822 and 1856. There was a review in the 1838 issue of Anna Jameson's *Winter Studies and Summer Rambles.* I also read through *The Literary Garland,* published in Montreal, from 1838–1851, but did not find anything I could definitively attribute to Eliza.

42. See, for example, a letter from July 8, 1833 from Eliza in Toronto to Bessie, who was in New York at the time: "Maria had come over for a short holiday & having invited her to pass the day here, I asked the Philpotts, Miss Ghent, Miss Phillips, Miss Jarvis to tea to meet her. The Philpotts talked of nothing but *you,* & the previous evening concert. Miss Hughes & Mr. Ham gave a vocal concert of Song & Duets both here & at Niagara & now we have Madame Feron & Mr Walton doing the same thing."

43. The population estimate comes from Janet Carnochan's *History of Niagara* (Toronto: William Briggs, 1914). She was reporting a reference from *The Gleaner* of 1826. She also makes specific reference to the Niagara Seminary, citing both an 1830 advertisement and the 1833 note from when Eliza moved to York/Toronto. Carnochan cites *The Niagara Gleaner* notice in which, "Mrs. Breakenridge appeals to the public and 'hopes for a continuance of public favor,' and suggests 'the additional claims of a long residence in town, heavy misfortunes, a large family to maintain and her experience for four years with Mrs. Fenwick'" (131).

44. I should note that in the 1830s, rail lines were just being built as steam trains were just becoming available. The first American ones only arrived in the late 1820s, and the term Underground Railroad apparently came into use at around the same time.

45. Anna's husband, Robert Jameson (1796–1854), had known Charles Lamb, and through Lamb, Henry Crabb Robinson. See Clara Thomas, *Love and Work Enough: The Life of Anna Jameson* (Toronto: University of Toronto Press, 1967) for a discussion on Anna Jameson's early life and her relationship with Robert.

46. In Niagara-on-the-Lake, Negro Town was said to have been bounded by Mary and Ann Streets and King Street and Mississauga Road.

47. There is even a surviving description of what the school was like. A black woman named Mary Anne Guillan described it: "I went to school upstairs in the schoolhouse of the Scotch church (St. Andrew's) . . . for the coloured children. It was a black man who taught it. How many? Oh, it was full-full of children. The benches were slabs with the flat side up and the bark of the tree down, with round sticks put in slanting for legs. The children all studied aloud and the one that made the most noise was the best scholar in those days." See Michael Power and Nancy Butler, *Slavery and Freedom in Niagara* (Niagara-on-the-Lake: Niagara Historical Society, 1993), 58–59.

48. Duncan Phyfe (1768–1854) did go on to become an iconic American furniture designer and maker.

49. With thanks to Murray Wilcox for suggesting that she might also have been thinking about the Niagara Commons.

Coda

1. In the odd way that narrative coincidence can happen, when I chanced to look up Dr. Savage's description of gorillas, a reference to Christa Knellwoof King and Jane R. Goodall, eds., *Frankenstein's Science: Experimentation and Discovery in Romantic Culture, 1780–1830* (Aldershot: Ashgate, 2008), popped up. On a page of endnotes containing Dr. Savage's name were references to various books in the Goldsmith's Geography series published by Richard Phillips early in the nineteenth century. What struck me was the way Eliza's connections ran like a vein through the page. The title allusion to Frankenstein links Eliza to the attendance at the birth of its author, Mary Shelley, in 1797. The references to the works by Richard Phillips link to Eliza's time as one of the "drudges" in his employ in the early 1800s. And the reference to Dr. Savage's discovery links Eliza to a man she never knew, her granddaughter Bessie's husband in the 1840s.

2. William Rutherford Savage Papers 1826–1953, Chapel Hill, University of North Carolina, File #49.

3. William Rutherford Savage Papers 1826–1953, File #43.

4. L11 WW Baldwin Papers L11, Box 106-7, 3rd Folder #54.

5. As mentioned in the Prelude, Wollstonecraft referred to herself as "a particle broken off from the grand mass of mankind" in *Letters Written During a Short Residence in Sweden, Norway and Denmark* (1796).

References

Archives Consulted

Abinger Papers. Bodleian Library Special Collections. University of Oxford. Oxford, UK.

Archive of British Publishing and Printing (Longmans archive). University of Reading, UK.

Baldwin Collection Manuscripts. Toronto Public Library.

Baldwin Library of Historical Children's Literature. University of Florida.

Barbados Historical Society. Bridgetown, Barbados.

Barbados National Archive. Bridgetown, Barbados.

Barbados National Library. Bridgetown, Barbados.

Barrell Family Papers, Rare Book & Manuscript Library. Columbia University Libraries, New York.

Beinecke Rare Book & Manuscript Library. Yale University, New Haven, Connecticut.

Bristol New Rooms. Reference Library. Bristol, UK.

British Library. London, UK.

Blythe House. Victoria and Albert Museum. London, UK.

Cambridge University Library. Cambridge, UK.

City of Toronto Archives. Toronto, Ontario.

Cole, T. C. Papers. Archives of American Art. Smithsonian Washington D.C.

Cotsen Children's Library, Firestone Library, Princeton University.

Cork Archives Institute. Cork, Ireland.

Cork City Library. Cork, Ireland.

Dr. Williams's Library. London, UK.

Frick Art Reference Library. New York, New York.

Hockliffe Project: Early British Children's Literature. Available at http://www.sd-editions.com/hockliffeNew/.

Huntington Library, Art Collections, and Botanical Gardens. Los Angeles, California.

James Gibson Library, Special Collections and Archives. Brock University, St. Catharines, Ontario.

John Ryland's Library. University of Manchester, Manchester, UK.

Morgan Library and Museum. New York, New York.

National Archives. London, UK.

National Army Museum. London, UK.

New Haven Museum and Historical Society. New Haven, Connecticut.

New-York Historical Society. New York, New York.

Niagara Historical Society. Niagara-on-the Lake, Ontario.

Ontario Provincial Archives. Toronto, Ontario.

Orlando Project. http://www.artsrn.ualberta.ca/orlando/.

Osborne Collection of Early Children's Books. Toronto Public Library.

Pforzheimer Collection of Shelley and His Circle. New York Public Library.

Renier Collection, Victoria and Albert Museum at Blythe House. London, UK.

Thomas Fisher Rare Book Library. University of Toronto.

UCLA Research Library (Charles E. Young). Los Angeles, California.

Wesley College. Cambridge, UK.

Wesley College Library Archives. Bristol, UK.

William Rutherford Savage Papers. The Wilson Library, University of North Carolina, Chapel Hill.

Chronological List of Works Written or Edited by Eliza Fenwick

Secresy, or The Ruin on the Rock. London: W. Lane, 1795; Reprint, with an Introduction by Gina Luria. New York: Garland, 1974; Reprint, with an Introduction by Janet Todd. London: Pandora, 1989; Edited, with an Introduction by Isobel Grundy, Peterborough: Broadview Press, 1998.

Mary and her Cat. London: Tabart, 1804.

The Life of Carlo, the Famous Dog of Drury-lane Theatre. London: Tabart, 1804.

Presents for Good Girls. London: Tabart, 1804.

Presents for Good Boys. London: Tabart, 1805.

Visits to the Juvenile Library: or, Knowledge Proved to be the Source of Happiness. London: Tabart, 1805.

Songs for the Nursery: Collected from the Works of the Most Renowned Poets, and Adapted to Favourite National Melodies. London: Tabart, 1805.

The Class Book: or Three Hundred and Sixty-Five Reading Lessons, Adapted to the Use of Schools; For Every Day in the Year. London: Tabart, 1806.

Six Stories in English and French. London: Tabart, 1809. Republished as *Six Stories from the Nursery.* London: Godwin, 1819, 1824.

Infantine Stories, Composed Progressively, in Words of One, Two, & Three Syllables. London: Tabart, 1810. Also Boston: Munroe & Francis, No. 4, Cornhill, 1818.

Rays from the Rainbow. London: Godwin, 1812.

Lessons for Children. London: Godwin, 1813.

Works Cited

Aikin, Lucy. *Poetry for Children.* London: Tabart, 1801.

The Albion, or, British, Colonial, and Foreign Weekly Gazette. New York. 1822–56.

Alleyne, Warren. "A Tradition of the Theatre." *The Bajan and South Caribbean Magazine* (August 1981): 16–7.

Asiatic Annual Register, or A View of the History of Hindustan, and the Politics of Commerce and Literature of Asia. Volume IX—for the year 1807. London: T. Cadell and W. Davies (Booksellers to the Asiatic Society in the Strand); and Black Parry and Kingsbury, Booksellers to the Honourable the East India Company in Leadenhall Street, 1809.

Atmore, Charles. *The Methodist Memorial: Being an Impartial Sketch of the Lives and Characters of the Preachers who have Departed this life since the commencement of the work of god among the people called Methodists, late in connection with the Rev. John Wesley, deceased.* London: Hamilton, Adams & Co, 1871.

Atwood, Margaret. *The Journals of Susanna Moodie*. Toronto: Oxford University Press, 1970.

———. *The Illustrated Journals of Susanna Moodie*. Ill. Charles Pachter. Toronto: Cormorant, 2014.

Austen, Jane. *Sense and Sensibility* (1811), ed. Kathleen James-Cavan. Peterborough, Ontario: Broadview Press, 2001.

———. *Pride and Prejudice* (1813). Oxford: Oxford University Press, 2010.

Baldwin, Maria. *The Bonnet Box Letters: Maria, Her Family and Friends*. Unpublished Manuscript (interior notes indicate it was assembled in the late nineteenth century by her unnamed nieces and nephews). Baldwin Collection, Toronto Public Libraries.

Ballstadt, Carl. "Secure in Conscious Worth: Susanna Moodie and the Rebellion of 1837." http://www.uwo.ca/english/canadianpoetry/cpjrn/vol18/ballstadt.html.

Ballstadt, Carl, Elizabeth Hopkins, and Michael Peterman, eds. *Letters of Love and Duty: The Correspondence of Susanna and John Moodie*. Toronto: University of Toronto Press, 1993.

Barbauld, Anna Laetitia. *Lessons for Children*. 4 vols. London: Joseph Johnson, 1787–88.

Barbados Mercury Gazette (known variously as the *Barbados Mercury* and *Bridgetown Gazette*), 1811–25.

Barber, J. W. *History and Antiquities of New Haven, (Conn.): From Its Earliest Settlement to the Present Time. Illustrated with Engravings*. New Haven: Published and Sold by J. W. Barber, 1831. Courtesy of the New Haven Historical Society.

Barthes, Roland. "Authors and Writers." *A Barthes Reader*. Ed. Susan Sontag. New York: Hill & Wang, 1960: 185–93.

Beckles, Hilary. *A History of Barbados: From Amerindian Settlement to Nation-State*. Cambridge: Cambridge University Press, 1990.

———. *Black Rebellion in Barbados: The Struggle Against Slavery 1627–1838*. Bridgetown, Barbados: Antilles Publications, 1984.

Bernstein, Robin. *Racial Innocence: Performing American Childhood and Race from Slavery to Civil Rights*. New York: New York University Press, 2011.

Binns, John. *Recollections of the Life of John Binns*. Philadelphia: Printed and for Sale by the Author and by Parry and McMillan, 1854.

Blake, William. *The Complete Poetry and Prose of William Blake*. Ed. David. V. Erdman. Garden City, New York: Anchor, 1892.

Blouet, Olwyn M. "Mrs. Fenwick and Her School for Girls in Barbados, 1814–1822." *Journal of Caribbean History* 34.1–2 (2000): 1–20.

Borrow, George. *Lavengro; the Scholar—the Gypsy—the Priest*. London: John Murray, 1861.

Boulukos, George. *The Grateful Slave: the Emergence of Race in Eighteenth-Century British and American Culture*. Cambridge: Cambridge University Press, 2008.

Brown, Vincent. *The Reaper's Garden: Death and Power in the World of Atlantic Slavery*. Cambridge: Harvard University Press, 2010.

Bundock, Christopher. "The (Inoperative) Epistolary Community in Eliza Fenwick's *Secresy*." *European Romantic Review* 20.5 (2009): 709–20.

Burnett, Frances Hodgson. *From the One I Knew Best of All: A Memory of the Mind of a Child*. New York: Charles Scribner's Sons, 1893.

Butler, Marilyn. *Jane Austen and the War of Ideas*. Oxford: Oxford University Press, 1975.

————. *Maria Edgeworth: A Literary Biography.* Oxford: Clarendon, 1972.

————. *Romantics, Rebels and Reactionaries: English Literature and its Background, 1760–1830.* Oxford: Oxford University Press, 1982.

Byatt, Antonia Susan. *Possession: A Romance.* London: Chatto and Windus, 1990.

Byrne, Paula. *Perdita: The Life of Mary Robinson.* London: Harper Collins, 2004.

Canadian Literary Magazine. York, Upper Canada: G. Gurnett. Vol 1, No. 1–3 (April, May and October 1833).

Cannon, Mercy. "Hygienic Motherhood: Domestic Medicine and Eliza Fenwick's *Secresy.*" *Eighteenth-Century Fiction* 20.4 (2008): 535–61.

Carnall, Geoffrey. "The Monthly Magazine." *The Review of English Studies* 5.18 (1954): 158–64.

Carnochan, Janet. *History of Niagara.* Toronto: William Briggs, 1914.

Carroll, Lewis. *The Annotated Alice: The Definitive Edition.* ed. Martin Gardner. New York: Norton, 1999.

Chiu, Frances. "From Nobodaddies to Noble Daddies: Writing Political and Paternal Authority." *Eighteenth-Century Life* 26.2 (2002): 1–22.

Clairmont, Claire. *The Letters of Claire Clairmont, Charles Clairmont, and Fanny Imlay Godwin.* Ed. Marion Kingston Stocking. Baltimore: Johns Hopkins University Press, 1995.

Clairmont, M. J. *Tabart's Collection of Popular Stories.* London: Tabart, 1804.

Coe, Patricia. "The Walls of Her Prison: Madness, Gender and Discursive Agency in Eliza Fenwick's *Secresy* and Mary Wollstonecraft's *The Wrongs of Woman.*" *European Romantic Review* 23.6 (2002): 671–87.

Cohen, Michèle. "Gender and 'Method' in Eighteenth-century English Education." *History of Education* 33.5 (September 2004): 585–95.

Colley, Linda. *The Ordeal of Elizabeth Marsh: A Woman in World History.* New York: Anchor Books, Random House, 2008.

Connecticut Herald. 18 November 1823. Courtesy of the New Haven Historical Society.

Cook, Daniel and Amy Cully. *Women's life Writing 1700–1850: Gender, Genre and Authorship.* Basingstoke: Palgrave, 2012.

Copeland, Edward. *Women Writing About Money: Women's Fiction in England 1790–1820.* Cambridge: Cambridge University Press, 2005.

Courtney, Winifred. *Young Charles Lamb 1775–1802.* London: Macmillan, 1982.

Craton, Michael. "Proto-Peasant Revolts: The Late Slave Rebellions in the British West Indies 1816–1832." *Past & Present* 85 (1979): 99–125.

————. *Testing the Chains: Resistance to Slavery in the British West Indies.* Ithaca: Cornell University Press, 1982.

————. "The Passion to Exist: Slave Rebellions in the British West Indies 1650–1832." *Journal of Caribbean History* 13 (1980): 7–20.

Crookshank, Anne and the Knight of Glin. *Irish Watercolours and Drawings.* New York: Harry N. Abrams, 1995.

Darton, F. J. Harvey. *Children's Books in England: Five Centuries of Social Life.* (1932) 3rd ed. Rev. Brian Alderson. Cambridge: Cambridge University Press, 1982.

d'Aulnoy, M. C. *The History of Fortunio.* London: Tabart, 1804.

Davenport, Hester. *The Prince's Mistress: A Life of Mary Robinson.* Stroud: Sutton, 2004.

Davies, Robertson. *At My Heart's Core.* Toronto: Clarke-Irwin, 1950.

Davis, Michael T. *London Corresponding Society 1792–1799*. 6 vols. London: Pickering & Chatto, 2002.

Daytona Beach Morning Journal. "War, Romance Scandal," 20 April 1958.

de Genlis, Stéphanie Félicité. *Les Veillées du Château* (1784) Paris: Maradan, 1804.

de Genlis, Stéphanie Félicité, and Thomas Holcroft. *Tales of the Castle: or, Stories of Instruction and Delight*. London: G. Robinson, 1785.

de Laclos, Pierre Choderlos. *Les Liaisons dangereuses*. Oxford: Oxford University Press, 1995.

de Waal, Edmund. *The Hare with Amber Eyes: A Hidden Inheritance*. New York: Picador, 2010.

Duncombe, Charles. *Doctor Charles Duncombe's Report Upon the Subject of Education, Made to the Parliament of Upper Canada. 25th February 1836*. Toronto: M. Reynolds, 1836.

Edgeworth, Maria. *Letters for Literary Ladies*. London: J. Johnson, 1795.

———. *Parent's Assistant; or, Stories for Children*. London: Longman, 1858.

Eliot, T. S. *Four Quartets*. 1944. London: Faber & Faber, 1959.

Elmsley, Sarah. "Radical Marriage." *Eighteenth-Century Fiction* 11:4 (1999): 477–98.

Equiano, Olaudah. *The Life of Olaudah Equiano, Or, Gustavus Vassa, the African*, ed. Vincent Carretta. (1789). London: Penguin, 2003.

Favret, Mary A. *Romantic Correspondence: Women, Politics and the Fiction of Letters*. Cambridge: Cambridge University Press, 2005.

Fenn, Ellenor. *Cobwebs to Catch Flies*. (1783). London: John Marshall, 1800.

———. *Juvenile Correspondence or Letters Suited to Children from Four to Above Ten Years of Age*. London: Marshall, 1783.

Fenwick, John. *The Indian: A Farce. As it was Performed at Drury-Lane Theatre*. London, 1800.

———. *On the Trial of James Coigley for High Treason*. London: Printed for the Author, 1798.

———. "William Godwin," *Public Characters of 1799–1800. To Be Continued Annually*. London: Phillips, 1799.

Filmer, Robert. *Patriarcha and Other Political Works*, ed. Peter Laslett. Oxford: Blackwell, 1949.

Freud, Sigmund. "Beyond the Pleasure Principle" (1920). *A General Selection from the Works of Sigmund Freud*. Ed. John Rickman. New York: Doubleday Anchor, 1957.

Frost, Robert. *The Road Not Taken, Birches, And Other Poems by Robert Frost*. Claremont California. Coyote Press, 2010.

Gaggio, Dario. "Gold and Silver Industry," *The Oxford Encyclopedia of Economic History*, ed. Joel Mokyr. Oxford: Oxford University Press Online, 2005.

Gladwell, Malcolm. *The Tipping Point: How Little Things Can Make a Big Difference*. Boston: Little Brown, 2000.

Godwin, William. *An Enquiry Concerning Political Justice*. (1793) Ed. Mark Philp. Oxford: Oxford Worlds Classics, 2013.

———. *Bible Stories*. London: Tabart, 1802

———. *The Diary of William Godwin*. Eds. Victoria Myers, David O'Shaughnessy, and Mark Philp. Oxford: Oxford Digital Library, 2010. http://godwindiary.bodleian.ox.ac.uk.

———. *The Letters of William Godwin: 1778–1805*, 2 vols. Ed. Pamela Clemit. Oxford: Oxford University Press, 2011.

———. *Memoirs of the Author of A Vindication of the Rights of Woman.* Peterborough, ON: Broadview Press, 2001.

———. *Of Population. An Enquiry Concerning the Power of Increase in the Numbers of Mankind, Being an Answer to Mr. Malthus's Essay on That Subject.* London: Longman, Hurst, Rees, Orme & Brown, 1820.

———. *Things as They Are; or, The Adventures of Caleb Williams.* Ed. Maurice Hindle, London: Penguin, 2005.

Goldsmith, Rev. J [pseudonym for Richard Phillips]. *Geography for the Use of Schools, And Young Persons in General.* London: Richard Phillips, 1803.

Golightly, Jennifer. *The Family, Marriage and Radicalism in British Women's Novels of the 1790s.* Lanham, Maryland: Bucknell University Press, 2012.

Goodall, Jane and Christa Knellwolf, eds. *Frankenstein's Science: Experimentation and Discovery in Romantic Culture: 1780–1830.* Aldershot, England; Burlington VT: Ashgate, 2008.

Green, V. H. H. *John Wesley.* London: Nelson, 1964.

Gregory, Gayle and Carolyn Chapman. *Differentiated Instructional Strategies.* Thousand Oaks: Corwin Press, 2002.

Grenby, M. O. *The Child Reader, 1700–1840.* Cambridge: Cambridge University Press, 2011.

Habermas, Jürgen. *The Structural Transformation of the Public Sphere: An Inquiry into a Category of Bourgeois Society.* Trans. Thomas Burger with the assistance of Frederick Lawrence. Cambridge: MIT Press, 1989.

Hague, William. *Wilberforce: The Life of the Great Anti-Slave Trade Campaigner.* London: Harper Press, 2007.

Hammill, Faye. *Literary Culture and Female Authorship in Canada 1760–2000. Cross/Cultures* Vol. 63. Amsterdam: Rodopi, 2003.

Hastling, H. L., W. Addington Willis and W. P. Workman. *The History of Kingswood School by Three Old Boys.* London: Charles H. Kelly, 1898.

Hays, Mary. *Family Annals: or, The Sisters.* London: W. Simpkin and R. Marshall, 1817.

———. *Female Biography: Or Memoirs of Illustrious and Celebrated Women . . . Alphabetically Arranged.* London: Richard Phillips, 1803.

———. *Memoirs of Emma Courtney.* (1796) Oxford: Oxford University Press, 2009.

———. *Memoirs of Queens: Illustrious and Celebrated.* London: T. and J. Allman, 1821.

———. *The Correspondence of Mary Hays (1779–1843): British Novelist.* Ed. Marilyn L. Brooks, Lewiston, New York: Edwin Mellen Press, 2004.

Heffernan, Margaret. *Willful Blindness: Why We Ignore the Obvious.* Toronto: Doubleday, 2011.

Hempton, David. *Methodism and Politics in British Society 1750–1850.* London: Hutchinson, 1984.

Heuman, Gad. "Runaway Slaves in Nineteenth-Century Barbados," *Slavery & Abolition* 6,3 (1985): 96–111.

Hilton, Mary and Jill Shefrin Ed. *Educating the Child in Enlightenment Britain: Beliefs, Cultures, Practices.* Farnham: Ashgate, 2009.

Hilton, Mary, Victor Watson and Morag Styles. *Opening the Nursery Door: Reading, Writing and Childhood 1600–1900.* London: Routledge, 1997.

Holcroft, Thomas. *Memoirs of the Late Thomas Holcroft, Written by Himself and Continued to the Time of his Death from his Diary, Notes and other Papers.* Ed. William Hazlitt. London: Longman, Brown, Green, 1852.

Holcroft, Thomas, and Mrs Inchbald. *The Road to Ruin: Comedy in Five Acts.* Vol. 24. As performed at the Theatre Royal, Covent Garden. Printed from the Prompt Book with Remarks by Mrs. Inchbald. London: Longman, Hurst, Rees & Orme, 1808.

Hughes, Ted. "Myth and Education." *Winter Pollen: Occasional Prose,* Ed. William Scammell. London: Faber 1994: 136–53.

———. *Poetry in the Making.* London: Faber, 1967.

Immel, Andrea. "'Mistress of Infantine Language': Lady Ellenor Fenn, Her *Set of Toys,* and '*The Education of Each Moment.*'" *Children's Literature* 25: 1997: 215–28.

Immel, Andrea and Michael Whitmore. *Childhood and Children's Books in Early Modern Europe.* New York: Routledge, 2006.

Inchbald, Elizabeth. *Nature and Art.* Ed. Shawn L. Maurer. Peterborough, ON: Broadview Press, 2004.

Irving, D. *The Elements of English Composition.* London: Tabart, 1801.

Issitt, John. "The Natural History of a Textbook." *Publishing History* 37 (2000): 5–30.

———. *Jeremiah Joyce: Radical Dissenter and Writer.* Aldershot: Ashgate, 2006.

Jackson, Thomas. *Early Methodist Preachers.* Vol. 2. London: Paternoster, 1876.

———. ed. *The Lives of Early Methodist Preachers, Chiefly Written by Themselves, Edited with an Introductory Essay by Thomas Jackson.* Vol. 1. London: Wesleyan Conference Office, 2 Castle Street, 1865.

James, Felicity and Ian Inkster, Eds. *Religious Dissent and the Aikin-Barbauld Circle, 1740–1860.* Cambridge: Cambridge University Press, 2012.

Jameson, Anna Brownell. *Winter Studies and Summer Rambles in Canada.* Afterword by Clara Thomas. New Canadian Library, Toronto: McClelland & Stewart, 2009.

Janeway, James. *A Token for Children: Being an Exact Account of the Conversion, Holy and Exemplary Lives, and Joyful Deaths, of Several Young Children.* Religious Tract Society, 1825.

Johnston Judith. *Anna Jameson: Victorian, Feminist, Woman of Letters.* London: Scolar Press, 1997.

Jones, Frederick E. Ed. *Maria Gisborne & Edward E, Williams: Shelley's Friends, Their Journals and Letters.* Norman: University of Oklahoma Press, 1951.

Kadar, Marlene. *Essays on Life Writing: From Genre to Critical Practice.* Toronto: University of Toronto Press, 1992.

Kegan Paul, Charles. *William Godwin: His Friends and Contemporaries.* London: Henry S. King, 1876.

King, Christa Knellwolf, and Jane R. Goodall, eds. *Frankenstein's Science: Experimentation and Discovery in Romantic Culture, 1780–1830.* Aldershot: Ashgate, 2008.

Kingston Chronicle and Gazette. 19 April 1834: 2.

Kingston Stocking, Marion. Ed. *The Claire Clairmont Correspondence: Letters of Claire Clairmont, Charles Clairmont, and Fanny Imlay Godwin.* Baltimore: Johns Hopkins University Press, 1995.

Knowlton, Steve A. "Contested Symbolism in the Flags of New World Slave Risings," *Raven* 21 (2014): 71–94.

Kruks, Sonia. "Simone de Beauvoir." *Encyclopedia of Human Rights.* Oxford: Oxford University Press, 2009.

Lamb, Charles. *Essays of Elia and Last Essays.* The World's Classics. London: Oxford University Press, 1964.

———. *Everybody's Lamb: Being a Selection from the Essays of Elia the Letters and the Miscellaneous Pros of Charles Lamb*, Edited by A. C. Ward. Illustrated by Ernest H. Shephard. London: G. Bell and Sons, 1933.

———. *The Letters of Charles and Mary Lamb*. Edited by E. V. Lucas. London: Methuen, 1912.

———. *The Letters of Charles and Mary Anne Lamb*. Ed. Edwin W. Marrs, Jr. Ithaca: Cornell University Press, 1975.

———. *The Letters of Charles Lamb*. Edited by Alfred Ainger. London: Macmillan and Co., 1904.

Langford, Paul. *A Polite and Commercial People: England 1727-1783*. London: Clarendon Press, 1989.

Larkin, Philip. *High Windows*. London: Faber, 1974.

le Carré, John. *Tinker, Tailor Soldier Spy* (1974). London: Hodder & Stoughton, 2011.

Ledoux, Ellen Malenas. "Gothic Space and Female Agency in *Emmeline, The Mysteries of Udolpho* and *Secresy*," *Women's Writing* 18.3 (August 2011): 331–47.

Lenton, John. *John Wesley's Preachers: A Social and Statistical Analysis of the British and Irish Preachers Who Entered the Methodist Itinerancy before 1791*. Milton Keynes: Paternoster, 2009.

———. "Support Groups for Methodist Women Preachers 1803–1851," *Religion, Gender, and Industry: Exploring Church and Methodism in a Local Setting*. Ed. Geordan Hammond and Peter S. Forsaith. Eugene, Oregon: Pickwick Publications, 2011.

Literary Garland. Montreal. 1838–51.

Lockhart, John Gibson. *Peter's Letters to his Kinsfolk*. CS Van Winkle, 101 Greenwich Street, 1820.

Mavor, William. *The British Nepos*. London: Tabart, 1802.

———. *The English Spelling Book*. London: Tabart, 1802.

McCarthy, William. *Anna Letitia Barbauld: Voice of Enlightenment*. Baltimore: Johns Hopkins University Press, 2008.

———. "Mother of all Discourses: Anna Barbauld's *Lessons for Children*," in *Culturing the Child: 1640–1914: Essays in Memory of Mitzi Myers*. Ed. Donelle Ruwe, 85–111. Lanham, MD: Scarecrow, 2005.

Moodie, Susanna. *Roughing it in the Bush: Forest Life in Canada* (1852), New and Revised Edition. Toronto: Hunter, Rose and Company, 1871.

Moody, Jane and Daniel O'Quinn. *The Cambridge Companion to British Theatre 1730–1830*. Cambridge: Cambridge University Press, 2007.

Moon, Marjorie. *Benjamin Tabart's Juvenile Library: A Bibliography of Books for Children Published, Written, Edited and Sold by Mr. Tabart, 1801–1820*. London: St. Paul's Bibliographies, 1990.

Myers, Mitzi. "Impeccable Governesses, Rational Dames and Moral Mothers: Mary Wollstonecraft and the Female Tradition in Georgian Children's Books." *Children's Literature* 14 (1986): 31–58.

O'Callaghan, Evelyn. *Women Writing the West Indies 1804–1849: A Hot Place Belonging to Us*. London: Routledge, 2003.

O'Connor, Adrian. "Nature, Nurture and the Social Order: Imagining Lessons and Lives for Women in Ancien Régime France." *French Culture, Politics and Society* 31.1 (Spring 2012): 1–22.

———. "Support Groups for Methodist Women Preachers 1803–1851," *Religion, Gender, and Industry: Exploring Church and Methodism in a Local Setting*. Ed. Geordan Hammond and Peter S. Forsaith. Eugene, Oregon: Pickwick Publications, 2011.

Ouellette, David. "James Crooks." *Dictionary of Canadian Biography*, Vol 8, Toronto: University of Toronto/University of Laval. 2003.

Old Times: Upper Canada College Alumni Magazine (Winter 1977; 19 January 1985: 39).

Opie, Iona and Peter Opie. *The Oxford Dictionary of Nursery Rhymes*. Oxford: Oxford University Press, 1997.

Osborn, Matthew Warren. *Rum Maniacs: Alcoholic Insanity in the Early American Republic*. Chicago and London: University of Chicago Press, 2014.

Parker, Matthew. *The Sugar Barons: Family, Corruption, Empire and War in the West Indies*. New York: Walker, Bloomsbury, 2011.

Paul, Lissa. *The Children's Book Business: Lessons from the Long Eighteenth Century*. New York: Routledge, 2011.

Perrault, Charles. *Bluebeard*. London: Tabart, 1804.

———. *Cinderella*. London: Tabart, 1804.

———. *Hop o' my Thumb*. London: Tabart, 1804.

———. *Puss in Boots* and *Diamonds and Toads*. London: Tabart, 1804.

———. *Riquet with the Tuft*. London: Tabart, 1804.

———. *The Sleeping Beauty*. London: Tabart, 1804.

Pope, Alexander. *Essay on Criticism*. London: T. Daniel and J. Steele in Paternoster Row, 1758, ECCO Range 11750.

Porter, J. *The Two Princes of Persia*. London: Tabart, 1801.

Power, Michael and Nancy Butler. *Slavery and Freedom in Niagara*. Niagara-on-the-Lake: Niagara Historical Society, 1993.

Priestman, Martin. *Romantic Atheism: Poetry and Freethought 1780–1830*. Cambridge: Cambridge University Press, 2004.

Probyn, Elspeth. *Sexing the Self. Gendered Positions in Cultural Studies*. New York: Routledge, 1993.

Public Ledger and Daily Advertiser. London: 5 October 1829.

Remarks on the Insurrection in Barbados and the Bill for the Registration of the Slaves. London: Ellerton and Henderson, 1816.

Report from a Select Committee of the House of Assembly Appointed to Inquire into the Origin, Causes and Progress of the Late Insurrection. Bridgetown: *Mercury and Gazette*: 1818.

Rhodes, Jewell Parker. *Towers Falling*. New York: Little Brown and Co., 2016.

Robinson, Henry Crabb. *Diary, Reminiscences, and Correspondence of Henry Crabb Robinson 1776–1867*. London: Macmillan, 1869.

Robinson, Mary. *The Poetical Works of the Late Mrs. Robinson Including Many Pieces Never before Published*. Vol. 1. London: Richard Phillips, 1806.

Rodgers, Lawrence. "Migration." *The Oxford Companion to Women's Writing in the United States*. Edited by Linda Wagner-Martin and Cathy N. Davidson. Oxford: Oxford University Press, 2005, 565–68.

Rolph, Thomas. *A Brief Account together with Observations made during a visit in the West Indies and Through a Tour through the United States of American in Parts of the Years 1832–3 Together with a statistical Account of Upper Canada*. Dundas, Upper Canada: Heyworth, Hackstaff, 1836.

Rousseau, Jean-Jacques. *Emile or On Education.* Trans. Christopher Kelly and Allan Bloom. (1979) Lebanon, New Hampshire: Dartmouth College Press, 2009.

Ruddick, Sara. *Maternal Thinking: Toward a Politics of Peace.* New York: Ballantine, 1989.

Russell, Gillian. *Women, Sociability and Theatre in Georgian London.* Cambridge: Cambridge University Press, 2007.

Runia, Robin. Ed. *The Future of Feminist Eighteenth-Century Scholarship: Beyond Recovery.* New York: Routledge, 2018.

Saul, John Ralston. *Louis-Hippolyte La Fontaine and Robert Baldwin.* Toronto: Penguin, 2010.

Schiller, F. *The Death of Wallenstein: A Tragedy in Five Acts.* Trans. S. T. Coleridge. London: G. Woodfell, 1800.

Sewell, John. *A Political Biography of William Lyon Mackenzie.* Toronto: Lorimer, 2002.

Shefrin, Jill. *Such Constant Affectionate Care: Lady Charlotte Finch, Royal Governess, and the Children of George III.* Los Angeles: Cotsen Occasional Press, 2003.

Shields, Carol. *Small Ceremonies.* London: Fourth Estate, 1995.

Shelley, Mary Wollstonecraft. *Frankenstein, the 1818 Texts, Contexts, Criticism.* Ed. J. Paul Hunter. New York: W. W. Norton, 2012.

Smith, Charlotte. *Letters of Charlotte Smith.* Ed. Judith Phillips Stanton. Bloomington: Indiana University Press, 2003.

Snow, Malinda. "Habits of Empire and Domination in Eliza Fenwick's *Secresy.*" *Eighteenth-Century Fiction* 14.2 (2002): 159–75.

Southey, Robert. *The Life of Wesley; and Rise and Progress of Methodism.* 2 vols. London: Longman, Green, Longman, Roberts, & Green, 1864.

Spivak, Gayatri. "Diasporas Old and New: Women in the Transnational World." *Textual Practice* 10.2 (1966): 245–69.

St. Clair, William. *The Godwins and the Shelleys: The Biography of a Family.* London: Faber, 1989.

Steedman, Carolyn. *Dust: The Archive and Cultural History.* Manchester: Manchester University Press, 2001. Print.

Stokes, Peter John. *Old Niagara on the Lake.* Illustrated with sketches by Robert Montgomery. Toronto: University of Toronto Press, 1971.

Stowe, Harriet Beecher. *Uncle Tom's Cabin* (1852) Oxford: Oxford University Press, 2008.

Thale, Mary. *Selections from the Papers of the London Corresponding Society 1792–1799.* Cambridge: Cambridge University Press, 1983.

Thomas, Clara. *Love and Work Enough: The Life of Anna Jameson.* Toronto: University of Toronto Press, 1967.

Thomson, James. *Poems, Viz. Spring. Summer. Autumn, Winter. A Hymn to the Seasons. To the Memory of Isaac Newton.* Dublin, Printed by S. Powell, for George Risk, at the Shakespeare's Head, George Ewing, at the Angel and Bible, and William Smith, at the Hercules, Booksellers, (1730): 53. Eighteenth Century Collections Online: Range 1552.

Todd, Janet. *Feminist Literary History.* New York: Routledge, 1988.

———. *Death and the Maidens: Fanny Wollstonecraft and the Shelley Circle.* London: Profile, 2007.

———. *Mary Wollstonecraft: A Revolutionary Life.* London: Bloomsbury, 2014.

———. ed. *A Wollstonecraft Anthology*. New York: Columbia University Press, 1990.

Tolstoy, Leo. "Anna Karenina. 1877." Trans. Louise and Aylmer Maude. New York: Oxford University Press, 1995.

Tomalin, Claire. *The Life and Death of Mary Wollstonecraft*. London: Viking, 2012.

Traill, Catharine Parr. *The Backwoods of Canada: Selections*. Introduction by Clara Thomas. Toronto: McClelland & Stewart, 1965.

Vallone, Lynne. *Disciplines of Virtue: Girls Culture in the Eighteenth and Nineteenth Centuries*. New Haven: Yale University Press, 1995.

Walker, Gina Luria. *Mary Hays (1759–1843): The Growth of a Woman's Mind*. London: Ashgate, 2006.

Wallace, Miriam. *Revolutionary Subjects in the English "Jacobin" Novel, 1790–1805*. Lewisburg: Bucknell University Press, 2009.

———. "Constructing Treason, Narrating Truth: The 1794 Treason Trial of Thomas Holcroft and the Fate of English Jacobinism." *Romanticism on the Net: Université de Montréal. Érudit* 45: paragraph 11 (February 2007).

———. *Revolutionary Subjects in the English Jacobin Novel, 1790–1805*. Lewisburg: Bucknell University Press, 2009.

Walpole, Horace. *The Letters of Horace Walpole, Earl of Orford. Vol 1: 1735–1745*. London: Richard Bentley, 1846.

Wedd, A. F., ed. *The Fate of the Fenwicks; Letters to Mary Hays (1798–1828)*. London: Methuen, 1927.

Welch, Pedro L. V. *Slave Society in the City: Bridgetown, Barbados, 1680–1834*. Oxford: James Currey, 2004.

Wesley, John. "Reasons against a separation from the Church of England." (1875).

———. *Letters of John Wesley*. Edited by George Eayrs. New York: George H. Doran Co., 1916.

Wilder, Laura Ingalls. *The Little House Complete* (9 volume set). New York: HarperCollins, 2008.

White, James. *Falstaff's Letters*. London: B. Robson, 1877.

Whyman, Susan. *The Pen and the People: English Letter Writers 1600–1800*. Oxford: Oxford University Press, 2009.

Williams, Karina. *Contrary Voices: Representations of West Indian Slavery, 1657–1834*. Kingston, Jamaica: University of West Indies Press, 2008.

Wollstonecraft, Mary. *The Collected Letters of Mary Wollstonecraft*. Ed. Janet Todd. London: Allen Lane The Penguin Press, 2005.

———. *The Works of Mary Wollstonecraft*. 7 vols. Eds. Janet Todd and Marilyn Butler. London: Pickering, 1989.

Wordsworth, William. *Wordsworth Poetical Works With Introductions and Notes*. Ed. Thomas Hutchinson and revised by Ernest de Selincourt. New. Oxford: Oxford University Press, 1936.

Wright, Angela. "'To Life the Life of Hopeless Recollection': Mourning and Melancholia in Female Gothic, 1780–1800." *Gothic Studies* 6.1 (2004): 19–29.

Index

Italic page numbers refer to illustrations.

www.ingramcontent.com/pod-product-compliance
Lightning Source LLC
Chambersburg PA
CBHW021407110726
47901CB00008B/2084